# EARLY MODERN KNOWLEDGE SOCIETIES AS AFFECTIVE ECONOMIES

*Early Modern Knowledge Societies as Affective Economies* researches the development of knowledge economies in early modern Europe. Starting with the Southern and Northern Netherlands as important early hubs for marketing knowledge, it analyses knowledge economies in the dynamics of a globalizing world.

The book brings together scholars and perspectives from history, art history, material culture, book history, history of science and literature to analyse the relationship between knowledge and markets. How did knowledge grow into a marketable product? What knowledge about markets was available in this period, and how did it develop? By connecting these questions the authors show how knowledge markets operated, not only economically but also culturally, through communication and affect. Knowledge societies are analysed as affective communities, spaces and practices. Compelling case studies describe the role of emotions such as hope, ambition, desire, love, fascination, adventure and disappointment – on driving merchants, contractors and consumers to operate in the market of knowledge. In so doing, the book offers innovative perspectives on the development of knowledge markets and the valuation of knowledge.

Introducing the reader to different perspectives on how knowledge markets operated from both an economic and cultural perspective, this book will be of great use to students, graduates and scholars of early modern history, economic history, the history of emotions and the history of the Low Countries.

**Inger Leemans** is Professor of Cultural History at Vrije Universiteit Amsterdam, the Netherlands, and Principal Investigator of *NL-Lab* at the Humanities Cluster of the Royal Netherlands Academy of Arts and Sciences. She has published on the history of emotions and the senses, radical Enlightenment, financial crises and digital humanities. Her current project is on 'Affective Economies. A Cultural History of Stock Trading'.

**Anne Goldgar** is Garrett and Anne Van Hunnick Professor of European History at the University of Southern California. From 1993 to 2020 she taught at King's College London, where she was Professor of Early Modern European History. She is a social and cultural historian who has written numerous works, including *Impolite Learning: Conduct and Community in the Republic of Letters 1680–1750* and *Tulipmania: Money, Honor, and Knowledge in the Dutch Golden Age.*

# Knowledge Societies in History

The expertise of the history of knowledge is essential in tackling the issues and concerns surrounding present-day global knowledge society. Books in this series historicize and critically engage with the concept of knowledge society, with conceptual and methodological contributions enabling the historian to analyse and compare the origins, formation and development of knowledge societies.

**Series Editors:** Sven Dupré, Utrecht University and University of Amsterdam, Netherlands, and Wijnand Mijnhardt, Utrecht University, Netherlands.

**In this series:**

For more information about this series, please visit: https://www.routledge.com/Knowledge-Societies-in-History/book-series/KSHIS

# EARLY MODERN KNOWLEDGE SOCIETIES AS AFFECTIVE ECONOMIES

*Edited by Inger Leemans and Anne Goldgar*

Routledge
Taylor & Francis Group

LONDON AND NEW YORK

First published 2020
by Routledge
2 Park Square, Milton Park, Abingdon, Oxon OX14 4RN

and by Routledge
52 Vanderbilt Avenue, New York, NY 10017

*Routledge is an imprint of the Taylor & Francis Group, an informa business*

*British Library Cataloguing-in-Publication Data*
A catalogue record for this book is available from the British Library

*Library of Congress Cataloging-in-Publication Data*
Names: Leemans, Inger, editor. | Goldgar, Anne, editor.
Title: Early modern knowledge societies as affective economies / edited by Inger Leemans and Anne Goldgar.
Description: Abingdon, Oxon ; New York, NY : Routledge, 2021. | Includes bibliographical references and index.
Identifiers: LCCN 2020037240 (print) | LCCN 2020037241 (ebook) | ISBN 9780367219949 (hardback) | ISBN 9780367219963 (paperback) | ISBN 9780429270222 (ebook)
Subjects: LCSH: Knowledge economy--Europe--History. | Economics--Europe--Sociological aspects. | Emotions--Economic aspects--Europe. | Europe--Economic conditions--17th century. | Europe--Intellectual life--17th century.
Classification: LCC HC240.9.I55 E433 2021 (print) | LCC HC240.9.I55 (ebook) | DDC 338.94/02--dc23
LC record available at https://lccn.loc.gov/2020037240
LC ebook record available at https://lccn.loc.gov/2020037241

ISBN: 978-0-367-21994-9 (hbk)
ISBN: 978-0-367-21996-3 (pbk)
ISBN: 978-0-429-27022-2 (ebk)

Typeset in Bembo
by MPS Limited, Dehradun

# CONTENTS

# FIGURES

# CONTRIBUTORS

**Tina Asmussen** is Assistant Professor of Early Modern Mining History at the Deutsches Bergbau-Museum Bochum (DBM) and the Ruhr-Universität Bochum (RUB). Before joining the DBM she held an *Ambizione* fellowship by the Swiss National Science Foundation at the Chair for Science Studies at ETH Zurich and was a postdoctoral fellow at the Max Planck Institute for the History of Science in Berlin. Her main research interests are early modern history of science and knowledge, environmental and economic history as well as the history of natural resources. Her main book projects are *Theatrum Kircherianum: Wissenskulturen und Bücherwelten im 17. Jahrhundert* (co-authored with Lucas Burkart and Hole Rößler, Wiesbaden 2013) and *Scientia Kircheriana: Die Fabrikation von Wissen bei Athanasius Kircher* (Affalterbach 2016). She currently works on a book project with the working title: *Subterranean Œconomies: Mining and Resource Cultures in Early Modern Europe*.

**Kaspar Beelen** obtained his PhD in History at the University of Antwerp (2014). As a digital historian, Kaspar investigates how artificial intelligence can contribute to historical debates. He has worked as a post-doctoral fellow at the University of Toronto (Computer Science and Political Science Departments) and the University of Amsterdam (Institute of Informatics), where he also served as assistant professor in Digital Humanities (Media Studies Department). Kaspar currently works as a research associate at the Alan Turing Institute, London, where he investigates – as part of the 'Living with Machines' project – the lived experience of the industrial revolution using data-driven techniques.

**Feike Dietz** is Assistant Professor in Early Modern Dutch Literature and Culture at Utrecht University. She is project leader of the NWO Vrije Competitie Project 'Language Dynamics in the Dutch Golden Age' (together with Marjo van Koppen). Her PhD-project (2007–2011) focused on the interconfessional and international exchange of illustrated religious literature in the Dutch Republic. Her current research focuses on the relationship between early modern literature and knowledge production: texts for children and adolescents as instruments of (medial, visual, information) literacy. Within the context of this research group, she aims to understand how youngsters were skilled to participate in the new knowledge market that arose after the advent of print.

**Sebastian Felten** (PhD, King's College London) is a historian of finance, science and bureaucracy in early modern Europe. He is a visiting assistant professor at the Department of History at the University of Vienna and was a fellow at the Max Planck Institute for the History of Science Berlin (MPIWG) between 2015 and 2018. He currently works on three larger projects: (1) a monograph on money as a social technology in the Dutch Republic; (2) a collective volume about the history of bureaucratic knowledge and (3) a second book on knowledge production in early modern Saxony across mining officials, workers, merchants and scholars.

**Anne Goldgar** is Garrett and Anne Van Hunnick Professor of European History at the University of Southern California. Previously she taught from 1993 to 2020 at King's College London, where she was Professor of Early Modern History. She is author of a number of works on early modern cultural history, notably *Impolite Learning: Conduct and Community in the Republic of Letters 1685-1750* (Yale, 1995) and *Tulipmania: Money, Honor, and Knowledge in the Dutch Golden Age* (Chicago, 2009). She is currently working on Dutch expeditions to the arctic in the 1590s and the role of their subsequent representations in national identity.

**Vera Keller** is Associate Professor of History at the University of Oregon. She researches the origins of experimental science by looking at the intersections between technology, industry and political economy; craft and philosophy; sociability and science; and ideas of innovation, projects and the public interest. She has published, amongst others, *Knowledge and the Public Interest, 1575 -1725* (Cambridge, 2015). She is currently working om a book project, tentatively entitled *The Experimental Century: Curating the Early German Enlightenment* looks at how late 17th-century German academics sought to reign in, winnow, connect and re-order three previous epistemic cultures: the court culture explored in her first book, mercantile and medical collecting networks, and pansophic erudition. Along with Markus Friedrich and Christine von Oertzen, she is co-editing a new book series from De Gruyter, *Cultures and Practices of Knowledge in History*.

**Inger Leemans** is professor of Cultural History at Vrije Universiteit Amsterdam and PI of NL-Lab at the Humanities Cluster of Royal Netherlands Academy of Arts and Sciences She researches early modern cultural history, specifically the history of emotions and the body, the history of knowledge and digital humanities. Her most recent publication is *Worm en Donder:* a text book on 18th-century Dutch literature. Inger Leemans is member of the scientific board of the EU JPI Cultural Heritage, of the Dutch National Research Council for Cultural Heritage, and of the National Council for Dutch Language and Culture. She is co-founder of ACCESS, the Amsterdam Centre for Cross-Disciplinary Emotion and Sensory Studies. She has been a visiting professor/fellow at UCLA, the Getty Research Institute, and NIAS - the Institute for Advanced Study in the Humanities and Social Sciences. Her research group collaborates with partners from heritage institutes, industry and creative industries. Currently, she is working on a project 'A Cultural History of Stock Trading'.

**Martin Mulsow** is Professor of Intellectual History at the University of Erfurt and Director of the Gotha Research Centre for Early Modern Studies. From 2005 to 2008 he was professor of history at Rutgers University. He is member of several German academies and was member of the Institute for Advanced Study in Princeton, the Wissenschaftskolleg in Berlin and the NIAS in Amsterdam. His work on Renaissance philosophy, the history of early modern scholarship and the radical Enlightenment received many prizes, among them the prize of the Berlin-Brandenburg Academy of Sciences (2012), and the Anna-Krüger Prize (2014). He is the author of *Die unanständige Gelehrtenrepublik* (2007), *Prekäres Wissen: Eine andere Ideengeschichte der Frühen Neuzeit* (2012) *Enlightenment Underground: Radical Germany, 1680-1720* (2015), and *Radikale Früaufklärung in Deutschland (1680-1720* (2018).

**Claartje Rasterhoff** is project leader of the National Culture Monitor of the Boekmanstichting. She was Assitant Professor at University of Amsterdam and a postdoctoral researcher in the project 'Creative Amsterdam: An E-Humanities Perspective (CREATE)', where she coordinated the Amsterdam Time Machine project. As a historian of arts, culture and economics, she specializes in the relationship between cities, culture and economics, and has published and taught on art markets and cultural industries from the early modern period to the present. She is author of *Painting and Publishing as Cultural Industries: The Fabric of Creativity in the Dutch Republic 1580–1800* (2016), for which she got a prize of the Provinciaal Utrechts Genootschap voor Kunsten en Wetenschappen. Her current research projects focus on the development of historical cultural datasets and digital infrastructures as well as their application in other societal domains.

**Ulinka Rublack** is Professor of Early Modern European History at the University of Cambridge and elected Fellow of the British Academy. Rublack has published widely on 16th- and 17th-century culture as well as on methodological concerns. Her books have been translated into German, Italian and Chinese. In 2018 the Humboldt and Thyssen Foundations jointly awarded her a life-time achievement award for outstanding research and fostering academic exchange, the Reimar-Lüst Prize. In 2019, her work as a historian and her book *The Astronomer and the Witch* were recognised with Germany's most prestigious prize for historians, awarded every three years, the Deutsche Historikerpreis. She has edited the *Oxford Concise Companion to History* (2011), and the *Oxford Handbook of the Protestant Reformations* (2016). Her monographs include *Reformation Europe* (2005), *The Crimes of Women* *in Early Modern Germany* (1999) and *Dressing Up: Cultural Identity in Renaissance Europe* (2010), which won the Roland H. Bainton Prize.

**Claudia Swan** is the inaugural Mark S. Weil Professor of Early Modern Art History in the Department of Art History & Archaeology at Washington University in St. Louis, Missouri. She has edited and authored five books and has published numerous articles and book chapters on early modern art, science and collecting and on Dutch visual culture. Swan has been a resident fellow at the Institute for Advanced Study in Princeton, NJ; the Max-Planck-Institut für Wissenschaftsgeschichte, Berlin; CRASSH, Cambridge University; and the Netherlands Institute for Advanced Study. Her most recent book *Rarities of these Lands: Art, Trade, and Diplomacy in the Dutch Republic* is forthcoming (2021) from Princeton University Press

**Karel Vanhaesebrouck** is a professor and chair of theatre studies at the Université Libre de Bruxelles. Prior to coming to Brussels, Vanhaesebrouck was an assistant professor at Maastricht University. Karel Vanhaesebrouck is a member of the 'Jonge Academie'. He acts as a co-director of the THEA Research Group, a cross-institutional (VUB, ULB, RITS) research group facilitating artistic and scientific research within the broad fields of theatre and performance. In 2013 Vanhaesebrouck's research was awarded the Prize 'Laureaat van de Koninklijke Vlaamse academie voor Wetenschappen en Kunsten in de Klasse van de kunsten' by the Royal Flemish Academy of Sciences and Arts in Belgium). Vanhaesebrouck was a visiting professor at the Université Paris Ouest Nanterre La Défense, and a fellow at the Netherlands Institute for Advanced Study (NIAS) in Amsterdam. Vanhaesebrouck supervises several research projects funded by FNRS, Innoviris and FWO. He also supervises a number of artistic PhD projects (Doctorat en Arts et Sciences de l'Art) in the field of theatre, performance and documentary research.

# ACKNOWLEDGEMENTS

This book is produced in the context of the research project *Creating a Knowledge Society in a Globalizing World (1450–1800)*, resulting from a collaboration between the Descartes Centre for the History and Philosophy of the Sciences and the Humanities (University of Utrecht), the Max Planck Institute for the History of Science (Berlin), and the Netherlands Institute for Advanced Study in the Humanities and Social Sciences (NIAS – KNAW).

We thank the initiators and principal investigators of the project Wijnand Mijnhardt (University of Utrecht) and Sven Dupré (University of Utrecht & University of Amsterdam) for giving us the opportunity to start a working group on 'Knowledge and the market' and for their intellectual and practical support in the subsequent process. Wijnand Mijnhardt has sat in on all our meetings and brought great inspiration to the team. We have also very much enjoyed working and discussing our plans with the PI's of the other working groups of *Creating a Knowledge Society in a Globalizing World*: Bert de Munck, Fokko Jan Dijksterhuis, Thijs Weststeijn and Marieke Hendriksen.

We sincerely thank the staff of the NIAS for hosting our Theme group in 2017. The NIAS provided a stimulating research environment. We would like to thank Lissa Roberts, Laurence Fontaine, Herman Roodenburg, Reinier Munk, Joost Hengstmengel and Olav Velthuis, who acted as keynotes and discussants in our workshops. The presentations and discussions at the workshops at NIAS and Vrije Universiteit Amsterdam have improved this book considerably. Also, they helped our group to form into a 'Faszinationsgemeinschaft', an affective community, passionate about knowledge. We hope that this volume will reflect the pleasure with which we have collaborated in this project.

# 1

# INTRODUCTION

## Knowledge – market – affect: knowledge societies as affective economies

*Inger Leemans and Anne Goldgar*

In the anonymous painting 'Glorification of Commerce and Science' we find a colourful visualization of an early modern knowledge economy (Figure 1.1).[1] Painted sometime between 1625 and 1645 in the Southern Netherlands, it depicts a world full of knowledge which is directly connected to trade, commerce, and prosperity. In the building at the left, producers of knowledge are busy at work: men of letters read books, examine globes, discuss their findings and write them down. They study geology, geometry, astronomy, and the fine arts: all aspects of useful knowledge that might result in better fortifications, safer navigation or other practical results. One of the scholars points out the three young consumers of knowledge in the centre of the picture, assiduously acquiring forms of literacy such as writing, reading, and – as the books and instruments around them indicate – also medicine, philosophy, mathematics, accounting, cartography, and the arts.

This studious and industrious knowledge society is presided over by Mercury, god of commerce and of the arts. Through Mercury the painting seems to indicate that the search for knowledge is strongly connected to the economy. This is also underlined by the urban landscape and harbour in the right-hand corner, and by the riches Mercury distributes across the land. The implication is that those who sail out in search of knowledge can return with ample credit, a cornucopia full of riches. Economic prosperity can both be the cause and the effect of the development of knowledge.

The painting also indicates that the knowledge economy is a highly affective phenomenon. The younger and older learners seem passionate about gathering knowledge. Mercury's golden chariot is drawn forward by desire: roosters, symbols of watchfulness and lust, are lured to new heights by the exotic birds flying before them. The search for knowledge and profit is propelled by fascination for the unknown, by the promises of the market, the desire for more, and – for these roosters – maybe even by the wish to become a better version of one's own species.

FIGURE 1.1 Attrib. to Jan Brueghel II, *Glorification of Commerce and Science (The Children of Mercury)*, c. 1649. Oil on canvas, 70 × 92,3 cm. Rijksmuseum Amsterdam: SK-A-3027

This desire, however, is also mocked in the 'underworld', where monkeys experiment with alchemical equipment, trying to distil new, powerful elixirs and thereby a shortcut to riches. This is a place of animal spirits, of excess, and of comic inversion. That these creatures are trying to stretch the limits of knowledge too far is not only implied by their nature – they are monkeys aping the natural order – but also by the pile of books between them and the children, where Virgil and Galen lie next to Dr. Faustus. Solid knowledge can contribute to a broader human enterprise and to economic benefits, but the possible profit can also turn out to be risky, a monkey's game. Mercury's cornucopia not only distributes pearls, tobacco, music, and joy, but also masks and dice. The open theatre and the masked *commedia dell'arte* figures further warn against the possibly hazardous and idle nature of human endeavour.

This anonymous painting was not anomalous, but instead can be placed in a series of similar depictions of the relation between knowledge, commerce, and affect. We take this image, and comparable images from the period, as an emblem for our enterprise in this book, where we examine the complex relations between these three crucial entities in the early modern period. The fact that the painting was one of several on this theme signals that in this period a change occurred in the way knowledge was valued.[2]

## The value of knowledge

What is the value of knowledge? What is the relation between knowledge, market, and affect? These questions have gained urgency as our current global knowledge economies are undergoing fundamental shifts. Traditional bastions of the consolidation, valuation, and transmission of knowledge, such as universities, media, and publishers, are currently being challenged. Criticism is growing about educational institutions which run their 'business' like factories, reducing knowledge to numbers and income. In the political realm, terms such as 'post-truth politics', 'alternative facts', and 'emocracy' indicate a re-evaluation of knowledge versus beliefs, lies, and emotions. The global information network is now perceived as a disconnected series of social media bubbles, while at the same time information flows are increasingly monitored and controlled by states and corporations.

These current shifts in the global knowledge society demand critical analysis, historical perspectives, and methodologies to analyze such complex and problematic notions as 'knowledge', 'marketed knowledge', 'global knowledge society', and 'knowledge economy'. When and how did knowledge become a commodity: a fixed and reproducible product that can be distributed and sold through markets? How did large groups of people become so passionate about knowledge that they did not hesitate to regularly invest a considerable percentage of their income in knowledge products? How can we study the valuation of knowledge?

This volume aims to analyze the connection between knowledge, market, and affect, by turning to one of the defining moments in the history of knowledge societies: the early modern period. This period witnessed an explosive expansion in the production, distribution, and consumption of knowledge on a global scale. It was a period of rapid change which posed challenges to existing modes of the organization of knowledge. New media developed, and the landscape of traditional knowledge authorities was thoroughly reorganized. Through the invention of the printing press, the growth of state bureaucracies, the founding of academies and of knowledge-hungry trading companies, the production and distribution of knowledge evolved into an international, even global, interactive process.[3]

In 2015, the international research project *Creating a Knowledge Society in a Globalizing World (1450–1800)* was established to study the development of knowledge societies in the early modern period, with the Northern and Southern Netherlands as primary case studies.[4] Our volume results from this project. We focus on the economics of knowledge societies by analyzing the interrelation between knowledge and markets, specifically from the aspect of affect and emotion.[5] Our claim is that the commodification of knowledge in the period 1500-1750 has been under-researched, and that in order to understand the development of knowledge economies in the early modern period, we need to take emotions, or *affects*, into account. This volume provides eleven case studies, which analyze the interrelation between knowledge, markets, and affects. Before we introduce these three key concepts, we will first explain why we have focused particularly on the Netherlands.[6]

## The Southern and Northern Netherlands as knowledge economies

The highly developed, commercialized and urbanized Southern and Northern Netherlands provide a useful case study for studying the connection between knowledge and market. These were societies in flux, undergoing rapid changes to their politics, economy, and culture, which posed challenges to the existing modes of the organization of knowledge. With their decentralized political power structures and their fast-expanding global trade networks, the Southern and Northern Netherlands offered a fertile breeding ground for the development of knowledge communities. In the urban trading zones of the Netherlands, different cultures and divergent social and professional groups mixed, forming new kinds of exchanges and interactions. Changing structures, and the new products beginning to flow into these markets, demanded new forms of knowledge, as did new connections with cultures abroad.

In the historiography of the early modern Southern and Northern Netherlands, strong claims have been made about their unique nature, both in terms of their economy and their political systems, and to their knowledge culture. The Dutch Republic has been described as the 'first modern economy', a 'miracle', a 'world power' and a 'financial might' with a worldwide trading network.[7] Antwerp and Amsterdam have been labeled as 'world cities', and 'hubs' in an emerging capitalist world economy.[8] The development of these urban, commercial societies is considered the backbone for the development of a quite remarkable climate for knowledge in the 16th and the 17th century, with an open public sphere and a central position in the international republic of letters, producing innovative scientific and philosophic research.[9] One of the underlying assumptions of this historiography is that in the early modern Netherlands, knowledge processes came to depend heavily on markets and commerce, with information and knowledge growing into an essential element for economic growth.[10]

This claim is most recently made by Jan Luiten van Zanden, who in his study *The Long Road to the Industrial Revolution: The European Economy in a Global Economy* labels the Southern and Northern Netherlands as the first knowledge economy.[11] While the concept of 'knowledge economy' is generally reserved for industrial and post-industrial societies, Van Zanden states that the strong economic performance of the North Sea region, especially the Netherlands and England, should be understood in the context of the development of an advanced knowledge economy, in which human capital, knowledge, and knowledge-intensive products accumulated. During the 14th and 15th centuries, the demand for manuscripts and books shifted from clergy and the church to the lay public, mostly urban elites. This led to a spectacular growth in European book production, from around 1,000 books per million inhabitants in Western Europe, to 10,000 around 1400, and 100,000 in the 17th century.[12] The Southern and Northern Netherlands became leaders in this market in the 16th and 17th centuries, with England taking over in the 18th century.

Recent studies in the history of knowledge also describe the Dutch Republic in the Golden Age as an example of an early knowledge economy, where scholars, traders, and the creative industries helped to turn knowledge into a commodity. These studies position the Netherlands as a truly *global* knowledge economy, building a knowledge market within the context of expanding trade networks, inventing exoticism in print, and developing cosmopolitan ideals for the world of letters.[13] The vast literature on the history of collecting and the exchange of goods and knowledge products also highlights this interconnectedness of knowledge and the market, through the need for connoisseurship, the display of wealth and expertise, and the combination of the exchange of goods and epistemic gifts. These studies have shed a new light on the structure of knowledge-making, showing for instance that merchants were directly involved in the production and circulation of knowledge about the natural world.[14]

Current historiography has thus brought together a number of claims and expectations about the development of a global knowledge economy in the Southern and Northern Netherlands:

- The early modern Netherlands developed into a knowledge hub, with centres in which a large-scale production and distribution of knowledge was connected to the production, distribution, and use of knowledge-intensive artefacts and technologies.
- These developments were stimulated by the self-sustained and accelerating growth of the urban centres. In urban areas, advanced commercial and financial systems and global trade networks strongly relied on the exchange of information, and stimulated new literacies and forms of knowledge.
- The Dutch knowledge hubs witnessed a large-scale commoditization of knowledge: knowledge was turned into a reproducible good, valued economically.
- A considerable percentage of the population (of different social classes, genders, religions) participated in knowledge-making processes, acquiring various kinds of literacies (textual, material, visual, mathematical, calligraphic), while new participants were recognized as producers of valid knowledge.
- Knowledge became an essential motor for economic development, for instance through the growing dependency of institutions on 'knowledge workers' and the stable input of knowledge.

We should not envision this as a linear process, with knowledge constantly building up in a commercial, open exchange environment. Knowledge societies are characterized by a tension between open and free transfer and exchange of knowledge, and constant attempts at control, secrecy, and regulation.

## Knowledge markets and market knowledge

Our volume aims to analyze the history of knowledge economies from the perspective of cultural history. We study here the interrelation of *knowledge* and *markets* from two angles. Firstly, we examine the development of *knowledge markets*. How did knowledge grow into a marketable product in the early modern period? Secondly, we start from the presumption that commercial societies develop through the expansion of knowledge. So how knowledge-intensive were early modern markets? What *market knowledge* – knowledge about markets and commerce – was available, and how essential was this for commercial projects? In examining these questions, we assume as well that *knowledge markets* and *market knowledge* intersect. Commercial societies need consumers and producers who are able to navigate markets. How dependent was the development of the knowledge market on the development of knowledge *about* markets, and vice versa: how was knowledge about markets furthered by marketed knowledge, for instance by books on accountancy, or stock trading?[15]

Market knowledge does not only encompass commercial skills, literacies, and practical knowledge about products and prices; it also functions on a different, more abstract level. Deirdre McCloskey has stated that the positive appreciation of commerce developed in the Dutch collective imaginary made capitalism seem 'natural' and thus stimulated commercialization.[16] Dutch 'commercial republicanism' developed a discourse in which merchant practices were balanced with civic virtue.[17] Studies in this area open up to one of the urgent questions underlying the history of capitalism: how were early modern societies able to stimulate commercial expansion and extensive consumption patterns, while the dominant discourses generally rejected sins such as greed, luxuriousness, and the hubris informing the open display of wealth?[18]

Our approach, to investigate the interrelation between marketed knowledge and knowledge about markets, underlines our interest in the way knowledge markets operate, not only economically but also culturally. The need to research knowledge economies from a cultural historical perspective has also recently been stressed by Joel Mokyr, who in *Culture of Growth* states that 'For quite a few years now, economists have become increasingly open to the idea that long-term economic change cannot be seriously analyzed without some concept of "culture" and some idea of how it changes and why these changes matter.'[19]

Two important operators in knowledge markets, or even *conditions* for their successful development, need to be considered. Firstly: *communication*. As the market needs inter-subjectivity, or agreement on the idea of what is valuable knowledge, communication is central. How was inter-subjectivity shaped, established, and 'distributed'? It is important to stress that communication encompasses discourses and practices. For instance, artistic practices established embodied ways of knowing, which helped to attribute quality to and establish trust in new products.[20] Secondly, we argue that *affects* are important operators in the market. Affects operate on many different levels in the market: the market consists

Caudior alter eques mullo falebrofa labore
Conuxus durum per iuga carpit iter.

Hos tenuere locos qui iam ubijnque, iocifque
Altius humanis exeruêre caput.

Vnica cura quibus caelum fpectantibus altum
Quod uerum atque decens quaerere, idemque fequ

**FIGURE 1.2**  Collecting Knowledge. Antwerp 1570. Design: Jan van der Straet. Engraver: Pieter Jalhea Furnius. Publisher: Hieronymus Cock. Courtesy of Rijksmuseum Amsterdam, RP-P-OB-102.543

of producers passionate about products and projected profits, and it needs consumers who desire something, who are convinced they need more. Markets operate by stimulating and balancing vehement passions. In the end affects might even be turned into marketed products themselves.

In order to analyze the affective conditions and operations of the early modern knowledge markets, we need to establish the key concepts of this volume: knowledge, market, and affects – three contested concepts. Below we will explain our understanding of these concepts, while positioning our research within the most relevant historiographies which have dealt with these issues.

## Knowledge

In his 2016 textbook *What is the History of Knowledge?* Peter Burke recalls that in the 1990s, when he was composing his two-volume study *A Social History of Knowledge*, he thought he was pioneering in this research field.[21] The history of knowledge was considered an exotic or even eccentric topic. However, even at that time interest in this topic was expanding, and has continued to do so. A new school of scholarship has developed, a discipline even, with its own societies, journals, chairs, textbooks, and educational programs.[22] This new discipline is a combination of established fields such as the history of ideas, the history of science and technology, and the sociology of knowledge, but is setting its own path, to explore new questions.[23] What, then, is the *knowledge* studied by historians of knowledge? Burke states (with a wink to Lévi-Strauss): 'Information is raw, knowledge is cooked.'[24] *Information* or *data* seems unordered or merely factual (but of course is already somehow selected, interpreted, and structured), while *knowledge* can be the effect of a long process of selection, verification, classification, systematization, valuation, comparison, evaluation, criticism, or other forms of processing. The concept of *knowledge* intersects with a long list of related terms: information, truth, science, belief, ideas, *mentalité, Wissen, ars*, concepts, theory, and so forth. Although the term knowledge itself indicates a certain 'fixedness', a certain stability, in fact knowledge can be highly unstable. In his recent study, *Prekäres Wissen*, Martin Mulsow challenges the presumed solidity of knowledge, pointing to the fact that knowledge can be invisible, problematic, unstable, delicate, and easily revoked.[25] Mulsow's statements are backed up by a growing body of studies about lost knowledge and the intentional destruction of knowledge.[26] *Knowledge* is situated: its form and valuation depends on the location where it is produced or digested, for instance in monasteries, households, guilds, governmental bodies, universities, industries, laboratories, media networks, archives, museums. There are different *forms of knowledge* and *ways of knowing*, such as artistic, empirical, hermeneutical, practical, or technical knowledge.[27] *Knowledge* can be *embodied* or *tacit*: inherent, enacted, transmitted, or learned through bodily actions.[28] What is considered *valuable knowledge* depends on culture, religion, political climate, social class, gender, or other factors.[29]

In this volume, we will work with an open definition of *knowledge*. One thing we aim to investigate is what *kinds of knowledge* were commodified. It is important to note that studies in the history of knowledge until recently have expressed little interest in economic aspects of *knowledge societies*. Such studies provide insight into the history of knowledge production, classification, selection, valuation, and distribution, but they mostly do so by focusing on academia, religious institutions, governments or other 'gatekeepers' of knowledge, while ignoring the market as a gatekeeper and as a site for knowledge formation. Taking Burke's textbooks as an example: in the long list of key concepts for studying the history of knowledge, 'market', 'commerce', and 'economy' are absent. However, this tide is turning: Dániel Margócsy has recently described the 'commercial visions' of 17th-century scholars, while Martin Mulsow has discussed the 'economy of knowledge', and David Heidenblad has identified 'financial knowledge' as a specific form of knowledge.[30]

The original absence of interest in markets and economies as part of the history of knowledge can probably be put down to the fact that the economics of knowledge already had a separate historiographical tradition: the history and theory of *knowledge economies*. The (global) knowledge economy has for some time been a topic of interest for scholars and practitioners working in economics, management, sociology, anthropology, history, and political science.[31] More than

**FIGURE 1.3** Meeting in a bookstore. Scene from A.J. Montfleury's theatre play *L'Impromtu de Condé* (1698). Engraving: Caspar Luyken. Publisher: Adriaan Braakman. Courtesy of Rijksmuseum Amsterdam, RP-P-1896-A-19368-1595

in the history of knowledge, this area is informed by political and ideological agendas, producing appraisals of the economic potential of the global knowledge economy, both for western nations and for emerging economies. In knowledge economy theory, two developments are considered essential for emerging knowledge economies: (a) knowledge becomes a commodity, a marketed good; and (b) knowledge becomes a productive asset of the economy, highly valued and necessary for economic growth. In this respect knowledge economies are opposed to economies that rely more on physical labour or natural resources: where agrarian societies harvest grain, knowledge economies harvest data.[32] Knowledge economy studies often focus on the second aspect, on knowledge-intensive activities that stimulate technological advance and economic growth. They research human capital, wage inequality based on knowledge intensity in the job market, advanced technology, or the political economy of knowledge.

Studies concerning the history of knowledge economies usually begin around the year 1750. The first knowledge economy is generally placed in the era of the Industrial Revolution (1760s–1850s), first in Britain and then in selected parts of northern and western Europe.[33] The criterion for this localization and periodization is the continuity of economic growth based on technological innovation. In his seminal study *The Gifts of Athena*, Joel Mokyr describes how new knowledge helped to create modern material culture, economic growth, and prosperity. Mokyr limits the concept of knowledge mostly to 'useful knowledge', a term coined by Kuznets in 1965.[34] This focus shows the inherent tendency in knowledge economy studies to narrate the story of western civilization and the great divergence in terms of the rise of *useful knowledge*.[35] The term, however, is contested. *Useful knowledge* often values one type of knowledge (technological knowledge, knowledge that can control and predict) over other forms of knowledge (household knowledge, religious knowledge, artistic knowledge, descriptive, theoretical or interpretative knowledge), and separates knowledge from practices, thus overlooking embodied knowledge.[36] As Margaret Jacob stated in her critique of the historiography of the knowledge economy: 'this top-down conception of knowledge ignores the fundamentally dynamic character and plural contours shaping its production and generation.'[37]

In this volume, we will use of the concept of *knowledge economies*, but we will disconnect this concept from the industrialization-modernization theory, and from the limiting notion of useful knowledge. Although we discuss human capital formation (mostly in terms of literacies and the socialization of new groups of knowledge actors), we will focus more on the *commoditization of knowledge*.

## Markets

Some of the most interesting questions about commerce in history revolve around the question how the demand for and value of certain goods developed.[38] How can we explain the creation of a market for knowledge? How can we explain the readiness with which people wanted to buy and consume commodified knowledge products? How was the valuation of knowledge products established? To answer these questions, we combine the concept of the *market* from economics and economic history with anthropological visions of market processes. In standard economic theory, *markets* are places or systems where goods and services are exchanged for other goods or for money, and value is established through the interplay of supply and demand. For the early modern period, many of the assumptions and distinctions made in standard models are problematic, such as the distinctions between production and exchange, and between producers and consumers.[39]

To engage with more open, dynamic market concepts, we turn to anthropological approaches to economics, such as the work of Igor Kopytoff, which contests the presumption that commodities are somehow fixed in their status: 'For the economists, commodities simply are. That is, certain things and rights to things are produced, exist, and can be seen to circulate through the economic system as they are being exchanged for other things, usually in exchange for money'.[40] Commoditization is a process, where the value and status of things are constantly negotiated. 'The only time when the commodity status of a thing is beyond question is the moment of actual exchange'; otherwise its status is inevitably ambiguous 'and open to the push and pull of events and desires, as it is shuffled about in the flux of social life'.[41] Monetary commoditization is a specific form of reciprocal exchange, which can function in connection with other kinds of markets, such as gift economies.[42] Although the chapters of this volume mainly focus on monetary commoditization, they work with a process-oriented interpretation of commoditization, analyzing the negotiations, inter-subjectivity and moral economy behind the 'objective' economy of monetized transactions. This approach also helps to show how the different agents in the knowledge networks (producers, consumers, intermediaries, and institutions) intersected in the early modern period. Producers were often also merchants, and merchants also produced markets, instead of merely interacting with and exchanging in them. Producers were also consumers, as much as consumers helped to produce knowledge products.

For the analysis of the consumption of knowledge, this project can build on a vast body of studies on the history of consumerism. The development of knowledge societies and the growth of the market for knowledge are directly connected to changing consumer patterns in the early modern period. As with studies of the knowledge economy, the dominant body of work in consumer studies has long focused on the 18th century and on England and western Europe as the cradle of the consumer society.[43] This has changed as work appeared on earlier periods, foremost Lisa Jardine's groundbreaking work *Worldly Goods: A New History of the Renaissance*, which argues that Renaissance Italy anticipated modern consumer society. Jardine retold the conventional story of an age of learning and virtue as one of ostentation and unparalleled global commerce, with luxury objects beginning to fill the lives of those endowed with a restless entrepreneurial spirit and a desire for self-fashioning.[44] Other studies traced comparable changes in consumer patterns outside the core Atlantic economies of western Europe.[45] For the Southern and Northern Netherlands, a growing number of studies have also indicated the 16th and 17th centuries as a foundational period for consumer society.[46]

One of the pressing questions we take from this field is how we can explain changing patterns in *consumer behaviour*. Does the consumption of knowledge follow the same patterns as the consumption of luxury goods or foodstuffs? Various studies have moved on from the traditional structural connection between economic growth and consumer demand, starting with Jan de Vries in his *The Industrious Revolution*. De Vries argues that in 17th-century Holland people started to work harder and for longer hours in order to improve their economic status, in

**FIGURE 1.4** Drinking cup in the shape of a book. Amsterdam 1651. Rijksmuseum Amsterdam. BK-NM-12573

order to be able to acquire more (luxury) goods.[47] De Vries places this change within the context of an emerging urban bourgeoisie which abandoned the traditional moral restraints on luxury to turn into active consumers, in search of comfort, pleasure, novelty, and a grasping at modernity.[48] The development of consumer societies requires explanations which take cultural practices and sensitivities seriously. Taste and social status and respectability were major driving forces for stimulating luxury consumption, as were comfort, politeness, gentility, or the romantic ethic.[49] Informed by these cultural reinterpretations of the consumer revolution, our volume asks similar questions for consumers of knowledge: what are the moral and affective challenges in the process of the commoditization of knowledge and the expansion of the knowledge market? This question also takes us to the third concept underlying our research: *affect*.

## Affects

One of the innovative aspects of this volume is that it studies *knowledge markets* and *market knowledge* in terms of *emotions* and *affects*. What role did affects play in the development of knowledge economies? How did producers try to stimulate an eagerness for knowledge products? How passionate were entrepreneurs and trading companies about gathering new knowledge? How did scientists turn knowledge into a spectacle? Was the market perceived as a passionate place? Since the 1990s, various disciplines have made a so-called affective turn: linguists, historians, anthropologists, sociologists, and philosophers became interested in the production, expression, and transmission of emotions and the determining role emotions play in political, social, cultural, and individual processes.[50] In the humanities, the rise of the history of emotions has led to the founding of centres for emotion studies in various countries.[51] So far, however, the history of emotions has paid remarkably little attention to economics. In the encyclopedic overview *Early Modern Emotions* hardly any attention is paid to markets and economics.[52] Merridee Bailey, in her lemma on 'Economic Records', also recognizes this historiographic vacuum. She presumes that 'the absence of systematic work into the presence of emotions in early modern Europe's economic records and the lack of explicit methodologies to investigate the role emotions have played in historic economic systems' is due to the fact that 'historians have understandably shied away from supposedly drier source materials, assuring that emotions will be absent from certain bodies of sources.'[53]

On the other hand, economic theory has traditionally neglected emotions. Capitalism has mostly been perceived as a rational system, either through the (neo) liberal focus on the *homo oeconomicus* and rational interest as the driving force of economic processes, or through the Marxist conceptualization and criticism of 'cold capitalism'.[54] In the last decades, however, economists have started to recognize the role of emotions in finance and economics, resulting in behavioural economics and behavioural finance as new research fields.[55] Historians, anthropologists, and philosophers also stress that we need to reconsider the 'cool' stereotype of economics and investigate the historicity of the connection between economics and emotion. Sociologist Eva Illouz states that if we realize that our 'hyper-modern, hyper-capitalistic lives are also hyper-emotional', we need to reconsider where this connection was forged.[56] Ute Frevert, director of the 'Geschichte der Gefühle' group at the Max-Planck Institut für Bildungsforschung, studies emotional regimes of capitalism in the 19th century, such as the operation of trust and greed in the financial world.[57] Other studies have discussed the role of the imagination, of hope, and of trust and honour in economic processes.[58]

Although economics and the history of emotions are finding more connections, this has not yet resulted in extensive research into the early modern period, a period which witnessed the development of capitalism as well as a fundamental shift in emotional culture. This volume will help to bridge this gap by studying early modern knowledge societies as affective communities. The term *affect* needs explanation. We have chosen this term, and not the more common word *emotion*, because the latter only became the preferred term for feeling during the 19th century. In the early modern period terms such as 'passion', 'affect', 'sentiment' and 'feeling' were far more common. We do not presume to make any kind of ontological claim about the operation of emotions, and we will also try to avoid the vast discussions around *affect*.[59] The term *affect* helps to underline various aspects that we consider of importance for understanding early modern market processes. Firstly, the term *affect* connects emotional responses with bodies and the world outside the body. Emotions are often perceived as intense mental activity, mainly aroused through the nervous system. However, early modern humoural theory firmly connected the passions with a wide variety of bodily functions *and* with the macrocosm.[60] Passions were seen as affecting the body, which could be triggered from both within or without. This underscores the importance of taking bodily expressions and locations into account when analyzing knowledge markets: affective knowledge practices are acted through the body and influenced by the material context in which the body operates.[61] A damp and crowded coffee house, for example, was prone to trigger different emotional trading behaviour than an open market place.[62] Market behaviour is an affective practice, communicated through the body, and shaped by locations which can therefore be seen as affective spaces.[63]

Secondly, the term *affect* helps to underline that emotions are also *emotives*: they are performative means of communication.[64] Emotional expression (both through words and through body language) functions as an instrument for communication with others. The term *affect* highlights this communicative and performative aspect. Emotions affect people and transform situations; they do something to the world.[65] In knowledge markets this concept of affective communication might turn out to be very relevant.

Thirdly, emotions also have an active *social life*. Barbara Rosenwein has coined the term 'emotional community' for 'groups in which people adhere to the same norm of emotional expression and value—or devalue—the same or related emotions'.[66] This aspect of emotions is highly relevant for the history of knowledge, as it might help us understand how *knowledge communities* were formed through emotional behaviour and language. What role did emotions play in the shaping of knowledge communities? What shared *vocabularies of feeling* helped to construct affective knowledge communities, and what *emotional scripts* or *feeling rules* helped to discipline (newcomers to) the group?[67] Emotions provide the self and others with meaning and value, while they can also exclude the other.[68] This point is also made by Martin Mulsow, who stresses that knowledge is not only about classification and paradigms, it is also about habitus and feeling. Mulsow describes the development of *Faszinationsgemeinschaften*: communities of learners passionate about and fascinated by knowledge.[69]

Finally, we acknowledge that emotions are not merely irrational impulses, but also *instruments of appraisal*.[70] Martha Nussbaum's *Upheavals of Thought,* drawing on pre-modern models of analysis, suggests that emotions should be regarded as a complex interplay between personal judgment and social norms. Emotions therefore should not be seen as separate from ratio and morals but as ethical and social factors in answering questions such as 'What is worth caring about' and 'How should I act?'.[71] This connects to Susan James' description of how in 17th-century philosophy, knowledge became more closely connected to emotion, as the conception of knowledge included volition, which was regarded as a passion.[72]

Built on these interpretations of affect, we argue that the concept of *affective economy* will provide a useful model for the analysis of historical market-emotion-negotiations, by considering the role of bodies, locations, performativity, ethics, and cognition.

## Analyzing knowledge societies as affective economies

In this volume we will investigate the development of knowledge economies in the early modern period, offering examples of how to analyze such complex concepts as knowledge societies and the interrelation between knowledge, markets, and affects. We locate the development of knowledge markets in a variety of spaces: in the urban areas of the Netherlands, the book market, merchant networks, global trading companies, stock exchanges, courts, laboratories, mints, playhouses, scaffolds and anatomical theatres, art collections, and private households. The chapters investigate the commodification of knowledge from the perspective of different actors: scholars, publishers, designers, literary authors, merchants, entrepreneurs, amateurs, princes, diplomats, minters, children, and teachers. They explore knowledge-intensive products (such as books, objects, art collections, shares and derivatives, or coins) and the literacies they required. Dynamics in the knowledge market are analyzed in a wide variety of sources: egodocuments, records of trading companies, notarial archives, criminal records, catalogues of collections, mining archives, theatrical plays, travel literature, images, objects, and large data sets. Together, these stories portray the Northern and Southern Netherlands as early examples of an advanced knowledge economy, in which knowledge was commoditized, and in which commoditized knowledge acquired an important role in economic and social processes. The chapters furthermore analyze the role affects played in this process. While all chapters address this question on different levels, the chapters in the first part of the volume focus more on the affects of actors in the market, while the chapters in the second part investigate how knowledge economies market and manage affects.

The chapters by Ulinka Rublack, Vera Keller, Martin Mulsow, Tina Asmussen, Claudia Swan and Feike Dietz focus mostly on the knowledge cultures and the emotional drives of *actors* in early modern knowledge markets: merchants, entrepreneurs, prince-projectors, collectors, authors, publishers, and readers. These chapters show what types of knowledge these actors possessed and made valid to other sections of society, as well as their own desire to collect, make, distribute, and consume goods. How can we understand the emotional dimensions of early modern mercenary and entrepreneurial engagements with commodities and commercial projects? The most common assumption has been that merchants sought to rationally maximize profit and reproduce distinction through goods as social markers. These chapters all contest this assumption, while bringing in various new perspectives and concepts, such as *wish economies*, *affective projecting*, *market sensibility*, and *affective knowledge communities*.

Ulinka Rublack investigates the early modern entrepreneurial spirit through a case study on the famous Augsburg merchant Hans Fugger (1531-1598). Fugger's remarkable collection of over 4500 letters reveal him as a consumer and co-creator of values, often in regard to innovative products or sourcing mechanisms. The chapter highlights the substantial role of merchants in early modern knowledge-making processes. It furthermore shows that early modern merchants were not simply figures who calculated the reduction of transaction costs to optimize supply, cultivating rational price management and disenchantment. Fugger's letters clearly show his affective investment in the goods he ordered, whether shoes, feathers, animals, or oysters. Fugger's case indicates that the early modern affective economy was built around categories of *newness*, *liveliness*, *freshness*, and *vitality*. The Netherlands played a key role in the emergence of new types of knowing tied to the world of the senses – the material and natural worlds. The merchants' consumer demands and relation to matter corresponded to and further explored understandings of the body, the passions and the soul.

Tina Asmussen and Martin Mulsow analyze two noblemen: German dukes with a passion for profitable knowledge. The authors argue that the prioritization of useful knowledge as a motor for the economic development of early modern Europe and its path towards modernity has overlooked the role of hope, desire, fear, and the imagination in these processes. Tina Asmussen brings in the case study of the Duke Julius of Braunschweig-Lüneburg (1529-1589) and his wish to revive ore mining and metal production, and turn Wolfenbüttel into a prospering town of industry and commerce. To enable this, the duke aimed to build a large-scale inland waterway system. This required expert knowledge and skilled engineers whom he attracted, amongst others, from the knowledge market of the

Southern Netherlands. Asmussen investigates the planning, implementation, and failure of this waterway project as steps in an affective economy, highlighting the impact of *imaginaries, promises, and desires* on the duke's economic practices. While other princes and electors were obsessed with the 'hunting devil', Duke Julius was obsessed with the 'mining devil', attracted by the highly contingent and capital-intensive nature of mining. In order to stimulate his imagination and keep his entrepreneurial zeal oriented towards the promising profits of the mine and waterworks, the duke commissioned colourful paintings of the mining area and of the inland navigation project. Asmussen shows that these imaginaries and passions did not hinder business, but helped the duke to envision future profits, make plans, set goals, attract investors, and overcome risk aversion.

A comparable case of *affective projecting* is described by Martin Mulsow, in his chapter on Frederick I, Duke of Saxe-Gotha-Altenburg (1646-1691). In the case of this business-oriented duke, the passion for profitable knowledge resulted in the activation of an international network of researchers interested in alchemy and in the development of an alchemist laboratory. Mulsow starts the duke's story from the 'whodunnit' question: why did Frederick, in July 1688, suddenly feel a pressing need to go to Amsterdam? To answer this question, Mulsow follows the duke in a complicated fabric of activities: stock market speculation, troop rental, art purchases, political negotiations, and alchemical experiments. As it turns out, in order to reach his goals, Frederick was navigating different markets: the (alchemical) knowledge market, the art market, the Amsterdam stock market and shopping zones, and the markets for army building and territorial gain. Mulsow describes these complex negotiations of the prince-entrepreneur as an affective economy, a precarious balancing between hope and disappointment, trust and mistrust, secrecy and open knowledge exchange.

Both Asmussen and Mulsow state that the emerging knowledge economies seem to have attracted actors who were willing to take risks. The urban centres of the Northern and Southern Netherlands acted as an accelerator, providing a certain breathlessness and enticing a thirst for speculation. *Alchemy* played an important role in this *wish economy*, with its promise of sudden riches for those who could find the key. Furthermore, the exotic aspects of alchemy were part of the attraction of the emerging global knowledge economy, and the knowledge field also brought innovation and inspiration, e.g. ideas for a new physics, with new conceptions of matter. This we can also see visualized in the anonymous painting 'Glorification of Trade and Science' (Figure 1.1), described at the beginning of this introduction, where alchemical experiments and exotic birds are envisioned as drives towards new knowledge and prosperity.

The painting also helps to highlight the importance of aesthetics and of the arts in economic processes. *Ars* and *technē* were essential instruments in the economy of promise, as is shown in various chapters in this volume: whether it is the colourful paintings of his projects which the Duke of Braunschweig-Lüneburg wanted to hang on his palace walls, the early modern interest in calligraphy, the artful knowledge collections of connoisseurs, or the way authors of children's books played on the imagination to attract new readers. The arts reified future imaginaries, turning them into tangible elements of economic practice.

At another level, art itself was a prized commodity, subject to the contingencies of open markets. The chapter by Claudia Swan discusses the interrelation between knowledge, affect and the art market through the role of *liefhebbers* – amateurs, or 'lovers', as the Dutch word *liefhebber* indicates. Swan shows how *liefhebbers*, learned non-professionals whose knowledge of a given subject or practice enabled them to exercise discernment, functioned as knowledge brokers through the use of affects. This phenomenon has been described in affective terms of *curiositas* and wonder, but not in terms of love.[73] Swan uses the concept of *market sensibility* to analyze the nature of the 'love' of *liefhebbers*: how they connected knowledge, value, and affect. Highlighting the emotive investment in these practices, Swan describes the importance of social values of *liefhebberij*: friendship was key to acquisition and valuation in a market which mainly operated in private spaces. By opening up their cabinet of curiosities for visitors, and publishing beautiful catalogues of their collections, amateurs were able to attract new groups of knowledge lovers to the market for collecting. *Liefhebbers* thus helped to form communities of shared tastes and interests, microcosms bound by social and market values.[74]

Feike Dietz analyzes the development of another *affective community* in the knowledge economy: the community of young readers. The early modern Dutch book market is a fruitful case study because of the Republic's high literacy rate and extensive book production.[75] The fact that the market for youth literature eventually became a flourishing literary subsystem suggests that early modern producers of such literature were highly successful in presenting their wares as desirable and favourable. Dietz describes the strategies employed in the book market to attract youngsters as new consumers to the knowledge market and turn them into eager consumers of knowledge. For this, producers and distributors needed to overcome the negative connotations of addiction to knowledge and overstimulation of the imagination. Despite these fears and objections, youth literature became a very successful market product, with a growing product differentiation over the 18th century. One of the strategies employed to overcome contemporary sensitivities and anxieties was to present reading as a physical act of eating, drinking, or digesting: books as honey for the mind. Here we can link back to Rublack's chapter, which highlighted the importance of sensorial experience in the commoditization of knowledge, and the role the Netherlands played in this process. Just as with Fugger's world of goods, the affective economy of children's books was built around categories of newness, liveliness, freshness, vitality, and health. The healthy habit of reading was also presented as a social act. Children were lured by the prospect of becoming a member of an affective reading community. Dietz traces a possible trend from seeing reading as a social economy, a cycle of gift and reciprocity, based on interactions and binding obligations, to considering reading a rational investment, a rewarding form of labour in terms of profit. The flourishing early modern book market thus invited young consumers to 'practise books' as commodities to consume and buy, to embody and crave.

Dietz also makes a plea for revising the presumed passive role of consumers: children not only bought and consumed, but also helped to shape knowledge products. They functioned as *prosumers*. The same observation is made by Rublack, who shows that producers and traders like Hans Fugger were also passionate consumers, sensitively attracted by fine fabric, and bodily engaged through smell, touch, and taste to test out materials.[76]

## 'We merchants are like resty horses': global knowledge economies

The chapters by Rublack, Keller, Swan, Asmussen, Mulsow, and Goldgar describe aspects of an emerging *global knowledge economy*, with an open eye to the challenges expanding global trade networks brought to existing modes of knowledge. Merchants, investors, collectors, and other knowledge brokers operated in global trade networks, reshaping traditional European knowledge models along global horizons. The global market also intertwined worldwide emotions. Exotic luxury goods and curiosities excited desire and wonder among European investors and consumers. Yet, as Vera Keller states, we must remember that the development of global knowledge economies also entangled the lives and emotions of peoples outside Europe with the emotions and doings of the European consumers and producers. The excitement and apprehension experienced by the European investors related, in an unequal nexus of power and affect, to the fear and pain experienced by the enslaved individual upon whose labour that investor's success depended. Recent studies have also shown this to be true for the Dutch Republic, where visual and literary media purposefully engaged Dutch desires for global mastery, including through the depiction of enslaved and mastered peoples.[77]

Vera Keller analyzes the global ambitions of Sir Balthazar Gerbier (1592-1663), calligrapher, secretary, spy, double agent, miniature portraitist, costume and masque designer, architect, military engineer, cartographer, art collector and connoisseur, colonizer, academy founder, pamphleteer, promoter of investment schemes and proponent of slavery, and author of many works in Dutch, English, and French. This short summary of Gerbier's accomplishments already indicates how he combined a wide variety of knowledge domains and aesthetics in the making of a global knowledge economy. In his far-ranging career Gerbier, like many others of his merchant peers, projected ambitious global projects. He aimed to shape a new world, overriding longstanding knowledge assumptions of climatic bounds and human nature, planting African crops in Southeast Asia, and African people in the Americas. The mixture of types of knowledge in Gerbier's practice illustrates that in the rise of global trade, forms of knowledge previously reserved for the courts of princes became newly available not only to commonwealths and trading companies, but to individual private actors in the global marketplace. As Keller argues, Gerbier developed existing global views into an *aesthetic*, offering both verbal and visual languages for reshaping Europe along global horizons.

Through his monumental calligraphic hand, Gerbier expressed the majesty of his enterprise. Keller shows that Gerbier's interest in calligraphy should be understood in the context of the Dutch Republic's role in the emerging global knowledge economy. At its most expansive period of overseas settlement, 17th-century Dutch calligraphy reached a scale, grandeur, and luxury unmatched elsewhere in Western Europe. Mastering calligraphic literacy could be instrumental in the display of military control and political *savoir-faire*. Gerbier's calligraphic mastery suggests that the seemingly manic nature of his wild-eyed global projects was in fact a carefully calibrated aesthetic. Gerbier emphasized that manipulating the emotions of investors and settlers in the new world, through the creation of alluring fictions, was a form of knowledge vital to global trade. With the description of the role of aesthetics and the imagination to highlight the promises of the market in the global *wish economy,* Keller's chapter connects to the articles by Asmussen and Mulsow.

Various essays in this volume show that the value of knowledge was balanced between its quality of uniqueness, often requiring secrecy, and its quality to attract large audiences in the open public sphere. Martin Mulsow describes how the Duke of Saxe-Gotha-Altenburg balanced political and economic interests in the communicative radius of his activities: what was public, what was secret, and what should be kept very secret? Keller's chapter on Gerbier shows comparable strategies of secrecy in the global trade network: according to Gerbier, it was not always wise to know too much and to educate all populations on the same level. These insights seem to be in line with current historiography, which holds that international trading companies such as the VOC and West India Company (WIC) were not major promotors or instruments of scientific research, and safeguarded information their employees collected through strict policies of secrecy.[78] However, although secrecy played an important role in global knowledge markets, and although the VOC and WIC might not have been the most active promotors of knowledge, the global trade networks they helped to develop did form the basis for an extensive system of knowledge transfer and appropriation. They enabled the exchange of knowledge-intensive goods, exotic products, and naturalia, and facilitated explorers who set out to research and describe the cultures and natural environments the trade routes connected.[79]

## Marketing affects and knowledge: familiar surprises and spectacular knowledge

Anne Goldgar takes up this point of the role trade companies played in the expansion of the global knowledge economy through the case study of the explorations of the Dutch *Noordsche Compagnie*, the monopoly whaling company. The Nordic Company had a strong interest in collecting knowledge, setting up advanced and quite brutish empirical experiments with human bodies and lives as test cases in the ice cold Nordic regions. The company staged overwinterings on

Spitsbergen and Jan Mayen Island to investigate the possibility of year-round occupation of the whaling stations. Goldgar's case study shows the prominence of the market for knowledge around 1630. Although the Nordic expeditions turned out to be a failure, they were turned into a commercial success through the book market. Publishers took the travelogues, tailored them to consumers' expectations and craving for adventure stories and put them on the market. In these journals, readers could experience the horror through detailed accounts of the challenges of daily life on the islands, which gave readers a means of grasping the state of mind of the sailors as they lay helpless, contemplating their end. What might have been useful information for trade companies (for instance, information on wind and weather), essential knowledge even to pursue future overwinterings, for a publisher looking for a wider market, could be relatively boring, and was removed or adapted. Publishers would much rather highlight that one of the journals was found between the legs of the longest-lived of the sailors. Marketing adventure, the new genre of 'overwintering' brought chilling narratives about whales, icebergs, bears, scurvy, starvation, and freezing to death, for 'Lief-hebbers of strange Voyages'.

However, we should not make too sharp a distinction between knowledge and emotion – between the rational assessments of the trade companies and the craving for adventure in the book market. References to emotion in a journal of overwinterings were also a source of information for the company and its investors. Emotion is in itself a form of knowledge. In the case of the overwinterings, the ability of a sailor to withstand emotionally the hardships of a lonely and miserable Arctic winter would have been as helpful a piece of information as the availability of scurvy grass. At the other hand, the adventure stories educated the European public about the Nordic regions. Trade science was turned into knowledge about explorations, the Arctic and its wildlife, about human endeavour and perseverance.

Goldgar's case study shows that affects were turned into marketed products in the early modern period. The chapters by Goldgar, Dietz, Swan, and Vanhaesebrouck, on travel narratives, children's books, cabinets of wonders, and (anatomical) theatres, all show that emotions became market products in the developing knowledge economy. Excitement, horror, wonder, health, and happiness could be bought in affordable units. Consumers could 'addict' themselves to series of comparable products, with small changes in the product line, to guarantee consumer involvement. In the published accounts of the Nordic explorations, trade moved to the background, while adventure took centre stage. For early modern readers, emotion became a way of marketing knowledge.

Claartje Rasterhoff and Kaspar Beelen trace these dynamics through a digital analysis of product differentiation and coordination in the early modern Dutch book markets. In line with the chapter by Feike Dietz, their article sees the book market as a site where market actors shape knowledge products and where the knowledge products themselves also shape the behaviour of market actors. Rasterhoff and Beelen start from the presumption that books developed from luxury goods into *populuxe goods*: new, affordable, non-essential products and product variants.[80] In line with Van Zanden's thesis concerning the Netherlands as knowledge economy, the authors map the mushrooming production of books in the Dutch Republic. In the 17th century, the Dutch book market generated a knowledge culture in which novelty was an important source of value. Mining the rich database of the Short Title Catalogue of the Netherlands (STCN), Rasterhoff and Beelen trace how Dutch publishers introduced product and process innovations that could lower costs and increase profit. By analyzing the patterns of co-ordination via products, through multiple measures related to product innovation (diversity, similarity, and 'burstiness'), Rasterhoff and Beelen are able to trace how the creative industries introduced 'familiar surprises' – small differences, diverging just enough from traditions and norms to create a sense of novelty, without losing touch with established genres and expectations.[81] Explorations with sentiment mining techniques furthermore underline the findings of Goldgar: emotions were indeed marketed in the Dutch book world. The overall 'positive' sentiment of the first half of the century seems to have shifted towards higher levels of anxiety and negative emotions in the second half of the century, while 'bursty', sudden, significant changes in affective language appear to have declined in the 18th century.

Karel Vanhaesebrouck's chapter can help to understand this burstiness of negative sentiments, as he traces the development of a commercial spectacular culture with specific interest in violence and horror. The chapter takes us further along the line of the marketing of affects through its analysis of how knowledge was made into a spectacle in the early modern Netherlands. Vanhaesebrouck follows the body, as it was displayed and dissected in anatomical theatres and atlases, on scaffolds, and on the theatre stage. In the 17th-century Dutch Republic, knowledge about bodies was commodified through spectacle. As it turns out, the presumed 'classicist' Northern Dutch theatrical realm was fond of Senecan drama, with its overtly violent, gruesome horror scenes. Vanhaesebrouck shows that this spectacular theatre not only exploited the passions of the public commercially, but can also be labelled as an exploration of knowledge, diving deep into the souls and senses of the viewers to investigate and manipulate their bodily actions and passions. The chapter thus describes the changing relationship between science, theatricality, spectacle, and commercialization in the Dutch Republic.

## Managing affects in the knowledge market

As various chapters in this book demonstrate the high level of emotional involvement of producers, distributors, and consumers in the early modern knowledge market, it becomes urgent to ask how these emotions were managed, and whether early modern societies were aware of the involvement of affect in commercial processes. How 'emotionally literate' were early modern market actors?

Sebastian Felten approaches these questions through the topic of money and coins, and the challenges these knowledge-intensive products posed for the various groups of handlers. In the early modern period money was a thing about which the essentials eluded the knower. All users of metallic money, from lay people to financial experts, were sometimes mystified by money. This is quite understandable if we realize that the Dutch Republic alone housed over 800 different types of coins. Money handling required a specific, advanced literacy. Learning one's coins required constant effort. Scholars have often presumed that this 'chaotic' system posed many challenges to the users and that therefore the 'rationalization' or harmonization of the coin system was naturally welcomed. Felten poses the question *how* commensurability of value was achieved across social and cultural contexts, and what affective aspects were in play in this process. He shows that the establishment of commensurability between multiple coins was a highly affective phenomenon, drawing the actors of the Dutch *entrepôt des savoirs monétaires* into highly emotional battles about the clash between private gains and passions and the true interest of the commonwealth.

Inger Leemans finds comparable patterns of the management of affect in the context of the Amsterdam stock exchange. She first describes the Amsterdam bourse building as a microcosm of the Dutch knowledge economy. Since its foundation in 1611, the Amsterdam Stock Exchange functioned as a global market place and as a hub of knowledge, bringing together an impressive variety of forms of knowledge, while schooling new groups to participate in this fast-expanding and dynamic market. This hub can be described as an affective space. Affects played a central role in the organization of bourse life, in the day-to-day practices of the commercial communities in and around the building. The building was organized to incite desire, for products and for profit; to create enthusiasm in both trader and consumer, but also to regulate excessively passionate behaviour and to avoid violent clashes. This tension between exciting and taming passions was all the more visible in the corner of the bourse where shares and derivatives were traded. What was new and challenging about the stock market is not only that it was knowledge-intensive, but also that it was highly excitable: share trading depends on volatility and fast negotiations. This formed a challenge to the established moral economy of the wise, honourable, and trustworthy merchant, who acted with prudence and restraint. Leemans shows that the regulation of affect was engineered through the organisation of the building (by the roofed shopping floor, or by ordering trade around pillars), through regulations and law enforcement, but also through an advanced public discourse, in textual, visual, and performative form. A 'natural philosophy of trade' emerged which described the trade floor as an affective economy, in which passions functioned as embodied knowledge on which merchants could act. Knowledge about the passions that drive markets was stimulated, in order to improve successful operation within the market. The Amsterdam exchange thus presents an excellent case study for the intersection of market knowledge and the knowledge market.

## Conclusion: affective knowledge economies

The chapters of this volume show the importance of taking affects into account when analyzing knowledge markets. They present the early modern knowledge society as a lively affective economy, with entrepreneurs and merchants full of hope and enthusiasm, *prosumers* and *liefhebbers* passionate about knowledge, minters fighting over the value of money, publishers and authors exploiting the market with spectacular knowledge, and jobbers educating themselves in theories of the passions to better navigate the market. We trace the desires and anxieties of the actors in the knowledge market – their eagerness, hope, and frustration – and show how emotions were used as techniques of knowledge. Furthermore, we show how early modern entrepreneurs, collectors, and consumers of knowledge formed *Faszinationsgemeinschaften*, emotional communities shaped around fascination for new knowledge and for knowledge products.

All in all, these case studies stress that in order to understand the dynamics of early modern knowledge markets, we need to understand market sensibilities. Market processes are dependent on affects. We cannot otherwise fully understand why producers, entrepreneurs, and consumers were so eager and persistent in their efforts to develop and consume new products and open up new markets. Adventure, the lure of the unexpected, and other promises of the market helped to overcome risk and anxiety. By advocating knowledge products as fresh, healthy, and alive, and as fulfilling the needs of the body, those selling knowledge lured new groups of consumers to the market. These affective strategies can be seen as universal and timeless, but, as the chapters in this book will show, they are also contingent, depended on contemporary sensitivities and normative systems. Early modern consumer patterns had to be balanced with anxieties about sin, conspicuous consumption, risk, and loss of honour, and with the drama the global knowledge economy caused to people across the globe. The new knowledge economy with its altering consumption culture also required a specific affective economy, tailored to the needs and knowledges of the early modern society.

## Notes

1 Two other versions of this painting have been attributed to Jan Brueghel the Younger: "Landscape with Mercury and his children" (https://rkd.nl/explore/images/209264) "Allegorie der verkehrten Welt" (http://www.artnet.com/artists/jan-brueghel-the-younger/allegorie-der-verkehrten-welt). The painting has been described in: R. Bastiaanse and H. Bots, *Glorieuze Revolutie*, 129; K. Ertz, *Jan Breughel der Jüngere*, 388, 389; A. P. de Mirimonde, "Les Allégories de la Musique," 351; Van Lennep, 'l'Alchemiste', 153.

2 The painting shows remarkable resemblances to earlier prints, such as: "Planet Mercury and his Children" (1566-1570), by Harmen Jansz Muller, after a design of Maarten van Heemskerck, Rijksmuseum Amsterdam, RP-P-1891-A-16487, to Jan Sadeler I, 'Children of Mercury (Wednesday)' (1585), after a drawing by Maarten de Vos (1532–1603), and to Sebastian Vrancx's painting of the port of Antwerp, which also depicts the 'Children of Mercury' in a commercial setting. Tarbes, Musee Massey. We thank Elizabeth Honig for her comments and suggestions on this topic.

3  P. Burke, *A Social History of Knowledge,* 32–80.
4  The project is a collaboration between the Max Planck Institute for the History of Science, the Descartes Centre for the History and Philosophy of the Sciences and the Humanities, a number of Dutch and Flemish universities, and the Netherlands Institute for Advanced Study (NIAS) of the Royal Academy of the Netherlands (KNAW). See for further information on the project: http://www.globalknowledgesociety.com. We are grateful to the NIAS for its generous support, and to Wijnand Mijnhardt and Sven Dupré for setting up this project and guiding us through the process.
5  The first volume was published in 2019: B. De Munck and A. Romano, *Knowledge and the Early Modern City.*
6  We will use the term "the Netherlands" and "Dutch" to refer to both the Southern and Northern Netherlands.
7  J. De Vries and A. Van der Woude, *The First Modern Economy*; J. Israel, *Dutch Primacy in World Trade*; M. Prak, *The Dutch Republic in the Seventeenth Century.*
8  G. Marnef, *Antwerp in the Age of Reformation*; Mielants, "Early Modern Antwerp."
9  M. Prak, *The Dutch Republic in the Seventeenth Century*; K. Davids, *The Rise and Decline of Dutch Technological Leadership*; K. Davids and B. De Munck, *Innovation and Creativity*; J. Israel, *Radical Enlightenment.*
10  C. Lesger, *The Rise of the Amsterdam Market.*
11  J. Van Zanden, *The Long Road to the Industrial Revolution.* Van Zanden aims to provide a new historical timeline for the Great divergence debate.
12  The development of the Northern European knowledge economy was rooted in earlier developments, e.g. long-distance trade networks, urbanization, guild structures, proto-industry, income per capita, rising literacy, and changing consumption patterns. J. Van Zanden, *The Long Road,* 80–90.
13  P. H. Smith and B. Schmidt, *Making Knowledge in Early Modern Europe*; H. J. Cook, *Matters of Exchange*; D. Margócsy, *Commercial Visions*; B. Schmidt, *Inventing Exoticism*; J. Mokyr, *The Gifts of Athena*; M. C. Jacob, *The First Knowledge Economy*; M. C. Jacob, *Strangers Nowhere in the World.*
14  Smith and Findlen *Merchants and Marvels*; Miller, *Peiresc's Mediterranean World.* For the Dutch Republic as the center of the European book trade in the seventeenth century C. Rasterhoff, *Painting and Publishing*; Hoftijzer, "The Dutch Republic."
15  J. Soll, *The Reckoning,* Chap 5; S. R, Epstein and M. R. Prak, *Guilds, Innovation, and the European Economy.*
16  D. McCloskey, *Bourgeois Virtues*; D. McCloskey, *Bourgeois Dignity.*
17  A. Weststeijn, *Commercial Republicanism.*
18  M. C. Jacob and C. Secretan, *The Self-perception of Early Modern Capitalists.* D. Sturkenboom, *De Ballen van de Koopman*; T. Wijsenbeek-Olthuis, "A Matter of Taste."
19  J. Mokyr, *A Culture of Growth,* 7.
20  B. De Munck and A. Romano, *Knowledge and the Early Modern City*; Smith, Meyers and Cook, *Ways of Making and Knowing*; J. Östling, D. L. Heidenblad and A. N. Hammar, *Forms of Knowledge.*
21  P. Burke, *A Social History of Knowledge,* Vol. I and II.
22  P. Burke, *What Is the History of Knowledge?*
23  S. Lässig, "The History of Knowledge"; L. J. Daston, "The History of Science and the History of Knowledge"; S. Dupré and G. Somsen, "The History of Knowledge and the Future of Knowledge Societies"; M. Mulsow and L. Daston, "History of Knowledge."
24  P. Burke, *What Is the History of Knowledge?*
25  M. Mulsow, *Prekäres Wissen*; M. Mulsow, "Ökonomie des Wissens."
26  D. Schäfer, *Cultures of Knowledge*; K. Davids, "Public Knowledge and Common Secrets"; S. Dupré and G. Somsen, "The History of Knowledge and the Future of Knowledge Societies"; M. Mulsow and L. Daston, "History of Knowledge".

27 L. J. Daston and P. L. Galison, *Objectivity*; L. J. Daston and E. Lunbeck, *Histories of Scientific Observation*; P. H. Smith and B. Schmidt, *Making Knowledge*; J. Östling, D. L. Heidenblad and A. N. Hammar, *Forms of Knowledge*.

28 M. Polanyi, *The Tacit Dimension*; L. Roberts, "Circulation of Knowledge"; B. De Munck, "Disassembling the City."

29 L. J. Daston and K. Park, *Wonders and the Order of Nature*; L. J. Daston and P. L. Galison, *Objectivity*.

30 D. Margócsy, *Commercial Visions*; M. Mulsow, "Ökonomie des Wissens."

31 In 2010, Springer founded the *Journal of the Knowledge Economy*.

32 W. W. Powel and K. Snellman, "The Knowledge Economy."

33 M. C. Jacob, *The First Knowledge Economy*.

34 Kuznets as Mokyr define useful as useful in economic production, but whereas Kuznets sees useful knowledge as interchangeable with tested knowledge, Mokyr is specifically interested in technology - in propositional knowledge (what) and prescriptive (how to) knowledge that can help manipulate natural phenomena. J. Mokyr, *The Gifts of Athena*, 3–5.

35 J. Black, *The Power of Knowledge*.

36 M. Polanyi, *The Tacit Dimension* ; L. Roberts, "The Circulation of Knowledge"; B. De Munck, "Disassembling the City."

37 M. C. Jacob, *The First Knowledge Economy*, 9.

38 K. Pomeranz, "Ten Years After"; P. H. Smith and B. Schmidt, *Making Knowledge*; M. Hutter and D. Throsby *Beyond Price*; Klamer *Value Economics*.

39 K. Pomeranz, "Ten Years After". H. J. Cook, *Matters of Exchange*.

40 I. Kopytoff, "The Cultural Biography of Things," 83.

41 I. Kopytoff, "The Cultural Biography of Things," 69–70, 83.

42 M. Mauss, *The Gift*.

43 The field of consumer studies has witnessed a boom since the 1990's seminal work has been done in this field by Roy Porter, John Brewer, Maxine Berg and Daniel Roche: J. Brewer and R. Porter, *Consumption and the World of Goods*; J. Brewer and L. Fontaine, "Homo Creditus"; J. Brewer and F. Trentmann, *Consuming Cultures*; C. Berry, *The Idea of Luxury*; D. Roche, *A History of Everyday Things*; M. Berg and E. Eger, *Luxury in the Eighteenth Century*; M. Berg, "In Pursuit of Luxury"; M. Berg, *Luxury and Pleasure*; D. Miller, "Consumption as the Vanguard of History"; F. Trentman, *The Oxford Handbook of the History of Consumption*.

44 L. Jardine, *Worldly Goods*.

45 L. Peck, *Consuming Splendor*.

46 T. Wijsenbeek-Olthuis, "A Matter of Taste"; B. De Munck, "Artisans, Products and Gifts"; B. Blondé, "Shoppen met Isabella d'Este"; C. De Staelen, *Spulletjes en hun betekenis*; R. Rittersma, *Luxury in the Low Countries*. For a recent overview see: W. Ryckbosch "Early Modern Consumption History."

47 J. De Vries, *The Industrious Revolution*. De Vries's thesis has been challenged: did workers work harder to buy more goods, or to overcome economic hardship? R. C. Allen and J. L. Weisdorf, "Was There an 'Industrious Revolution'."

48 J. De Vries, *The Industrious Revolution*, 44–58.

49 Cf. studies by Berg, Berry, Brewer, Eger, Fontaine, Miller, Porter, cited above.

50 A. Rechwitz, "Praktiken und ihre Affekte." The 2019 volume *Affective Societies* presents a social science approach to this topic, discussing the domination of affect and emotion in social and political life as a recent phenomenon. J. Slaby and C. von Scheve, *Affective Societies*.

51 J. Plamper, *The History of Emotions*.

52 S. Broomhall, *Early Modern Emotions*.

53 M. L. Bailey, "Economic Records," 108.

54 A. O. Hirschman, *The Passions and the Interests*.

55 G. A. Akerlof and R. J. Shiller, *Animal Spirits*; A. Shleifer, *Inefficient Markets*; C. Zaloom, *Out of the Pits*.

56  E. Illouz, *Cold Intimacies*.
57  U. Frevert, "Gefühle und Kapitalismus."
58  J. Beckert, *Imagined Futures*; U. Stäheli, "Hoffnung als ökonomischer Affekt"; U. Stäheli, *Spectacular Speculation*; S. Teuscher, *The Moral Economy*.
59  B. Massumi, *Parables for the Virtual*; S. Triggs, "Affect Theory."
60  G. Paster, K. Rowe, and M. F. Floyd-Wilson, *Reading the Early Modern Passions*; J. R. Solomon, "You've got to have Soul"; M. Scheer, "Are Emotions a Kind of Practice."
61  I. Leemans,"Embodied Emotions from a Dutch Historical Perspective."
62  K. Barclay ,"Space and Place"; I. Leemans, "Verse Weavers and Paper Traders."
63  Reckwitz, "Affective Spaces."
64  W. M. Reddy, *The Navigation of Feeling*.
65  J. Plamper, *The History of Emotions*.
66  B. Rosenwein, *Emotional Communities*.
67  Ibid. W. M. Reddy, *The Navigation of Feeling*; A. Hochschild, *The Managed Heart*.
68  S. Ahmed, *The Cultural Politics of Emotion*.
69  M. Mulsow, *Prekäres Wissen*.
70  M. Scheer, "Are Emotions a Kind of Practice"; E. Ikegami, "Emotions."
71  M. Nussbaum, *Upheavals of Thought*; J. D. Greene, "Emotion and Morality."
72  S. James, *Passion and Action*.
73  L. J. Daston and K. Park, *Wonders*.
74  A. Goldgar, *Tulipmania*.
75  E. Buringh and J. Van Zanden, "'Charting the 'Rise of the West'".
76  U. Rublack, "Matter in the Material Renaissance."
77  Hochstrasser, "Visual Impact"; Sutton, *Capitalism and Cartography*; Van Groesen, "Visualizing the News."
78  K. Van Berkel, *Citaten uit het Boek der Natuur*, 146; H. J. Cook, *Matters of Exchange*, 338; S. Huigen, J. L. de Jong, and E. Kolfin, *The Dutch Trading Companies*.
79  S. Huigen, J. L. de Jong, and E. Kolfin, *The Dutch Trading Companies*.
80  C. Fairchilds, "The Production and Marketing of Populuxe Goods."
81  M. Hutter, "Familiar Surprises."

# Bibliography

Ahmed, Sara. *The Cultural Politics of Emotion*. New York: Routledge, 2004.

Akerlof, George A. and Robert J. Shiller *Animal Spirits. How Human Psychology Drives the Economy, and Why it Matters for Global Capitalism*. Princeton: Princeton University Press, 2009.

Allen, Robert C.  and Jacob Louis Weisdorf. "Was There an 'Industrious Revolution' before the Industrial Revolution?: An Empirical Exercise for England, c. 1300-1830." *Economic History Review* 64 (2010): 715–29.

Bailey, Merridee L."Economic Records." In *Early Modern Emotions*, edited by Susan Broomhall, 108–10. London: Routledge, 2017

Barclay, Katie "Space and Place." In *Early Modern Emotions*, edited by Susan Broomhall, 20–23. London: Routledge, 2017.

Bastiaanse, René and Hans Bots. *Glorieuze Revolutie: De wereld van William en Mary. Een korte biografische schets en een beeld van de tijd*. Den Haag: SDU, 1988.

Berkel, Klaas van. *Citaten uit het Boek der Natuur: Opstellen over Nederlandse Wetenschapsgeschiedenis*. Amsterdam: Bakker, 1998.

Black, Jeremy. *The Power of Knowledge: How Information and Technology Made the Modern World*. New Haven: Yale University Press, 2014.

Beckert, Jens. *Imagined Futures: Fictional Expectations and Capitalist Dynamics*. Cambridge, MA: Harvard University Press, 2016.

Berg, Maxine. "In Pursuit of Luxury: Global History and British Consumer Goods in the Eighteenth Century." *Past and Present* 182 (2004): 85–142.

Berg, Maxine. *Luxury and Pleasure in Eighteenth-Century Britain*. Oxford: Oxford University Press, 2005.

Berg, Maxine and Elizabeth Eger, eds., *Luxury in the Eighteenth Century: Debates, Desires and Delectable Goods*. Basingstoke: Palgrave Macmillan, 2003.

Berry, Christopher. *The Idea of Luxury: A Conceptual and Historical Investigation*. Cambridge: Cambridge University Press, 1994.

Blondé, Bruno. "Shoppen met Isabella d'Este: De Italiaanse Renaissance als Bakermat van de Consumptiesamenleving." *Stadsgeschiedenis* 2 (2007): 139–51.

Brewer, John, and Roy Porter, eds., *Consumption and the World of Goods*. London/ New York: Routledge, 1994.

Brewer, John, and Frank Trentmann, eds., *Consuming Cultures, Global Perspectives: Historical Trajectories, Transnational Exchanges*. Oxford/New York: Berg, 2006.

Brewer, John, and Laurence Fontaine. "Homo Creditus et Construction de la Confiance au XVIIIeme Siècle." In *La Construction Sociale de la Confiance*, edited by Philippe Bernoux and Jean Michel Servet, 161–76. Paris: Montchrétien, 1997.

Broomhall, Susan,ed. *Early Modern Emotions: An Introduction*. Abingdon: Routledge, 2017.

Buringh, Eltjo, and Jan Luiten Van Zanden, "Charting the 'Rise of the West': Manuscripts and Printed Books in Europe, A Long-Term Perspective from the Sixth through Eighteenth Centuries."*Journal of Economic History* 69, no. 2 (2009): 409–45.

Burke, Peter. *A Social History of Knowledge: From Gutenberg to Diderot*. Cambridge: Polity Press, 2000.

Burke, Peter. *A Social History of Knowledge: From the Encyclopaedia to Wikipedia*. Cambridge: Polity Press, 2012.

Burke, Peter. *What Is the History of Knowledge?* Cambridge: Polity Press, 2016.

Cook, Harold J. *Matters of Exchange: Commerce, Medicine, and Science in the Dutch Golden Age*. New Haven/London: Yale University Press, 2007.

Daston, Lorraine J. "The History of Science and the History of Knowledge." *KNOW: A Journal on the Formation of Knowledge* 1, no. 1 (2017): 131–54.

Daston, Lorraine J. and Katharine Park, *Wonders and the Order of Nature: 1150-1750*. New York: Zone Books, 1998.

Daston, Lorraine J. and Peter Louis Galison. *Objectivity*. New York: Zone Books, 2010.

Daston, Lorraine J., and Elizabeth Lunbeck, eds. *Histories of Scientific Observation*. Chicago: University of Chicago Press, 2011.

Davids, Karel. "Public Knowledge and Common Secrets: Secrecy and its Limits in The Early Modern Netherlands." *Early Science and Medicine* 10 (2005): 411–27.

Davids, Karel *The Rise and Decline of Dutch Technological Leadership: Technology, Economy and Culture in the Netherlands, 1350–1800*. Leiden: Brill, 2008.

Davids, Karel and Bert De Munck, eds. *Innovation and Creativity in Late Medieval and Early Modern European Cities*. Farnham: Ashgate, 2014.

Dupré, Sven, and Geert Somsen. "The History of Knowledge and the Future of Knowledge Societies." *Berichte zur Wissenschaftsgeschichte* 42, no. 2–3 (2019): 186–99.

Epstein, Stephan R., and Maarten R. Prak, eds. *Guilds, Innovation, and the European Economy, 1400–1800*. Cambridge: Cambridge University Press, 2010.

Ertz, K. *Jan Breughel der Jüngere (1601–1678): Die Gemälde mit kritischem Oeuvrekatalog* (Flämische Maler im Umkreis der grossen Meiser, 1). Freren: Luca-Verlag, 1984.

Fairchilds, Cissie. "The Production and Marketing of Populuxe Goods in Eighteenth-Century Paris." In *Consumption and the World of Goods,* edited by John Brewer and Roy Porter, 228–48. London: Routledge, 1993.

Frevert, Ute. "Gefühle und Kapitalismus." In *Kapitalismus: Historische Annäherungen,* edited by Gunilla Budde, 50–72. Göttingen: Vandenhoeck & Ruprecht, 2011.

Goldgar, Anne. *Tulipmania: Money, Honor and Knowledge in the Dutch Golden Age.* Chicago: Chicago University Press, 2009

Greene, Joshua D. "Emotion and Morality: A Tasting Menu." *Emotion Review* 3 (2011): 1–3.

Hirschman, Albert O. *The Passions and the Interests: Political Arguments for Capitalism before Its Triumph.* Princeton: Princeton University Press, 1977.

Hochschild, Arli *The Managed Heart: Commercialization of Human Feeling.* Berkeley: University of California Press, 1983.

Hoftijzer, Paul G. "The Dutch Republic, Centre of the European Book Trade in the 17th Century." *European History Online* (EGO), Leibniz Institute of European History (IEG), Mainz, 2015. Accessed July 2020. http://www.ieg-ego.eu/hoftijzerp-2015-en.

Huigen, Siegfried, Jan L. de Jong, and Elmer Kolfin. *The Dutch Trading Companies as Knowledge Networks.* Leiden/Boston: Brill, 2010.

Hutter, Michael. "Familiar Surprises: Creating Value in the Creative Industries." In *The Worth of Goods,* edited by Patrik Aspers andJens Beckert, 201–20. Cambridge: Cambridge University Press, 2010.

Hutter, Michael & David Throsby. *Beyond Price: Value in Culture, Economics, and the Arts.* Cambridge: Cambridge University Press, 2008.

Ikegami, Eiko. "Emotions." In *Concise Companion to History*, edited by Ulinka Rublack, 333–53. Oxford: Oxford University Press, 2011.

Illouz, Eva. *Cold Intimacies: The Making of Emotional Capitalism.* Cambridge: Polity Press, 2007.

Israel, Jonathan. *Dutch Primacy in World Trade, 1585–1740.* Oxford: Oxford University Press, 1990.

Israel, Jonathan. *Radical Enlightenment: Philosophy and the Making of Modernity 1650–1750.* Oxford: Oxford University Press, 2001.

Jacob, Margaret C. *The First Knowledge Economy: Human Capital and the European Economy, 1750–1850.* Cambridge: Cambridge University Press, 2014.

Jacob, Margaret C. *Strangers Nowhere in the World: The Rise of Cosmopolitanism in Early Modern Europe.* Philadelphia: Univ. of Pennsylvania Press, 2006.

Jacob, Margaret C. and Catherine Secretan. *The Self-perception of Early Modern Capitalists.* New York: Palgrave Macmillan, 2008.

Jardine, Lisa. *Worldly Goods: A New History of the Renaissance.* New York: W.W. Norton, 1998.

Klamer, Arjo, *The Value of Culture: On the Relationship between Economics and Arts.* Amsterdam: Amsterdam University Press, 1996.

Kopytoff, Igor. "The Cultural Biography of Things: Commoditization as Process." In *The Social Life of Things: Commodities in Cultural Perspective,* edited by Arjun Appadurai, 64–94. Cambridge/New York: Cambridge University Press, 1986.

Lässig, Simone. "The History of Knowledge and the Expansion of the Historical Research Agenda." *Bulletin of the German Historical Institute* 59 (2016): 29–58.

Leemans, Inger. "The Economics of Pain. Pain in Dutch Stock Trade Discourses and Practices 1600-1750." In *The Hurt(ful) Body: Performing and Beholding Pain, 1600–1800,* edited by Kornee van der Haven and Karel Vanhaesebrouck, 273–99. Manchester: Manchester University Press, 2017.

Leemans, Inger. "Embodied Emotions from a Dutch Historical Perspective." *Emotion Review* 8 (2015): 278–80.

Leemans, Inger. "Verse Weavers and Paper Traders: Speculation in the Theater." In, *The Great Mirror of Folly: Finance, Culture, and the Crash of 1720*, edited by William Goetzmann and Catherine Labio, et al., 175–90. New Haven: Yale University Press, 2016

Lennep, J. van. "l'Alchemiste: Origine et Développement d'un Thème de la Peinture du Dix-septième Siècle." *Revue belge d'archéologie et d'histoire de l'art*, 35 (1966-68): 149–168.

Lesger, Clé. *The Rise of the Amsterdam Market and Information Exchange: Merchants, Commercial Expansion and Change in the Spatial Economy of the Low Countries, c.1550–1630*. Florence: Taylor and Francis, 2006.

Margócsy, Daniel. *Commercial Visions. Science, Trade, and Visual Culture in the Dutch Golden Age*. Chicago/London: University of Chicago Press, 2014.

Marnef, Guido. *Antwerp in the Age of Reformation: Underground Protestantism in a Commercial Metropolis, 1550–1577*. Baltimore: Johns Hopkins University Press, 1996.

Massumi, B. *Parables for the Virtual: Movement, Affect, Sensation*. Durham/London: Duke University Press, 2002.

Mauss, Marcel. *The Gift: Forms and Functions of Exchange in Archaic Societies*. London: Cohen & West, 1966 (French 1st ed. 1925).

McCloskey, Deirdre. *Bourgeois Virtues: Ethics for an Age of Commerce*. Chicago: Chicago University Press, 2006.

McCloskey, Deirdre. *Bourgeois Dignity: Why Economics can't explain the Modern World*. Chicago: Chicago University Press, 2010.

Mielants, Eric. "Early Modern Antwerp: The First 'World City'?" *Journal of Historical Sociology* 30 (2017): 262–83.

Miller, Daniel. "Consumption as the Vanguard of History: A Polemic by Way of an Introduction." In *Acknowledging Consumption: A Review of New Studies*, edited by Daniel Miller, 1–57. London: Routledge, 1995,

Miller, Peter N. *Peiresc's Mediterranean World*. Cambridge: Harvard University Press, 2015.

Mirimonde, A.P. de. "Les Allégories de la Musique II: Le retour de Mercure et les Allégories des Beaux-arts." *Gazette des Beaux-Arts* 73 (1969): 343–62

Mokyr, Joel. *The Gifts of Athena: Historical Origins of the Knowledge Economy*. Princeton: Princeton University Press, 2002.

Mokyr, Joel. *A Culture of Growth: The Origins of the Modern Economy*. Princeton: Princeton University Press, 2016.

Mulsow, Martin. *Prekäres Wissen: Eine andere Ideengeschichte der Frühen Neuzeit*. Berlin: Suhrkamp, 2012.

Mulsow, Martin. "Ökonomie des Wissens, Wissen der Ökonomie und Wissensökonomie." In *Eigennutz und gute Ordnung: Ökonomisierungen der Welt im 17. Jahrhundert*, edited by Sandra Richter and Guillaume Garner, 295–300. Wiesbaden: Harrassowitz Verlag, 2016.

Mulsow, Martin, and Lorraine Daston, "History of Knowledge." In *Debating New Approaches to History*, edited by Marek Tamm and Peter Burke, 159–79. London: Bloomsbury Academic, 2019.

Munck, Bert De. "Disassembling the City: A Historical and an Epistemological View on the Agency of Cities." *Journal of Urban History*, 43, no. 5, 2016: 1–19.

Munck, Bert De. "Artisans, Products and Gifts: Rethinking the History of Material Culture in Early Modern Europe." *Past & Present*, 224 (2014): 39–74.

Munck, Bert De, and Antonella Romano. *Knowledge and the Early Modern City: A History of Entanglements*. Abingdon/New York: Routledge, 2019.

Nussbaum, Martha  *Upheavals of Thought: The Intelligence of Emotions*. Cambridge: Cambridge University Press, 2001.

Östling, Johan, David Larsson Heidenblad,  and Anna Nilsson Hammar, eds. *Forms of Knowledge: Developing the History of Knowledge*. Lund: Nordic Academic Press, 2020.

Paster, Gail Kern, Katherine  Rowe,  and Mary Floyd-Wilson. *Reading the Early Modern Passions: Essays in the Cultural History of Emotion*. Philadelphia: University of Pennsylvania Press, 2004.

Plamper, Jan. *The History of Emotions: An Introduction*. Oxford: Oxford University Press, 2015.

Peck, Linda. *Consuming Splendor: Society and Culture in Seventeenth-Century England*. Cambridge: Cambridge Press, 2005.

Polanyi, Michael. *The Tacit Dimension*. London: Routledge & Kegan Paul, 1966.

Pomeranz, Kenneth. "Ten Years After: Responses and Reconsiderations." *Historically Speaking* 12, no. 4 (2011): 20–25.

Powell, Walter W. and Kaisa Snellman. "The Knowledge Economy." *Annual Review of Sociology* 30 (2004): 199–220.

Prak, Maarten. *The Dutch Republic in the Seventeenth Century: The Golden Age*. Cambridge/New York: Cambridge University Press, 2005.

Rasterhoff, Claartje. *Painting and Publishing as Cultural Industries: The Fabric of Creativity in the Dutch Republic, 1580–1800*. Amsterdam: Amsterdam University Press, 2017.

Reckwitz, Andreas  "Praktiken und ihre Affekte." *Mittelweg 36. Zeitschrift des Hamburger Instituts für Sozialforschung* 24 (2015): 27–45.

Reddy, William M. *The Navigation of Feeling: A Framework for the History of Emotions*. Cambridge: Cambridge University Press, 2001.

Rittersma, Rengenier ed. *Luxury in the Low Countries. Miscellaneous Reflections on Netherlandish Material Culture, 1500 to the Present*. Brussel: Pharo Publishing, 2010.

Roberts, Lissa. "The Circulation of Knowledge in Early Modern Europe." *History of Technology* 31 (2012): 47–68.

Roche, Daniel. *A History of Everyday Things: The Birth of Consumption in France, 1600–1800*. Cambridge: Cambridge University Press, 2000.

Rosenwein, B. *Emotional Communities in the Early Middle Ages*. Ithaca: Cornell University Press, 2006.

Rublack, Ulinka. "Matter in the Material Renaissance." *Past and Present* 219 (2013): 41–85.

Ryckbosch, Wouter. "Early Modern Consumption History: Current Challenges and Future Perspectives." *BMGN Low Countries Historical Review*, 130 (2015): 57–84. DOI: http://doi.org/10.18352/bmgn-lchr.9962.

Schäfer, Dagmar. *Cultures of Knowledge: Technology in Chinese History*. Leiden: Brill, 2012.

Scheer, M. "Are Emotions a Kind of Practice (and is that what Makes them have a History)? A Bourdieuian Approach to Understanding Emotion." *History and Theory* 51 (2012): 193–220

Schmidt, Benjamin. *Inventing Exoticism: Geography, Globalism, and Europe's Early Modern World*. Philadelphia, PA: University of Pennsylvania Press, 2015.

Shleifer, Andrei. *Inefficient Markets: An Introduction to Behavioral Finance*. Oxford: Oxford University Press, 2000.

Slaby, Jan and Christian von Scheve, ed. *Affective Societies. Key Concepts*. London: Routledge, 2019.

Soll, Jacob. *The Reckoning: Financial Accountability and the Making and Breaking of Nations*. London: Allen Lane/Penguin Books, 2014.

Smith, Pamela and Paula Findlen, eds. *Merchants and Marvels: Commerce, Science, and Art in Early Modern Europe*. New York: Routledge 2002.

Smith, Pamela H., Amy R. W. Meyers, and Harold Cook. *Ways of Making and Knowing. The Material Culture of Empirical Knowledge*. Ann Arbor: The University of Michigan Press, 2014.

Smith, Pamela H. and Benjamin Schmidt. *Making Knowledge in Early Modern Europe: Practices, Objects, and Texts, 1400-1800*. Chicago/London: University of Chicago Press, 2007.

Solomon, Julie R. "You've Got to Have Soul: Understanding the Passions in Early Modern Culture." In *Rhetoric and Medicine in Early Modern Europe*, edited by Stephen Pender and Nancy S. Struever, 195–228. Farnham/Burlington: Ashgate, 2012.

Stäheli, U. "Hoffnung als ökonomischer Affekt." In *Kultur der Ökonomie. Zur Materialität und Performanz des Wirtschaftlichen*, edited by Inga Klein and Sonja Windmüller, 283–300. Göttingen, 2014

Stäheli, Urs *Spectacular Speculation: Thrills, the Economy, and Popular Discourse*. Stanford: Stanford University Press, 2013.

Staelen, Carolien de. *Spulletjes en hun Betekenis in een Commerciële Metropool: Antwerpenaren en hun Materiële Cultuur in de Zestiende Eeuw*. Antwerp: University of Antwerp, 2007.

Sturkenboom, Dorothee. *De Ballen van de Koopman: Mannelijkheid en Nederlandse Identiteit in de Tijd van de Republiek*. Gorredijk: Sterck & De Vreese, 2019.

Teuscher, S. *The Moral Economy: Poverty, Credit, and Trust in Early Modern Europe*. Cambridge, Cambridge University Press, 2014.

Trentman, Frank, ed. *The Oxford Handbook of the History of Consumption*. Oxford: Handbooks Online, 2012.

Trigg, Stephanie "Affect Theory." In *Early Modern Emotions*, edited by Susan Broomhall, 10–13. London: Routledge.

Vries, Jan de. *The Industrious Revolution: Consumer Behavior and the Household Economy, 1650 to the Present*. Cambridge: Cambridge University Press, 2008.

Vries, Jan de and Ad van der Woude. *The First Modern Economy: Success, Failure, and Perseverance of the Dutch Economy, 1500–1815*. Cambridge: Cambridge University Press, 1997.

Weststeijn, Arthur. *Commercial Republicanism in the Dutch Golden Age: The Political Thought of Johan & Pieter de la Court*. Leiden: Brill, 2012.

Wijsenbeek-Olthuis, Thera. "A Matter of Taste: Lifestyle in Holland in the 17th and 18th Centuries." In *Material Culture: Consumption, Life-Style, Standard of Living, 1500–1900*, edited by Anton Schuurman and Lorena Seebach Walsh, 43–55. Milan: Università Bocconi, 1994.

Zaloom, Caitlin. *Out of the Pits: Traders and Technology from Chicago to London*. Chicago: University of Chicago Press, 2006.

Zanden, Jan Luiten van. *The Long Road to the Industrial Revolution: The European Economy in a Global Economy*. Leiden/Boston: Brill, 2009.

# PART I

# Wish economies and affective communities

# 2

# KNOWING THE MARKET

## Hans Fugger's affective economies

*Ulinka Rublack*

Societies are built on producing, distributing and consuming things. Attitudes to objects therefore are central to an analysis of cultural meaning as well as arguments about values. The early modern world (1450–1750) witnessed major transformations in the quantities and qualities of object worlds as well as in debates about them. This chapter addresses the question of how we can understand the affective dimensions of an early modern merchant's engagements with such commodities. The most common assumption has been that merchants sought to rationally maximize profit and reproduce distinction through goods as social markers. Lisa Jardine's bestselling account *Worldly Goods: A New History of the Renaissance* thus influentially retold the conventional story of an age of learning and virtue as one of ostentation and unparalleled global commerce. Art indexed these new commercial desires. Jardine thus argued that Giovanni Arnolfini simply requested the painter Van Eyck to celebrate his ownership of possessions in the famous panel that hangs in London's *National Gallery* – a light, luxurious house, a fertile wife, a pet, overshoes and oranges, and a fancy bed. In this reading, Renaissance paintings typically mirrored the many luxury objects which began to fill the lives of those endowed with a restless entrepreneurial spirit, a desire for self-fashioning and cross-cultural curiosity in their race for status.[1]

Yet conceptually it is now increasingly recognized that material culture plays constitutive rather than merely expressive roles in social life and social transformation. Anthropologists powerfully argue that the materiality of objects constitutes relationships and perceptions, and archaeologists likewise show how the material world provides both sensory information and an extended cognitive system.[2] I have previously shown that in an age of craft this required a client's involvement with the emergence of an object in the making. Above all, matter was not necessarily treated as dead and inferior to form in the early modern period but could be regarded as imbued with life and specific affective qualities, or capable of animating them.[3] We can therefore better understand the meaning of materiality if we re-create its making and follow what types of cognitive and sensuous involvement it pertained to in a particular period. The archaeologist Nicole Boivin likewise has criticized accounts in which the 'material world is little more than a theatre, with objects as kind of props in a story that has already been written by human agents'.[4] The challenge is to formulate approaches which overcome the notion that matter only becomes part of culture through disembodied cognition. This leads to questions such as the following: How do ideas and cultural understandings in part emerge through material worlds and human engagement with them?[5] How can materiality enable human thought, imagination and emotion? How does it relate to cognitive, emotional and sensate processes, especially in view of the fact that humans themselves are materially constituted and often share bodily qualities with goods – as leather was akin to skin, or fur and feathers to hair, and colour pigment can correspond to organic matter, such as blood, for example? A historical account then amounts to more than a story of things as social markers in a diversifying world. Rich relationalities between materialities, things and humans could ensue, to entangle them in possibilities and constraints. This material world surrounded and shaped early modern people – yet we still need to learn much about its role in people's lives as markets diversified and expanded.

My study focuses on Hans Fugger (1531–98), an Augsburg merchant active during the second half of the 16th century, and in particular his correspondence with his Antwerp agents in surviving letters. Around 4,600 letters by Fugger are extant, nearly all of which concerned commercial goods. Fugger's correspondence is so remarkable because it tells us about him as a consumer and co-creator of values, often in regard to innovative products or sourcing mechanisms. He sourced goods for a network of friends and clients of the Fugger company without taking any commission, as well as for his own household.[6]

Recent research has highlighted the crucial role of merchants in early modern knowledge-making processes and cultural exchange.[7] Peter N. Miller in particular has drawn attention to the way the French polymath Nicolas de Pereisc (1580–1637) relied on the factual information, geographical, social and political knowledge of merchants he collaborated with and treated as colleagues. Pereisc also replicated some of their communicative methods, as he wrote in the vernacular and paid great attention to the objects he wanted to be sourced. Early modern merchants thus emerge as 'thinkers with wide interests and multiple competences'.[8] Moreover, Miller draws attention to Aby Warburg's commitment to see in Florentine portraits of Renaissance merchants an enactment of a collective identity defined by authority, innovation, strength and piety, and argues that in Pereisc's correspondence we see the engagement of merchants in the cause of 'curiosity', 'their desire to collaborate in the pursuit of the new, and their range of geographical vision'.[9] He finally reminds us of Fernand Braudel's vision for his influential book series of European merchant correspondence, to reveal an economic history 'as seen day by day, explained by its actors'.[10] This means that we have to approach anew the question of what types of knowledge merchants possessed and made valid to other sections of society, as well as their own desire to collect and make rare and novel goods. Fugger's correspondence tells us much about the practical information about the market he required; the ways in which he sought to control commerce, through his networks as well as the very elaborate use of samples in an age before pattern books; and his information-gathering about prices. All this is of great interest to a new cultural history of early modern economic practices. For this article I want to focus on this 'Merchant of Augsburg' in his relation to Antwerp.

During the 16th century, Antwerp itself became eulogized as 'marketplace of the world'. It emerged, as Christine Göttler puts it, as a

> hub of colonial knowledge and artistic expertise as it became a trading centre where goods were available that could not be found elsewhere … With the arrival of new artefacts, new types of speciality markets and a new culture of collecting emerged that reflected and reinforced an increased preoccupation with 'special' or precious things, the materials and technologies employed in their making, and their cognitive, affective, and sensory dimensions.[11]

Fugger's correspondence shows that this remained true even during an extremely challenging period of trade.[12] Cities such as Antwerp brought together international mercantile elites and their agents, makers, lovers of knowledge as well as knowledge experts, such as geographers and mathematicians, in unique ways which made them conducive to innovation through artisanal knowledge translation in an age of *mondialization* – an age of global trade which inspired local networks and cultural blendings.[13] In this attempt to work towards a historical anthropology of the merchant, I first set out the function of goods as enlivening, next discuss the material literacy Fugger needed, and finally explore the affective dimensions of his relationship with goods.

## Enlivening matter

Exchange relations in many cultures can be regarded in part as symbolic systems to facilitate life and well-being.[14] Historians and anthropologists thus study objects not for their aesthetic value. They are interested in how they functioned as actors in a network of social relationships.[15] They are also interested in how their qualities emerged through the way they were made. We can ask how technical virtuosity enhanced particular properties which could emphasize lifelikeness, such as lustre and sheen, and how they were experienced. What qualities mattered to whom, and which were invested with social and moral meaning?[16] How were they linked to particular social and cultural sensory practices? These in turn could interlink with the positive evaluation of novelty and aliveness in consumptive practices that were valued as invigorating. In the early modern period conceptions of human aliveness were certainly linked to a humoral world view which associated dry and cold qualities with ageing, and freshness and health with youth and with masculine attributes. 'Freshness' thus was a potent category of value across different commercial goods and resonated with the high valuation of 'rare', novel and ingenious goods.

In relation to food consumption this means that it is interesting to note how much effort was made to source fresh produce over long distances rather than solely preserved or dried goods. Food in this way can not only be seen in terms of the binaries raw and cooked, but fresh and dried, and cultures differ in relation to how these qualities are given meaning and seen to influence health. Hans Fugger invested a great deal in his ability to integrate fresh delicacies, and fish in particular, into ceremonial occasions as much as his regular fasting diet. In 1566, for example, he requested oysters, fish and other '*gentilezzi*' from Antwerp for his sisters' wedding in October, noting that the family had already sourced sufficient quantities of preserved foodstuffs, especially from Portugal. Now they wanted to receive something 'unknown'. He was therefore delighted to hear, on the first of October, that his Antwerp agent Hans Keller was confident that these items of '*Fremdigkait*', of 'strangeness', could be supplied.[17] In November, Fugger noted that the fish, mussels and crabs which had arrived in Augsburg in rapid succession encased in small barrels had 'served well' at the wedding, except that the sturgeon and crabs had not been completely fresh. Such weddings could be described in great detail to business partners, as they indicated the wealth and distinction of guests and thus ideally increased a merchant's reputation, which was all-important to enlarge his network. Indeed, one of Fugger's most remarkably persistent requests was to source sea urchins from the Mediterranean, which likewise would have been prestigious objects to present in a land-locked German town.[18] He kept reminding his Antwerp agent that the season for oysters was about to end in March, or that exotic vegetables like artichokes were dried out by the heat in September.[19] An excess of heat and dryness in turn was associated with immoral action, such as impetuous, fiery behavior.[20]

As Sandra Cavallo and Tessa Storey have outlined, the cultivation of cheerfulness was regarded as a health preservative in the early modern period, as it filled the body with "good nourishment", kept the senses vigorous and conserved the intellect, thus increasing health and prolonging life. It was linked to the right amount of body heat and vitality, and to delightful objects or animals.[21] Wonderful meals, drinking great wine, listening to birdsong in gardens of the villa, smelling invigorating, subtle scents, seeing delightful sights, and wearing clothes in lovely colours, enjoying expensive horses, hunting dogs and sporting were among the pursuits which were seen to resonate with the life of a merchant as gentleman, so much so that by the mid-17th century the medical writer Domenico Auda recommended:

> One must be cheerful, since happiness excites natural heat, tempers the spirits, makes them purer … prolongs life, sharpens the intellect, and puts a man in a state of readiness for his business dealings.

It was recognized that orators, scholars and merchants particularly needed to cultivate these practices in order to cope with the ambitious, highly competitive environment they found themselves in.[22]

Caring for one's health played an increasingly important role in the construction of the elite self during the sixteenth century.[23] The significance of food was obviously its incorporation, and the fact that it could delight the senses and strengthen the body or conversely weaken it if its properties deteriorated.

This similarly applied to drugs. Fugger thus wrote to Keller in 1567 that he did not object to the delay in sourcing 'sarsaparilla', a plant used to cleanse the blood and against syphilis which came from South-America.[24] The most important thing was that it needed to be 'fresh and good'. Yet when the plant arrived in Augsburg one month later Fugger was disappointed and thought it slightly old and 'worn out' (*verlegen*), and reprimanded Keller, saying that he should have sent it earlier. He nonetheless started to take the drug straight away as a cure, which was so intense that he referred to it in another letter to justify a slower response than usual to a correspondent. Access to such drugs in turn allowed elites to create knowledge about their correct use and disseminate recipes and advice within their network. As Regina Dauser has shown, Fugger was ahead of local doctors in the medical information he acquired.[25] He disseminated his advice and care through a wide-ranging network of contacts. In 1574, for instance, Fugger reported to the high-ranking courtier Don Juan Manrique de Lana in Vienna that his brother Marx was taking *sarsaparilla* because of a bad 'flow which has taken much of his hearing in the right ear'.[26] In 1574 he provided detailed medical advice and recipes for his Antwerp agent Jacob Mair, while in 1557 he sent a recipe from one of his medical books to a correspondent in Rome.[27]

Fugger used the same expression about inferior *sarsaparilla* as 'old and worn out' in relation to a pair of leather gloves he once received from Antwerp. He immediately told his agent Römer that these gloves were too expensive and inferior in relation to what he could buy in Rome; he was never to send any gloves again.[28] Fugger was a connoisseur of leather; he put tremendous effort into sourcing high-quality cordovan leather from Antwerp, in particular shoes, and he provided precise feedback for shoemakers via his agents to optimize their products, a point to which I shall return. Antwerp imported and exported leather from the Indies, either as raw material or as manufactured in Spain with Arabic traditions of craftsmanship, ranging from gloves of Ocaña to the gilded leather used for walls and cushions.[29] Like no other material, leather for gloves or shoes functioned as a second skin, especially as Fugger preferred to wear tight-fitting shoes, fashionable knee-high boots as well as jerkins. Old, wrinkled leather would have made him look faded, and thus he insisted on receiving newly alumed and often gleaming white shoes of light, soft cordovan leather, and invested in many pairs to keep this pristine look.

This might seem 'natural' but is of course a highly relevant choice which stands in opposition, for instance, to contemporary aesthetic preferences today which can demand the manufacturing of faded looks in dress items. Sixteenth-century elites preferred new, fresh, and in this sense vivacious, enlivening sensuous effects of clothing – which were particularly cultivated through shiny, lustrous silk fabrics and slashing, which created light effects. This preference was, however, challenged by the custom of wearing mourning dress for prolonged periods. Veit Konrad Schwarz (b.1541) may have been typical of many young men in struggling emotionally to keep wearing black mourning attire after the death of Anton Fugger, Hans Fugger's father and former head of the company. Veit Konrad threw these mourning clothes off to go dancing.[30] If we wish to reconstruct the experience of commodities and their affective potential, it thus seems relevant that Hans Fugger ordered black shoes for cold seasons, which of course served the practical purpose of not showing dirt as easily as white shoes. But it does seem significant that one of his most determined letters in which he requested a new product to be made coincided with the period of winter and his mourning for his uncle Hieronimus Fugger. In 1573 he thus wrote to Philip Roemer in Antwerp that, as winter was on the door-step and he was in mourning, he would like two pairs of black Poursequines, with the smooth rather than the flesh side to the outside. Over them he would like to wear a pair of mules 'a la Portuguesa'. He would order more if they pleased him. Otherwise, he continued, he had observed that the Spaniards had black boots made 'a la gineta', with single soles, which could also be worn together with mules. Even if they 'were somewhat wider and did not fit tightly' onto the leg, one could wear them in periods of mourning and in winter.[31] In other words: he responded to the simplicity and restraint imposed by traditional mourning clothes with a demand for fashion innovation that enabled him to act as open to novelty and Southern European cultural styles.

In 1571, 101 Portuguese men belonged to the members of the "nation" in Antwerp; at least 15 of them belonged to established families in the city. Together with the Spanish, the Portuguese inhabitants in total constituted about 5 percent of the population in 1570 of ca. 85,000 people.[32] For Guicciardini, merchants made Antwerp so special because they knew how to imitate 'foreigners, with whom they easily enter into relationships' and showed their experience of the world.[33] Shoes materialized this. Fine shoe-ware in this way emerges as a knowledge-intensive good, which Fugger helped to optimize through his material literacy. It can be viewed as an excellent example of small product innovation which followed new consumer tastes. Their feedback and requirements led to new artisanal practices and trial-and-error learning, which has been termed 'learning on the shopfloor' rather than formal education. Yet it is problematic to characterize the aesthetic of such products as un-Italian, exotic or mannerist and neatly separate national styles in craft production. Rather, Fugger presented consumer preferences of an international elite which often shared decorative languages.[34]

Books likewise not only invited a rational cognitive but also an affective response. As Feike Dietz shows in her contribution to this volume, children's literature, for example, could be seen as a process of physical incorporation, of eating and digesting – just as mystics in the Middle Ages and afterwards tasted the word of God. We might note a similar emphasis on enlivening freshness in Fugger's typical requests for books which came straight from the printer. On the one hand this was of course linked to practices of social distinction, as Fugger could demonstrate his knowledge of and access to the most recent products. In 1571, Fugger thus noted with irritation that others already possessed an engraved portrait of the duke of Alba, but that his agent Hans Keller had not taken the initiative to send one to him from Antwerp. He instructed Keller to report on what had been newly published in print.[35] In 1573, he asked for a Latin grammar by Cornelius Valerius to be sent as soon as it was printed, and sent one of the books he duly received immediately on to the teacher of his son in Ingolstadt, emphasizing that he had just received it from Antwerp. Valerius made his name through systematizing the teaching of Latin grammar in new ways. In December, Fugger told his Antwerp agent Römer that only two of the grammar editions he had sent were from that year, but another one dated from 1569 – he was to send another current edition. As this was a teaching book it is perfectly possible that this was an updated edition, but it can also make us think further about the material qualities of print. Would the ink have looked fresher in the year a book was published, and would it and the paper have smelt and felt different? Did a thirst for books fresh from the printer, in other words, not also impart enlivening, invigorating qualities? Was it part of a passionate relationship with the creation of new knowledge or the aesthetic nature of knowledge production? It certainly seems characteristic that the French scholar Pereisc exclaimed that 'craftsmen are among my best friends' when he sought out specific kinds of leather, presumably to bind his books.[36] Connoisseurship certainly applied to the acquisition of the Plantin bibles, and in 1572 Fugger replied to a letter in which his Antwerp agent had informed him that the printer sold his newly printed bible in eight books on two types of paper and sold them unbound – one book for 80 Carolus guilders and the other for 70. Fugger asked for three bibles of the expensive edition, but instructed Keller to negotiate the price. Soon after he received these he requested two more of these large bibles, to be sent at the earliest possibility. They arrived alongside the Braun Hogenberg edition of the most notable cities of Europe, which he had likewise asked for.[37]

Live animals are a final material complex which seems suggestive in this context. The Fuggers requested them regularly.[38] Discussions of elite collecting practices often focus on durable and dried parts of unusual animals and plants, whereas an 'important form of collecting concerned rare and often exotic animals ... that were still alive'.[39] Rare or expensive animals required particular care to keep them alive, sometimes through experts, and thus involved owners in forms of cultural labour of care which further focused on the goal of enlivening and were particularly mindful of environmental factors: the cold or heat which would damage animal health. The breeding of such animals became a major pursuit, not least for women in German elite families who frequently became entrepreneurs in the agrarian economies attached to their territory.[40] Hans Fugger's wife Elisabeth, whose family belonged to the Imperial nobility, thus spent much time on their farm, the *Meierhof*. Fugger meanwhile helped to build up a zoo in Augsburg from 1570. He ordered different types of animals via

Antwerp, ranging from exotic parrots, canaries and young monkeys to English whippet dogs and horses.

In 1566, Fugger was sorry to see that one of these horses was ill, and wondered whether this had been caused by heat on its way to Augsburg or whether it had previously been unwell.[41] As a result, he no longer trusted his agent to competently judge how horses should be selected and instructed him to either choose experts or send Fugger's own stable master to inspect the Antwerp horse market held at Pentecost. He repeatedly specified the type of horse he was looking for – brown or dappled, 'young, well-proportioned and tall'. Just before the market took place he affirmed in late May 1567 that he was waiting for the tall horse he had requested 'with great desire'. Keller, however, did not find a horse taller than 14/15 hand widths, to which Fugger responded in turn that he had heard about two tall stallions for sale in Bruges. Keller was to look for horses at least 24 hand widths tall in the western parts of Flanders and otherwise go to Bruges but involve experts before any deal. They were to be taken to Augsburg after the summer to avoid any damage. In the end, Keller reserved the two tall stallions for 33 Flemish pounds, and Fugger's trusted stable master Servat Preyt was dispatched to buy and take them with him.[42] Fugger could thus control the quality of his acquisitions through his ability to draw on expert knowledge.

Just like horses, dogs were an important status symbol in courts as well as increasingly in cities. Fugger had a clear sense of the type of breed and colour he wanted to source either for himself or the Bavarian court.[43] In 1568, he thus was surprised to receive English whippet dogs via Antwerp which differed in colour to what Keller had led him to expect. He asked Keller why he had described one of them as pike-coloured when in fact to Fugger he seemed to have the colour of a wolf. The other one was red, as described, but in fact Fugger was going to write to the Englishman to tell him that neither of them was of the kind he desired. This suggests that long-distance trade furthered the need for precise observation and description, as the effort involved in transporting and inspecting live goods was considerable. In May 1568, Fugger told Keller that the whippet dogs all had to be sent together, and that the climate was still sufficiently mild to send them if they travelled only in the evening, at night and during the morning, and rested during the day.[44]

The sourcing of exotic animals could be complicated by a lack of knowledge about foreign species. This turns us to the question of what information was needed to access the right goods and how it could be transmitted in the right way. In December 1567, Fugger was extremely frustrated to receive two doves from Venice, which the lutenist Michel Merk astonishingly enough had managed to transport over the Alps 'diligently and fresh'. Yet they were not at all what he wanted. Fugger had ordered 'Beckhin grossi', Indian doves with a large beak, whereas he had received 'Becketin', a completely different type. These had small beaks, which did not tolerate air and thus they perished in winter. He requested three to five doves, with short and thick beaks, but he instructed to wait at least until early February to send them, as the lutenist had reported on all the bad weather and cold on his way. Fugger closed demandingly: 'send me something beautiful and good, or nothing!' In the same year he noted that doves were more expensive in Antwerp than in Germany, but he nonetheless ordered three pairs, for breeding.[45]

As the comments on Indian doves suggest, Fugger possessed knowledge about exotic birds, which enabled him to access the market in informed ways. This presumably relied on his access to scholarly or other types of expert knowledge, although it is interesting that he did not specifically refer to a standard work of ornithology.[46] It nonetheless underlines – as Renate Pieper's work on information flows in the Habsburg empire as well as Pamela Smith's and Paula Findlen's important *Merchants and Marvels* first brought out, and Peter Miller has recently shown in relation to Pereisc – that merchants were involved in the production and circulation of knowledge about the natural world.[47] Fugger's knowledge of course extended to pricing. In 1568, he thus reminded Keller in Antwerp that he was looking for small parrots and supplied the following information: these usually were exported via Malacca, and those with a yellow beak were called 'Noyres'. In Lisbon they cost 20 or 30 Portuguese Cruzados. Keller was to ask Sebald Linns, their agent in Spain and Portugal, for one or two birds. Fugger now commented on their qualities: they were very beautiful, 'but not common, very delicate, which is why they require great diligence and good care' and could only be transported in spring. He was curious to know more about how they should be properly fed and kept and was going to ask his agent Christoph Hörmann to find out information in relation to this.

This means, in other words, that Fugger used a network of three agents to source one or two small, fragile birds of this kind from the East Indies and acquire expert knowledge about how to keep them alive in Germany. The desire for animals involved him in the appreciation of super tall, strong, male horses as much as the most delicate birds, and each case involved him in the accumulation of knowledge, networks and practices which focused on controlling the diet and environmental conditions which would extend care and avoid their death.

## Controlling communication

Fugger sought to control much of his communication about decorative objects or materials through sending lists but mostly through receiving samples and sketches.[48] This – as he knew – had its own traps. In 1571, for instance, he let Hans Keller know that he had received his two samples of flax, one for flax costing six and the other for 11 *stuivers*, and actually preferred the less expensive one. Keller was to buy 50 pounds of the first and only 25 of the higher quality flax, and it would be even better if he could negotiate the price of it down. He then announced that he wanted to keep the sample, 'as they are often more beautiful than the goods which are later sent' – and he could therefore check up on divergences.[49] In 1574, Römer had to mediate between an instrument maker and

Fugger, to explain why parts he had sent did not correspond with the quality of an original sample.[50]

Another way of controlling quality was to send patterns and samples in both directions, as when Fugger in March 158 sent a pattern – perhaps an image – of 12 ruffs as well as cuffs for his wife and asked Keller to return a sample of what could be sourced in Antwerp.[51] The samples arrived in late April and were approved by Elisabeth. She then asked for others in the same manner but asked for two cuffs for each ruff, as the starched linen (Kress) wore out much more quickly on the arms. By December the whole order was ready to transport, and, as Renate Pieper's work on the Fugger-*Zeitungen* has shown, the need for political information of course went hand in hand with the knowledge of when to transport goods. In May 1568, Fugger thus advised Keller that these were quiet times and he should think about sending the whippet dogs and green parrots, as well as the shoes, ruffs and cuffs for his wife.[52]

A rare glimpse of how artisans could gain more power in these exchanges during years of crisis is offered by a letter Fugger wrote to Wilhelm of Bavaria in November 1575. The crown prince had shown an interest in dolls, which he wanted to use as gifts for St Niclaus Day – the sixth of December. Fugger assured him that he had 'run around all day' without finding anything suitable. He had been promised that something could be made for St Niclaus Day, but the makers wanted to be assured that the crown prince would buy the dolls, as Fugger had only been told to inquire after their price. Fugger added: 'the people here are almost poor, and they cannot make something to be sold', which implies to be sold without a clear order, as there would not have been a free market for such goods. He added as a postscript that he had indeed received four dolls, which he was sending with the letter, and that they could be finished before the Santa Claus celebrations in a manner just as Wilhelm wished. He had also been comforted by receiving information that such dolls had been shown at the wedding celebrations of the duke of Württemberg on the seventh of November and that beautiful dolls were being brought for sale to Augsburg. As Fugger was absent from Augsburg in early December, his wife Elizabeth sent the dolls to Wilhelm on the first and fourth of December, adding a request for them to be paid for soon, as their makers were poor.[53]!

For some decorative luxury items, samples were sent alongside detailed instructions. This underlines that the involvement with making in the period required elites to be materially literate; we can see how Fugger led in material conversations, which validated and modified understandings of the material world. When ordering 12 night-caps from Antwerp, Fugger thus asked for them to be lined with cotton, specifying 'but there must not be too much cotton in it', 'just a little'. In addition, the seamstress was to take special care not to make them too tight-fitting.[54] This in turn meant that merchants were inquisitive about new techniques and drove their development through exchanging knowledge in the household and through male and female networks.

Fugger's connection to the Bavarian court was particularly important. In October 1571 Fugger thus sent Keller a sample of wood from which he wanted a paternoster made for Wilhelm of Bavaria. Paternosters were strings of beads designed to help say prayers, and further devotional objects such as a crucifix or small devotional image might be attached to them. They became increasingly important for Catholic devotion in the sixteenth century, as Protestants rejected them. But they were also part of the consumer revolution in devotional objects and could be highly luxurious. Rachel King explains that 'there was no Europeanwide rule about how many beads a prayer rope should have or in what combination they should be threaded; hence beads were, most often, first arranged on a string when they reached their final destination.'[55] This in turn means that consumers were very much involved in the customization of prayer beads in terms of their material, and that other consumers appreciated these with informed craft spectatorship. Fugger specified that seven large balls were to be made in the damscene manner from iron and then decorated with gold and silver. Damascening was a Middle Eastern technique of working with metal and used arabesque patterns. It was popular among European elites for a range of decorative objects ranging from ewers to incense burners. The incisions enhanced the haptic experience of running the fingers through beads repetitively. Gold decorations further added to their preciousness and surface texture. Fugger further specified that – just like incense burners – the damascened prayer beads were to be hollow inside, to avoid them being overly heavy. Interestingly Keller did not agree a fixed price with the master craftsman until the paternoster was finished. As with other technically virtuoso objects, Fugger affirmed that he knew that their making required time, even if he waited for them impatiently and told Keller to keep inquiring after them.[56] Even in relation to the delivery of canvas he could affirm that he was happy to tolerate delays if it was made with diligence, and that the work would be charming – *possierlicher* – if more time was taken.[57]

As with the Indian doves, exotic goods required rare knowledge. In 1569, Fugger thus wrote to duke Albrecht of Bavaria to thank him for a sample of Indian wood. He would send it on to Spain and try to source a piece 'as large as possible'. But he remarked that it would have been helpful for his own enquiries if the duke had told him about the wood at greater length.[58] In turn he sent the sample to Mair in Antwerp and asked him to send it on to Christoph Hörmann at the soonest. He regretted being unable to say whether the wood had originally been imported via Lisbon, as it apparently came from India.[59] A later letter affirmed that he did not know any more about the wood, and that one had to try to source it via Lisbon.[60] In the same letter Fugger was pleased to enclose an exact image of a unicorn's twisted horn, which weighed ten and a half pounds and had been sent by a friend. This made it more trustworthy, and Fugger underlined that the unicorn apparently looked exactly as depicted. He asked for the image to be returned and advised that he would be obliged to source the horn in case Albrecht wished to look at it.[61]

Fugger believed in the authenticity of the unicorn horn, but concerning other goods was well aware of fakes. The circulation of fakes further explains why material literacy among merchants was high. Dealing with pearls, Fugger explained to Christoph Hörmann in 1574, requires much knowledge, as they could be faked in very high quality.[62] He also reported on fake Portuguese Cruzsdos made from gilded lead.[63]

Concerning the flourishing diamond trade in Antwerp, Fugger could be very specific in his price and quality requests – but also insist that goods were sent directly for him to inspect. The cutting of precious stones was unrestricted and not guilded in the city until 1582, and this meant that the quality of products was less controlled. The Portuguese were particularly actively involved in the sourcing and cutting of stones. In April 1571, Fugger thus instructed his agent Jakob Mair, who was entrusted with financial services and the trade in diamonds in Antwerp, that he required two similar diamonds within a price range of 25 to 30 florins, which were to be used for a collier. After Mair declared himself unable to find them, Fugger decided to look for them in Augsburg itself.[64] For duke Albrecht of Bavaria, he looked for a precious diamond simultaneously in Augsburg, Venice and Antwerp. His Antwerp agent had told him about a 17-carat stone, but it did not possess the required weight. If the duke wanted to inspect it, Fugger affirmed, he would need to undertake the transport at his own cost and risk.[65]

Keller also mediated craftsmen's requests for more specific information. In 1572, Fugger wrote with some concern that as it had been 'desired to know how large the uncut diamonds' were meant to be, he wanted to make clear that he only required common diamonds of the simple kind. They were for a cross which 'a woman can wear on her bare skin'.[66] Three weeks later he showed himself surprised that Keller was unable to source seven of these uncut diamonds and told him to send him strong, cut ones. Fugger wanted to inspect them, and now specified that they were for his wife, who wanted to wear them on her bare skin. He planned to look for them in Augsburg at the same time.[67] It then turned out his wife had intended to use them as protection when giving birth, for in April Fugger reported that he had received the cut diamonds, but his wife had delivered 18 weeks early, so that he returned them. He remained keen to receive seven uncut diamonds – 'bad, common things' – as they were not for a jewel but would be applied to the skin in a simple mould. Now the couple was waiting for Elisabeth to become pregnant again, so there was no hurry.[68] This underlines that the Fuggers used goods not just for social distinction, but to preserve and enhance health, and that they ordered goods across a broad spectrum of value.

After receiving sketches for blankets for mules – *Repusteros* – he therefore instructed Römer in 1574 to find a good tapestry maker and ask him to send an estimate for work that would be carried out with 'good colours' and even more beautifully than in the sketch. However, he also underlined that no silk should be used and not much silver and gold thread, but only wool, as in tapestry.[69] These blankets were for Wilhelm of Bavaria, and the case provides another excellent example of how merchants could help to optimize products that were more affordable but retained a high aesthetic appeal.[70] Fugger himself sent gold and silver thread to the Bavarian court and knew its high price well.

Where some goods were concerned, of course it mattered enormously that they helped to compare the Fuggers or their network to Italian or Spanish elites. Hans instructed Keller in 1569 to look for the type of fabric Spanish women used for coats, which could not be sourced in Augsburg, and requested sufficient fabric for two cloaks.[71] With such requests, there could be misunderstandings about just how much time, effort and money his agents were expected to invest. In April 1569, Fugger thus instructed Keller that he would like two tall, identical dappled horses for a ladies' carriage, as used in Italy. Keller was to report about whether he could find them 'in perfection'.[72] In July he specified that their colour was in-different, but that brown dappled horses, whether or not they were light or dark, were the most beautiful. He had assumed that Keller could mobilize his own network to find out whether they could be sourced without having them brought to Antwerp, which would be too expensive.[73] By August he reprimanded Keller that he should have inquired more diligently himself, rather than employing a man to visit different places in Flanders to look for them. On the other hand, he affirmed that he knew how difficult it was to find two similarly-coloured, able horses, and that there was no rush.[74] By December he agreed that one needed to wait for the right opportunity and that the horse had to be suitable to pull a carriage rather than for riding.[75] His request was never fulfilled.

## Affect

There were other instances where Fugger needed to be patient, cope with frustration or simply cancel a commission. The making of fur coats for winter, for instance, required careful planning to source a specific number of individual skins of high quality which could be sewn together. In December 1570, Fugger thus requested six 'bisottas' of sable like those he had been previously sent in order to widen a fur and make it longer – that is, more impressive. He asked for the fur to be sent in waxed cloth.[76] By January he had to accept that the sable could not be sourced and told Keller not to look for it for this winter. But he returned to his quest in 1574 and 1579, finally hopeful that he might source these sable skins through the Frankfurt spring fair, as they were still not to be had via Antwerp.[77]

His agents were either told to strike off goods from the list of goods to source, or to keep trying to obtain them. In 1569, for instance, Fugger replied to Keller, writing that he well imagined that it was impossible to find Portuguese parrots at the moment, but that he should try a better opportunity.[78] Markets for goods of this kind were not predictable, and the notion that a good opportunity had to offer itself and then be seized is recurrent throughout the correspondence. Wide networks of informants in key locations of trade ready to help thus were crucial. In 1567, Fugger was resigned that he might be unable to source a paternoster made of coral but was awaiting news from Mair in Antwerp, who had a friend in Genoa. Yet, Fugger concluded, if this friend did not possess better contacts than he himself, he would likewise achieve nothing – and so it proved to be.[79]

Fugger certainly expressed his enthusiasm about different types of products. He enthused about two 'precious' (köstlich) Turkish horses sourced for him by Earl Egk von Salm in 1569.[80] Such value judgements related to his material literacy and helped him to optimize products, as when in 1569 Fugger rejected a sample of raw silk from Venice, requesting it to be spun 'somewhat more subtly' so that it would please him more.[81] This required knowledge and experience of what quality could be achieved in luxury products or delicatessen and was important as 'subtlety' in turn linked to a valuation of acuteness and thus bestowed virtue on its owner.[82] His brother Marx commented in March 1569 that the preserved ginger sent to the courtmaster Trautson in Vienna from the Netherlands was too bitter and not of the kind one needed to preserve it in India. Hans Fugger now sent a barrel of ginger he himself used and sourced via Portugal.[83] In relation to cordovan leather he instructed Keller in 1569 to look for two pair of porsequine of smooth leather, one with double soles, and emphasized the need for good, elastic, soft leather which was not slashed and boots which were wide and easy to get into.[84] He optimized this challenging product in a whole series of letters which contained instructions to the shoemaker – for instance that the thickness of the leather had to be carefully taken into account so that they could be appropriately worn.[85] In 1568, he had even coined a new word to describe the patterning of Porsequines when he thanked for receiving a pair which was wide enough, but a little 'pa-tagramic' to look at. Keller was to order another pair of these slashed shoes, and just have them made a little tighter around the thigh.[86]

What this means is that we can recognize many objects that at first appear mundane to be in fact knowledge intensive. Comfortable, fine shoes were one of the most challenging dress objects to make, and Fugger's detailed feedback could then be used for other customers. In relation to painters, he trusted in the qualities of Anthonis Mor as acknowledged expert, writing in 1568 that Keller should find a good painter for a posthumous portrait of his father Anton, but that Mor would be preferable as the 'best portraitist far and wide'.[87] Similarly, work with fine linen-shirts – presumably embroidery – for Renata of Bavaria was entrusted to a named female expert in Antwerp, Antoinetta von Exsel, who was paid very substantial sums of money.[88] The engagement of women beyond guilds in the buoyant, innovative textile trades has recently begun to attract more attention.[89]

The fact that Fugger ordered goods across a spectrum of value meant that he differentiated between goods such as girdles for a monastery, for instance, which he wanted to be 'pretty' but not too expensive, and, as we have seen, his insistence to be sent nothing but something 'beautiful and good!' in the case of the Indian dove. In 1571, he was pleased about a large, beautiful piece of coral sourced for crown prince Wilhelm, while in 1569 he specified that he wished to order an ivory crucifix, about 30-cm long, as well as several other devotional items made from ivory; so that he required about one or two pounds of ivory which needed to be beautiful and as white as possible.[90] Such pure white ivory was more expensive but is likely to have been especially prized because of the affective qualities it lent crucifixes. It brought out the deadness of Christ's sacred body and the emotional power of the colour which indicated his loss of a spirit of liveliness. This in turn was believed to shape a viewer's affective empathy and thus his moral personhood more deeply.[91] Fugger's Catholicism was profound, and the same was true for other leading merchants – his contemporary Simon Ruiz, for instance, owned a house in Medina del Campo with two lavishly equipped oratories.[92]

Such raw materials were then often given to local master craftsman whose work was in demand, and whom Fugger regularly visited to look after gifts and orders. This had the additional benefit that they acquired a sense of their trustworthiness, ability and how much time they usually needed to work. In 1574, Fugger thus told crown prince Wilhelm that he would have a gemstone turned into an *Agnus Dei*; he was already in negotiation with an Augsburg master named Ulrich Möringer (d.1582), a good Catholic, who was particularly suited to such work, if a little slow in execution.[93] This underlines that consumers like Fugger responded to the production of highly skilled objects through proud guildsmen, which retained qualities of their makers as inalienable.[94] Devotional objects were further enhanced through their blessing, which turned them into efficacious sacramentals. Fugger thus asked his Madrid agent for candles which had been blessed at Candlemas at Monserrat, no matter what size.[95] He enthusiastically thanked Andreas Fabricius, the Leiden professor who now served Albrecht V of Bavaria as spiritual counsellor and had accompanied him to Rome, for sending a blessed rosary, assuring him that he always wanted to hold it in highest honour.[96]

Fugger repeatedly referred to the notion that good craftsmanship took time and paid off by increasing the aesthetic appeal of an object: in 1574, for instance, he informed the Earl of Lodron in Naples that weapons he had ordered would still take a while to make, but they were in the process of becoming very beautiful.[97] The weapons for Lodron, alas, caused further communication, as Fugger had to admit that Master Sterz kept telling him that they were about to be finished; this meant that Lodron, writing from different places in Italy, had to keep reminding Fugger, and Fugger needed to exert further pressure on Sterz.[98] He sent them one month later to Lodron's brother in Trent, and expressed his wish that they would please Lodron.[99] In May 1574, Fugger was delighted to employ an Italian sculptor (the young Giambologna) for repairs as he had no German and therefore no time to lose (*verbummeln*).[100]

Fugger could applaud goods as 'perfect', pretty or beautiful.[101] He regretted not being able to source seeds for the 'beautiful' cauliflower, after Cyprus had fallen to the Ottomans.[102] Dogs and horses were usually referenced with the adjective beautiful, and a key criterion for horses was the beauty of their proportions: Fugger asked for a horse to be sold although it was good, because it had an 'annoyingly large head'. He quantified how much this might devalue the price.[103] He could further show himself 'very content' with the work of a craftsman or, as in the case of his disastrous experience with the making of leather wall-paper, feel deeply betrayed, so that he would never trust the man again.[104]

The Augsburg merchant reserved some of his most enthusiastic remarks for featherwork he received from French makers.[105] They naturalistically imitated flowers and were to be used on sledges and in tournaments. Their price was precious: 200 crowns for a large barrel, which he apparently had paid for upfront and now wrote about to a courtier at the Inner-Austrian court of Charles II, Jörg Earl of Nogarola. They were 'so beautiful', he noted in August 1574, 'as I have never seen' and then again, towards the end of the letter: 'in sum, they' (the lifelike flowers) 'could just not be more beautiful'.

One might well object that Fugger used such affective registers in order to gain a better value for goods he sought to sell. In Kopytoff's terms, affect thus played a role in the process of commodification, in which the price and value of an object emerged through negotiation, and, we might add, affective regimes. Two months after his first letter to the Earl, Fugger reminded him that he would like to be paid for the featherwork, especially as he had taken a lot of trouble to get it.[106] By November, Fugger realized that the Earl might not want to acquire the feathers, and he wrote to a contact in Vienna to see whether they could be sold in the coming winter, perhaps on the occasion of one of the court's outings with decorated sledges. If this should prove difficult, Fugger was happy to exchange the feathers for a Turkish *Haupt*-horse – which underlines the high value of the featherwork.[107] In a further letter in December he referred to them as feather panaches rather than just flowers and acknowledged that the Earl might find them too expensive. Yet he added that he should have told Fugger earlier if he had wanted to receive them as presents.[108] Fugger had to mobilize further members of his network to see how they could be sold, and in December received news from his brother-in-law how to sell them, and told his Vienna contact to take his advice.[109] In November 1575, he wrote a final letter regarding these feathers, this time to Wilhelm of Bavaria. The crownprince had approached Fugger as he had heard that he possessed beautiful silk. Fugger replied that the crown prince had been misinformed, but that he had once sourced 'various curiously dyed feather panaches from France', which he had sent to Graz. They had been bound together like flowers. If they had been made from silk, he would have instantly sent them to Wilhelm.[110] Fugger nonetheless now sprang into action, as the crown prince had actually requested him to source silk flowers a long time ago. In December, he wrote to Wilhelm that he had never been able to find these, but that he had now found a talented woman who was a master of this art. If the crownprince was still interested, he would send samples and an estimate.[111] This suggests that Fugger in writing to Wilhelm glossed over how beautiful the featherwork had been, as he had not offered them to him, and was anxious to instantly affirm his wish to serve him in relation to other requests.

But Fugger's enthusiasm was certainly matched by his other comments on featherwork, which he often sourced for himself and admired. They underline that feathers used in head-wear were now bound up with fashionability and the creation of affective atmospheres. Feathers imparted *gentilezza* through their very materiality and embodied the ideal of *sprezzatura*, a natural elegance and lightness to signal the aesthetic and moral ideals of gracious gentlemen, whose choice of accessories resonated with the beauty of his soul. They were among a range of objects which delighted the eye with beautiful colours and thus furthered moral affects. Fugger mobilized his international trade networks to source them. In January 1576, for instance, Fugger wrote to an agent in Italy to acquire feathers for his daughters' bonnets and asked for 'a pair each of different *fazon*', which indicated the manner of manufacture rather than type of bird. He thought they might best be available in Milan or Mantua.[112] Within two weeks, he was sent four pairs of feather-panaches in different colours for his daughters as well as two white panaches, and in addition further panaches from Antwerp. By February, his Milan agent promised a box of feathers for bonnets.[113] A few days later, Fugger wrote to his Nuremberg agent about the fashionable new Saxon hats for his servants, whose liveries indicated status.[114] He kept inspecting deliveries from Nuremberg to check their quality as well as sending patterns for hats he wanted to have made and accessorized. Each time he noted how much the feathers which adorned them pleased him – as soft, translucent matter, they enabled particular qualities of sensual and affective experience.[115]

## Conclusion

The early modern period was an age of intensified global exchange, which was driven by merchants, and at the same time investigated and prized the local. Claartje Rasterhoff and Christine Göttler have recently drawn attention to Giovanni Botero's 1588 *Treatise Concerning the Causes of the Magnificencie and Greatness of Cities*, which prized excellence of local skill and product sophistication and explained it in relation to environmental factors or 'the subtlety of inhabitants' and their hidden knowledge, rather than natural resources in minerals, for instance.[116] Added to this, as we have seen, was the belief in the sacred power of particular locales, objects or people, and, as Göttler shows, 'counter-reformation spirituality increased sensitivity regarding the efficacy of sacred materials and in turn affected collecting practices and considerations at home'.[117] In this article I have sought to outline how Fugger interacted with his agents in Antwerp, one of Europe's foremost 16th-century knowledge hubs, in which Botero himself would have seen new artefacts and commodities.[118] Fugger possessed considerable material literacy and knowledge about a wide range of goods and their uses. He is typical of merchants who needed to know about far more than prices and politics. He was part of and shaped an emotional community which was excited about these goods and understood them to be as enlivening, invigorating and able to inject novelty and cultural distinction into life.

One of the Fugger's steady Antwerp trading partners were the Ximenes. An analysis of the 1617 inventory of Emmanuel Ximenes (1564–1637) underlines similarities in the valuation of goods which marked out such international merchants. As Birgit Borkopp shows, silk fabrics were the most costly materials used for both household furnishings and for clothes, and silk thus merited particular attention in the inventory; different qualities of silk – light-weight or heavy, plain or patterned – were therefore carefully recorded. 'A delightful contrast', she writes, 'would have been achieved with a fur lining in a garment otherwise fashioned from a silk damask, a patterned fabric with a smooth, shiny surface ('a violet damask night robe lined with marten')' – and this is exactly how we see Fugger portrayed as mature man.[119] Both Ximenes and Fugger highly valued gilt leather as a wall covering. The Ximenes inventory does not record shoes, which, as I have argued, could be a knowledge-intensive, sophisticated product for which merchant elites helped to shape demand, and an object of cultural exchange for Fugger, as he imitated the Portuguese style, perhaps even of the Ximenes family. Both families of course possessed libraries and precious devotional objects. They also cared greatly about medical knowledge. Ximenes owned a distilling chamber, which, as Lawrence Principe explains, was 'used primarily for the manufacture of simple medicinal waters, cordials, and oils, presumably for the use of Ximenez's family and friends – perhaps most of all for his wife Isabel da Vega, who suffered a long illness'.[120] Fugger likewise extended medical care to his employees, serfs, family and friends, as well as to his wife, for whom he sourced stones which were ascribed protective powers when she gave birth and intimately put them 'on her bare skin', as if to infuse herself directly with their power. In 1584, Fugger wrote to the Spanish merchant Simon Ruiz to ask whether he could source the seeds and small plants of some Latin American flowers in the park of the Escorial, 'of various and rare colours'.[121]

What I have charted, therefore, forms part of a new history of the merchant: as a figure whose fears, hopes and enjoyment entangled with the commodities he ate, wore or turned into medicine as well as, to be sure, good money. It would be wrong to project Eva Illouz's statement that modern capitalism shapes 'hyper'-emotionality into the past.[122] But early modern merchants like Fugger certainly were not just figures who calculated the reduction of transaction costs to optimize supply, cultivated rational price management, disenchantment and emotional numbness. They located experience not just in a disembodied intellect, but substantially in the body and senses. They lived in a time which provided much guidance on the question of how the world was to be experienced sensorially – in relation to sight, smell, sound and touch – and emotionally, not least through a new emphasis on the preservation of health. Objects were implicated in moral and not just social self-formation. Antwerp and the Southern Netherlands, it has been argued, 'played a key role in the emergence of new types of knowing tied to the world of the senses – the (new) material and natural worlds – but also imbued with virtue and morality'.[123] The merchants' own consumer demand and relation to matter corresponded to and further explored understandings of the body, the passions and the soul.

## Notes

1 L. Jardine. *Worldly Goods.*
2 L. Malafouris and C. Renfrew, "Introduction."
3 U. Rublack, "Matter in the Material Renaissance."

4  N. Boivin, *Material Cultures*, 21.
5  Ibid., 47
6  C. Karnehm, ed., *Die Korrespondenz Hans Fuggers*; Dauser, *Informationskultur*.
7  See, for instance, M. North, *Kultureller Austausch*; M. Klebusek, "Mercator Sapiens."
8  P. N. Miller, *Peiresc's Mediterranean World*; the quotation is from A. Grafton, "A Hero of the European Mind."
9  P. N. Miller, *Peiresc's Mediterranean World*, 19
10  Ibid.
11  C. Göttler, "Indian Dagger," 101.
12  This is outlined for the period of Hans Fugger's correspondence with his agents by Van der Wee, *The Growth of the Antwerp Market*, vol. 2, 252–67, for his dealings with jewelery see K. Siebenhüner, *Die Spur der Juwelen*.
13  C. Göttler, B. Ramakers, and J. Woodall, "Introduction," 13, and 15 for this engagement with Gruzinski's work on mondialisation.
14  N. Thomas, *Oceanic Art*, 11.
15  C. Van Eck, *Art, Agency*, 19, reference to Gell.
16  C. Van Eck, *Art, Agency*, is stimulating in calling for a consideration of a historical dimension of Gell's work, 55.
17  C. Karnehm, ed., *Die Korrespondenz*, I 1, 7, 12, for the following see 18.
18  Some of the Italian fish supplies were sent to southern Germany pre-cooked: see G. Lill, *Hans Fugger*, 23, fn.2.
19  C. Karnehm, ed., *Korrespondenz*, II 192, 302.
20  S. Cavallo and T. Storey, *Healthy Living*, 184.
21  Ibid., 184–85.
22  Ibid., 195, 196–97; 207.
23  Ibid., 276.
24  L. Schiebinger, *Plants and Empire*, 28, 178.
25  R. Dauser, "Stainlin für griess," 54, 71; Hyden-Hanscho, "Beaver-hats," 161–62.
26  C. Karnehm, ed., *Korrespondenz*, II 255.
27  Ibid., II 26, 658.
28  Ibid., II 892.
29  V. Vazquez de Prada, *Lettres marchandes*, I 109.
30  U. Rublack and M. Hayward, ed., *The First Book of Fashion*.
31  C. Karnehm, ed., *Korrespondenz*, I 184.
32  H. Pohl, *Die Portugiesen in Antwerpen*, 66–67; 74, 87.
33  C. Göttler, B. Ramakers, and J. Woodall, "Introduction," 16.
34  This problematizes S. Dupré and G. Vanpaemel, "The Circulation of Knowledge," 45. The question clearly is a complex one and requires comparative research among merchant elites. The important concept of learning on the shop-floor is discussed on p.7 1.
35  C. Karnehm, ed., *Korrespondenz*, I 542.
36  P. N. Miller, *Peiresc*, 181.
37  C. Karnehm, ed., *Korrespondenz*, I 800, 915, 943.
38  Extensive discussion in K. S. Mathew, *Indo-Portuguese Trade*.
39  S. Dupré and G. Vanpaemel, *Embattled Territory*, 199.
40  For Anna of Saxony: U. Schlude, "Naturwissen und Schriftlichkeit."
41  C. Karnehm, ed., *Korrespondenz*, I 6.
42  Ibid, I 60, 70, 75, 167
43  S. Steuscher, "Hunde am Fürstenhof."
44  C. Karnehm, ed., *Korrespondenz*, I 281, 242
45  Ibid., I 125, 110, 117.
46  See also R. Pieper, *Die Vermittlung einer neuen Welt*.
47  P. H. Smith and P. Findlen, eds., *Merchants and Marvels*.
48  C. Karnehm, ed., *Korrespondenz*, example for lists II 0, II 156, for books.

49 Ibid., I 615. When it arrived, the flax was inspected by his wife Elisabeth and found to be acceptable, 747

50 Ibid., I 246.

51 Ibid., I 192.

52 Ibid., I 237, 300, 300, 237.

53 Ibid., II 654.

54 Ibid., I 578.

55 R. King, "'The Beads," 158ff.

56 C. Karnehm, ed., *Korrespondenz*, I 556, 570, 578, 598.

57 Ibid., I 679, 701.

58 Ibid., I 454.

59 Ibid., I 458. He advised Mair to separate it into two pieces in case of doubt that it might reach Hörmann. If Hörmann was able to source it he was to transport it via Genua, as current shipments to the Netherlands were currently complicated by the English.

60 C. Karnehm, ed., *Korrespondenz*, I 474.

61 Ibid., I 45. In 1557, Adam Freiherr of Dietrichstein, who represented the Habsburg Emperor in Spain beween 1564–1573, likewise intensely corresponded with his brother about the acquisition of unicorns.

62 Ibid., II, 4.

63 Ibid., II 62, 68.

64 Ibid., 635

65 Ibid., I 454.

66 Ibid., I 679.

67 Ibid., I 701.

68 Ibid., I 717, In the case of other precious stones he first sent a pattern for emeralds and rubies he required, then inspected pieces and chose most of them, 634.

69 Ibid., II 62, 68.

70 Ibid., II 163.

71 Ibid., I 446.

72 Ibid., I 448.

73 Ibid., I 461.

74 But after a fortnight he reminded Keller of his wish, as he was also asking for an Italian earl who wished to source Dutch young, beautiful quality horses of a common variety for his carriage. Perhaps both requests could be dealt with at the same time to reduce costs? C. Karnehm, ed., *Korrespondenz*, I 473, 479.

75 Ibid., 620.

76 Ibid., 491.

77 Ibid., II 224, 1459.

78 Ibid., 383.

79 Ibid., 123, 145.

80 Ibid., 386.

81 Ibid., 390.

82 L. Syson and D. Thornton, *Objects of Virtue*.

83 C. Karnehm, ed., I *Korrespondenz*, 393.

84 Ibid., 434.

85 Ibid., 322.

86 Ibid., 333.

87 Ibid., 268.

88 Ibid., 951, 976, 985.

89 See, for instance, A. Caracausi, "Textiles Manufacturing," 131–60, and on innovation on ribbon-making in Italy, 141–44.

90 C. Karnehm, ed., *Korrespondenz*, I 579, 480.

91 C. W. Bynum, *Christian Materiality*.

92  H. LaPeyre, *Une Famille de Marchands: Les Ruiz*, 76–78, on the Catholicism of leading merchant-bankers see also 599.
93  C. Karnehm, ed., *Korrespondenz*, II 65.
94  B. De Munck, "Artisans, Products and Gifts."
95  C. Karnehm, ed., *Korrespondenz*, II 137.
96  Ibid., II 20.
97  Ibid., II 80.
98  Ibid., II 88.
99  Ibid., II 121.
100  Ibid., II 118.
101  Ibid., II 123.
102  Ibid., II 136.
103  Ibid., II 177.
104  Ibid., II 154, 172
105  Ibid., II 193.
106  Ibid., II 223.
107  Ibid., II 257
108  Ibid., II 279.
109  Ibid., II 299.
110  Ibid., II 620.
111  Ibid., II 655.
112  Ibid., II 702.
113  Ibid., II 708, 728.
114  Ibid., II 704.
115  Ibid., II 1790, 1796, 1903.
116  C. Rasterhoff, "The Spatial Side of Innovation," 161, see also the extended discussion in C. Göttler, 'Indian Daggers', 102.
117  C. Göttler, "Indian Daggers," 102.
118  Ibid.
119  See the Ximenes inventory website at Bern university, http://ximenez.unibe.ch/material/clothing/.
120  Ibid., http://ximenez.unibe.ch/laboratory/.
121  H. Pohl, *Portugiesen*, 331.
122  E. Illouz, *Cold Intimacies*, 5.
123  On this in relation of Amsterdam: C. Goettler, B. Ramakers, and J. Woodall, "Introduction," 14.

## Bibliography

Boivin, Nicole. *Material Cultures, Material Minds: The Impact of Things on Human Thought, Society, and Evolution*. Cambridge: Cambridge University Press, 2008.

Bynum, Carline Walker. *Christian Materiality: An Essay on Religion in Late Medieval Europe*. New York: Zone, 2011.

Caracausi, Andrea. "Textiles Manufacturing, Product information and Transfers of Technology in Padua and Venice between the Sixteenth and Eighteenth Centuries." In *Innovation and Creativity in late Medieval and Early Modern European Cities*, edited by Karel Davids and Bert de Munck, 131–60. London: Routledge, 2016.

Cavallo, Sandra and Storey, Tessa . *Healthy Living in late Renaissance Italy*. New Haven: Yale University Press 2013.

Dauser, Regina. *Informationskultur und Beziehungswissen: Das Korrespondenznetz Hans Fuggers (1531–1598)*. Tübingen: Niemeyer, 2008.

Dauser, Regina. "Stainlin für griess und andere Wundermittel: Hans Fuggers Korrespondenz über medizinische Exotica." In *Die Welt des Hans Fugger, 1531–1598,* edited by Hans Karg, 51–59. Augsburg: Wissner, 2008.

Dupré, Sven and Geert Vanpaemel. "The Circulation of Knowledge in the Spanish Netherlands. Introduction." In *Embattled Territory. The Circulation of Knowledge in the Spanish Netherlands,* edited by Sven Dupré, Bert de Munck, Werner Thomas, and Geert Vanpaemel, 7–22. Gent: Academia Press.2015.

Eck, Caroline van. *Art, Agency and Living Presence: From the Animated Image to the Excessive Object.* Leiden: Amsterdam University Press, 2015.

Göttler, Christine. "'Indian Daggers with Idols' in the Early Modern Constcamer: Collecting, Picturing, and Imagining "Exotic" Weaponry in the Netherlands and Beyond." In *Netherlandish Art in its Global Contexts. Netherlands Yearbook for History of Art,* edited by Thijs Weststeijn, Eric Jorink, and Frits Scholten, 80–111. Leiden: Brill, 2016.

Göttler, Christine, Bart Ramakers and Joanna, Woodall. "Introduction." In *Trading Values in Early Modern Antwerp. Netherlands Yearbook for History of Art,* edited by Christine GoettlerRamakers, Bart, and Woodall, Joanna, 8–37. Leiden: Brill, 2015.

Grafton, Anthony. "A Hero of the European Mind." *New York Review of Books* November 19, 2015, 15–18.

Hyden-Hanscho, Veronika. "Beaver-hats, Drugs and Sugar Consumption in Vienna around 1700." In *Cultural Exchange and Consumption Patterns in the Age of Enlightenment: Europe and the Atlantic World,* edited by Veronika Hyden-Hanscho, Renate Pieper, and Werner Stangl, 153–68 Bochum: Winkler, 2013.

Illouz, Eva. *Cold Intimacies: The Making of Emotional Capitalism.* Cambridge: Polity, 2007.

Jardine, Lisa. *Worldly Goods: A New History of the Renaissance.* New York: Norton, 1996.

Karnehm, Christl, ed. *Die Korrespondenz Hans Fuggers von 1566 bis 1594: Regesten der Kopierbücher aus dem Fuggerarchiv.* III vols. Munich: Bayerische Landesgeschichte, 2003.

King, Rachel. "'The Beads with which we Pray are Made from it': Devotional Amber in Early Modern Italy." In *Religion and the Senses in Early Modern Europe,* edited by Wietse de Boer, and Christine Goettler, 153–75. Leiden: Brill, 2012.

Klebusek, Marika. "Mercator Sapiens: Merchants as Cultural Entrepreneurs." In *Double Agents: Cultural and Political Brokerage in Early Modern Europe,* edited by Marika, Klebusek and Badeloch Vera Noldus, 95–111. Leiden: Brill, 2011.

LaPeyre, Henri. *Une Famille de Marchands: Les Ruiz.* Paris: Colin, 1955.

Lill, Georg. *Hans Fugger (1531–1598) und die Kunst: Ein Beitrag zur Spätrenaissance in Süddeutschland.* Leipzig: Dunker und Humblot, 1908.

Malafouris, Lambros and Colin, Renfrew. "Introduction." In *The Cognitive Life of Things: Archaeology, Material Engagement and the Extended Mind,* edited by Lambros, Malafouris, and Colin, Renfrew, 1–12. Cambridge: McDonald Institute Monographs, 2010.

Mathew, Kuzhippalli Skaria. *Indo-Portuguese Trade and the Fugger of Germany.* New Delhi: Manohar, 1997.

Miller, Peter N. *Peiresc's Mediterranean World.* Cambridge.: Harvard University Press, 2015.

Munck, Bert de. "Artisans, Products and Gifts: Rethinking the History of Material Culture in Early Modern Europe." *Past & Present* 1/224 (2014): 39–74.

North, Michael, ed. *Kultureller Austausch: Bilanz und Perspektiven der Frühneuzeitforschung.* Cologne: Böhlau, 2009.

Pieper, Renate. *Die Vermittlung einer neuen Welt: Amerika im Kommunikationsnetz des habsburgischen Imperiums (1493–1598).* Mainz: Van Zabern, 2000.

Pohl, Hans. *Die Portugiesen in Antwerpen (1567–1648): Zur Geschichte einer Minderheit.* Wiesbaden: Steiner, 1977.

Rasterhoff, Claartje. "The Spatial Side of Innovation. The Local Organization of Cultural Production in the Dutch Republic, 1580–1800." In *Innovation and Creativity in Late Medieval and Early Modern European Cities*, edited by Karel, Davids and Bert de Munck, 161–88. Farnham: Ashgate, 2014.

Ribeiro, Ana Sofia. "The Evolution of Norms in Trade and financial Networks in the First Global Age: The case of the Simon Ruiz's Network." In *Beyond Empires: Global, Self-organizing, Cross-imperial Networks, 1500-1800*, edited by Catia Antunes, and Amelia Polonia, 12–40. Leiden: Brill, 2016.

Rublack, Ulinka. "Matter in the Material Renaissance." *Past & Present* 219 (2013): 41–85.

Rublack,, Ulinka and Maria, Hayward, eds., *The First Book of Fashion: The Book of Clothes of Matthäus and Veit Konrad Schwarz of Augsburg*. London: Bloomsbury, 2015.

Schiebinger, Londa. *Plants and Empire. Colonial Bioprospecting in the Atlantic World*. Cambridge: Harvard University Press, 2004.

Schlude, Ursula. "Naturwissen und Schriftlichkeit." In *Die natur ist überall bey uns': Mensch und Natur in der Frühen Neuzeit,* edited by Tina Asmussen, Bott, Sebastian, and Münch, Paul, 95–108. Zürich: Chronos, 2009.

Siebenhüner, Kim. *Die Spur der Juwelen: Materielle Kultur und transkontinentale Verbindungen zwischen Indien und Europa in der Frühen Neuzeit*. Cologne: Böhlau, 2018.

Smith,, Pamela H. and Paula Findlen, eds., *Merchants and Marvels. Commerce, Science, and Art in Early Modern Europe*. London: Routledge, 2001.

Syson, Luke and Thornton, Dora. *Objects of Virtue: Art in Renaissance Italy*. Los Angeles: Getty Publications, 2002.

Teuscher, Simon. "Hunde am Fürstenhof: Köter und "edle wind" als Medien sozialer Beziehungen vom 14. Bis 16. Jahrhundert." *Historische Anhropologie* 6/3 (1998): 347–69.

Thomas, Nicholas. *Oceanic Art*. London: Thames and Hudson, 1995.

Vazquez de Prada, Valentin. *Lettres marchandes D'Anvers, vol. 1*. Paris: Colins, 1961.

Wee, Herman van der. *The Growth of the Antwerp Market and the European Economy*. The Hague: Nijhoff, 1963.

# 3

## PENNETREK

### Sir Balthazar Gerbier (1592–1663) and the calligraphic aesthetics of commercial empire

*Vera Keller*

### Introduction: the grasping hand

The global market intertwined worldwide emotions. Exotic luxury goods and curiosities excited desire and wonder among European consumers; high-risk long-distance trade investments evoked apprehension; the prospect of mastering far-flung parts of the world raised new ambitions, and the practical abilities required to sustain trade around the world showcased new forms of technological bravado. Yet, we must remember that what was global about such trade was not just nature, commodities and spaces but people. The history of emotions of peoples outside of Europe entangled with the emotions of the European consumer, merchant and investor. The excitement and apprehension experienced by the European investor related in an unequal nexus of power and affect with the fear experienced by the enslaved individual upon whose labour that investor's success depended.[1]

Perhaps no image illustrates this more than the allegory of Count Friedrich Casimir of Hanau-Lichtenberg's plan for a Guyanese colony (Figure 3.1). The dramatically lit hand of the Count reaches for the riches held by a young African boy, who, rather than willingly presenting it, turns aside. The boy's body, trapped between the arms of the count and of the god of commerce, shrinks away, his eyes remaining trained on the approaching threat and his lips slightly parted, perhaps from rapid breath.

For once, the boy need not have feared. While the Count acquired the colony on paper through signed contracts with the Amsterdam Chamber of the West India Company (WIC), he never sent colonisers there and never profited from it. The artist Johann David Welcker transformed the entire episode into a *vanitas* painting, with Mercury, the god of eloquence pointing ultimately not to the alluring riches, but past them to a roughly written manuscript note, signed by the artist Welcker: *vanitas vanitatum et omnia vanitas*. The dream of New World slave-based wealth proved to be but a paper fiction.

**FIGURE 3.1** Johann David Welcker, *Allegory of the Acquisition of Surinam in 1669 (1676)*, Oil on canvas, 162,5 × 134 cm. Inv. 1164. Photo Credit: bpk Bildagentur/ Staattliche Kunsthalle Karlsruhe/ Wolfgang Pankoke/ Art Resource, NY

The arm of the Count is confusingly placed; it looks like it might belong to the mysterious individual lurking behind him. The painting, besides for highlighting the lust of the nobleman and the fear of the boy, thus asks us to consider who the real mastermind behind the project was. Who, from the shadows, manipulated the affective relationships on display in the painting's foreground? It has been suggested that this figure represents the count's advisor, the alchemist, commercial theorist and entrepreneur Johann Joachim Becher (1635–82), who sold the idea of the colony to the Count.[2] Yet, even now, the painting still conceals the ultimate mastermind behind the colony, as it was not originally Becher's idea. Becher, fishing for useful inventions, alchemical secrets and investment opportunities in Amsterdam, had been sold the idea of a late Dutchman, Sir Balthasar Gerbier (1592–1663). Gerbier is known today primarily as an early Stuart political and artistic agent.[3] He is little studied as a proponent of slavery, yet he pursued slave-based colonial schemes throughout a long career.[4] Born in Middelburg of Huguenot descent, Gerbier zig-zagged through Spain, Italy, France, the Netherlands and England. One of his fondest projects was a scheme to establish the Duke of Buckingham, shortly before the latter's assassination in 1628, as the ruler of a new Caribbean state.[5] He ultimately founded a trading company, the Nieuwe Geoctroyeerde Guiaansche Compagnie (NGC), with a slave-based colony in Guyana in 1659.

It was this colony whose acquisition Becher negotiated for on behalf of the German Count. From beyond the frame of the painting, even from beyond the grave, Gerbier attracted investors into his paper fantasies of slave-based wealth, with their attendant emotional extremes of desire and fear. Even the savvy commercial theorist, Becher, was enticed. The ultimate commercial savoir-faire, this painting suggests, was the ability to recruit investment by creating colonial visions playing upon investors' emotions. The tool that Gerbier used to do this, far more beautifully than Welcker's painted note suggests, was the calligraphic hand and the assurances it offered in an array of media, from map legends to contract signatures.

This essay explores Gerbier's original project and the scribal aesthetics he deployed in order to manipulate global affective relationships of slave-based wealth. Such a viewpoint has much to add to the investigation of the Dutch global knowledge society, since the history of slavery has been long underplayed in accounts of the Dutch Golden Age. Slavery played a fundamental role in the Dutch colonial empire in both Asia and the Americas.[6] The VOC, for instance, 'shipped African, Indian, and Asian slaves to Batavia, commercial emporia such as Malacca (Melaka), its spice plantations in the Moluccas (Malukus) in eastern Indonesia, and its settlements in coastal Ceylon (Sri Lanka) and the Cape of Good Hope'.[7] According to the latest estimates, 554,300 slaves were 'carried from the African coast in Dutch vessels in 1596–1829'.[8] The phase of the trade in the years between 1651–75, with which this essay is concerned, is 'the least known and in some ways most interesting' of this period; with shipments beginning to the Caribbean and the Guianas, the trade jumped from 26,000 slaves shipped in the previous 25-year period to 70,800.[9]

It might be assumed that Dutch consumers and investors were unaware of the role of slaves in global Dutch trade. We might imagine early modern consumers and investors smoking tobacco, sipping coffee, eating sweets and enjoying tropical woods while remaining oblivious to the suffering through which goods were produced, much as Western consumers today often give little thought to overseas factory conditions. Yet, this essay shows how one prolific, international image-maker, Gerbier, intentionally made the overseas context present in an aesthetics deliberately tailored to the world of global commercial empire. Gerbier believed this would appeal to his audience. An aesthetic showcasing European violence enacted upon enslaved peoples overseas aggrandized emotions of triumph and mastery for the European economic actor.

This account runs counter to an influential strand of scholarship arguing that the Dutch visual relationship to global territories (in contrast with the English) was peculiarly masterless. According to both Donna Marks and Svetlana Alpers, Dutch maps implied an egalitarian political structure.[10] Alpers argued that though 'mapping can serve to mark ownership, it does not, by its nature, display pictorial marks of authority'.[11] Alpers emphasized mechanical means of visual image production, such as that of the camera obscura, rather than images shaped by the human hand; the optical projection of images supposedly offered an objective description of reality liberated from human dominance and power structures, as well as from emotions.

By contrast, more recent studies have showcased how visual and literary media purposefully engaged Dutch desires for global mastery, including through the depiction of enslaved and mastered peoples.[12] Dutch maps not only served global exploitation as useful 'management tools'.[13] They also narrated 'the spaces of European conquest, colonialism and empire', 'encouraging an intense sense of touch, depth and space,' and arousing 'wide-ranging colonial desires'.[14]

This essay expands this more recent strand of scholarship by focusing on a medium less often related to colonialism: calligraphy. The history of calligraphy offers a signal means to explore the relationship between the history of knowledge and the history of emotions in the age of global trade. While many accounts relate the history of knowledge and global trade through practices of verification and the production of useful, reliable knowledge, as the editors to this volume discuss, the history of calligraphy instead emphasizes a growing importance placed on aesthetic flourish. It thus allows us to delve into the emotional and performative aspects of commercial transactions and intelligence.

During the era of trade's globalization, calligraphy transformed in terms of its audience, its aesthetic and in the forms of knowledge it promised. Calligraphic exemplar books expanded into large-scale, impractical, luxury objects – and none more so than one mammoth calligraphic copy or exemplar book executed by Gerbier. The aesthetic developments of calligraphy in the period point towards an increased emphasis on social ambition and mastery in a commercial setting.

The premier calligraphic achievement of the era was the single-line unbroken flourish, technically known as a paraph, or in Dutch a *pennetrek*. Utilitarian in origin, the paraph began as the inimitable mark of a notary that guaranteed authenticity. Gerbier made ample use of signatures and manuscript signs as guarantees, even within the printed pamphlets promoting his colonization projects. Yet the *pennetrek* also developed into an independent art form that went far beyond the conveyance of trusted information.

The calligraphic flourish is an embodied gesture, often performed in high-stakes commercial settings such as the signing of contracts. It participated in Gerbier's aesthetic vocabulary of triumphal architecture and festoons that he would explicitly connect to the bonds restraining enslaved bodies. In the mastery of the pen it demonstrated and the inventiveness of the forms it produced, the flourish showcased the pen-man's control and independence, as calligraphers made new spaces for themselves. From Gerbier's hand flowed a constant stream of proposals, encrypted documents, maps and secrets, creating a paper version of overseas wealth within which even such a canny schemer as Becher was entrapped.

## Manipulating desires through legend: a form of market knowledge

Martijn van den Bel and Lodewijk Hulsman have argued that Dutch settlers typically did not search for fabled cities of gold. Gerbier's settlement on the Approuague river in today's French Guiana in 1659, they say, was the best-known exception. Gerbier's plantation was the stuff of legend, of wild dreams of immense riches for the Dutch colonists lured to settle there between 1659 and 1678 and of nightmares for the enslaved Africans transported there by the West India Company, upon whose labour those riches were to be based.[15] The clash of these visions led to a personal disaster for Gerbier as mutineers shot his two daughters, killing one of them. Gerbier was quick to publish the scene in lurid detail, including improbable scenes of the native inhabitants mourning at his daughter's deathbed.

One vision for the colony involved a supposed mine of gold and various alchemical secrets that Gerbier had allegedly acquired from a renegade Flemish secretary in Spanish employment. Another vision, coming fast on the heels of the fall of Dutch Brazil, promised a New Brazil, that is, 'a great and profitable tropical colony based on coerced labour that facilitated the realization of dreams of wealth and power'.[16] Gerbier had recruited Otto Keye, a veteran of Dutch Brazil and an enthusiastic promoter of slave-based sugar plantations, to help found his settlement. The competing visions of mineral versus slave-based wealth eventually devolved relations in the settlement, leading to the attack of Keye and Johannes Rhenanus, a German chymist Gerbier had hired, on Gerbier and his family.

Even after the mutiny and the murder, Gerbier immediately set about, on his return to Europe, promoting additional schemes for explorations of West and North Africa. Yet, Gerbier's commitment to his own stories of El Dorado, or any sense of contradiction between them and slavery-based agriculture he also pursued, should not be taken at face value. He prided himself on remaining immune from the temptations surrounding him; he claimed to be 'of such a temper as that I might be Court proofe, were its allurements never so great'.[17] Meanwhile, he represented himself as an expert in how to tempt others.

In one anonymously published pamphlet describing how to lure colonists to far-off lands, Gerbier revealingly describes the instrumentality of crafting legends such as El Dorado. In his 1652 pamphlet, *A Sea-Cabbin Dialogue*, an English sea captain and a Dutch merchant on shipboard discussed another pamphlet –

Gerbier's *Remonstrance,* and the tales of golden cities it contained.[18] According to the *Remonstrance*, the normal, careful, time-consuming ways of seeking wealth, such as that of the 'Merchant with the buying of Negros' or that of 'Myne-masters', could be replaced with an instant path to wealth through a chymical secret, like that which Queen Elizabeth had sought in vain from Edward Kelly.[19] The English captain in the *Sea-Cabbin Dialogue* had heard of such rumours, and so had the Dutch merchant – not surprisingly, since Gerbier marketed these projects to both English and Dutch audiences.[20]

The discussion of such legends tested the patience of another passenger, a Frisian. He warned that not every proposer of overseas ventures was equally honest; there were 'sundry propounders' who 'goe about to Cozen'.[21] One propounder, or projector, who meant to deceive his audience, was Sir Thomas Dishington, the Frisian claimed.[22] However, although Dishington's wild projects proved unreliable, an aspect of his project was true, the Frisian continued. Dishington knew that one must lure colonizers 'with the hopes of conquesting some great matter, and the which must be hard to come by, for that else it would not seem to be a worthy undertaking for them'. Such great designs as 'the conquesting of the golden Fleece' or the 'pulling of that dayled beast, Anti-Christ out of his Romish seate' were of sufficient magnitude and difficulty to tempt settlers to try life in a new land. The propositions must be pleasing and, while challenging, not entirely impossible in order 'to keepe the peoples mind in a longing expectation, and in a constant resolution'.[23]

In other words, any colonial wealth-seeking venture would in fact need to engage practical commercial ventures such as Merchants' 'buying of Negros' and the efforts of 'Myne-masters'. Yet, such pedestrian business plans would not inspire individuals to travel around the world. Veneering proposals with a superficial chymical or apocalyptic sheen could tempt and control participants. The English captain, impressed by the Frisian's savoir-faire, noted that such abilities in discovering and manipulating the secret desires of others granted the Dutch their freedom and made them the masters of other men. This was the means by which the 'Hollanders Common-Wealth' 'have shaken the Monarchicall Yoaks from their Necks, have made themselves masters of Armies, of Treasures, as well as of the meanes and lives of men'.[24]

The Captain queried why the Dutch merchant did not take up the project of overseas settlement himself. The merchant sighed. 'Alas! we Merchants (at least many of us) are like resty Horses that neither can, nor will be beaten out of their old Track, according unto our several vocations; if you tell me of a Balthazar de Moucheron, or a Curtin, and such like; why they I graunt have been fit for such undertakings'.[25] He referred to the visionary Flemish merchants of an earlier era, such as Balthasar de Moucheron, Balthasar Gerbier's relative and namesake, and Willem Courten, who both moved north and established Dutch global trade in the Americas, Africa, and Asia. de Moucheron's activities outside of Europe began in the 1590's in West Africa. The Courten-de Moor company sent out two fleets to South America in 1616. One built a fort on the Amazon River and planted tobacco, but the colony was disbanded in 1621. The second went to the Essequibo in Guyana, where Fort Kijkoveral was founded.[26] By relating his projects to earlier global ventures, Gerbier sets his Caribbean and South American plans in context. Projects and global trade are generally historiographically separated by the anachronistic and contingent criterion of success. Yet, when first proposed, every global trading venture was itself a project. Gerbier thus explicitly pointed to such earlier ventures as the role model for his own projects; moreover, he suggested that it was this older generation's ability to uncover and exploit the hidden desires of other humans that won them freedom and made them masters of other men.

Gerbier's realpolitik account of El Dorado as a useful lure for colonists sheds a new light on his seemingly wild-eyed global projects. Gerbier emphasizes that manipulating the emotions of investors and settlers through the creation of alluring fictions was a form of knowledge vital to global trade. In this pamphlet, he revealed that the seemingly manic nature of his project, which included prophecies, quests, alchemical secrets, assassinated Dukes and Spanish renegades, was in fact a carefully calibrated aesthetic that he saw as part of a tradition in Dutch global trade.

## Calligraphic forms of secret knowledge

Gerbier's colonial projects promised his settlers ultimate power and freedom through their grand exploitation of nature and subject populations; all the while, Gerbier sought to control the colonizers themselves as well. Although Gerbier's attempts to control his colony were not successful, given the mutiny he quickly faced, his art of selling its vision initially was. One key tool in Gerbier's marketing of his scheme lay in his calligraphic performance.

Gerbier made his penmanship his calling card, as can be seen his first overture to George Villiers, Duke of Buckingham (1592–1628), the royal favourite and arbiter of fashion in the early Stuart court, whom Gerbier would serve as image-maker.[27] In a letter in French offering his services to Villiers, Gerbier led a flourish or *pennetrek* in a single unbroken line from the name of George Villiers down to a calligraphic image of a hand holding a compass. In a poem, Gerbier characterized his flourish as though it flowed from Villiers' own hand through Gerbier's in an infinite extension. Gerbier thus developed his penmanship into an emblem of his potential patron's effortless, long-distance control of his would-be agent, at the same time as celebrating Villiers' 'debonnaireté'. [28]

Precisely because he attempted to appear *debonnaire*, Villiers himself could never have achieved such calligraphic flourish. He, in fact, 'cultivated a large scrawl that reflects his power and influence'.[29] At this time, a good hand could be associated with subservience, not something at which anyone with pretensions to political power wished to excel. The servile status of calligraphy was, however, shifting, precisely due to the inventiveness and *sprezzatura* exemplified by the single-line flourish or *pennetrek* popularized by Jan van de Velde (1568–1623). Van de Velde was one of over 400 writing masters who emigrated from the South to the Dutch Republic, making it the new centre of European calligraphy.[30] This calligraphic emigration intersected with the mercantile one, since it was in inexpensive 'French schools' that writing masters taught calligraphy alongside ciphering, accounting and French, the language of trade.[31] Like Gerbier, writing masters enjoyed versatile, international careers.[32] Yet, while calligraphers often developed diverse interests, the curriculum for their schools remained conservatively targeted at a commercial audience. They did not offer a noble education.

Conversely, noble forms of education did not offer instruction in penmanship. Courtiers and princes had long exercised several forms of physical and manual arts, such as hunting, horsemanship, dance, ivory-turning or even amateur painting and engraving.[33] Riding academies sprang up all over Europe offering such an education. All such training of the hand and the body was supposed to illustrate not only military valour and vigour but also control and political *savoir-faire*. Such schools, generally speaking, excluded penmanship and accounting.[34]

Exceptionally, the academy that Gerbier briefly ran in London in 1648–9 included *both* 'riding the great horse', military fortifications, 'noble exercises' and courtly arts, as well as calligraphy, accounting, arithmetic, double-writing, stenography, history, modern languages, and even, extremely innovatively, 'Experimentall Naturall Philosophie'.[35] He published the curriculum's contents in several works, including in a bilingual French-English edition called *The Interpreter*. After the academy's closure in London, Gerbier continued to advertise it in the Netherlands, including in an excerpt from *The Interpreter* on military architecture published in Delft in 1652, where he proposed the opening of a 'Public Art School' (*Publique Constleerplaatse*) specifically aimed at poorer students in Middelburg.[36] In 1658, he also remarketed the lectures from his academy as an education fit for the young Prince William III of Orange, in a volume entitled *Princely Virtuous Academical Discourses,* as well as in a calligraphic manuscript mirror for princes.[37] Gerbier's academy reflects a fusion of the political education aimed at the nobility and a commercial one geared for aspiring merchants. To both audiences, he offered a single form of education, one conflating the traditional roles of political master and his secretary.

This fusion relates to an evolution in the history of economic thought. In turn-of-the-century political treatises, the manipulation of secrets of empire, *arcana imperii,* was part of the reason of state and exclusively the province of the prince. Secretaries served princes as keepers of their secrets. However, given the economic slant of Giovanni Botero's *Reason of State* (1589), this body of political secrets was inflected with new forms of commercial manoeuvring, more akin to the forms of knowledge to be gained in the training of a secretary than in that of a prince.[38] Eventually a Dutch commercial reason of state would be codified in the political writings of the De la Court brothers.[39]

Global empire required calligraphic performances that could transmit an imperial presence further afield. It was said of the Spanish Phillip II, 'His body was only active at one place, but the activity of his soul spread and stretched out across both continents and created with strokes of the pen as much as all his ancestors did with the point of their sword'.[40] In England, King James established a Master of

Ceremonies, whose job entailed overseeing 'the writing and decorating of ambassadorial letters of credence'.[41] Gerbier was appointed to the position of English Master of Ceremonies in 1641. However, his views of secretarial identity were in tension with his court service.

Beneath the wide linguistic and stylistic array he could so skilfully assume, Gerbier owed allegiance to nobody and kept his own views tight to the chest. As he wrote in one defence of his career, as 'a free man borne in Zeeland,' he was 'not bound to answer to any man living'.[42] His pen was for hire, but he was not, he claimed. In his anonymously published 1652 *Sea-Cabbin Dialogue,* the English sea captain and the Dutch merchant at first nearly came to blows discussing the Amboina massacre and the Anglo-Dutch animus it ignited. They didn't, though, because the captain admitted that 'I know thou art a Pen-man, and hast the liberty and prerogative of thy Counting-House'.[43] The sea captain thereby suggested that as a mercantile professional, the Dutch merchant's primary loyalty was to profit, not to nation. What has been interpreted as Gerbier's disloyalty, or service to many masters, could likewise be seen as his service to himself, as a figure following in the footsteps of merchants like Courten and de Moucheron, who used business savvy to make themselves the masters of other men.

In his widely advertised economic projects, Gerbier claimed to make the political secrets to which he had access available to his investors, and he deployed calligraphy as a means of giving his forms of knowledge an air of secret intelligence. Far from a trustworthy secretary, or keeper of secrets, Gerbier excused his divulgences by noting that 'secrets are secrets but for a time'.[44] Secrets continually flowed from his pen. Of course, more often than not, Gerbier's claim to offer privy intelligence was another form of deceptive image-making for luring investors and backers through contrived legends that he did not himself believe.

## The convergence of calligraphy and architecture

In 1654, Gerbier produced a monumental calligraphic display of his secret knowledge in an atlas folio manuscript. This volume attests to a more general elevation of commercial and secretarial ambition. In the Netherlands in the 17th century, calligraphy achieved an unparalleled grandeur and luxury. Text painting, the sometimes 16-feet tall inscriptions replacing paintings on the walls of otherwise white-washed Calvinist church interiors, intervened between calligraphy, cartography and architecture.[45] The text painting of the ten commandments in the Dutch Church in Austin Friars, London, has been attributed to Gerbier.[46] Maps stretching across the walls of wealthy houses also included calligraphic inscription as part of their aesthetic since Gerhard Mercator; it was also Mercator who published one of the first calligraphy manuals in 1540.[47]

By the early 17th century, engraved Dutch calligraphy manuals also reached an unrivalled size and expense. Jan van de Velde's *Spieghel der schrijfkonste* of 1605, a 'large oblong folio', was the 'largest and most sumptuous writing book'. Virtuosic ships and elephants, sea monsters and centaurs, flowed from van de Velde's pen as a single, unbroken line, their massive size making his control of the pen all the more impressive.[48] Compared to Van de Velde's *Spieghel* at 26.5 × 38 cm, English copy-books were much smaller oblong quartos, such as Richard Gething's *Calligraphotechnia* (1642), at 18 × 28 cm. The oblong format in which these books appeared was supposed to be functional; it was meant to allow the book to lie open more easily on its own, allowing the copyist to make use of their hands.[49] Yet the Dutch luxury 'exemplaarboeken' were too expensive to actually function as practical copybooks, as opposed to smaller, cheaper writing books ('materieboeken').[50] Their size illustrated their status as a newly prestigious art form.

Even compared to van de Velde's folios, the manuscript exemplar book Gerbier produced in Middelburg in 1654, now Wellcome MS 2505, was mammoth. As an atlas, rather than an oblong folio, at 45 × 35 cm (some pages of smaller dimension, 33 × 23 1/2 cm, were laid down on sheets), Gerbier's exemplar book does away with the pretence that it was made for copying by others. This was also apparent in its unusual content. Exemplar books were meant to display a versatility of hands for copying, and thus their content consisted in stock phrases in various languages and hands. Gerbier too included such phrases – either prayers or political maxims in an array of languages. The main text, however, comprised his own proprietary knowledge, partially enciphered. In other words, the book was doing double duty, displaying to potential backers not only Gerbier's calligraphic skills and linguistic range but the valuable secret content his calligraphy contained.

It has two title-pages. The first, *A Secret Mirror of Virtues and Sciences … and Several Secrets Useful to Princes and Peoples* (*Secretum virtutis et scientiarum speculum. Miroir de la vertu. Et quelques secrets utiles aux Princes et aux Peuples*), is followed by crayon drawings on biblical subjects by Gerbier. The second section is en-titled *Sampler, concerning the scribal art, and a secret language and cipher, very useful for Princes, on Drawing, Geometry, Military Architecture, Perspective, Cosmography, Geography, Miniature, Painting, Architecture and experimental natural philosophy, in examples of secrets, very rare and useful.* Such secrets included tools for intelligence-gathering, such as an 'expedient for hearing what is said at night and far away', a method of 'imitating all sorts of characters perfectly', and a secret language so that, for example, if a prince wished to say in public to another prince or to an ambassador, 'The people is a beast that does not know why it loves or it hates (Le Peuple est une beste, que ne scait pourquoy il ayme ou hayt)', he should say 'pela Celpuepo atsea benuo cetsebi bijuge nena atiaso tyourqruopa alis permyar tuor etiyaho'.[51]

Gerbier's secrets also offered abilities needed for overseas conquests: from chymical and medicinal secrets to techniques for the long-term preservation of foods, to methods for preserving ships' hulls, to the 'laws, ordonnances and statutes for a new state'. This was his secret plan, his 'Project for a New State in America,' that Gerbier had developed, he claimed, in concert with the first Duke of Buckingham for a Caribbean state. In calligraphy of an architectural scale, Gerbier designed every detail of this new state, down to the text-painting for the walls of the dining halls for new chivalric orders to be established in America (Figure 3.2).

**FIGURE 3.2** Chivalric assembly room wall text-painting for a new state. Balthasar Gerbier, Miroir, 1654, Wellcome Collection, MS.2505, 34

## A Commander at last: Gerbier recruits for Guyana

Gerbier's manuscript proved persuasive. In 1655, an anonymous pamphlet appeared in Middelburg mourning the loss of Dutch Brazil and calling on patriots for renewed conquests.[52] In this context, Gerbier convinced a group of Zeeland merchants to send out a ship to collect ore for testing. In a series of four pamphlets, he recounted how, although the ship did return with minerals, he and the merchants fell out.[53] The Zeeland associates got their own patent for a Guyanese settlement from the Zeeland Chamber of the WIC, which allowed them (among other terms that Gerbier would repeat in his own eventual colony), the 'liberty to go to the coast of Africa and fetch as many negroes as they shall have need of or may desire to offer for sale'.[54] This chamber included members of the original generation of Dutch global merchants among whom Gerbier was raised. Pieter Boudaen Courten and Jan de Moor, members of the Zeeland Chamber of the WIC, were involved in a project on the Berbice river in Guyana in 1627; de Moor also sent several expeditions to Tobago.[55] De Moor's patroon-ship on Tobago established in 1628 'was arguably the first Dutch plantation colony in the Americas'.[56]

Gerbier turned to the States General and received a patent for his own colony, the Nieuwe Geoctroyeerde Guiaansche Compagnie (NGC), with himself in the position of Commander, on November 15, 1658.[57] He offered colonizers many enticements. They were promised exemption on taxes on an alluring array of natural goods. The climate of the land was described as 'just as good as Brazil's (immers so goet als dat van Brasil)'. The area abounded in sugar, indigo, cotton, tobacco, as well as good dyes, balsams, gums, skins, costly wood, salt, saltpetre, delicate fruit and many kinds of wild prey and fish, and fowl, as well as rich mines of gold, silver, gems, and pearl fisheries. The WIC would supply slaves at the same rates at which they supplied the Zeeland Chamber's colony at Essequibo. Abraham Becker and Gerard Demmer, representing the NGC, signed a contract with the Amsterdam Chamber of the WIC for the delivery of slaves.[58]

A 'Further specification concerning the outfit, the capital, and the unusual present profits in the affair' reported that the raised capital would equip a fleet of two ships and purchase four hundred slaves. It would include equipment for mining, agriculture, felling valuable woods, and building houses, warehouses and watermills. Otto Keye also came out with a pamphlet in favour of the colony in 1659.[59] The recruitment succeeded. Although Gerbier sailed almost at the same time as two other expeditions (one led by the experienced Jan Claes Langendijck and another by David Nassy), he succeeded in bringing at least four ships of settlers to Guyana.[60]

## The politics of signatures

Gerbier recruited directors for his company from among the most successful merchants and well-connected politicians of the era. They were Johann Hulft (1610–77), an alderman of the city of Amsterdam and a director of the VOC, Arnout Hellemans Hooft (1629–80), the infamous Admiral Gerard Demmer (formerly a member of the Council of the VOC based in Batavia and governor of Amboina), the lawyer Abraham Becker (aka Backer), Philip van Harlem, Pieter Ruttens (likely the Dutch merchant who sailed to Batavia), and Amsterdam merchant Steffen von Schoonevelt.[61] Gerard Demmer invested the most, to the tune of 6000 guilders, with another 2000 guilders added at the end of May; Abraham Becker also added 1000 guilders to his original investment of 6000. By June 4, the board of directors had shifted a bit; Philip van Harlem and Steffen van Schoonevelt dropped out and were replaced by Anthony Casteleyn, a wealthy director of the VOC's chamber in Amsterdam, who had contributed 2000 guilders on behalf of Jacob Motte, a Rotterdam merchant (and his relative), and 3000 for himself by the 8th of April.[62]

Of the 26 investors in the company who added their inscriptions between April 5 and August 8, 1659, many were prominent figures. They included Albert Snouckaert van Schauburg (1637–78), the Venetian-Dutch merchant scion, Giovanni Battista van Axel, and Cornelius Sladus (1599–1678), rector of the Latin school in Amsterdam. These were savvy, experienced, and successful investors.

Their signatures offer a window onto their social jockeying and positioning within the company (Figure 3.3). The clarity and choice of hand, of order, of position, of the nature of the flourish, were tools deployed for negotiating roles in this colonial enterprise. James Daybell's discussion of the 'politics of handwriting' in the case of English epistolary exchange applies here as well. As he suggests, everything about the material rhetoric of the manuscript page down to the 'placement and performance of the signature' was freighted with significance easily 'understood by contemporaries familiar with epistolary cultures'.[63]

Signing a document such as this, with fortunes at stake and in the presence of fellow investors, sea captains, and a future colonial governor, dramatizes the relationship between handwriting and gesture. The signing was itself a bodily performance, and one which, moreover, was intended to leave its mark upon a legally binding document. As the pen passed from hand to hand, each individual had choices to make about how to present themselves.

The following analysis of signatures is not intended to graphologically reveal the characters of the inscribers but rather to suggest the performative politics of handwriting. In performing one's inscriptions, the inscriber had many choices to make, and bigger was not always best. Arnout Hellemans Hooft's demure signature is a case in point. Hooft, known today for his travels and art connoisseurship, was the son of the poet P.C. Hooft, and a scion of a family that had successfully raised itself from traders to learned regents. His uncle was Jacob Pergens, a wealthy merchant and a relative of Gerbier's hero, Willem Courten. Hooft himself invested in Amsterdam, Middelburg, Dordrecht, Delft and Enkhuizen, and in 1667 would be elected to the Amsterdam Chamber of the WIC.[64]

Both Gerard Demmer, former governor of Amboina, and Gerbier (aspiring governor of Guyana), took a more aggressive route in their dramatic changes of scale, loose Italianate hand, and occupation of space. In the bravado of his flourish, Gerbier even signed over the signatures of the two witnesses, one of whom was his subordinate (and later rebel), Otto Keye. Demmer, similarly, let the pen run over the hand of the notary, Emmanuel de Lavello.

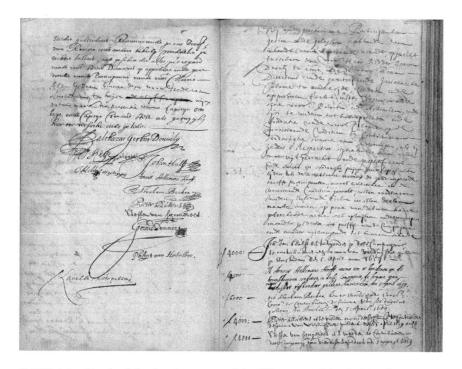

**FIGURE 3.3**  On the left, the signatures of the Directors of the NGC, the notary, Emanuel Lavello, and two witnesses. On the right, the commitments of investors. Amsterdam City Archives, entry number 5075, inventory (inv.) 2989, 112–3, April 5, 1659, not. Emmanuel de Lavello

Gerbier was keenly attuned to the affects of documentary and scribal assurances upon potential investors and colonists. Gerbier's printed patent for the colony, like many of his other pamphlets, included many virtual notarial marks of authenticity. For instance, an addendum of February 12, 1659, attested by the Amsterdam notary Emmanuel de Lavello, appointed Godefroy Lauterbach to serve as Gerbier's agent in collecting inscribers to the colony because Lauterbach was a figure 'well known to all the parties involved' who could authenticate Gerbier's signature.[65] Lauterbach collected signatories to Gerbier's manuscript contract, and he would attest that Gerbier's hand was authentic.

Gerbier also printed a note attested by the Hague notary Guiliaum Lecoeur that the printed copy of the patent matched the archival version. According to this note, potential investors could learn more about the colony at the home of the broker Jeronimo de la Croix, behind the stock exchange, where a map of the land and other required information could be found. This was likely Jeronimo de la Croix the younger; his father, originally from Middelburg, served as an agent for the de Moucheron family.[66] Investors might also inscribe in four other cities, in Haarlem with the journalist Abraham Casteleyn, in Leiden with the broker

Swanenvelt, in The Hague with the notary Guiliaum le Coeur, and in Rotterdam with the notary de Paus. Gerbier left space in two different versions of this printed pamphlet for Godefroy Lauterbach to add his manuscript signature, 'G. Lauterbach', which in two copies in The Hague is filled in by hand in pen, creating a hybrid print/manuscript pamphlet.[67]

## Counterintelligence: cartography and calligraphy

The Guyanese venture quickly turned deadly, and Gerbier published all the horrid details of Keye's mutiny in a luridly illustrated pamphlet of 1660.[68] Nevertheless, he immediately continued his colonizing projects upon his return to Europe. Amazingly, he even included an English account of Keye's treachery within a promotional tract encouraging plantation drawn from Keye's own text, which he dedicated to the returning English monarch Charles II in 1660.[69] Gerbier sets out, in the accompanying *Advertissement for Men inclyned to Plantasions in America* , terms largely drawn from the old patent for the NGC. He claimed that the original paper of the patent, as well as other 'papers which did not concerne that dessyne' had been violently taken from him in Guiana. He was now starting afresh, drafting new papers for an English colony in 'Surename'.

In this text, the extremes of liberty and slavery to be found in the plantation were still more emphasized than in Gerbier's previous pamphlets, with an explicit mention of the price for slaves and the addition of a promise of liberty of conscience (standard in Dutch colonies and one of Gerbier's lifelong goals for English settlements) for planters. Planters were tempted with a freedom from taxes for ten years. Slaves could be had on credit. Each planter could 'have slaves for fifthien pound a peece, pay them either in reddy monny or with the commodities off thire owne plantations, taking the tyme of five yeares for the same'. They might 'freely enjoy' the riches of mines they discovered on their lands.[70] The many invocations of liberty and freedom for the settlers were at the expense of the imported enslaved labour force, unequal trade with the local population, and the exploitation of nature.

One of Gerbier's printed advertisements still includes a manuscript leaf inviting subscription to the colony, tempting potential investors with many assurances. Gerbier promised that 'their Signature shall nott bee Obligatory untill after the signing of a competent Stock', as well as until they have been assured of the 'quallity of Associates', until the King granted a patent, and until 'the propounder [Gerbier] shall have engaged himself in person to conduct the Colloniers to the fitt place'. This colony was based on secret intelligence Gerbier was not ready to divulge to the investors. They were to elect representatives to hear from Gerbier 'all what hath ben told him and offered unto him concerning the good which with the blessing of God and by Juditious dextrous conduct may bee attayned unto in that part of the American world.' The elected members would promise to keep this knowledge 'unrevealed' until two months after the departure of the colonizers.[71] This pamphlet illustrates Gerbier's continuing strategy of employing hybrid print/manuscript pamphlets as investment prospectuses, offering investors an alluring entrée into the world of scribal secrets.

Nearing the age of 70 years, Gerbier continued to promote a slave-based Guyanese settlement, led by himself, to an English audience, and specifically to Charles II. This continued his long-standing proposal that the English should capture the West African slave trade from the Dutch. In one 1651 pamphlet of commercial advice for Cromwell's Interregnum government (as the first Anglo-Dutch War heated up), he noted that the Hollanders 'serve the King [of Spain] with Blacks, which proves a great Traffique, when as one Black being bought for nine Ryals, is sold at an exorbitant price to the said King'.[72]

By proferring intelligence regarding Dutch Guyana and the slave trade to Charles II, Gerbier hoped to secure his position with the returning monarch, despite the services he had rendered Cromwell. He illegally copied a map of the 1649 Fort Schoonenburgh in Ceará (Siara) from a map still in the WIC archives. The residents in that place, he argued, could show the way to El Dorado.[73] He also presented Charles further plans for exploring North and West Africa.[74] He offered to supply intelligence on the WIC and the VOC.[75] He noted that the WIC offered more favourable terms to settlers than the English did, and that the States of the United Provinces 'to make them yet more great' were 'hastening to a treaty with the King of China, the secret and depth of which a zealous person offers to discover to his Majesty, or to the East India Company'. He still (!) promoted his idea from the 1620s of a gold mine in the Caribbean, about which 'which a Spaniard told his late Majesty existed in Jamaica'. As in his earlier anonymous *Sea-Cabbin Dialogue*, Gerbier here openly addressed the instrumentality of that legend. If Charles II wished to extend 'his power in the West Indies', the stories of this gold mine would serve him well, since it would lure 'a number of adventurers far more considerable than bare planters'.[76]

The elderly Gerbier transformed another aged piece of intelligence into another slave-trading proposal, in the form of two monumental vellum maps, 1 foot by 4 foot, presented to Charles II and the Secretary of State, Frances Gwynne. These, some of the earliest extant maps of the Gambia River, represent an effort to secure state funding for a voyage to expel the Dutch from the area and to gain control of the slave trade (British Library Additional 16371 and King/ Topographical CXVII, 98) (Figure 3.4).[77] Gerbier's vigorous, sure hand across this wide expanse is all the more impressive if you consider his age.

The map includes all the imperialist four and two-footed staffage typical for the maps of the period. Gerbier detailed exactly how they were to be exploited through a lengthy, partially enciphered French inscription on the map itself; the land thus appears as an agenda for action. He writes how

> … there was … a mountain in a place where the sun shines at midday within
> which lies a great mass of gold …. The one who gave this relation noted that
> the inhabitants only bothered to collect the gold from the shores, which
> they sold for cloth of little value, and scarlet ribbons, knives, hatchets, glass

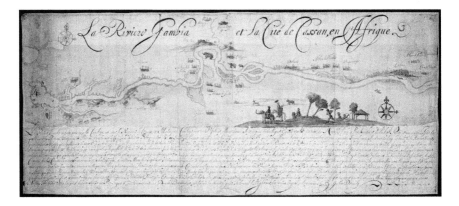

**FIGURE 3.4** The British Library Board, Additional MS 16371

beads of any color, and pins. These inhabitants are very subtle and adept in goldworking, in bracelets, and chains, and gold thread, which the goldsmiths in Europe could not make any better. However, one can only trade them for gold ore, since they are great deceivers and will mix it with silver whenever they can. These inhabitants trade in elephant teeth, rhinoceros horn, and elemi gum. The land abounds in meat, fish, fowl, and palm wine; and in slaves which they have to transport to America, where the gold mines are, to make them work there. One should also note the great quantity of salt in the Gambia river, which one could have for free and use to store the fish, which will give a great profit, and this is an advantage of which nobody has taken notice. There is also a great deal of wax, and the one who gave this relation to Sir Frobisher, visited the most secret places in this part of the world and assured him that the locations noted here in cipher were not known by the inhabitants and therefore not by other Nations. Frobisher gave the original relation of this to King James, who recommended it to the Duke of Buckingham, the Admiral, from whose hands I received it.[78]

The map was not just a description of topography but a guide through a dizzying array of relations between natural resources, manufactures and varying peoples. Profit could be extracted from this array, brought together in the right way. The extraction demanded by the map is insatiable. Besides for the easily acquired Gambian gold, Gerbier also described how slaves must be taken from there to work the apparently more difficult to extract mineral resources in America.

Gerbier's monumental calligraphic hand on the map serves to enhance the majesty of the enterprise as well as the atmosphere of secret intelligence, tracing the passage of this intelligence from the unnamed informer to the explorer Frobisher, to James, to Buckingham, and from his hands directly to Gerbier, placed Gerbier in an unbroken line of privileged knowledge. This was the line connecting Gerbier to the hand of Buckingham and on to global action, covertly looping and swirling around the world, that his original flourish to Buckingham had requested. Yet, this lineage leaves out a few inconvenient truths, such as Prince Rupert of the Rhine's previous voyage and the map of Gambia he had John Vermuyden create for him, of nearly the same dimensions, shortly beforehand.[79] Upon the basis of such intelligence, Prince Rupert helped found the Royal Adventurers into Africa, which did indeed establish the British African slave trade to the West Indies, formerly monopolized, from 1638 to 1661, by the Dutch.[80]

## Slavery, body ornament and architecture

With the return of the English monarchy in 1660, Royalists were eager to compete with Dutch commercial empire. The City of London turned to the elderly Gerbier to communicate the power of global trade to Charles II. They commissioned him to design the ephemeral triumphal arches through which the royal entry would wind into the city. In the arch he devoted to trade near the Exchange, Gerbier celebrated the merchant companies' exploitation of the world by positioning atop the arch 'living Figures, representing Europe, Asia, Africk, and America, with Escutcheons, and Pendents, bearing the Arms of the Companies trading into those parts'.[81] Europe alone wore armour; the other continents, mostly naked, illustrated the goods they offered to her.[82] It is extraordinary to image the bodies of the actors perched atop the arch so exposed to public view as the returning monarch entered below them, taking control of the city and its commercial centre.

As Christine Stevenson has argued, Gerbier's designs for his ephemeral architecture stressed a triumph over human bodies, an aesthetic upon which he centred his architectural theories more generally. As Gerbier had explained in a 1648 work intended for his academy, Grecian columns were based upon the 'form of slaves bearing the burden of their buildings, that those graines (as bead drops pendans garlands, enterlassed knots, fruitages, and an infinite number of ornements ... did signify the spoills which the vancours had braught away from their ennemies ...'.[83] According to this, Stevenson has claimed, 'architectural sculpture is, ultimately, a trophy made up of victory spoils, both human and inanimate'.[84] Gerbier's triumphal arch, with its columns surmounted by living enactors, makes this passage between human and inanimate architecture manifest.

Rather than obscuring the human subjugation fundamental to global trade, Gerbier further highlighted it. As Stevenson pointed out, Gerbier revised his 1648 account of Greek ornament in the architectural *Discourse* he issued in 1662; in his later work, the number of columns ranged around a building explicitly represented 'the number of Slaves which they had taken'.[85] He would go on to offer prescriptions for architecture based on Caribbean body piercings, updating ancient Greek models of military triumph with examples of conquered bodies drawn from transatlantic trade.[86]

Gerbier's integration of architecture and overseas colonization was both aesthetic and practical, as he inserted global investment proposals into his most basic construction manuals. One of the many dedicatees of his 1663 *Counsel and Advice for Builders* was Francis Willoughby, 5th Baron of Parham (1614–66). The Governor of Barbados, Willoughy was the 'most ambitious and aggressive' of a group of 'elite planters who had grand visions for the spread of the Barbadian plantation system and its satellite resource colonies through the greater Caribbean world'. Willoughby directed 'the outward migration of settlers, slaves and capital through the Lesser Antilles and towards the Guianas – and in particular toward a colony in Surinam', intending to spread the 'sugar plantation frontier'.[87] Just the year before Gerbier published his book, Willoughby received a patent granting him the 'power to plant settlements, erect cities, towns, manors, markets, schools', and so forth, in his new colony, thus allowing construction on a grand scale.[88]

Gerbier suggested that, against received wisdom, his European building advice could be employed in Surinam. It was already sufficiently global and mobile to serve in a region of the world where all architecture, he claimed, was ephemeral. As he wrote in his dedication to Willoughby, he predicted he would live to see his construction advice enacted there, even though Willoughby was bent upon

> the populating of such a part on the American Coast, where Houses are builded in two hours time, because they have no second story, less third or fourth; the Inhabitants whereof affecting no other livery then that of the first naked; and who conceive that leaves of Trees do thatch their domiciliums with less danger to their naked parts, then if covered with Dutch Pan, or English-hard-burnt Tiles.[89]

Conversely, in the main text of the work, Gerbier cast himself, via Willoughby, as a vehicle of information concerning tropical woods available in Surinam ('as the Right Honourable the Lord Willouby of Param well knoweth') that could easily be brought to Europe for construction. Beautiful timbers were a far better investment opportunity, he argued, than 'Furr from Norway'; other profits to be gained in Surinam included a 'very gainfull returne of Amber Greese and vendible commodities in exchange of Iron Tools, Siffers, Knives, old Linnen and trifles'.[90] In an ostensibly practical guide to construction mainly aimed at a European audience, Gerbier inserted yet another tempting overseas commercial prospect.

Gerbier would not succeed in recruiting Willoughby. Not only would Gerbier die that year, but three years later, Willoughby sent a force attacking the remaining settlers of Gerbier's plantation, making off with 'their Armour, Slaves and Goods [and] Ingenious [engines] to make sugar'.[91] However, Gerbier's settlement survived Willoughby's attack and endured until 1678. Even today, historians Martijn van den Bel and Lodewijk Hulsman have observed the settlement's ruins, including Dutch rooftiles and yellow bricks, showing that the European building materials Gerbier discussed in his manual were indeed utilized there.[92]

## Conclusion

At a particular moment in the rise of global trade, theories, forms of knowledge and practices previously reserved for the courts of princes became newly available not only to commonwealths and trading companies but to individual private actors in the global marketplace. The mixture of varied forms of knowledge in Gerbier's academy curriculum and exemplar book, as well as the convergence of architecture and calligraphy in Gerbier's aesthetic practice, illustrates this. While architecture for Gerbier had its origins in military triumph and enslavement, calligraphy had begun as a servile art, used for keeping secrets and accounting books on behalf of masters, and more associated with commerce than warfare. His stress on ephemerality and ornament in architecture (a point he argued earlier in his career with Inigo Jones, who promoted a more solid Vitruvian aesthetic) undermined the distinction between calligraphy and architecture. Gerbier's calligraphy expanded to architectural dimensions, while his architecture turned calligraphic, both in service to an aesthetic fit for the hybridization of trade and violence, that is, for commercial empire.

Gerbier offered the European consumer or investor visions of their newly empowered participation in the unequal affective relationships structuring this commercial empire. All the while – and this is how market knowledge relates to the history of emotions in Gerbier's case – Gerbier artfully manipulated potential investors and colonizers by glorifying their sense of mastery and liberty of action. Gerbier's premier form of market knowledge, explicitly celebrated in his *Sea-Cabbin Dialogue* and in his overtures to Charles II, was how to play upon such emotions.

As a calligrapher, Gerbier could draw from a world of ciphers, notaries and scribal tools of statecraft. Through scribal aesthetics, he endowed his global proposals with an aura of privileged intelligence. He did so most dramatically in his mammoth exemplar book/book of secrets or his beautiful map of the Gambia river. Even when working in print, however, he created the illusion of a scribal aesthetic, whether through precise mention of signatures, seals and notarial marks, through hybrid print/manuscript pamphlets, or through offering directions to where manuscript materials, such as a map of Approuague river, could be consulted.

Gerbier's strategies proved compelling for many. His was the alluring vision that tempted Johann Joachim Becher, who had come to Amsterdam to seek a colonial opportunity for his patron. Becher was hunting for Dutch commercial intelligence in order to lever his German patron out of debt, and Gerbier's project appeared to offer it.

Becher's journey was itself a testament to the Dutch Republic as a locus of knowledge about new global enterprise, as also illustrated by Martin Mulsow's chapter in this volume. The shifting locus of empire demonstrated to many contemporaries the overturning of traditional noble roles and prohibitions against engaging in trade. As Pamela Smith points out, 'The fact that the court of Hanau sought favors from a merchant company in the Dutch Republic appeared to many people of the seventeenth century to be an inversion of natural order'.[93] Becher assured his patron that by importing Dutch global commercial savviness, even if it went against noble mores, he was offering the Count a wonder-working *lapis politicorum*, or stone of the politicians, on the model of the immense powers promised by the alchemical philosophers' stone.[94]

In Amsterdam, Becher encountered a barrage of persuasive tools originally assembled by Gerbier. The documentary evidence, as well as a collection of specimens of natural resources that Gerbier had curated, were brought out by the WIC to persuade Becher of the Guyanese colony's investment potential. It worked. Much pomp and circumstance, including a rich present of many works from the Duke's *Kunstkammer* to the WIC, attended Becher's signing of the contract. As a critic noted, Becher then sent back ahead the signed contracts to Hanau 'enclosed in an ivory capsule… with this ridiculous pomp, as though celebrating a triumph'; when the contract arrived, the Count affixed his own signature, the document was read publicly, fireworks ignited and a hundred cannon shots fired.[95]

The story of Becher's Amsterdam trip and the contract's triumphal return has been well told by Pamela Smith. But behind it, and undergirding Becher's confidence in global commercial schemes and the fetishized contracts in which they appeared, lies a whole other tale explored in this essay. If the Count was deceived by Becher, as so many complained, Becher haplessly fell prey to Gerbier and the scribal aesthetic of global commercial secrets in which he dealt. In a printed defence of the Guyanese colony, Becher republished the many assurances of Gerbier's printed patent, including allusions to its marks of scribal notarial authenticity by Guillaume de Coeur and Emmanuel de Lavello, as well as to Godefroy Lauterbach's manuscript authorizations.[96]

A hidden story thus lurks behind the *Allegory of the Acquisition of Surinam* (Fig 3.1). Friedrich Casimir's grasping of slave-based wealth is all too obvious. Behind him stands Becher, thinking himself a savvy operator pulling strings from the shadows. Smugly confident of the commercial *arcana* he has fished for in Amsterdam, Becher remains unaware that he in fact was the prey. Even more hidden than the grasping hand of the Count/Becher was the aspiring grasp of Gerbier's *pennetrek*. Through the control, versatility, and bravado of his pen, Gerbier demonstrated his ability to design and carry out global schemes, to assure and to excite investors, to navigate the worlds of notaries, brokers, journalists, alchemists and merchants, and to do so with a flourish.

## Notes

1 The history of emotions is a new development in the history of slavery. J. Sharples, "Discovering Slave Conspiracies" and J. Sharples, "Slavery and Fear." Special thanks for comments on this research from my fellow participants in Working Group III of the Global Knowledge Society, as well as from my UO colleagues, Stephen Dueppen and Michelle McCormick.

2  V. Von Flemming, "Alles Lüge," 104–109.

3  H. R. Williamson. *Four Stuart Portraits*, 26; J. Wood, "Gerbier, Sir Balthazar." E. Chaney, "Notes Towards a Biography." M. Keblusek, "Cultural and Political Brokerage." B. Hoxby, "The Government of Trade." J. Peacey, "Print, Publicity, and Popularity."

4  J. Chaplin, *Subject Matter*, 220.

5  K. Vera V. Keller, "The 'Framing of a New World.'" See also P. R. Sellin, "Michel le Blon and England III"; Idem, *Treasure, Treason and the Tower*.

6  R. van Wellie, "Slave Trading and Slavery."

7  R. B. Allen, "Ending the History of Silence," 297.

8  J. Vos, D. Eltis, and D. Richardson, "The Dutch in the Atlantic World," 232.

9  Ibid., 233–34.

10  D. Merwick, *Possessing Albany*.

11  S. Alpers, *The Art of Describing*, 144–45.

12  J. B. Hochstrasserulie, "Visual Impact"; E. Sutton, *Capitalism and Cartography*; M. van Groesen, "Visualizing the News."

13  K. Zandvliet, *Mapping for Money*, 263. For other paper regimes of the global slave trade: N. Worden, "Cape Slaves."

14  B. Schmidt, "Response," 181.

15  M. van den Bel and L. Hulsman, "Une colonie néerlandaise." Earlier accounts include M. G. De Boer, "Balthazar Gerbier."

16  S. B. Schwartz, "Looking for a New Brazil," 46.

17  B. Gerbier, *A Manifestation*, 7.

18  Gerbier claimed authorship of this anonymously published pamphlet in a February 16, 1652, letter to Bulstrode Whitelocke. The Whitelocke papers from the archives of the Marquess of Bath [microform] (Yorkshire: EP Microform, 1972). *A Sea-Cabbin Dialogue… Translated out of Dutch*. I have not found a Dutch original for this pamphlet.

19  B. Gerbier, *To the Parliament*, 8.

20  *Sea-Cabbin Dialogue*, Part II, 19.

21  *Sea-Cabbin Dialogue*, Part II, 24.

22  Gerbier had been drawn into this projector's schemes; as he revealed in another pamphlet, one story about a mountain of gold in the Gambia River that he later would associate with Frobisher in fact originated with Dishington. *Derde Verclaringe aeengaende de Goude ende Silvere Mijne*.

23  *Sea-Cabbin Dialogue*, Part II, 25.

24  *Sea-Cabbin Dialogue, Part II*, 27.

25  *Sea-Cabbin Dialogue, Part II*, 29.

26  V. Enthoven, "Early Dutch Expansion; Ebert, 'Dutch Trade with Brazil"; O. Gelderblom, *Zuid-Nederlandse kooplieden*.

27  C. Hille, *Visions of the Courtly Body*.

28  Gerbier to Villiers, Bodleian Library, MS Tanner 73, 119.

29  M. Bland, *A Guide to Early Printed Books*.

30  M. Peters, "'Trekt Heuvelman voor ons gezicht?'", 318.

31  N. Ellerton and K. Clements, *Rewriting the History*. M. Ogborn, "Geographia's pen."

32  H. De la Fontaine Verwey, "The Golden Age of Dutch Calligraphy," 73–75. Keblusek compares Frisius and Gerbier in "The Pretext of Pictures," 152.

33  J. Connors, "Ars Tornandi."

34  M. E. Motley, *Becoming a French Aristocrat*, 139.

35  B. Gerbier, *The Interpreter,* 3–4.

36  B. Gerbier, *Cryghs Architecture ende Fortificatien*. Gerbier's advertisement for the Middelburg school in this work was described by Nagtglass, *Lebensberichten van Zeeuwen*, 257. It does not appear in the copy I consulted, however, Gerbier frequently tailored even print publications to varied audiences.

37  KW 138 D 6 and Kw 76 H 22. On these volumes: Keblusek, *Boeken in de hofstad*.

38  V. Keller, "Mining Tacitus."
39  A. Weststeijn, *Commercial Republicanism*, 207.
40  A. Brendecke, *The Empirical Empire*, 20.
41  M. Jansson, *Art and Diplomacy*, 77–78.
42  *Baltazar Gerbier Knight to all men that loves love truth*, 14.
43  *Sea-Cabbin Dialogue, Part II*, 10.
44  Sloane 4181, quoted in I. D'Israeli, "Curiosities of Literature," 395.
45  M. M. Mochizuki, "The Dutch Text Painting."
46  O. P. Grell, *Calvinist Exiles*, 134.
47  G. Mercator, *Literarum latinarum, quas italicas, cursoriasque vocant, scribendarum ratio*.
48  H. De la Fontaine Verwey, "The Golden Age," 74.
49  K. Van Orden, *Materialities*.
50  H. De la Fontaine Verwey, "The Golden Age," 78.
51  Wellcome MS 2505, 14.
52  *Cort, Bondigh ende Waerachtigh Verhael*.
53  B. Gerbier, *Waerachtige Verklaringe Nopende*. B. Gerbier, *Waarachtige Verklaringe vanden Ridder*. On Gerbier's use of print to promote projects: J. Peacey, 'Print, Publicity, and Popularity'.
54  Translated in 'Conceptie van notificatie', 138–39.
55  Nat. Arch., Den Haag, Oude West-Indische Compagnie (OWIC), nummer toegang 1.05.01.01, inventarisnummer 20, Resolutie Boeck, May 4, 1626–August 30, 1629, f. 70, April 22, 1627. C. K. Kesler, "Tobago: Een vergeten Nederlandsche Kolonie."
56  R. Van Welie, "Slave Trading and Slavery," 58, n. 30.
57  *Octroy… aengaende de Colonie op de Wilde Kust van America*.
58  Stadsarchief Amsterdam 1309/46–48, November 10, 1659, not. Schaeff.
59  O. Keye, *Het Waere onderscheyt*. On this pamphlet: K. Davids, "Nederlanders en de natuur."
60  L. Hulsman, "Nederlands Amazonia," 148.
61  Stadsarchief Amsterdam, 5075/2989/108–112, April 5, 1659, not. De Lavello.
62  On the Castelein and Motte cartels: H. De Bruyn Kops, *A Spirited Exchange*.
63  J. Daybell, *The Material Letter*, 229.
64  E. M. Grabowsky and P. J. Verkruijsse, *Een naekt beeldt*. N. H. Schneeloch, *Aktionäre der Westindischen Compagnie*, 292–93.
65  *Octroy… aengaende de Colonie op de Wilde Kust van America*. A Gottfried Lauterbach worked as an agent for several courts, including both Dutch and German members of the House of Nassau. See J. A. Pastorius, *Europaischen Flori Historici*, 308, 312–13.
66  http://research.frick.org/montiasart/browserecord.php?-action=browse&-recid=25165.
67  KB 8175a and KB 4724.
68  B. Gerbier, *Sommier verhael*.
69  B. Gerbier, *A Sommary description*.
70  *Advertissement for men inclyned to Plantasions*, A3v.
71  B. Gerbier, *A Sommary description*. James Ford Bell Library, 1660 Ge 1, manuscript insertion into printed pamphlet.
72  B. Gerbier, *Some Considerations*, 2.
73  K. Zandvliet, *Mapping for Money*, 196–97. Bodleian, Clarendon MS 92, 177–180. Fort Schoonenburgh, like Gerbier's later settlement on the Approuage, was founded in order to support a search for a silver mine in the interior. M. Meuwese, "From Dutch Allies to Portuguese Vassals."
74  State Papers SP 29/40 f.189.
75  W. N. Sainsbury, *Calendar of State Papers*, 69. January 22, 1662. Sir Balthazar Gerbier to the King. E. B. Sainsbury, "A Paper sent from Antwerp."
76  E. B. Sainsbury, *Calendar of State Papers*, 69. January 22, 1662. Sir Balthazar Gerbier to the King.

77 D. P. Gamble and P. E. H. Hair, eds., *The Discovery of River Gambra*. K. Zandvliet, *Mapping for Money,* 194–97.
78 D. P. Gamble and P. E. H. Hair, eds., *The Discovery of River Gambra*, 231–32. Gerbier's map survives in two copies in the British Library, Additional MS 16371 h and King's/ Topographical CXVII, 98.
79 R. C. Anderson, "The Operations of the English Fleet." K. Roper, "Prince Rupert, the Cavalier," 207. The map associated with Vermuyden is "The Map of the River of Gambia," 3 f. 6 in. × 1 f. 2. in., King's CXVII, 96, 97.
80 M. Govier, "The Royal Society." M. Makepeace, "English Traders on the Guinea Coast." K. Dewhurst, "Prince Rupert as a Scientist." C. Wilson, *Profit and Power*, 115.
81 J. Ogilby, *The Entertainment*, 67.
82 J. Ogilby, The *Entertainment,* 81.
83 B. Gerbier, *The Interpreter*, 177.
84 C. Stevenson, "Occasional Architecture," 36.
85 B. Gerbier, *A Brief Discourse*, 6.
86 Ibid, 6–7. See also Balthasar B. Gerbier, *Counsel,* 4.
87 J. Roberts, "Surrendering Surinam," 225. S. Barber, "Power in the English Caribbean."
88 W. N. Sainsbury, *Calendar of State Papers*, 131.
89 B. Gerbier, *Counsel,* [dvr-v].
90 B. Gerbier, *Counsel,* 108–109.
91 Journal of William Byam, British Library, Sloane MS 3662, cited in M. van den Bel and L. Hulsman, 9.
92 M. van den Bel and L. Hulsman, 10.
93 P. Smith, *The Business of Alchemy*, 147.
94 P. Smith, 165.
95 P. Smith, 162–63.
96 J. J. Becher, *Politische Discurs*, 1216. "Diese Privilegien seynd gedruckt/ in Holländsich zu finden in Quart/Anno 1659. und authorisirt von G. de Coeur, G. Lauterbach/ Emmanuel de Lavello, Notariis Publicis."

# Bibliography

*Manuscript*

Amsterdam, Stadsarchief, 5075, not. Lavello, inventory (inv.) 2989, 108–113, April 5, 1659.
Amsterdam, Stadsarchief, 1309/46–48, not. Schaeff, November 10, 1659.
Bodleian Library, Clarendon MS 92.
Bodleian Library, MS Tanner 73. British Library, Additional MS 16371.
The Hague, Nationaal Archief, Oude West-Indische Compagnie (OWIC), 1.05.01.01, Inventarisnummer 20, Resolutie Boeck, 4 May 1626–30 August 1629, f. 70, 22 April 1627.
The Hague, Nationaal Archief, 1.05.01.01, Inventarisnummer 18A. Octrooi verleend door de W.I.C. aan Frederik Casimir graaf van Hanau voor het oprichten van een kolonie op de Wilde Kust van Amerika tussen de rivieren Orinoco en Amazone.18 juli 1669.
Kew, UK National Archives. Papers SP 29/40 f.189. *Summary of papers presented to Council by Sir Balt. Gerbier, April 10, 1661.*
Wellcome MS 2505. Gerbier, Balthasar. *Miroir,*1654.

*Print*

Allen, Richard B. "Ending the History of Silence: Reconstructing European Slave trading in the Indian Ocean." *Tempo* 23, no. 2 (2017): 294–313.

Alpers, Svetlana. *The Art of Describing: Dutch Art in the Seventeenth Century*. Chicago: University of Chicago Press, 1983.

Anderson, R. C. "The Operations of the English Fleet, 1648-1652." *The English Historical Review* 31, no. 123 (1916): 406–28.

1655 Anonymous. *Cort, Bondigh ende Waerachtigh Verhael van't schandelijk over-geven ende verlante vande voornaemste Conquesten van Brasil*. Middelburg: Brouwers-haven, 1655.

Barber, Sarah. "Power in the English Caribbean: The Proprietorship of Lord Willoughby of Parham." In *Constructing Early Modern Empires: Proprietary Ventures in the Atlantic World, 1500–1750*, edited by Louis H. Roper and Bertrand Van Ruymbeke, 189–212. Leiden: Brill, 2007.

Becher, Johann Joachim. *Politische Discurs*. Frankfurt: Zunner, 1673.

Bel, Martijn van den and Lodewijk Hulsman, "Une colonie néerlandaise sur l'Approuague au début de la deuxième moitié du XVIIe siècle." *Bulletin de la Société d'Histoire de la Guadeloupe* 164 (2013): 1–15. doi:10.7202/1036800ar.

Bland, Mark. *A Guide to Early Printed Books and Manuscripts*. London: Wiley-Blackwell, 2010.

Brendecke, Arndt. *The Empirical Empire: Spanish Colonial Rule and the Politics of Knowledge*. Berlin/Boston: De Gruyter, 2016.

Chaney, Edward. "Notes Towards a Biography of Sir Balthazar Gerbier." In *The Evolution of the Grand Tour: Anglo-Italian Cultural Relations since the Renaissance*, edited by Edward Chaney, 215–25. London: Frank Cass, 1998.

Chaplin, Joyce. *Subject Matter: Technology, the Body, and Science on the Anglo-American Frontier, 1500-1676*. Cambridge: Harvard University Press, 2001.

1898 Zeeland, Chamber, West India Company. "Conceptie van notificatie van allen de geenen die desen sullen sien ofte hooren lesen, doen to weeten." *British Guiana Boundary. Arbitration with the United States of Venezuala. Appendix to the Case on Behalf of the Government of Her Britannic Majesty* 1 (1898) , no. 1593-1723: 137–39.

Connors, Joseph. "Ars Tornandi: Baroque Architecture and the Lathe." *Journal of the Warburg and Courtauld Institutes* 53 (1990): 217–36.

Davids, Karel. "Nederlanders en de natuur in de Nieuwe Wereld: Een vergelijking van visies op de natuur in Brazilië, Nieuw Nederland en de Wilde Kust in de zeventiende eeuw." In *Jaarboek voor Ecologische Geschiedenis 2009, Natuur en milieu in Belgische en Nederlandse koloniën*, edited by Marjolein't Hart and Henk van Zon, 1–24. Gent: Academia, 2009.

Daybell, James. *The Material Letter in Early Modern England: Manuscript Letters and the Culture and Practices of Letter-Writing, 1512–1635*. Basingstoke: Palgrave-Macmillan, 2012.

De Boer, M. G. "Balthazar Gerbier." *Oud Holland* 21 (1903): 129–64.

De Bruyn Kops, Henriette. *A Spirited Exchange: The Wine and Brandy Trade between France and the Dutch Republic in an Atlantic Framework, 1600-1650*. Leiden: Brill, 2007.

De la Fontaine Verwey, Herman. "The Golden Age of Dutch Calligraphy." In *Miniatures, Scripts, Collections: Essays Presented to G. I. Lieftinck*, edited by John Peter Gumbert and M. J. M. de Haan, 69–78. Amsterdam: A.L. van Gendt, 1976.

Dewhurst, Kenneth. "Prince Rupert as a Scientist." *The British Journal for the History of Science* 1, no. 4 (1963): 365–73.

D'Israeli, Isaac. *Curiosities of Literature*. London: Moxon, 1849.

Ebert, Christopher. "Dutch Trade with Brazil before the Dutch West India Company, 1587–1621." In *Riches from Atlantic Commerce: Dutch Transatlantic Trade and Shipping, 1585–1817,* edited by Johannes Postma and Victor Enthoven, 49–76. Leiden: Brill, 2003.

Ellerton, Nerida and Ken Clements. *Rewriting the History of School Mathematics in North America 1607–1861: The Central Role of Cyphering Books.* Dordrecht: Springer, 2012.

Enthoven, Victor. "Early Dutch Expansion in the Atlantic Region, 1585–1621." In *Riches from Atlantic Commerce: Dutch Transatlantic Trade and Shipping, 1585–1817,* edited by Johannes Postma and Victor Enthoven, 17–48. Leiden: Brill, 2003.

Flemming, Victoria von. "Alles Lüge." In *Unter vier Augen: Sprachen des Porträts,* edited by Kirsten Claudia Voigt. Karlsruhe: Staatliche Kunsthalle, 2013, 104–109.

Gamble, David P. and P.E.H. Hair, eds., *The Discovery of River Gambra (1623) by Richard Jobson.* London: Hakluyt Society, 1999.

Gelderblom, Oscar. *Zuid-Nederlandse kooplieden en de opkomst van de Amsterdamse stapelmarkt (1578–1630).* Hilversum: Verloren, 2000.

Gerbier, Balthasar. *Advertissement for Men Inclyned to Plantasions in America.* Rotterdam: Goddaeus, 1660.

Gerbier, Balthasar. *A Brief Discourse Concerning the Three Chief Principles of Magnificent Building viz., Solidity, Conveniency, and Ornament.* London, s.n., 1662.

Gerbier, Balthasar. *Counsel and Advise to all Builders.* London: Mable, 1663.

Gerbier, Balthasar. *Cryghs Architecture ende Fortificatien.* Delft: Arnold Bon, 1652.

Gerbier, Balthazar. *Derde Verclaringe Aengaende de Goude ende Silvere Mijne Aenghewesen Door den Ridder Balthasar Gerbier, Baron Douvily.* The Hague: Rammazeyn, 1656.

Gerbier, Balthazar. *A Manifestation.* London: s.n., 1651.

Gerbier, Balthazar. *A Sea-Cabbin Dialogue … Translated out of Dutch.* London: T.M., 1652.

Gerbier, Balthazar. *Some Considerations on the Two grand Staple-Commodities of England: And on Certain Establishments, Wherein the Publike Good is Very Much Concerned.* London: Coles, 1651.

Gerbier, Balthasar. *A Sommary Description, Manifesting That Greater Profits Are to bee Done in the Hott Then in the Could Parts off the Coast off America.* Rotterdam: Goddaeus, 1660.

Gerbier, Balthasar. *The Interpreter of the Academie for Forrain Languages, and All Noble Sciences, and Exercises.* London [Paris]: s.n., 1648.

Gerbier, Balthasar. *Waerachtige Verklaringe Nopende de Goude en Silvere Mijne.* The Hague: J. Rammazeyn, 1656. *Tweede deel.* The Hague, s.n., 1656). *Derde Verklaringe.* The Hague, s.n., 1656.

Gerbier, Balthasar. *Waarachtige Verklaringe vanden Ridder, B: Douvilij; Noopende Sijn Saecke van Goude en Silvere Mynen, Waer over hy Ghecontracteert Hadde met Sekere Persoonen in Zeelant.* S.l: s.n., 1657.

Gerbier, Balthazar. *To the Parliament, the Most Humble Remonstrance of Sr. Balthazar Gerbier, Kt.* London: s.n., 1650.

Gerbier, Balthazar. *Sommier verhael van sekere Amerikaensche voyagie, gedaen door den Ridder Balthas. Gerbier…. Commandeur van een Guajaensche colonie.* S.l.: s.n., 1660.

Gerbier, Balthazar. *Subsidium Peregrinantibus.* Oxford: Gascoigne, 1665.

Gerbier, Balthazar. *Octroy, van de Hoog: Moog: Heeren Staten Generael, aengaende de Colonie op de Wilde Kust van America. Onder het beleyt van den Ridder Balthazar Gerbier Baron Douvily.* S.l.: s.n., 1659.

Govier, Mark. 'The Royal Society, Slavery and the Island of Jamaica: 1660–1700.' *Notes and Records of the Royal Society of London* 53 , no. 2 (1999): 203–17.

Grabowsky, E. M. and Verkruijsse, P. J., eds. *Een naekt beeldt op een marmore matras seer schoon: het dagboek van een 'grand tour' (1649–1651).* Hilversum: Verloren, 2001.

Grell, Ole Peter. *Calvinist Exiles in Tudor and Stuart England*. Brookfield: Ashgate, 1996.

Groesen, Michiel van, ed. *The Legacy of Dutch Brazil*. New York: Cambridge University Press, 2014.

Groesen, Michiel van. "Visualizing the News: The Amsterdam Spin Doctor Claes Jansz Visscher and the West India Company." In *Visualizing the Text: From Manuscript Culture to the Age of Caricature*, edited by Lauren Beck and Chrisina Ionescu, 95–116. Newark: University of Delaware Press, 2017.

Hille, Christiane. *Visions of the Courtly Body: The Patronage of George Villiers, First Duke of Buckingham and the Triumph of Painting at the Stuart Court*. Berlin: Akademie, 2012.

Hochstrasser, Julie Berger. "Visual Impact: The Long Legacy of the Artists of Dutch Brazil." In *The Legacy of Dutch Brazil*, edited by Michiel Groesen, 248–83. Cambridge: Cambridge University Press, 2014.

Hoxby, Blair. "The Government of Trade: Commerce, Politics, and the Courtly Art of the Restoration." *English Literary History* 66 (1999): 591–627.

Hulsman, Lodewijk. "*Nederlands Amazonia: Handel met Indianen tussen 1580 en 1680*." UvA, Ph.D. thesis, 2009. https://hdl.handle.net/11245/1.319499

Jansson, Maija. *Art and Diplomacy: Seventeenth-Century English Decorated Royal Letters to Russia and the Far East*. Leiden: Brill, 2015.

Keblusek, Marika. "Cultural and Political Brokerage in Seventeenth-century England: The Case of Balthazar Gerbier." In *Dutch and Flemish Artists in Britain 1550–1800*, edited by Juliette Roding, et al., 73–81. Leiden: Primavera Pers, 2003.

Keblusek, Marika. "The Pretext of Pictures: Artists as Cultural and Political Agents." In *Double Agents: Cultural and Political Brokerage in Early Modern Europe*, edited by Marika Keblusek and Badeloch Vera Noldus, 147–60. Leiden: Brill, 2011.

Keller, Vera. "Mining Tacitus: Secrets of Empire, Nature, and Art in the Reason of State." *British Journal for the History of Science* 45, no. 2 (2012): 189–212.

Keller, Vera. "The 'Framing of a New World': Sir Balthazar Gerbier's Project for Establishing a New State in America, ca. 1649." *William and Mary Quarterly* 70, no. 1 (2013): 147–76.

Kesler, C. K. "Tobago: Een vergeten Nederlandsche Kolonie." *De West-Indische Gids* 10 (1928/1929): 527–34.

Keye, Ottho. *Het Waere onderscheyt tusschen Koude en Warme Landen*. The Hague: Hondius, 1659.

Makepeace, Margaret. "English Traders on the Guinea Coast, 1657–1668: An Analysis of the East India Company." *History in Africa* 16 (1989): 237–84.

Mercator, Gerhard. *Literarum latinarum, quas italicas, cursoriasque vocant, scribendarum ratio*. Antwerp: Richard, 1540.

Merwick, Donna. *Possessing Albany, 1630-1710: The Dutch and English Experiences*. Cambridge: Cambridge University Press, 1990.

Meuwese, Mark. "From Dutch Allies to Portuguese Vassals: Indigenous Peoples in the Aftermath of Dutch Brazil." In *Legacy of Dutch Brazil*, edited by Michiel Groesen 59–76. Cambridge: University of Cambridge Press, 2014.

Mochizuki, Mia M. "The Dutch Text Painting. *Word and Image* 23 (2007): 1–17.

Motley, Mark Edward. *Becoming a French Aristocrat: The Education of the Court Nobility, 1580–1715*. Princeton: Princeton University Press, 1990.

Nagtglass, Frederik. *Lebensberichten van Zeeuwen*. Middelburg: Altorffer, 1890.

Ogborn, Miles. "Geographia's pen: writing, geography and the arts of commerce, 1660–1760." *Journal of Historical Geography* 30, no. 2 (2004): 294–315.

Ogilby, John. *The Entertainment of His Most Excellent Majestie Charles II, in His Passage through the City of London to his Coronation*. London: Roycroft, 1662.

Pastorius, Johann Augustijn. *Scharfsinniger Adler mit der Europaischen Flori Historici Continuation*. Frankfurt: s.n., 1659.

Peacey, Jason. "Print, Publicity, and Popularity: The Projecting of Sir Balthazar Gerbier, 1642-1662." *Journal of British Studies* 51 (2012): 284–307.

Peters, Meindert. "'Trekt Heuvelman voor ons gezicht?': The Library of Writing-Master Johannes Heuvelman.' *Quaerendo* 46 (2016): 307–28.

Roberts, Justin. "Surrendering Surinam: the Barbadian Diaspora and the Expansion of the English Sugar Frontier, 1650–1675." *William and Mary Quarterly* 73, no. 2 (2016): 225–56.

Roper, Hugh Trevor. "Prince Rupert, the Cavalier." In *From Counter-Reformation to Glorious Revolution* , edited by Hugh Trevor Roper, 195–211. Chicago: University of Chicago Press,1992.

Sainsbury, W. Noel. *Calendar of State Papers, Colonial Series. America and West Indies*, 1661-1668. London: Longman & Co, 1880.

Sainsbury, Ethel Bruce. "A Paper sent from Antwerp to Sir Balthazar Gerbier [undated] (Public Record Office: CO. 77, vol. viii, no. 87)." In *Calendar of Court Minutes of the East India Company, 1660-1663,* edited by Ethel Bruce Sainsbury, 66. Oxford: Clarendon Press, 1922.

Samson, Alexander, ed. *The Spanish match: Prince Charles's journey to Madrid, 1623.* Burlington, VT: Ashgate, 2006.

Schmidt, Benjamin. "Response: On the Impulse of Mapping, or How a Flat Earth Theory of Dutch Maps Distorts the Thickness and Pictorial Proclivities of early modern Dutch Cartograph (and Misses its Picturing Impulse)." In *The Erotics of Looking: Early Modern Netherlandish Art*, edited by Angela Vanhaelen and Bronwen Wilson, 170–83. West Sussex: Wiley-Blackwell, 2013.

Schneeloch, Norbert H. *Aktionäre der Westindischen Compagnie von 1674 Beiträge zur Wirstschafftsgeschichte Klett- Cotta.* Stuttgat: Kellenbenz and Schneider, 1982.

Schwartz, Stuart B. "Looking for a New Brazil: Crisis and Rebirth in the Atlantic World after the Fall of Pernambuco." In *The Legacy of Dutch Brazil,* edited by  Michiel Groesen, 41–58. Cambridge: Cambridge University Press, 2014.

Sellin, Paul R. "Michel le Blon and England III: Gustav II Adolf, Sir Walter Raleigh's Gold Mine, and the Perfidy of George Villiers, Duke of Buckingham." *Dutch Crossing* 23, no. 1 (1999): 102–32.

Sellin, Paul R. *Treasure, Treason and the Tower: El Dorado and the Murder of Sir Walter Raleigh.* Burlington: Ashgate, 2011.

Sharples, Jason. "Discovering Slave Conspiracies: New Fears of Rebellion and Old Paradigms of Plotting in Seventeenth-Century Barbados." *The American Historical Review* 120, no. 3 ( 2015): 811–43.

Sharples, Jason. "Slavery and Fear." In *Oxford Bibliographies in Atlantic History*, edited by Trevor Burnard. Oxford: Oxford University Press, 2018. Accessed October 15, 2020. https://www.oxfordbibliographies.com/view/document/obo-9780199730414/obo-9780199730414-0308.xml.

Smith, Pamela. *The Business of Alchemy: Science and Culture in the Holy Roman Empire.* Princeton, NJ: Princeton University Press, 1994.

Stevenson, Christine. "Occasional Architecture in Seventeenth-Century London." *Architectural History* 49 (2006): 35–74.

Sutton, Angela  and Charlton Yingling. "Projections of Desire and Design in early modern Caribbean Maps," *Historical Journal* 63, no. 4 (2020): 789–810.

Sutton, Elizabeth. *Capitalism and Cartography in the Dutch Golden Age*. Chicago: University of Chicago Press, 2015.

Van Orden, Kate. *Materialities: Books, Readers, and the Chanson in Sixteenth-Century Europe*. Oxford: Oxford University Press, 2015.

Vos, Jelmer, David Eltis and David Richardson. "The Dutch in the Atlantic World: New Perspectives from the Slave Trade with Particular Reference to the African Origins of the Traffic." In *Extending the Frontiers: Essays on the New Transatlantic Slave Trade Database*, edited by David Eltis and David Richardson, 228–49. New Haven: Yale University Press, 2008.

Wellie, Rik van. "Slave Trading and Slavery in the Dutch Colonial Empire: A Global Comparison." *NWIG: New West Indian Guide/ Nieuwe West-Indische Gids* 82, no. 1/2 (2008): 47–96.

Weststeijn, Arthur. *Commercial Republicanism in the Dutch Golden Age: The Political Thought of Johan & Pieter de la Court*. Leiden: Brill, 2012.

Williamson, Hugh Ross. *Four Stuart Portraits*. London: Evans Brothers, 1949.

Wilson, Charles. *Profit and Power: A Study of England and the Dutch Wars*. The Hague: Nijhoff, 1978.

Wood, Jeremy. "Gerbier, Sir Balthazar (1592–1663/1667)." In *Oxford Dictionary of National Biography* (online ed). Oxford: Oxford University Press, 2004, January 2008. Accessed October 23, 2011. http://www.oxforddnb.com/view/article/10562.

Worden, Nigel. 'Cape Slaves in the Paper Empire of the VOC.' *Kronos* 40, Special Issue: Paper Regimes (2014): 23–44.

Zandvliet, Kees. *Mapping for Money: Maps, Plans, and Topographic Paintings and their Role in Dutch Overseas Expansion during the 16th and 17th Centuries*. Amsterdam: Batavian Lion, 1998.

# 4

# AFFECTIVE PROJECTING

## Mining and inland navigation in Braunschweig-Lüneburg

*Tina Asmussen*

In early 1573, Duke Julius of Braunschweig-Lüneburg commissioned a merchant from Mechelen, Wilhelm de Voß, to obtain technical knowledge in the form of books, manuscripts and drawings from Antwerp. Duke Julius provided De Voß with a shopping list containing 22 entries. He was particularly interested in new books about the construction of watermills, locks, bridges, sluices and hoisting machines, as well as those on architecture, agriculture and fireworks. He also requested a number of experienced and skilled artisans.[1]

Willem de Voß wrote to Wolfenbüttel on May 27, 1573, to inform his contacts there that he had managed to acquire all the desired goods. He also asked for an official letter of passage to travel with his goods to Wolfenbüttel without hindrance and for the payment of an additional 200 thaler because shopping in Antwerp was so expensive.[2] In another (undated) letter, de Voß introduced a skilled practitioner named Willem de Raet to the duke.[3] He highlighted several of De Raet's inventions, mainly in the field of gunsmithing: for instance, he was able to construct a cannon made of wood, that was strong, robust and easily transportable; he had invented a special type of fire cannonball with an steel tip that guaranteed adhesion and had an enormous destructive force; he had invented arrows that inflame in the air; he was able to cast copper that looked like silver; he was also an expert in brass casting, created portraits [*conterfey*] and furniture made of crystal glass, and was able to make all sorts of perfume and oil from herbals and flowers. In 1575, De Raet was commissioned by the duke for a project of inland navigation. Astonishingly, none of the skills described by de Voß were in the field of hydraulic technology.[4]

The duke's dispatching of the merchant to Antwerp must be situated in the context of the particular importance of the Southern Netherlands as centre of commerce and trade, as well as distinguished site of knowledge production and distribution. For concerns such as how to improve the productivity of industry, trade and infrastructure in Braunschweig-Lüneburg, Julius regularly drew on the expertise of artisans, craftsmen and merchants from the Netherlands.[5] The latter possessed essential knowledge and skills for the management of his mines, the expansion of his infrastructure and his princely residence.

This article examines the relevance of carriers of knowledge to Duke Julius and what function they had within his economic and ruling practice. I am particularly interested in the role of the passions motivating the duke to acquire knowledge in the form of experts, books and technology in order to improve mining, metallurgy, navigation and commerce in his duchy. As is frequently stated, knowledge in the form of new technologies, instruments and other ingenious inventions played an essential role in the economic development of early modern Europe and set the path towards modernity.[6] This utilitarian perspective ignores how knowledge also fuelled of hopes, promises and desires, which in turn spurred economic and political action.

Specialists in Julius's economic and political thought have shown how the duke's particular interest in managing and improving the natural resources of his territory – for instance, through mining, forestry and agriculture – was embedded in his overarching reform plans aimed at increasing the wealth of the ducal chamber. The economic reforms undertaken by Duke Julius, they argue, aimed at the formation of a closed economic and industrial zone by interweaving the production areas of agriculture and forestry, mining, metallurgy and metal processing. All decisions regarding industry, finance, technology and trade were made by the ducal administration, which became more and more powerful, with the duke himself as Principal Director. This absolutist principle of state organization is known as the 'directorial system' [*Direktionssystem*].[7]

The objective of Duke Julius's economic and political developments is generally understood to be the setting of the economy on a path towards profit. The economic historian Hans-Joachim Kraschewski argues that for Julius the economy was a 'rational entity geared towards a rational and functional entity'.[8] From this perspective, Julius's obsession with implementing economic and administrative reforms was an entirely rational undertaking, which could be planned, measured and calculated. The aim of this article is to flesh out what Brian Massumi has referred to as 'the ability of affect to produce economic effect(s)'.[9] I use the duke's passions as a vehicle to show the impact of imaginaries, promises and expectations on his economic practice. I do not consider them to be irrational or non-rational, because they fundamentally helped the duke to envision future profits, make plans, set goals, generate investors or overcome risk aversion. The importance of the imaginary within economic theory and economic sociology has gained considerable attention in recent studies. Jens Beckert, among others, views economic action as oriented towards an uncertain future and analyses how ideas and imaginaries about the future fundamentally shape economic action.[10]

The present article is inspired by recent research on the constitution of markets as a specific form of social interaction for the exchange and circulation of goods and knowledge, commercial and scientific exchange, and the distribution, marketing and consumption of knowledge and knowledge products.[11] The case studies presented here zoom in on two areas essential to Duke Julius's economic and political practice: mining and inland navigation. The first part of the article takes the example of Julius's documentation and valuation of the mineral wealth of his duchy, examining the concept of an economy of promise and the techniques (surveying, documenting, visualizing and valuating) used to enact the promise and achieve economic effects. The second part concentrates on the duke's desire to implement his promises and expectations through the example of inland navigation, the so-called *Julius-Schiffahrt*. Here, I will analyse the economy of reputation and trust of knowledge carriers and how they helped to materialize desires, promises and hopes.

## Princely projecting and the economy of promise

In a letter to his stepmother, Sophia of Braunschweig-Luneburg (1522–75), in late November 1574, Julius confessed that he was passionate about mining. He explained that while other princes and electors were obsessed with the 'hunting devil' [*Jagdteufel*] he personally was obsessed instead with the 'mining devil' [*Bergteufel*, literally 'mountain devil'].[12] The highly contingent and capital-intensive nature of mining, where gain and loss followed on each other's heels, indeed had a special attraction for contemporaries.[13] The mixture of promises and fears, triggered on the one hand by ingenious machines, technological inventions and rich ore finds, and on the other hand by the destructive effects of mining on the human body, finances and on society as a whole could certainly be described as demonic.[14] Although such explicit statements about the emotional involvement in mining are rare, the analysis of affects is by no means only accessible via ego-documents. In the case of Julius, it is in particular the ardour with which he pursued his projects for improving the mines and working processes and with which he acquired knowledge about ore deposits and new modes of ore processing that gives us insights into what it meant to be 'obsessed with the mining devil'. This ardour was principally articulated in an abundance of documents that have emerged in the context of mining administration. They show a constant occupation with surveying, evaluating, calculating, ordering and visualizing natural riches, and they fuelled promises that were affectively charged.

Duke Julius's desire to acquire knowledge, in the form of books, instruments, artisans and craftsmen, as testified in the shopping list for De Voß, must in particular be situated in a broader social, political and economic context. Bruce Moran has shown how sovereigns' interest in machines, instruments, alchemy and astronomy was widely shared among late 16th-century German princes. He coined the term *prince-practitioner* to describe the aristocratic interest in precision and technology. Their preoccupation with surveying, mechanics or fortification had important political and economic implications, which resulted from efforts to achieve political consolidation and exploration as well as territorial and commercial expansion.[15] In order to comprehend the duke's actions and ideas of the political and commercial expansion of his state, it is useful to examine this concept of the *prince-practitioner* in combination with that of projecting. In the 16th century, projecting became closely connected with the application of new knowledge and technology benefitting the public good or leading to social and economic improvements.[16]

The attribution of the term 'projector' to a historical figure is mostly applied to artisans, practitioners and learned persons seeking noble patronage, not to princes. Indeed, there are several differences between a projecting prince and a common projector. The most obvious difference is that a prince, even if he failed, did not necessarily lose his social capital. The ability to remain in a certain position and in a certain place was also not connected to the success of the project. And finally, he did not invest his entire capital in a single project. The term 'entrepreneur' is more commonly used for the practices noble projecting encompassed. But the concept of the princely entrepreneur is closely connected to a narrative of economic improvement and innovation, leading to economic growth and to the broader process of state-building.[17] In contrast to the entrepreneur, the concept of projecting allows us to pay more attention to processual and dynamic modes of exchange, as well as to uncertainties. Consequently, it makes sense to acknowledge the utility of the concept to a broader range of actors.

Analysing the duke's activities through the lens of projecting means concentrating on promises directed towards the future that go beyond the calculable and the predictable and have an impact on actual thinking, acting and feeling. This perspective perceives economic actions and reasoning not as goal-oriented towards profit maximization but rather as a drive that requires constant fuelling through wishes, hopes and promises.

A substantial part of the outlined projects of Duke Julius and his contemporaries in the late 16th and 17th centuries were concerned with the promotion of 'useful' knowledge in agriculture, mining, forestry and navigation.[18] In particular, the subject of applied hydraulics gained a Europe-wide interest, not only at the courts but also in the major trading cities of the Holy Roman Empire. Hydraulic technology was needed to solve the problem of groundwater in mining, to drain lands or to expand the network of inland navigation. Artisans and practitioners from the Netherlands played a leading role in this field.[19] In Antwerp, the experiences and developments created in the context of its expansion through the Nieuwstad district turned this global hub on the river Scheldt into a distinct location for hydraulic theory and practice (construction of dams, sluices, locks and canals or drainage technology etc.).[20] However, acquiring knowledge and technological expertise was not all that Antwerp meant to the Duke of Wolfenbüttel. It was also one of his preferred places to sell his mining products, which were advertised extravagantly throughout the country and in major trading cities.[21]

From about the 1520s onwards, the Dukes of Braunschweig-Lüneburg systematically revived ore mining and metal production in the north-western part of the Harz Mountains.[22] Just as his father Heinrich the Younger had done, Julius regarded silver, copper, iron and lead mining as a major source of income for his state and even expanded his activities in this sector. But making the mines profitable was no easy task. Deep mining required complex operations such as the use of huge pumping and drainage machines to solve the ever-present problem of groundwater removal. Another problem was the decreasing metal content of the ores at greater depths. For these poor ores (i.e. ores with a low content of precious metal), new ore processing techniques had to be applied, including the use of large furnaces and smelters. Mining was therefore an undertaking that required knowledge, labour and capital to an extremely high degree.

In order to gather knowledge on how to improve the productivity of his mines by means of technology or better modes of transportation, the duke turned towards experienced miners, metalworkers and alchemists from within his territory and from abroad.[23] Large piles of paper that still survive to this day provide details of the duke's consultations and negotiations with the practitioners with mineral, technological or metallurgical expertise. Countless documents from the local mining administration are stored in the archives of Wolfenbüttel, Hanover and Clausthal-Zellerfeld, as well as inventories, maps, drawings and sketches. These practices of calculating, conceptualizing and visualizing should not only be regarded as a result of the emergence of centralized administrative structures, they are also inherent in the more dynamic and processual practices of projecting. The contemporary term 'project' can be deduced by the Latin term *projicere* meaning to 'throw forward'.[24] Vera Keller and Ted McCormick see the origins of the concept of projecting in the practice of drafting and mapping, which they aptly describe as a 'paper technology'.[25] In the following sections, I will analyse the various paper techniques of enacting promises, showing how these incited specific actions.

## Documenting and visualizing promise

The practices of inventorying material riches, surveying land and drawing maps were among the most common forms of rulership in the 16th and 17th centuries. By means of mapping, inventories of the dominions were made, to help consolidate political, legal and economic rights.[26] These maps or inventories do not provide an 'accurate' image of the conditions in the territories but, rather, are expressions of claims, material imaginaries and the concept of promise. The practice of conceptualizing and visualizing riches demonstrated the sovereigns' power of mastery and improvement of nature as well as the power to promote industry and innovation.[27] Both – conceptualizing and visualizing – were not only expressions of rulership but also essential practices of projecting. Therefore, projecting can be seen as a form of rulership as well.

Duke Julius regularly assigned artists to draw maps, machines and instruments, most prominently the Dutch artists Hans Vredeman de Vries (1527–1606) and Adam Lecuir (d. 1586).[28] A protocol between the duke and the painter David von Hemmerdey dated March 1572 shows that the former desired an elaborate visual representation of the potential of his lands for his private rooms in the ducal palace. The duke commissioned the painter to visit all the places that produced silver, lead, copper, brass, iron, sulphur, vitriol, magnet, salt, together with their mountains, valleys and landscapes, and paint them in 'delightful colours' [*lieblichen Farben*].[29] Von Hemmerdey's certificate of appointment as ducal court painter, issued on April 4, 1572, contains the duke's commission of four sample pieces [*Probestücke*], none of which is preserved today. One of these paintings was to depict his mines. The duke instructed von Hemmerdey to represent the workshops and buildings above and below the ground, together with their workers and tools, in such a way that the instruments and handicraft skills were accurately reproduced throughout. Similarly, the tunnels and shafts were to be painted in their entire depth, including the corridors, as well as the surrounding rivers, brooks, mountain waters, water arts, hammer works and foundries, winches, smithies, mints, streets and official buildings. The instructions were to depict all this accurately 'nach kontrafeiischer Art'[30] In a personal meeting between the duke and the painter on March 22, 1572, Julius expected that trough von Hemmerdey's art '[…] the wild and rough Harz becomes all the more joyful and pleasant to look at.' [*damit der rauhe und wilde Harz in seiner Art desto lustiger und lieblicher zu besehen*].[31] This *Contrafactur* of the mining industry in the Harz was to be raised on four panels 'in order to be a princely adornment in the ducal chamber' [*eine fürstliche zierde im Herzoglichen Gemach und Zimmer*].[32]

Another *Probestück* was to depict, similarly to the mining scene, a project of inland navigation entitled *Julius-Schiffahrt*. Julius built on the efforts of Heinrich the Younger to connect the mining regions in the Harz Mountains to the Wolfenbüttel ducal residence though a complex waterway floating system in order to improve the transport of natural resources.[33] Stones, wood, timber, metals and other building materials from the forests, mines and quarries in the Harz were to be floated into the city. Nevertheless, Julius had an even more ambitious plan: to transform the small river Oker that runs through Wolfenbüttel into a navigable and busy torrent of domestic trade. For that reason, he wanted to connect the Oker with the Elbe and Weser in order to provide direct transport to Hamburg and to the North Sea.

In the 16th and 17th centuries, inland navigation was paid close attention within the Holy Roman Empire as well as in England and the Netherlands. The idea of shifting the transport of goods from land to water promised to make logistics cheaper and faster. For Wolfenbüttel, accessing the Elbe and the Weser directly would enable a better distribution of the products from the Harz mines and quarries – mainly lead, brass, iron, vitriol and alabaster – and enhance domestic trade. Therefore, von Hemmerday was commissioned to depict this prestigious project of the Julius-Schiffahrt '[…] from the city of Goslar to the princely residence Wolfenbüttel and from here to Celle'. This painting was also to show the landscape of the Oker river surrounding Wolfenbüttel's fortress at a distance of six miles from the town.[34]

It is significant that these two *Probestücke* are designated as 'Contrafactur' or 'Conterfey'. In the context of 16th-century European art, the term meant a specific type of portrayal or replica of someone or something that designated a visual testimony. Contemporary lexicons translated the term into Latin not as *imago* but as *effigies,* meaning substitutes for the depicted object itself.[35] With the name 'conterfey', these visualizations acquired an enhanced sense of presence and offered a truthful testimony of the promising mine and waterworks.

This visualization of promise shows the effects of promise in its double meaning.[36] On the one hand, promise is related to auspicious expectations in the future while envisioning them in the present. On the other hand, it also had stabilizing effects which helped realize the expectations. For merchants, *promessa* served as an assurance with legal implications that aimed to secure the fulfilment of the desired expectations in the future.[37] Correspondingly, desiring and securing were permanently at play within the concept of promise and fuelled economic action.

The two meanings of promise become particularly evident in the authoritatively commissioned practice of surveying and inventorying land. Registering and documenting the mineral wealth of his territory was among Julius's major concerns from the beginning of his reign. In January 1572, Erasmus Ebner (1511–77), a councillor with broad metallurgical expertise and former mayor of Nuremberg, and already commissioned by Heinrich the Younger to improve the process of brass production, published an inventory of the most important mineral riches of the Harz Mountains, particularly at the Rammelsberg, the notable mining district next to the free imperial city of Goslar.[38] This inventory, headed 'Diverse presentation of all types of ore, metal and other compounds for exploitation which can be found at the Harz and particularly at the Ramesberg [sic]', contains 40 well-informed entries on ores containing gold and silver, and on copper, iron, steel and mercury, saltpetre, alum, sulphur, lime, gypsum, hard coal, marl and tar.[39] This catalogue of local mineral resources provides answers to possible applications of minerals and metals, the costs of certain mining and refining processes, as well as various sales opportunities. The purpose and use of this inventory were not made explicit, but the utilitarian perspective suggests that it was commissioned as a guide for the duke's financial investments and to attract foreign investors, and merchants, too.

Ebner's catalogue is an important document that has to be contextualized within Julius's reform and expansion of the mining administration, and the need of evaluating land from the point of view of its rentability.[40] But this perspective should not neglect the promising and rewarding character of the content of Ebner's text. In general, Ebner's catalogue documents the potential of the land while promising a prosperous future. His entire account of mining at the Rammelsberg builds on the promissory narrative of abundant mineral resources which have only been partially accessed at this stage. Ebner begins his entries with assertions about the most valuable metal, gold, and declares that all silver mined at Rammelsberg contains gold. But since the gold content is too low, he does not consider it worth extracting. However, Ebner does not leave it at this disappointing assessment but expresses his hopes for richer gold findings in the near future.[41] The evaluations of silver mining that follow are equally favourable: if the smelting technique were improved, rich quantities of silver could be produced.[42] While drawing a highly optimistic image of the promising future of the Harz mining industry, Ebner fuels the reader's hopes of obtaining access to these riches, while at the same time underlining the trustworthiness of his claims thanks to his status as an official counsellor and renowned mineral expert. It is very likely that Ebner's services are related to Julius's activities aimed at attracting foreign capital for his mines. Between January 2, 1569, and April 24, 1572, he called upon the entire aristocracy of his duchy and the neighbouring lands to participate in the mining industry by making capital investments of 200, 100 and 50 thalers.[43] It is therefore probable that Ebner's catalogue was also part of this campaign. This document served therefore to make desires tangible and calculable.

This example underlines the important role of practical and empirical knowledge in the economy of promise. The skills of Ebner or Hemmerdey helped to materialize immaterial desires. *Ars* and *technē* were thus essential instruments in the economy of promise, because they reified future imaginaries, turning them into tangible elements of economic practice.

## Staging and calculating promise

An inventory of the ducal palace, made on the occasion of the duke's death in 1589, mentions the navigation, but not the mining 'conterfey'.[44] This inventory provides a spatially organized description of the interior of the most representative rooms of the ducal palace. It is interesting that among the visual representations of cities, Antwerp is predominantly represented with four *vedute* and one painting of Antwerp's citadel. In Antwerp, the duke's interest in commerce, knowledge and technology coalesced, since it was the most important commercial and knowledge hub north of the Alps. The city also represented a 'prototype of a new city-plan based on a rigid grid pattern in which canals were situated parallel to each other', and so became a model for his own urban transformations.[45] As Barbara Uppenkamp has recently pointed out, Julius's projects to expand and reshape the city were similar to other urban planning in Renaissance Europe, indebted to function and utility, characterized by strong geometrical planning with a network of channels and straight roads. In Wolfenbüttel, from the 1570 onwards, the urban district of Heinrichstadt expanded according to an ideal plan.[46] A port was built for arriving ships, which supplied building materials, and straight canals crossed the city. In addition, it was also planned for Heinrichstadt to be extended by a suburb called Gotteslager. This town, due to its perfect location for transport, was to be developed into a large trading town with 36,000 hearths. This turned Antwerp into an imaginary realm of promises for the duke's urbanistic and mercantile projects. Julius's keen interest in Antwerp also encompassed more recent military events: two paintings listed in the inventory depict Alessandro Farnese's construction of a floating bridge of connecting ships that blocked the Scheldt and cut Antwerp off from its most important vehicle of trade in 1585.

Besides the prominent representation of Antwerp, the abundance of metal and mineral objects in the inventory is also striking. The majority of entries are objects made from products from the local mines and quarries – in particular, lead. Even before Julius's reign, along with silver and copper, lead was one of the most important resources of the duchy.[47] Although it was less important in terms of value than silver, it was significant because of its quantity. Most of the lead produced in the Harz region came from the district at the Rammelsberg, near Goslar on the north-eastern edge of the Harz mountains, and from the mines in the Upper Harz.[48] Among the mineral objects listed in the inventory is an abundance of animal heads made of lead (mostly stag and deer heads), portraits on lead plaques, lead cannonballs and even rolled lead, different kinds of brass furniture, brass buckets, iron chairs, tables made of alabaster, marble and slate.

As Thomas DaCosta Kaufmann has argued, the acquisition of knowledge about nature and its usefulness displayed through the princely collections in the *Kunstkammer* must not be misunderstood as some form of mere entertainment but rather served a specific political objective: self-advertisement, economic advancement and utility, and a display of learning.[49] The 1589 inventory clearly shows that the ducal collection of objects, paintings, instruments and books was not something outside the economic cycle. Far more than that, it played an integral and active part in the economic household, the state's oeconomy. It was where the local natural resources and the economic and political power of the territory were enacted. It was also where (utopian) visions become manifest, such as Wolfenbüttel as a prominent force in domestic trade.

This showroom of material wealth in Julius's palace had an equivalent in Heinrichstadt, a newly founded and continuously expanding city district that Julius named after his father. In 1578, during a short stay at Wolfenbüttel in Lower Saxony, the Silesian Hofmarschall Hans von Schweinichen admired the abundance of trading goods stocked in the newly established storehouse [*Faktoreihof*] in Heinrichstadt. Of all the stockpiled goods, the abundance of lead in particular amazed him: '[Julius] showed us such a stock of lead that lay in a heap on top of each other like a small mountain; at that time, he intended to plaster the whole city of Wolfenbüttel with lead instead of stone, which could be picked up and be used in times of need.'[50]

Two decades after this account, Franz Algermann (c. 1548–1613), Duke Julius's secretary and notary, discussed the copiousness of metal commodities. In Julius's biography, published almost a decade after the duke's death in 1598, Algermann quantifies the monetary value of this staple of trading goods made from the output of the local mines as being many hundred thousand thalers. In a similar vein to Von Schweinichen, Algermann highlights the masses of lead:

> For what was accumulated of lead, it is only known by those who saw it at that time; not to mention the other mining goods [*Bergwaren*], such as processed brass, copper, iron, green and blue vitriol, copper smoke, calamine etc., as well as rolled lead and roof tiles made of lead, garden borders and garden benches cast from lead and other decorations, stag and deer heads, chandeliers and all sorts of things, which were expensive to produce; this stock (which I, among others, helped to inventory in 1582, and according to my inventory) […] His Princely Grace had it estimated as a total of seven tons of gold and this even multiplied daily.[51]

The ostentatious presentation and valuation of objects made from the local mines in the representative rooms of the ducal palace as well as in the *Faktoreihof* turns these places into showrooms to demonstrate the fertility of the ducal land, the productivity of his mines and the industriousness of the local craftsmen. By means of *ars* and *technē*, the promising future of the principality was displayed in the ducal residence and in the city, challenging people to emulate this success. The idea behind both sites was to be a yardstick of material wealth put into practice.

Von Schweinichen's account of the stored goods and his remark that Julius intended to pave the streets of the city with the mineral wealth of his territory illustrates the complexity of 16th-century management of natural resources, which cannot be completely reduced to a utilitarian understanding of economy. This example shows how both promise and utility have been made visible though the piles of lead, which were not only presented but quantified and inventoried. Wolfenbüttel, a centre of bustling industry and trade, as becomes apparent from the ducal collection and urban storehouse, appears to anticipate Giovanni Botero's thoughts *On the Causes of Greatness and Magnificence of Cities* (1588). Botero's treatise addresses the European trading cities of the late 16th century under the rising power of the absolutist sovereign and emerging administrative structures. The main reasons why a city becomes great is, according to Botero, due to (1) the fertility of the land and the convenience of the place (meaning its accessibility by land or water), (2) the convenience of transport – whereas 'transport by water, if it is navigable, is incomparably better than transport by land, both for facility and speed'[52] – and (3) industry. Industry surpasses nature in many ways, Botero writes. He evokes iron mining, from which 'the revenues [...] are not very big, but an infinite number of people make their living from working the iron and trading in it; they mine it, refine it and melt it, they sell it wholesale and retail, they make it into engines of war and weapons for attack and defence, into endless kinds of tools for farming, building and every craft, and for the everyday needs and innumerable necessities of life, for which iron is no less needful than bread.'[53] What the iron mines were to Botero, the lead mines were to Julius: metal of low value that promised to turn into an unparalleled treasure through the processing industry.

Although Julius's project of transforming Wolfenbüttel into a magnificent and prospering town of industry and trade could ultimately only be realized on a small scale, his imaginaries and ideals show the projected dimensions of his economic and technological plans. A closer examination of Julius's endeavours in inland navigation will show how daring this project was and how closely it can be linked to other high-risk projects such as alchemy.

## Navigating promise

The promissory effects of knowledge were mediated by knowledge brokers or *expert mediators* – to use Eric Ash's concept – who claimed to master 'some rare, valuable and complicated body of useful knowledge'.[54] The expert mediators employed by Duke Julius, such as De Voß or De Raet, were mostly artisans, artists, mining foremen, metallurgists and merchants. They served as coordinators of the projects themselves and reported on their progress to the duke, constantly moving between managing the ongoing projects and communicating about and advertising them to the patron and other investors. The expert's knowledge, skill and expertise to plan and execute the project were highly sought commodities.[55] Their main task was thus to translate knowledge into economic activity.

In 1575, when De Raet entered in the duke's service, Julius's navigation project already had a considerable lifespan. The expansion of the rivers Oker and Nette (today Altenau) for shipping had always been a parallel venture to the expansion of the Harz water courses Radau and Ecker for floating.[56] The numerous experts Julius consulted on how to realize the navigation system and his various attempts to find investors confirm what Julius's valet, the Netherlandish artisan Ruprecht Lobri, described as 'great affection and desire that the duke had to the navigation'.[57] These experts enabled Julius to understand the technical details and requirements of the project and thus helped him appropriate and control it under his own name: *Julius-Schiffahrt*.

In autumn 1570, a group of practitioners and stone cutters, among them Lobri, who was already in the service of Duke Heinrich the Younger, visited the small river Radau. Their main concern was to find solutions for how to remove the rocks from the river 'with profit' in order to enable the floating of wood and peat.[58] Peat came from a location called the 'Grosse (Rote) Bruch'. This wetland extends 45 kilometres, between Oschersleben in Saxony-Anhalt in the east and Schladen–Werla in Lower Saxony in the west. It had a natural incline and connected the watercourses of the Oker and the Bode. The plan was to drain the area and build a channel (Schiffsgraben) to connect the Oker with the Elbe and reach Magdeburg. In February 1571, Julius attempted to convince his councils with a promissory report on its advantages in order to find support for the navigation project: he fuelled expectations while revealing untapped resources of wood and peat for heating and construction. Floating would enable the transport of wood from as yet inaccessible parts of the forest (where wood was still rotting because it was not being used) and the extraction of peat from the Grosse Bruch to where it was needed, such as in the saltworks in Juliushall, the brass foundry at Bündheim and to Heinrichstadt. The attractiveness of his projects was underlined with a remark on the redistribution of costs. He claimed to know of several people from the Netherlands who were interested in settling in the Harz in order to 'dig and dry peat at their own cost and at a respectable interest rate, as well as to burn lime and bricks at Büntheim [insertion in the duke's handwriting: 'all at their own cost'] [...]'.[59]

This report indeed attracted interest, because as early as July 1571 12 councillors accompanied by 2 merchants from Leipzig visited the Grosse Bruch.[60] After they had examined everywhere 'diligently', their hopes for rich profits turned to mistrust and scepticism. They concluded that the extraction and transport of peat would generate more costs than profit. Due to the steep gradient of the river and the many stones and cliffs, the floating of the peat would be very expensive, making the extraction unprofitable. They considered the idea of draining the Grosse Bruch too expensive as well. However, they supported the duke's idea of settling people from Holland who were experienced in the field of hydrological technology and could undertake this project at their own cost.[61] Lack of experience with this type of large-scale drainage projects among the local community was therefore one of the most important reasons for rejecting the project. Julius did make several attempts to get Dutch workers for this project. An extract within a ducal mandate on behalf of the military councillor [*Kriegs- und Kammerrat*] Jobst Kettwich in March 1573 even gives insights on the high number of workers that he envisaged. Kettwich was delegated, among other duties, to negotiate with 600 religious refugees to move to his duchy and take up work in the Grosse Bruch.[62]

After the failure to persuade the council members to join the navigation project and the 600 refugees to turn the moor into fertile and habitable land, the arrival of the skilled artisan De Raet raised new hopes. The following remarks do not intend to retell Julius's efforts to successfully establish navigation in his duchy but rather demonstrate the role of trust, persuasion and risk within the relationship between the duke and De Raet. The core of the economy of promise was the constant negotiation between desiring and securing, as well as between trust and mistrust. The practice of securing had trust-building effects that were essential to persuade investors or to overcome their risk aversion. The material and technical requirements of mining and inland navigation far surpassed the duke's knowledge. Employing trusted artisans thus had securing effects, because their knowledge helped him to anticipate the future, risks and profits.

A protocol of the first meeting of the duke with the artisan in autumn 1574 sheds light on the high expectations he had of De Raet's skills. What is particularly striking for us today is the fact that the duke juxtaposed his expectations of De Raet's artisanal skills with his earlier expectations of the skills of the (at that time imprisoned) alchemist Philipp Sömmerling.[63] This alchemist, who arrived at Wolfenbüttel in 1571, promised Julius he would transmute base metal into gold with a philosophical tincture. He declared that this art would produce a benefit of 200,000 thalers annually.[64] The promise could not be fulfilled. Sömmerling was imprisoned with his fellow alchemist Anna Zieglerin and several assistants on Pentecost 1574. After interrogation and a trial, the alchemists were condemned to death and executed on February 4, 1575.[65] The protocol between Julius and De Raet states that the duke expected the latter to deliver something 'enduring' so that he did not have to return to the Netherlands in disgrace and '[…] he declared how the imprisoned Duke Herzog Johann Friedrich [i.e. Johann Friedrich II of Sachsen-Gotha] recommended several alchemists, who had promised great things but achieved nothing. Moreover, they maliciously sought to kill the duke and his consort, and they caused him damages of 100,000 thalers […].' The protocol continues that they 'had promised a lot but could neither implement it nor make it prosperous, His Princely Grace does not want to grant this [i.e. punishment and disgrace] to De Raet, but rather he should make himself a good name through constant and eternal work.'[66]

Creating something durable, making a name for himself and avoiding disgrace and shame were the keywords of this discussion. The reputation of the artisan was at stake. Julius threatened De Raet with the negative example of the alchemists' failure and abuse of trust. The risks for the investor and for the artisan were both high, but whereas Julius conceived his own risks as primarily financial, he emphasized that the artisan risked losing his reputation. In the world of merchants and artisans, reputation was the most precious attribute one could lose, because all future employment relied on a good reputation.[67] In the subsequent certificate of appointment [*Bestallungsurkunde*] issued on July 25, 1575, Julius also attempted to secure himself from financial risk by transferring this to De Raet as well. The latter was to create a company of 'Burgunder' and other regions experienced in navigation and this type of projects.[68]

The expectations and ability to create prosperous and enduring work was therefore credited to both technological and alchemical arts. Julius invested – and lost, as he mentions – a considerable amount of money in alchemy.[69] For the duke alchemy served a practical economic or political purpose. Particularly in the field of mining, alchemy helped find technical solutions to problems of assaying or refining metals. By hiring skilled assayers and alchemists, sovereigns throughout Europe aimed to increase the productivity of their mines and the fertility of their lands.[70] The characteristic of mining as a risky and capital-intensive undertaking that promised rich rewards encouraged investments in alchemical arts, although these were just as risky, for the investor as well as for the alchemist. Julius's hope was not directed towards an immaterial good but materialized in poor but abundant ores. With the knowledge of a skilled and truthful alchemist the poor ores – i.e. ores with a low metal content – were perceived as a resource with the potential to become precious metals in the future.

The navigation project was equally risky and promised similar rewards: fallow and remote land that was to be transformed into fertile cropland and a highly frequented commercial zone. In De Raet's skills and good reputation, the duke's desire of a promising future of inland navigation materialized. The hopes and risks of De Raet's work become visible in the *Bestallungsurkunde*. Julius clearly points to the enormous rewards of the navigation project, although it is considered to be impossible by 'almost everyone in the countryside' and that 'this undertaking will bring envy and repulsiveness upon him [i.e. De Raet].'[71] In a new attempt to convince the councillors in 1575, Julius also uses De Raet's good reputation and undisputed expertise as a means to persuade the councillors and prelates. He mentioned that 'just recently, Wilhelm de Rath [sic] (born in Hartogenbosch under the reign of the Spanish King), who is known to everyone throughout the Netherlands for his skills in construction and waterworks' commenced his work on the navigation project.[72]

The first activity that the artisan undertook at the duke's command was an expedition to the Grosse Bruch on June 9, 1575. Besides De Raet, the expedition team consisted of principal mining official Christoph Sander and three artisans in ducal service, Ruprecht Lobri, Julius's personal valet originally from Grave in Brabant, Wilhelm Remmen from's-Hertogenbosch, painter, goldsmith and alchemist, and Jorien Schaefner, chamber trumpeter.[73] The report of the practitioners begins with promising words, which indicate a shift in strategy. Whereas in the letters to the council the transport of as yet untapped resources such as peat and its benefits for the local industry was always put in the foreground, now inland navigation advanced from a means to an end to the main promise made. This report was thus clearly designed to reach a broader group of investors, such as merchants and surrounding principalities and neighbouring countries:

> This report deals with the future navigation on the river Oker into the Elbe up to the city of Magdeburg and further with divine aid to the mines of the Elector in Saxony, in order to convert lead for money and other goods, to trade in the same way also with all other fruits of the country, so that each principality takes its products freely for nothing on the navigation, their grain and their victuals and other things, nothing is excluded and all in the same condition, since the various electorates and principalities, the spiritual and secular governments, the peasants, citizens, the nobility and the knighthood, the prelates, counts and chapters will have their various immured granaries and storehouses, their grain and their victuals in stock at the courses of the rivers of future navigation.[74]

After this promissory introduction, ample space is used for the presentation of the four experts. On four pages they are introduced with their full names, place of birth, age, current and former appointments. This information, which was intended to underline the trustworthiness of the expedition team, is more detailed than the account of the actual visit, which follows on the following six pages. The report lacks any deeper reflection on site specifics, necessary technologies or the amount of work needed. However, this lack of important information is due to the addressees of the text. It is aimed at potential investors. The report reveals the opinion that for investors the information of a cost-effective realization was sufficient, provided it came from trustworthy persons. The essential information that the navigation project was feasible and, according to De Raet, should also not cost much was repeated twice.[75] The reason for his optimism was again peat, but this time only as means to cover the costs for the construction of the canal. He predicted that peat could be sold at a high price in Halberstadt monastery because the wood there was scarce and expensive.[76]

Neither De Raet's nor Julius's attempts to find investors were successful. Therefore, the strategy of dispensing with all technical details about feasibility and implementation was ultimately not successful. De Raet even moved to Italy in 1576, where he acted in the service of the Republic of Lucca for a drainage project. He also signed a contract with Francesco I de' Medici concerning a similar navigation project between Florence and the mouth of the Arno.[77] The contract mentions that De Raet should be allowed to spend three months a year in the service of Braunschweig-Wolfenbüttel. Julius tried, with the aid of a diplomat, to push the project forward despite the lack of the project's principal practitioner. He sent his counsel and governor Heinrich von der Lühe to negotiate the terms of the navigation project with the Electorate of Saxony and Brandenburg.[78] In July 1584, it seems that the project gained renewed activity and Julius sent the report of De Raet, Lobri, Sander, Remmen and Jorien to a Dutch agent from Amsterdam in order to find skilled engineers and investors.[79] In 1587, the architect, painter and engineer Hans Vredeman de Vries entered ducal service and again fuelled hopes for the project with his designs and drawings of locks and dams. The individual stages of this project, which ultimately never came to fruition, clearly show the processual character of this undertaking, with the duke and his officials and artisans constantly adjusting their strategies with each setback. This demonstrates what a central role knowledge and knowledge carriers played in the economy of promise and persuasion.

## Affective projecting

While examining Duke Julius's undertakings in mining and navigation through the lens of projecting, the previous sections attempted to shift the deterministic narrative of the emergence of useful knowledge, innovation and progress to a more dynamic narrative that acknowledges the agency of affects and imaginaries. In particular, the 16th-century prince-practitioners' interest in alchemy, navigation, mining, fortification and large-scale drainage projects, in the context of their political consolidation as well as territorial and commercial expansion, required a growing number of technical experts and knowledge brokers. This turned the early modern states simultaneously into generators, consumers and products of expertise on knowledge and technology.[80] Various experts acted in the service of Duke Julius such as Ebner, von Hemmerdey or De Raet. Their techniques of documenting, inventorying, accounting and drawing, as well as their rhetoric of persuasion, helped to materialize the invisible imaginaries and promising futures of Braunschweig-Lüneburg.

Early modern resource management did not only have a material side, which could be calculated in terms of quantity, price and weight. It had an equally important immaterial and affective side, namely, the imaginaries of future wealth or profit and the hopes and desires connected with them. The material and the immaterial or the cognitive and affective are not in opposition to each other, however, but are inextricably linked. At the same time, they produce their own materiality, which becomes manifest in the practice of affective projecting. The latter is more 'rational' than we would expect since the duke and his artisans and practitioners attempt to visualize, conceptualize and calculate their hopes and promises. Affective projecting is consequently something we can explore while analysing its strategies and its impact. And taking the affective dimension of projecting, such as the promises of improvement and growth or the commodification of desires, into consideration adds another – more dynamic and complex – narrative to the linear plot of economic growth and the early modern origins of capitalism.

## Acknowledgement

I am grateful to Inger Leemans, Sven Dupré and Wijnand Mijnhardt for inviting me to this working group "Knowledge and the Market: Affective economies". The intellectual exchange, insightful suggestions and support of this group throughout the years were most valuable. Finally, I would like to thank the editors Anne Goldgar and Inger Leemans for supporting this project, for their suggestions and help. This research was funded by the Swiss National Science Foundation (SNSF) with an Ambizione grant. I am grateful to the SNSF for supporting this project.

## Notes

1 *Verzeichnis was meinem gnedigen Fürsten und Herrn der Niederländische Crämer Wilhelm die Vos genandt von Mechlem burtig aus dem Niederlandt und was alles davon zu bekommen sey mitbringen und ausrichten soll.* Cal. Br. 21, Nr. 1264, fols. $2^r$-$5^r$, Niedersächsisches Landesarchiv Standort Hannover [NLA HA],
2 '[…] dass die guetter sovill gekost sollten haben durch ursach das alle dieselbige Inn Anntorff Theur ist.' Willem de Voß to Herzog Julius, Anttorf 27 May 1573, Cal. Br. 21, Nr. 1264, fol. $10^r$, NLA HA.
3 Willem de Voß to Duke Julius, n.p., n.d. Cal. Br. 21, Nr. 1264, fols. $24^r$-$26^r$, NLA HA.
4 On De Raet: O.De Smedt, "Guglielmo de Raet"; O. De Smedt, "Willhem de Raet."
5 F. Thöne, "*Wolfenbüttel.*"
6 J. Mokyr, *The Lever of Riches*; J. Mokyr, *Gifts of Athena.*
7 H.-J. Kraschewski, *Wirtschaftspolitik.* This book builds upon extensive archival research as well as on older studies such as P. Zimmermann, "Herzog Julius in Volkswirtschaftlicher Beziehung"; E. Bodemann, "Die Volkswirtschaft des Herzogs Julius." See also J. Graefe ed., *Staatsklugheit und Frömmigkeit.*
8 'Zielsetzung dieser Maßnahmen war die Orientierung der Wirtschaft an Ertrag und Rentabilität. Wirtschaft wurde als rationales Zweckgebilde verstanden.' H.-J. Kraschewski, *Wirtschaftspolitik*, 173.
9 B. Massumi, *Parables for the Virtual*, 45.
10 J. Beckert, *Imagined Futures.* For the role of affects and emotions in economics: G. A. Akerloff and R. J. Shiller, *Animal Spirits*; U. Frevert, "Gefühle und Kapitalismus"; U. Stäheli, "Hoffnung als ökonomischer Affekt."
11 A. Goldgar, *Tulipmania*; H. J. Cook, *Matters of Exchange*; L. Roberts, *Centres and Cycles*; S. Dupré, B. De Muck and T. Werner, *Embattled Territory*; D. Margócsy, *Commercial Visions.*
12 "Wie andere Chur- und Fürsten meistentheils dem Jagdteufel anhängig, also hats mit Uns die Gelegenheit, wie E.G. u. L zum Theil wissen, daß Wir dem Bergteufel nachhängen." Letter of Duke Julius to Duchess Sophia of Braunschweig-Lüneburg, November 29, 1574, 1 Alt 23 Nr. 16, Niedersächsisches Landesarchiv Standort Wolfenbüttel [NLA WO]. See also E. Bodemann, "Die Volkswirtschaft des Herzogs Julius," 200.
13 This attractivity of mining is reflected in a growing number of mining related literature since the late 15th century. E. Darmstaedter, *Berg-, Probir- und Kunstbüchlein*; M. Koch, *Geschichte und Entwicklung*; P. O. Long, 'Openness of Knowledge'.

14 T. Asmussen, "Wild Man in Braunschweig."
15 B. T. Moran. , "German Prince-Practitioners"; B. T. Moran, *The Alchemical World.*
16 V. Keller and T. McCormick, "Towards a History of Projects," 424; K. Yamamoto, *Taming Capitalism,* esp. 3–19. The introductions of Yamamoto and Keller and McCormick give an in-depth discussion of the historiography of early modern projectors.
17 The most detailed study on Julius as princely entrepreneur is Kraschewski's standard work. He adopts the Schumpeterean concept of entrepreneur to Julius's economic thought. H.-J. Kraschewski, *Wirtschaftspolitik,* 151–65. See also H.-J. Kraschewski, 'Der ökonomische Fürst'.
18 V. Keller and T. McCormick, "Towards a History of Projects," 424.
19 K. Davids, *Rise and Decline.*
20 P. Lombaerde, "Antwerp in its Golden Age," 111.
21 C. Sack, "Herzog Julius von Braunschweig Lüneburg."
22 Of the numerous studies on the Harz mining industry in 16th and 17th centuries I only refer to the most essential literature: E. Henschke, *Landesherrschaft und Bergbauwirtschaft;* C. Bartels, "The Production of Silver, Copper, and Lead"; C. Bartels, *Vom frühneuzeitlichen Montangewerbe zur Bergbauindustrie;* H.-J. Kraschewski, "Organisationsstrukturen der Bergbauverwaltung"; H.-J. Kraschewski, "Bergbau und Hüttenwesen."
23 E. Henschke, *Landesherrschaft und Bergbauwirtschaft.*
24 V. Keller and T. McCormick, "Towards a History of Projects"; K. Yamomoto, *Taming Capitalism,* 1–25.
25 "While we think of projects conceptually today, the term first described a paper technology. Even as its primary meaning shifted, the project remained associated with a drafted image or written plan. Literally and figuratively, the project cast the future as an empty sheet." V. Keller and T. McCormick, "Towards a History of Projects," 427.
26 "Maps determined rights to forest lands and fields; offered proof of sovereign power and legal jurisdiction; specified taxable lands; and defined possession of economically productive regions such as mining areas, saltworks, woodlands, and transportation routes. Their construction required a general knowledge of geography as well as the development of accurate surveying techniques and instruments." B. T. Moran, "German Prince-Practitioner," 260.
27 On the connection of inventorying natural riches and economic thought: A. Cooper, "Possibilities of the Land."
28 F. Thöne, "Hans Vredeman de Vries in Wolfenbüttel." On Lecuir (or Liquir): A. Lipińska, "Alabasterdiplomatie."
29 E. Pitz, *Landeskulturtechnik,* esp. 74–75.
30 NLA WO 2 Alt Nr. 8105; A transcription of the Bestallungsurkunde is published in E. Bodemann, "Herzog Julius von Braunschweig," 237–39.
31 Quoted from E. Pitz, *Landeskulturtechnik,* 75.
32 E. Pitz, *Landeskulturtechnik,* 74.
33 On the floating and navigation project: T. Müller, *Schifffahrt und Flösserei,* esp. 52–91.
34 "2) Soll der ernannte David von Hemmerdey, Unser bestellter Hofmaler, Unser angerichtet Floßwerk ( Julius-Schiffahrt) von der Stadt Goslar an bis anhero nach Unserer Festung Wolfenbüttel, und von hier bis gen Celle, sammt allen Umständen abreißen und malen, und zugleich alle Gegend und Gelegenheit, was bei der Oker 6 Meilen Wegs um unsere Festung Wolfenbüttel gelegen ist.' E. Bodemann, "Herzog Julius von Braunschweig," 238.
35 P. Parshall, "Imago Contrafacta: Images and Facts in the Northern Renaissance," 561; C. Swan, "Ad vivum, naer het leven"; A. Goldgar, "Nature as Art."
36 An interdisciplinary research project on the cultural and economic history of markets in Early Modern Europe analyses the role of promise in Market practices. DFG-Netzwerk: *Das Versprechen der Märkte. Neue Perspektiven auf die Wirtschaftskulturgeschichte der Frühen Neuzeit.* http://versprechen-der-maerkte.de, accessed March 14, 2019.
37 "Promessa" derives from lat. 'promissio' and meant in canonic law a legal commitment to the moral and theological duties of truthfulness, sincerity, honorability and

faithfulness to promises. For the legal implications of promise: M.-P. Weller, *Die Vertragstreue*, 72; K.-P. Nanz, *Die Entstehung des allgemeinen Vertragsbegriffs*; B. Hamm, *Promission, Pactum, Ordinatio.*

38 Erasmus Ebner was lauded for having invented a new process of brass production and also funded the ducal brass foundry at Bündheim near Goslar. On Ebner's expertise in the service of Duke Heinrich the Younger see L. Ercker, *Rämelsbergk*, n.p. [45]. See also H. Kellenbenz, "Die unternehmerische Betätigung," 25; F. Tenner, "Die fürstliche braunschweigische Messinghütte," 88.

39 *Underschiedliche vorzeignus aller Bergart, Metall und anderer Nutzung so am Hartze und sonderlich am Ramesberg befunden werden.* E. Ebner, 'Bericht an Herzog Julius von Braunschweig'.

40 H.-J. Kraschewski, *Wirtschaftspolitik*, 127–128.

41 E. Ebner, "Bericht an Herzog Julius von Braunschweig," 494.

42 Ibid., 494–95.

43 F. Günther, "Versuch des Herzogs Julius zur Belebung des Bergbaus."

44 'Ab Conterfei der Schiffahrt uf der oker biß ke(en) Wulff(en)büttel," in *Inventarium über die im Wolfenbüttelschen Schlosse*, 1 Alt 25 Nr. 9 fol. 23r-34v, here 27 v, NLA WO. A transcription is published in B. Uppenkamp, "Ein Inventar von Schloß Wolfenbüttel," 79–91, here 84.

45 P. Lombaerde, "Hydraulic Projects," 104. The following publications classify Antwerp as model for the duke's urban transformations, O. De Smedt, "Wilhelm de Raet," 148; F. Thöne, "Wolfenbüttel unter Herzog Julius"; B. Uppenkamp, "Politische Macht – Architektonische Imagination," 62.

46 B. Uppenkamp, *Pentagon von Wolfenbüttel*.

47 Heinrich the Younger had already signed a contract with one of the most powerful merchants from Leipzig, i.e. Heinrich Cramer von Clausbruch, for the sale of an annual quantity of lead. Harz lead was mainly delivered to Thuringia and Saxony, where it was needed for refining silver ores. H.-J. Kraschewski, *Quellen zum Goslarer Bleihandel (525–1625)*; H.-J. Kraschewski, "Heinrich Cramer von Clausbruch."

48 For a very substantial overview on the Harz mining region, its subdivisions into different areas of dominion see: Bartels, "The Production." An in-depth analysis on financing and yields of lead mining at the Rammelsberg and the Upper Harz mining district in the years 1585–1586 is provided by H.-J. Kraschewski, "Zur Finanzierung"; H.-J. Kraschewski, "Relationen."

49 T. DaCosta Kaufmann, *The Mastery of Nature*, 174–94.

50 "Hat hernach einen solchen Vorrath von Bley gewiesen, welches übern Haufen gelegen, wie ein Berglein, hatte die Zeit Willens, die ganze Stadt Wolfenbüttel anstatt des Steinpflasters mit Blei zu besetzen, welches man in vorfallender Noth alle Zeit hätte wieder aufheben und gebrauchen mögen; welches Bleies Anzahl fast unglaublich gewesen." J. G. Büsching, ed. *Begebenheiten des Schlesischen Ritters Hans von Schweinichen*, 393f-384.

51 "Denn was allein an Bley allhier an Vorrath war, das wissen diejenigen, so es zur selben Zeit gesehen; geschweige derer anderen Bergwaaren, als von verarbeitetem Messing, Kupfer, Eisen, grünen und blauen Vitriol, Kupferrauch, Galmey, u.a., item an Rollen und Pfannenbley und von Bley gegossene Gartenleisten und Grasbänken und anderem Zierrath, Hirsch- und Reheköpfen, Kronenleuchtern, und allerley Sachen, daß auf solche Arbeit ein groß Geld gieng; daß solchen Vorrath (immaßen ich neben Andern ao. 1582 inventiren helfen, und laut meines Inventarii […] S. F. Gn. zusammen auf 7 Tonnen Goldes schätzen und denselben noch täglich vermehren ließen […]." F. Algermann, *Leben, Wandel und tödlichen Abgang*, 36.

52 G. Botero, *On the Causes of the Greatness*, 20.

53 Ibid., 44.

54 E. H. Ash, *Power, Knowledge, and Expertise*, 9.

55 Ibid., 216.

56  T. Müller, *Schifffahrt und Flösserei.*

57  "Dyses habe ich, Robbert Lobri, alz der elteste von ons vieren, ut befelch mins gnedigen Forsten und heren HH nach luyt minem pflicht und eyde mit eygner handt verzhegnet, nachdem ich vor lange jaeren von minem gnedigen Forsten und heren gesien und gehoert habe **dye goede zoeneygunge und begerte** [emphasis T.A.], dye sSin Forstlicher Gnaden alzeyt tzoe dusser Schipvart gehabt hat, darom dat Syn Forstlicher Gnaden woll gemerckt und gewost hatte, das soe grossen eindracht, comrespondens, verlichtung der armot, ockh Nutzs darin gelegen ist." 2 Alt Nr. 10376, fol. 12, NLA WO.

58  "Bericht von Heinrich Brocke und Ruprecht Lobri wegs Flössung der torffe uf dem Radau dem 25 octobris anno 70." 2 Alt Nr. 10349, 21r-24r, 21r, NLA WO.

59  "[…] das wir etzliche Niderländer wissen, die sich erbotten haben, uf ihre uncosten und um ein zimblich zinß, die dorf uff dem Rottbruch zustechen und zu drocknen, Ittem kalch und Ziegelstein bey Büntheim zu brennen [insertion from the duke: (?) alles auff zueselbst unkosten] sich auf deß ortts zubesetzen […]." 2 Alt Nr. 10349, fols. 50r-51v, 51rv, NLA WO.

60  2 Alt Nr. 10350, fols. 6r-8r, NLA WO.

61  "und darmit gleichwol E.F.G. eines solichen aufsehnlichen Platzes khünfftiglich geniessen möchten, were der beste weg, weil sy berichtet(?), das etliche Leutte, sonderlich auß Hollandt und der Ortt, da auß Morast albereit fruchtbar Landt gemacht worden, fürhanden, welche der ding erfahren, und alda ir heill, und soliches gleiche gestalt Zuverfügen und anzurichten verhofften, daß E.F.G. denselbigen underschiedliche Plez außtheilet, und ein zeitlang guete freyheit, auch zugeben im anfang notwendig holz geen und darnach wann die freiheit erloschen ein ziemlichen Zins […] [nehmen]." Ibid. fol. 7 v.

62  The passage in the ducal mandate is quoted in Ernst Rhamm's study: "Kettwig (soll) den 600 Niederländern, die ihres Glaubens halber bedrängt und ausgewandert, sofern sie sich der Kirchenordnung unterwerfen und ein mäßiges Schutzgeld zahlen, Aufenthalt anbieten, namentlich ihnen die Gelegenheit vermelden wegen des rothen Bruches auf dem harz, dabei von Alters her die Heerstraße gegangen, daß dort nicht allein guter tauglicher Torf die Menge vorhanden, sondern mit der Zeit bei anhaltendem Fleiße Ackerbau und Wiesenwachs gewonnen werden könne und solle ihnen nach Hufen und Morgen zugemessen werden." E. Rhamm, *Die betrüglichen Goldmacher*, 84, n. 64.

63  "Protocollum was In Julii obren Herren gemacht mit Wilhelmen de Rauh(?) am 5 Septembris anno 74 fürgelauffen." 2 Alt Nr. 10353 fols. 21r-30v, 21r, NLA WO

64  E. Rhamm, *Die Betrüglichen Goldmacher*, 9.

65  Ibid., 45.

66  "Wie D F. G. ihme bereit vermeldet, und sehen gern dass davon etwas bestendiges zur Probe mache angerichtet werde. Damit ehr nicht mit schimpf wieder hinein ins Niederlandt und von hinnen [..] und zeigt an wie der gefangene Herzog Johann Friedrich an S F G. ezliche Leute von Alchimisten verschrieben die sich ein hohes verheissen aber nichts Prestirt sondern bößlich und vergessentlich Sr F. G. und ihrem Gemahl nach leib und leben getrachtet und S. F. G. auff in die 100000 thaler schaden zugefügt. Dafür sie den jetze auch iren verdienst erhalten werden, und ein bößes geschrey hetten, das machte alles ihr böses wesen und das sie viel versprochen und nichts ins werck richten oder prosperiren konnten, Solichs möchte S. F. f. Ime Rath nicht gönnen, sondern vielmehr das ehr durch ein bestendig und ewig wehrendes werck einen gutten nahmen und also S. F. F. Landschafft gunst und (?) gewinnen möchte." 2 Alt Nr. 10353 fols. 21r-21v, NLA WO.

67  L. Fontaine, *The Moral Economy*, esp. 268–96.

68  "They should visit the places and consider how to realise floating and navigation. They should start and carry out the project from their 'own financial resources, at their own risk and at their own expense." (fol. 58–59) The conditions are followed by a number

of privileges relating to future profits. Should de Raet manage to realise the company as well as the shipping he will be rewarded with 10000 thaler (fol. 61). Bestallungsurkunde de Raet, 25th July 1575, 2 Alt Nr. 10354, fols. 57–63, NLA WO.

69 E. Rhamm, *Die betrüglichen Goldmacher*; T. Nummedal, *Alchemy and Authority*, esp. 73–95.

70 For further literature on Julius' interest in alchemy, his collections of alchemical literature and alchemical practices at his court, see: T. Nummedal, *Alchemy and Authority*; P. Feuerstein-Herz and S. Laube, eds., *Goldenes Wissen*.

71 "vormittelst gottlicher hulffe [es] soweit bringen […], das man zu waser mit pramschieffen aus der Oker bis in die Elbe und so hinwieder zuruckkommen […] ungeachtet das solchs fast von allen leuten dieser landorter vur unmuglich gehalten, ehr auch durch solchs sein furhaben vieler ungunst und wiederwertige verfolgung uf sich laden wurde [..]." 2 Alt Nr. 10354, fols. 57–63, 58, NLA WO

72 "[…] das in neulicher Zeitt unseren lieben getreuen Wilhelm de Rath (aus Harzogenbusch unter dem König zu Spanien geboren) welcher im ganzen Niderlandt seiner kunst halber und das er Baw: und wasserverstendig bey jedermann wolbescheint […]." 2 Alt Nr. 10354, fols. 27r-31r, 28 v. NLA WO.

73 2 Alt Nr. 10376, fols. 7–10, NLA WO.

74 "Dieser abriß bedeutet die zukünftige Schiffahrt von dem okerflus in die elbe an die stat magdeburgh und ferner mitt Gottlicher hülfe dem Churffurstlichen Sachsischen Berckwergk zum besten mit bley umb gelt oder ander wahren umbzusetzen, zu schiffen seien mochte, also mit allen anderen diversen Landesfruchte zu comresponderen und eines des anderen zu provenderen habe, und jdes Furstenthume, Landtstenden ihre selbsts eigene erworben Landesfruchten freyhe umbsünste auff die Schiffart zu passeren, ihre Getrede und Victualien und anders, nichts außgenommen, auch gleicher gestelt da der diversen Chur- und Furstenthumen, geistliche und weltliche regirunge, bauren, bürger, vom adel und die ritterschaft, prelaten, Grafen, der erblingen des thumcapites ihre diversen gemurte korn-heuisser und spicher, ihre getrette und victualia in vorrat zu habebn bei den wasserfleussen der zukünfftigen Schiffahrt." 2 Alt Nr. 10376, fol. 4, NLA WO.

75 "[…] eine Shipfahrt [kann] woll gemacht werden als nemlich mitten in dem vorschrieven Brogh, und das sollte mins erachtens nit voell kosten." 2 Alt Nr. 10376, fol. 11, NLA WO; "[…] und gleich Wilhelm de Raet nach besichtigung und nachdragent hier oenen vermelt das tzoe der verschrieven Schipfahrt van die oker nach die elbe mit nicht so groete kosten tzuemaken sy[…]." Ibid., 16.

76 "Alles, dat uth der Schipvart gegraeven werdet, das ist dem meysten deyl thorff, und der thorff solte voell mer wert sin, alzs dat Graevent kost, im Stift Halberstat an die Bronswighse Grentzs, dar alrede im Stift dat Holz düir ist." Ibid.

77 O. De Smedt, "Guglielmo de Raet."

78 2 Alt Nr. 10363, NLA WO

79 C. Römer, "Erste Schritte nach Amsterdam."

80 On the connection of expertise and the early modern state: E. H. Ash, "Introduction."

# Bibliography

*Manuscript*

Niedersächsisches Landesarchiv Standort Hannover, Cal. Br. 21, Nr. 1264.
Niedersächsisches Landesarchiv Standort Wolfenbüttel, 1 Alt 23 Nr. 16; 1 Alt 25 Nr. 9; 2 Alt 8105; 2 Alt Nr. 10349; 2 Alt Nr. 10350; 2 Alt Nr. 10353; 2 Alt Nr. 10354; 2 Alt Nr. 10363; 2 Alt Nr. 10376.

*Print*

Akerloff, George A. and Robert J. Shiller *Animal Spirits: How Human Psychology Drives the Economy, and Why It Matters for Global Capitalism*. Princeton: Princeton University Press, 2009.

Algermann, Franz. *Leben, Wandel und tödlichen Abgang weiland des Durchlauchtigen Hochgebornen Fürsten und Herrn, Herrn Juliussen, Herzogen zu Braunschweig und Lüneburg, hochlöblichen, christmilden Gedächtnisses [...] Anno 1598*, edited by Friedrich Karl von Strombeck. Helmstedt: C. G. Fleckeisenschen Buchhandlung, 1823.

Ash, Eric H. *Power, Knowledge, and Expertise in Elizabethan England*. Baltimore, MD: John Hopkins University Press, 2004.

Ash, Eric H. "Introduction: Expertise and the Early Modern State." *Osiris* 25 (2010): 1–24.

Asmussen, Tina . "Wild Man in Braunschweig: Economies of Hope and Fear in Early Modern Mining." *Renaissance Studies* 34, no. 1 (2020): 31–56.

Bartels, Christoph. "The Production of Silver, Copper, and Lead in the Harz Mountains from Late Medieval Times to the Onset of the Industrialization." In *Materials and Expertise in Early Modern Europe. Between Market and Laboratory*, edited by Ursula Klein and Emma C. Spary, 71–81. Chicago: University of Chicago Press, 2010.

Bartels, Christoph. *Vom frühneuzeitlichen Montangewerbe zur Bergbauindustrie: Erzbergbau im Oberharz 1635–1866*. Bochum: Deutsches Bergbau-Museum Bochum, 1992.

Beckert, Jens. *Imagined Futures: Fictional Expectations and Capitalist Dynamics*. Cambridge, MA: Harvard University Press, 2016.

Bodemann, Eduard. "Die Volkswirtschaft des Herzogs Julius von Braunschweig." *Zeitschrift für Deutsche Culturgeschichte* 1 (1872): 197–238.

Botero, Giovanni. *On the Causes of the Greatness and Magnificence of Cities 1588*. Translated by Geoffrey Symcox. Toronto: University of Toronto Press, 2012.

Büsching, Johann Gustav, ed. *Lieben, Lust und Leben der Deutschen des sechzehnten Jahrhunderts in den Begebenheiten des Schlesischen Ritters Hans von Schweinichen von ihm selbbst aufgesetzt*. Vol. 1. Breslau: Josef, 1820.

Cook, Harold J. *Matters of Exchange: Commerce, Medicine, and Science in the Dutch Golden Age*. New Haven, CT: Yale University Press, 2007.

Cooper, Alix. "'The Possibilities of the Land'. The Inventory of "Natural Riches" in the Early Modern German Territories." *History of Political Economy* 35 (2003): 129–53.

DaCosta Kaufmann, Thomas. *The Mastery of Nature. Aspects of Art, Science and Humanism in the Renaissance*. Princeton: University Press, 1993.

Darmstaedter, Ernst. *Berg-, Probir- und Kunstbüchlein*. Munich: Verl. d. Münchner Drucke, 1926.

Davids, Karel. *The Rise and Decline of Dutch Technological Leadership: Technology, Economy and Culture in the Netherlands, 1350–1800*. Vol. 1. Leiden: Brill, 2008.

De Smedt, Oskar. "Guglielmo de Raet e la Bonifica del Territorio Lucchese." *La Provincia di Lucca* 3, no. 2 (1969): 29–41.

De Smedt, Oskar. "Wilhelm de Raet, Baumeister und Ingenieur (ca. 1537–1583)." *Braunschweigisches Jahrbuch für Landesgeschichte* 46 (1965): 147–150.

De Smedt, Oskar. "Willem de Raet, Bouwmeester en Ingenieur (ca. 1537–1583). Een voorloping bestek." *Bulletin de l'Institut Historique Belge de Rome* 36 (1964): 33–68.

Dupré, Sven, Bert De Muck and Thomas Werner, eds. *Embattled Territory: The Circulation of Knowledge in the Spanish Netherlands*. Gent: Academia Press, 2015.

Ebner, Erasmus. "Bericht an Herzog Julius von Braunschweig vom 26. Jenner 1572. Mit mineralogischen, metallurgischen und chemischen Anmerkungen vom Zehntner Meyer und vom Bergamts-Auditor Hausmann." In *Hercynisches Archiv, oder Beiträge zur Kunde des Harzes und seiner Nachbarländer*, edited by Christian Erdwin and Philipp Holzmann, 494–540. Halle: Verlag der Buchhandlung des Waisenhauses1805.

Ercker, Lazarus. *Rämelsbergk und desselbigen Bergkwercks ein kurtzer bericht*. S.l.: s.n., 1565.

Kellenbenz, Hermann. "Die unternehmerische Betätigung der verschiedenen Stände." *Vierteljahresschrift für Sozial- und Wirtschaftsgeschichte* 44 (1957): 1–25.

Feuerstein-Herz, Petra and Stefan Laube, eds. *Goldenes Wissen: die Alchemie – Substanzen, Synthesen, Symbolik*. Wiesbaden: Harrassowitz, 2014.

Fontaine, Laurence. *The Moral Economy: Poverty, Credit and Trust in Early Modern Europe*. Cambridge: Cambridge University Press, 2014.

Frevert, Ute. "Gefühle und Kapitalismus." In *Kapitalismus. Historische Annäherungen*, edited by Gunilla Budde, 50–72. Göttingen: Vandenhoeck & Ruprecht, 2011.

Goldgar, Anne. *Tulipmania: Money, Honor, and Knowledge in the Dutch Golden Age*. Chicago: University of Chicago Press, 2007.

Goldgar, Anne. "Nature as Art: The Case of the Tulip." In *Merchants and Marvels: Commerce, Science, and Art in Early Modern Europe*, edited by Pamela H. Smith and Paula Findlen, 324–46. New York: Routledge, 2002.

Graefe, Julia, ed. *Staatsklugheit und Frömmigkeit. Herzog Julius zu Braunschweig Lüneburg, ein norddeutscher Landesherr des 16. Jahrhunderts*. Weinheim: VCH, Acta Humaniora, 1989.

Günther, Friedrich. "Ein Versuch des Herzogs Julius zur Belebung des Bergbaus." *Harz Verein für Geschichte und Altertumskunde* 43 (1910): 107–17.

Hamm, Bernd. *Promission, Pactum, Ordinatio: Freiheit und Selbstbindung Gottes in der scholastischen Gnadenlehre*. Tübingen: Mohr Siebek, 1977.

Henschke, Ekkehard. *Landesherrschaft und Bergbauwirtschaft. Zur Wirtschafts- und Verwaltungsgeschichte des Oberharzer Bergbaugebietes im 16. und 17. Jahrhundert*. Berlin: Dunker und Humblot, 1974.

Keller, Vera and TedMcCormick. "Towards a History of Projects." *Early Science and Medicine* 21 (2016): 423–44.

Koch, Manfred. *Geschichte und Entwicklung des bergmännischen Schrifttums*. Goslar: Hübener, 1963.

Kraschewski, Hans-Joachim. "Organisationsstrukturen der Bergbauverwaltung als Element des frühneuzeitlichen Territorialstaates. Das Beispiel Braunschweig Wolfenbüttel." *Niedersächsisches Jahrbuch für Landesgeschichte* 80 (2008): 283–328.

Kraschewski, Hans-Joachim. "Bergbau und Hüttenwesen." In *Die Wirtschafts- und Sozialgeschichte des Braunschweigischen Landes vom Mittelalter bis zur Gegenwart*, edited by Karl Heinrich Kaufhold,Jörg Leuschner, and Claudia Märtl, 689–735. Hildesheim: Olms, 2008.

Kraschewski, Hans-Joachim. *Quellen zum Goslarer Bleihandel (525-1625)*. Hildesheim: August Lax, 1990.

Kraschewski, Hans-Joachim. "Heinrich Cramer von Clausbruch und seine Handelsverbindungen mit Herzog Julius von Braunschweig Wolfenbüttel. Zur Geschichte des Fernhandels mit Blei und Vitriol in der zweiten Hälfte des 16. Jahrhunderts." *Braunschweigisches Jahrbuch für Landesgeschichte* 66 (1985): 115–28.

Kraschewski, Hans-Joachim. "Zur Finanzierung des Bergbaus auf Blei am Rammelsberg und dem Oberharz im 16. Jahrhundert am Beispiel der Wolfenbütteler Kammerrechnungen: Aus dem Rechnungsbook des Landesfürsten 'Camer Rechnung Trinitatis 1585 bis wieder Trinitatis 1586'." *Braunschweigisches Jahrbuch für Landesgeschichte* 70 (1989): 61–104.

Kraschewski, Hans-Joachim. "Über Relationen zwischen Produktionsmengen, Kosten und Preisen von Harzer Blei und Glätte in der zweiten Hälfte des 16. Jahrhunderts." *Der Anschnitt* 39: 2/3 (1987): 3–64.

Kraschewski, Hans-Joachim. *Wirtschaftspolitik im Deutschen Territoralstaat des 16. Jahrhunderts.* Köln: Böhlau, 1978.

Kraschewski, Hans-Joachim. "Der ökonomische Fürst. Herzog Julius als Unternehmer-Verleger der Wirtschaft seines Landes, besonders des Harz-Bergbaus." In *Staatsklugheit und Frömmigkeit: Herzog Julius zu Braunschweig Lüneburg, ein norddeutscher Landesherr des 16. Jahrhunderts*, edited by Julia Graefe, 41–57. Weinheim: VCH, Acta Humaniora, 1989.

Lipińska, Aleksandra. "Alabasterdiplomatie. Material als Medium Herrschaftlicher Repräsentation und als Vernetzungsinstrument in Mittel- und Osteuropa des 16. Jahrhunderts." *Kunsttexte.de/Ostblick* 2 (2014). www.kunsttexte.de/ostblick.

Lombaerde, Piet. "Antwerp in its Golden Age: 'One of the Largest Cities in the Low Countries" and "One of the Best Fortified in Europe'." In *Urban Achievement in Early Modern Europe: Golden Ages in Antwerp, Amsterdam and London*, edited by Patrick O'Brien, 99–127. Cambridge: Cambridge University Press, 2001.

Lombaerde, Piet. "Hydraulic Projects by Hans Vredeman de Vries and their Related Construction Problems." In *Hans Vredeman De Vries And the Artes Mechanicae Revisited*, edited by Piet Lombaerde, 101–15. Turnhout: Brepols Publishers, 2005.

Long, Pamela O. "The Openness of Knowledge: An Ideal and Its Context in 16th-Century Writings on Mining and Metallurgy." *Technology and Culture* 32 (1991): 318–55.

Margócsy, Dániel. *Commercial Visions: Science, Trade and Visual Culture in the Dutch Golden Age.* Chicago: University of Chicago Press, 2014.

Massumi, Brian. *Parables for the Virtual: Movement, Affect, Sensation.* Durham, NC: Duke University Press 2002.

Mokyr, Joel. *The Lever of Riches: Technological Creativity and Economic Progress.* Oxford: Oxford University Press, 1990.

Mokyr, Joel. *Gifts of Athena: Historical Origins of the Knowledge Economy.* Princeton: Princeton University Press, 2002.

Moran, Bruce T. "German Prince-Practitioners: Aspects in the Development of Courtly Science, Technology, and Procedures in the Renaissance." *Technology and Culture* 22 (1981): 253–74.

Moran, Bruce T. *The Alchemical World of the German Court: Occult Philosophy and Chemical Medicine in the Circle of Moritz of Hessen (1572-1632).* Stuttgart: Franz Steiner Verlag, 1991.

Müller, Theodor. *Schifffahrt und Flösserei im Flussgebiet der Oker.* Braunschweig: Waisenhaus-Buchdruckerei und Verlag, 1968

Nanz, Klaus-Peter. *Die Entstehung des allgemeinen Vertragsbegriffs im 16. bis 18. Jahrhundert.* Tübingen/München: Schweitzer, 1985.

Nummedal, Tara. *Alchemy and Authority in the Holy Roman Empire.* Chicago: Chicago University Press, 2007.

Parshall, Peter. "Imago Contrafacta: Images and Facts in the Northern Renaissance." *Art History* 16 (1993): 554–79.

Pitz, Ernst. *Landeskulturtechnik, Markscheide- und Vermessungswesen im Herzogtum Braunschweig bis zum Ende des 18. Jahrhunderts.* Göttingen: Vandenhoeck & Ruprecht, 1967.

Rhamm, Ernst. *Die betrüglichen Goldmacher am Hofe des Herzogs Julius von Braunschweig: Nach den Proceßakten.* Wolfenbüttel: Julius Zwißler, 1883.

Roberts, Lissa, ed. *Centres and Cycles of Accumulation in and Around the Netherlands During the Early Modern.* Period Berlin: Lit-Verlag, 2011.

Römer, Christof. "Erste Schritte nach Amsterdam. Die Niederlande Handels- und Kreditpolitik des Fürstenturms Braunschweig Wolfenbüttel nach 1576." In *The

*Interactions of Amsterdam and Antwerp with the Baltic Region, 1400–1800*, edited by Wiert Jan Wieringa, 43–50. Leiden: Nijhoff, 1983.

Sack, Carl. "Herzog Julius von Braunschweig Lüneburg als Fabrikant von Bergwerks-Erzeugnissen des Harzes sowie als Kaufmann. 1568ff." *Zeitschrift des Harzvereins für Geschichte und Altertumskunde* 3 (1870): 305–27.

Swan, Claudia. "Ad vivum, naer het leven, from the Life: Defining a Mode of Representation." *Word & Image* 11 (1995): 353–72.

Stäheli, Urs. "Hoffnung als ökonomischer Affekt." In *Kultur der Ökonomie. Zur Materialität und Performanz des Wirtschaftlichen*, edited by Inga Klein and Sonja Windmüller, 283–300. Bielefeld: Transcript, 2014.

Tenner, Friedrich. "Die fürstliche braunschweigische Messinghütte zu Bündheim." *Zeitschrift des Harzvereins für Geschichte und Altertumskunde* 67 (1934): 81–117.

Thöne, Friedrich. "Hans Vredeman de Vries in Wolfenbüttel." *Braunschweigisches Jahrbuch für Landesgeschichte* 41 (1960): 47–68.

Thöne, Friedrich. "Wolfenbüttel unter Herzog Julius (1568–1589): Topographie und Baugeschichte." *Braunschweigisches Jahrbuch für Landesgeschichte* 22 (1952): 1–74.

Thöne, Friedrich. *Wolfenbüttel: Geist und Glanz einer alten Residenz*. München: F. Brückmann KG, 1963.

Uppenkamp, Barbara. "Ein Inventar von Schloß Wolfenbüttel aus der Zeit des Herzogs Julius." In *Kunst und Repräsentation. Studien zur europäischen Hofkultur im 16. Jahrhundert*, edited by Heiner Borggrefe and Barbara Uppenkamp, 69–108. Lemgo: Weserrenaissance-Museum Schloß Brake, 2002.

Uppenkamp, Barbara. "Politische Macht – Architektonische Imagination? Zur Politik als architektonische Wissenschaft am Beispiel Wolfenbüttels um 1600." In *Machträume der Frühneuzeitlichen Stadt*, edited by Christian Hochmuth and Susanne Rau, 59–74. Konstanz: UVK Verlagsgesellschaft mbH, 2006.

Uppenkamp, Barbara. *Das Pentagon von Wolfenbüttel: Der Ausbau der welfischen Residenz 1568–1626 zwischen Ideal und Wirklichkeit*. Hannover: Hahn, 2005.

Weller, Marc-Philippe. *Die Vertragstreue: Vertragsbindung – Naturalerfüllungsgrundsatz – Leistungstreue*. Tübingen: Mohr Siebeck, 2009.

Yamamoto, Koji. *Taming Capitalism Before its Triumph: Public Service, Distrust & Projecting in Early Modern England*. Oxford: Oxford University Press, 2018.

Zimmermann, Paul. "Herzog Julius in Volkswirtschaftlicher Beziehung." *Hansische Geschichtsblätter* 32 (1905): 35–62.

# 5

# THE SECRET OF AMSTERDAM

## Politics, alchemy and the commodification of knowledge in the 17th century

*Martin Mulsow*

## Knowledge as a commodity

At the end of July 1688, Frederick I, Duke of Saxe-Gotha-Altenburg, suddenly and unexpectedly set off for Amsterdam.[1] He stayed there for a month, and then returned home by a circuitous route. What had he been doing in Amsterdam? In order to answer this question, it will be necessary to unravel a complicated network of activities: speculation on the stock market and trading in wood, hiring out troops and buying works of art, political negotiations and experiments in alchemy. We will have to establish the precise communicative radius of each of these activities (what was 'public', what was secret, what was top secret?), the political and economic strategies behind them, and the emotional or affective components that accompanied these strategies. We will see that at the heart of these activities, highly charged with expectations, lay the quest for practical knowledge of how to create gold. And this gold was to be used to support all the rest: increasing the number of troops, acquiring land, buying raw materials, and ultimately, exerting political influence.

Dániel Margócsy has recently described how 17th-century scholars turned knowledge into a commodity.[2] They had to consider the cost of transport and trade routes when sending each other books, fossils, drawings or impressions of coins;[3] they scored points over their competitors in the republic of letters as soon as they had valuable epistemic gifts to distribute along with goods;[4] they pragmatically sold the know-how they were able to offer.[5] The cultural grammar of these 'commercial visions' emerged early in the United Netherlands, which was perhaps the first knowledge society of modern times.[6] But what did this sort of commodification of knowledge look like from the perspective of a prince rather than that of a scholar? We are talking about a petty prince who, like many others in the same position, engaged in 'scientific' activities as a passionate alchemist, and also like many others in the same position, was an entrepreneur.[7] While Margócsy calls his active scientists and traders 'entrepreneurial practitioners', thus understanding scholarship in both its social[8] and economic sense, the entrepreneurial spirit had a much more tangible aspect for princes. They were active in politics, the military, economics and culture, all at the same time. Cultural entrepreneurship, as Joel Mokyr has shown, can have a potentially large impact on all sectors of society.[9] Yet the insight that the commodification of knowledge was always embedded in other commercial and cultural activities has, so far, had little impact on historiography. In general, scholars study the history of science *or* political history *or* economic history.

A modern history of knowledge, by contrast, provides a chance to see in context all the practices that surround different forms of knowledge – explicit and implicit, scholarly and social, administrative and political – in a sort of *histoire totale*.[10] A prince is an obvious choice of subject for such a study, as his 'entrepreneurship' consists of co-ordinating and weighing up against each other various forms of knowledge and options for action, as if in a game. This sort of 'game' can only be analysed in a case study offering a thick description of one actor over a few weeks, as we are attempting to do here; otherwise the complexity gets out of hand. But such a study should certainly generate insights from which further inferences may be drawn.

Amsterdam is an obvious place for this case study to focus on because in the late 17th century it was unparalleled as a point of interchange for worldwide trade, streams of information and political-military events.[11] Yet it is clear that any such study, even if it starts in one particular place, must be transnational, because as a crossroads, a location points beyond itself. We will soon see that our story is no longer just about relations between Amsterdam and Gotha but also about Paris and its expansionist ambitions, England and its Glorious Revolution and the obligations of the Holy Roman Empire.

By beginning with the micro-state of Gotha, we are, as it were, probing Amsterdam as a centre of knowledge from the outside: what was the duke doing? How did he behave in a town that must have far exceeded his expectations and knowledge of commerce? What was his emotional reaction? What practices did he employ? What information did he turn into economic capital, or try to? How can we decode the milieu of alchemy in Amsterdam using his contacts?

Many sources cast light on Frederick's stay in Amsterdam. Although the duke's diaries,[12] which otherwise provide the most productive basis for any reconstruction, are only extant up to 1686 and there is no research about his late years from 1687 to his death in 1691, a great deal of other material is available: letters from his agent, invoices for accommodation, his correspondence with an alchemist and with the administration in Gotha, his correspondence with his chancellor, an official travel diary, details about the political context, sources from Dutch archives, a diary listing the alchemical processes carried out and the statues acquired for the palace in Gotha, and even small scraps of paper containing the ciphers used to encode news. This wealth of material can be made to tell us what the duke was doing, in the greatest secrecy, during these summer months.[13]

In the following we will let Frederick guide us through the different milieus and activities that interest us. By following his journey bit by bit, we get into the problem of relations with France (Section "The official journey"), the information trade in Amsterdam, in particular with alchemical recipes (Section "Job Meyer – Amsterdam"), down to the canals where chemical substances were produced. At this stage, we will then come to the central point of the alchemical knowledge trade (Section "An alchemist appears"): Frederick met a true alchemist, who offered him new opportunities for the production of gold and universal medicine. How did a 'provider' and a 'buyer' behave in a 'market' that as such did not yet have fixed rules, let alone open ones? One problem for the buyer, Frederick, was that he had to keep the trade hidden from his own secret council at home in Gotha. He therefore chose – this will be our thesis – the pretext of a timber trade to satisfy the chamber councils (Section "Wood"). In reality, however, Frederick, with his Dutch agent and his alchemical expert, set about putting the alchemical prescriptions into practice on the spot, as we shall see. Since we have his alchemical diary, we will be able to reconstruct day after day what chemical experiments he has done (Section "Drinkable gold").

But the story is not over yet. As with a good drama, there are complications that delay it. Frederick had difficulty redeeming his bill at the bank (Section "Financial matters"). This gives us the opportunity to return to the economic and financial aspects of the journey. What did Frederick do? Why did the alchemist have debts that Frederick needed to pay? How much was he to pay? It will turn out that both Frederick and the alchemist were participants in speculative buying on the stock exchange (Section "On the stock exchange"). The new stock market thus cast its shadow over the covert market of the alchemical knowledge economy. We will learn that global aspects of the ore trade and transnational networks such as the Jewish black market traders played their part.

And then again – the last twist of the drama – there were political aspects. France was preparing for a campaign on the German territories on the left bank of the Rhine; in England, the Glorious Revolution began. For Frederick, it was a great lure to speculate not only on the secret alchemical market but also on the equally secret market of hiring out soldiers. His relations with France gave him hope to make the big money here as well (Section "Enticements of the French"). We will see him switching back and forth between steaming vials and couriers riding to Paris, all in great secrecy and euphoria. At this point we arrive at the affective parameters of the new knowledge economy. Speculation, euphoria, haste, risk-taking and secrecy were the ingredients that fuelled the entrepreneurialism of the prince, by which he was obviously swept away.

## The official journey

Frederick's visit to Amsterdam in August of 1688 was not his first. It was almost like a coda to a long journey which had begun the previous year and did not end until April 1688. This journey had been long prepared. Frederick had set out on

August 12, 1687, with a retinue of almost 60 people. His chamberlain, Johann Christoph Emmerling, was instructed to record all the details of the journey, and in particular, to describe all the sights that they intended to visit.[14] They arrived in Amsterdam on September 11 and stayed there for a week. Then, travelling via a number of other Dutch towns, they got to Brussels at the beginning of October, and were in Paris by the middle of that month. Paris seems to have been the main point of the journey, as Frederick was keen to be received by Louis XIV.

The official diary does not mention the deeper reason behind Frederick's audience. Louis XIV had, for some time, been wooing individual German princes in order to detach them from the alliance that had formed within the Holy Roman Empire against his aggressive policy of territorial expansion.[15] Now, as Louis was seeking more territory,[16] Frederick was sounding out what a clandestine collaboration with Gotha was worth to the French. Gotha, in fact, formed part of the Empire's defences in the Imperial circle of Upper Saxony, but the antagonism between Brandenburg and Saxony paralysed this circle's capacity to act, leaving the smaller actors such as Saxe-Gotha-Altenburg free to seek their own alliances. Competition within the Ernestine branch of the ruling family played a part in this: while Saxe-Weimar tended to support Electoral Saxony, which was part of the Albertine branch, Frederick I, although technically part of the League of Augsburg, was secretly also looking elsewhere. On November 12 in Paris, he made some calculations about troop contingents in his notebook (Figure 5.1)[17] – a rather ludicrous projection, according to which hiring out four regiments of soldiers would bring in 19,200 ducats per day, thus 87,600 per week, and as much as 5,990,400, or more than 11 million thaler, per year. '*Summa summarum*', he concluded, 'an outlay of 312,000 thaler, 3 million, 1 ton of gold' would yield a profit of '8 million, 8 tons of gold, 60,800 thaler'.

These are very strange calculations. Frederick played mind games of this sort from time to time;[18] he liked to imagine what he could do with the money to be made by hiring out soldiers, or with the gold to be produced by alchemy. These daydreams are the clearest expression of his entrepreneurial traits. But calculating was important for Frederick, as we will see again and again. It was a practice that should help to orient oneself in situations where there was little economic orientation. There was still no official 'market' – not, in any case, for hiring out troops – where it was easy to decide what the better offer was and how to weigh it against the risks. In Paris, the calculations provided the specific background for his cautious approach to Louis XIV, his talks with the Dauphin and his German wife, Maria Anna of Bavaria, and various diplomats.[19] We will see later how potentially explosive all this was. After all, Louis was the enemy of the Holy Roman Empire.

Before he left, Frederick received a most valuable present from Louis, a diamond-bordered miniature portrait of the king (Figure 5.2), worth more than 20.000 Reichsthalers.[20] These were the kind of gifts Louis used to commit the German princes to himself and signaled to them that they could possibly do business with him.

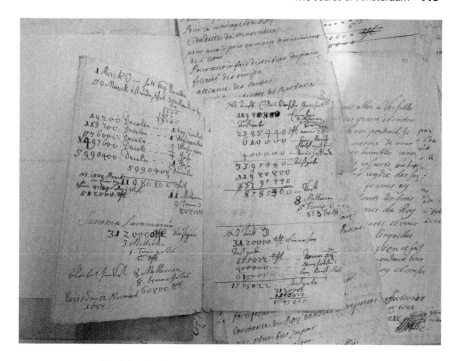

**FIGURE 5.1**  Frederick's calculations in Paris. ThStA Gotha, Kammer Immediate Nr. 1759, fol. 34v/35r. Courtesy of the Thüringisches Staatsarchiv Gotha

The travelling company continued on its way, going via Basel, Strasbourg, Stuttgart and Heidelberg to Darmstadt, where Frederick was able to see his sister, Elisabeth Dorothea, who was regent there. But he became seriously ill and spent the whole of February and March in bed, until he was able to rouse himself again to continue the journey via Frankfurt and Kassel, arriving back in Gotha on 15 April. We have a detailed medical report on Frederick, dated May, that lists the medicine he was given, and establishes that he was fully recovered.[21] And then, after just a few months in Gotha, he set off again. Why? Frederick said, somewhat enigmatically, that he was 'obliged, because of some letters received, to take a mail coach to Holland'.[22] This time, he travelled with the mail coach and a very small escort. This was not an official matter of state like the last trip. What letters had he received?

## Job Meyer – Amsterdam

In order to find out, we must turn our attention to the man who maintained a connection with Frederick from Amsterdam. During his brief stay in The Hague in September 1687, Frederick had met Job Meyer, who worked as an agent for the Archbishop-Elector of Trier, Johann VIII Hugo von Orsbeck.[23] Frederick had used his stay in The Hague to make enquiries about an alchemist he had employed

**FIGURE 5.2**   Diamond bordered Miniature Portrait of Louis XIV by goldsmith-jeweler Laurent Tessier Montarsy (?–1684): Miniature painting, silver, and diamond. OA12280 © RMN-Grand Palais/Art Resource, NY/Jean-Gilles Berizzi.

and paid a few years earlier, Rittmeister (cavalry captain) Johann Heinrich Vierorth. Alchemy was Frederick's favourite occupation, and he had invested large amounts of money in it since 1679. As we will see, it lay at the heart of his political

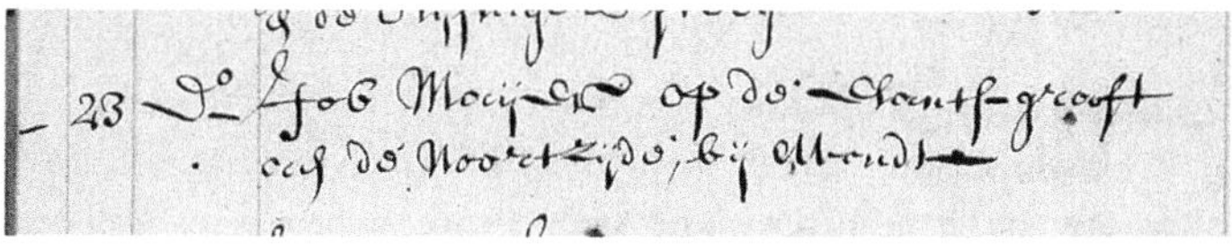

**FIGURE 5.3** Entry of Job Meyer as resident in the Elandsgracht. Stadsarchief Amsterdam

hopes of restoring Saxe-Gotha to significance.[24] Frederick had paid his first adviser in the field of alchemy, Baron von Gastorff, 60,000 gulden by the time he lost confidence in him in 1683 when, after years of experiments, Gastorff had achieved no results in terms of making gold.[25] Thereafter Frederick was more cautious about paying advances, but he nevertheless employed further advisers whom he paid at least a few thousand gulden. Vierorth had been one of them. Imprisoned for debt in Amsterdam in the spring of 1685, he had apparently died in an escape attempt.[26] He was thus unable to send Frederick the 'process', that is, the recipe for making gold, as he had intended. Thereupon Frederick had dispatched Johann Otto Hellwig to Amsterdam with instructions to look for Vierorth's papers. He was interested not only in the description of the 'process' but also in recovering his own letters to Vierorth, as they were potentially compromising.[27] Hellwig established contact with Isaak Telgens, a merchant with an interest in alchemy,[28] who had granted Vierorth some financial flexibility. In 1686 Telgens sent what he had of Vierorth's papers to Frederick. But there had also been highly secret papers which Vierorth had been wearing on his body when he died: in particular, a document containing a mysterious 'Processus', which probably described how to create gold. Telgens had no access to these because the authorities had confiscated them after the prisoner's death. Meyer was instructed to look for them, and this was the mission that Frederick paid him for.

Meyer lived as a trader in Amsterdam, dealing in art as well as information. This was typical of the new form of knowledge economy, which now was becoming more and more established. His house or apartment was full of pictures and sculptures, and when foreigners went to Amsterdam, they were shown around the apartment and made offers for anything they wanted to buy.[29] In particular, statues by the sculptor Bartholomäus Eggers, who was well known to Meyer, aroused great interest among princes and diplomats, who wanted to see likenesses of themselves in the Baroque manner. Meyer sold them sculptures, or brokered orders. In 1688 he was toying with the idea of moving to a larger house and setting up the sculptures in its back garden.[30] It seems that his business was doing well. Frederick had a price list drawn up for statues by Eggers for his palace: for example, a Maria, an Adonis and an Andromeda or a sculpture of Venus,[31] which cost 750 gulden.[32]

But Frederick was mostly interested in Meyer because he had many contacts in Amsterdam. Meyer promised to enquire about Vierorth's secret 'process' as soon as he was back in Amsterdam from The Hague. Finally, he received the complete text.[33]

Now it was a matter of seeing whether it would work, and Meyer began experimenting. Was he capable of doing it? At the time of his death in 1699, at least, Meyer was living on the Elandsgracht, two streets from the Looiersgracht (Figure 5.3).[34] There were industries in the area that worked with chemical processes. Galenus Abrahamsz had taken over Johann Rudolf Glauber's workshop there. Glauber had produced mineral (inorganic) acids and many other products, but Galenus concentrated mainly on manufacturing soap, while also continuing to experiment in alchemy.[35] 'We are seeking with great intensity an *Extractio Tincturae Auris*', Meyer wrote to Frederick on November 17, 1687.[36] His choice of words reveals that he had help, perhaps from the workers on the Looiersgracht.

## An alchemist appears

Frederick, in any case, was unusually excited about the alchemical possibilities he saw in his mind's eye. In the same year of 1687, he had a medal struck in Gotha to commemorate his activities in alchemy (Figure 5.4).[37] It was certainly not intended for the public but only for a small circle of initiated friends. Frederick had it engraved with his motto: 'Suscipio et reddo' ('I undertake and complete it'). That would reflect his entrepreneurial spirit. Or: 'I support and requite it.' A medal of this sort could, for example, be given to an expert alchemist as a token of thanks. It is said that this thaler was struck from alchemical silver.[38]

Meyer, for his part, was constantly busy. As early as March 1688 it became apparent that he had written letters seeking support for his somewhat uncertain excursions into alchemy. In the process, he had also turned to someone who lived mostly in England. Of this person we read: 'In England our good friend makes a universal medicine from salt [...] and sulphur, and achieves great cures with it.'[39] At first, Meyer knew this friend only from letters, but then he received a visit from him in Amsterdam, and Meyer was deeply impressed by his abilities. On April 27, 1688 – Frederick had only been back in Gotha for two weeks – Meyer wrote the duke an excited letter. Meyer's own opinion of the tincture, he said, was no longer so important: 'my eyes have been opened [...] in the field of philosophy [= alchemy] and I can now see that this process cannot achieve everything that is claimed for it. [...] The reason for my enlightenment is that last week one of my philosophical [= alchemical] correspondents, a very honest, upright, and intelligent man who is also highly experienced came to me here and revealed to me in confidence that he had received the true, correct [...] universal process in a very direct manner, after he had for many long years sought for it in vain [...].'[40] There was somebody, it seemed, who knew how to make gold.

Who was this man who had impressed Meyer so much? He was Joseph Bürger, also known as Giuseppe Borghero, possibly an Italian, who had long travelled through Germany and Europe, offering his skills in alchemy to clients.[41] But Meyer did not hesitate to name the fly in the ointment: his correspondent had debts of 2,000 gulden, which would have to be paid for him before he would set to work and produce gold in a timeframe of approximately nine months.[42]

FIGURE 5.4    Alchemical medal, Frederick I. of Saxe-Gotha-Altenburg, 1687. Münzenhandlung Harald Möller GmbH

Everything was to be above board, as he wanted 'to work in my house and do everything in my presence […] and after its success[ful] completion […] leave the tincture with me […].'[43] So that Meyer would believe him, Bürger had given him 'a [small] glass of his *auro Potabile* or Universal Medicine.'[44] In exchange for a 'present' of 500 Reichsthaler, he would start work. Bürger also made it clear to Meyer that he was able 'clearly to understand' the 'true philosophers' such as Basilius Valentinus, Bernardus Trevisanus and George Ripley.[45]

The way in which Bürger promoted himself, which Meyer passed on to Frederick, is a good illustration of how alchemists sold their knowledge.[46] To start with, of course, no names were named. In addition to praising the expected result, advertising involved providing a material sample to guarantee that the result could really be achieved, and a number of texts, or at least references to them, to show that the alchemist had a proper theoretical grounding in his science. Later Bürger regularly sent Frederick small manuscript tracts on alchemy to keep him happy in this respect. The fact that Bürger wanted to receive his payment as a 'present' shows how alchemists often only entered into economic relations in a manner that Bourdieu calls 'veiled', namely, in the form of a gift that was reciprocated.[47] The ethos of a 'true' alchemist did not allow him to make gold for profit.

Bürger's demand for 2,000 gulden to pay off his debts was, of course, a problem. But the alchemist knew how to put pressure on. He let Meyer know that he had actually intended to offer the recipe to John George III, Elector of Saxony, who had also recently been in Amsterdam.[48] Competition was a highly effective means of increasing the urgency of an offer. The potential buyer was made to feel that he could not let the opportunity pass, otherwise he would lose his chance.

Bürger had obviously taken note of Meyer's urgent search for the correct extraction of tincture of gold, as he said that he had received 'a letter *de extractione tincturae auri* from his friend, who promises to come to London immediately'.[49]

This, too, was nothing unusual coming from an alchemist. They almost always had some unnamed 'friends' to whom they could refer, or whose preliminary work they were waiting for. This could have been a protective fiction, for alchemists lived dangerously and often needed a fictional alter ego so that they could remove themselves from the line of fire if necessary.[50]

Meyer's enthusiastic reports must have been why Frederick suddenly hurried off to Amsterdam again in July. On May 6 and again on June 31, as a later alchemical diary says, the 'secretum anglicanum' has been sent to Frederick, that is the alchemical recipe that Bürger received from his 'friend' in London. It was Bürger's intention to leave London for Amsterdam in late July or early August. They could then work together on the processes for the transmutation of base metals into gold, the instructions for which Frederick had now received in full from Vierorth's papers and for making the drinking gold that Bürger praised so highly. Frederick boarded a ship and sailed down the Rhine.

## Wood

On July 30, Frederick arrived in Amsterdam, still a bit groggy from the boat trip.[51] Had he informed his privy councillors in Gotha that he was travelling to Holland on matters relating to alchemy? It seems not. As far as they were concerned, he was on different business, but this was almost certainly just a pretext, as it did not require the prince's presence. Frederick set about this business as soon as he arrived. He wrote to Bachoff that he had 'met Baron Schwartzenstein, who is organizing my wood trade. I am therefore sending a number of people from here with letters to the chamber in Gotha tomorrow to have a look at the area and the wood on my lands around Gotha as far as the Werra.'[52] By the end of May, Frederick had granted the baron authority to look for people in Amsterdam who might be interested in buying wood from the Thuringian forest. 'We [have] decided to sell from our forests some trees that could be used as masts, and others suitable for planking for ship-building. To that end, we have given Baron Gottofried Momm von Schwarzenstein a commission to look out for people who are interested in buying this sort of material [...].'[53] The potential Dutch buyers who travelled to Thuringia were to check the quality of the wood, and see whether it was economically viable to transport it on rafts and then ships via the Werra, Weser, and the North Sea.

This had not been discussed with Meyer, who was surprised to find Schwartzenstein inquisitively looking over his shoulder in July to see what he was doing. Meyer did not dare to tell him anything because he did not know how much Schwartzenstein knew about Frederick's business with him. Meyer did recognize, however, that Schwartzenstein also 'had something going on with Your Highness',[54] but Schwartzenstein for his part was similarly reticent, and did not report any details about the wood trade. In any case, as soon as he arrived, Frederick, corresponding with Paul Künold and Georg Reichardt, his councillors in Gotha, drew up a draft contract in order to wrap up his wood-trading business.[55]

**FIGURE 5.5**   Frederick I: Diarium Chimicum, fol. 1r. ThStA Gotha, Geh. Archiv, E XI Nr. 100. Courtesy of the Thüringisches Staatsarchiv Gotha

## Drinkable gold

But this was just the official part of his business and could be dealt with quickly. Frederick did not tell his councillors what was really keeping him in Amsterdam.

On the day after his arrival, as soon as he had regained his strength, he set up the 'process' at Meyer's house. The alchemical diary that Frederick began on this day, July 31 (Figure 5.5), shows that he spent most of the month at Meyer's house on the Elandsgracht.[56] This was because the process had to be observed and kept running early in the morning and late at night, and this required someone to be present as much as possible. Frederick and Meyer placed a crucible on the fire, heated it until it glowed, and then placed a pound of – probably – vitriol in it. To this was added two and a quarter pounds of crushed sulphurous antimony (*Spießglanzglas*), and finally iron.[57] Frederick picked up his notebook and noted down exactly what he was doing.

Things went well on the first day of the experiment. A *regulus stellatus* or starry regulus was quickly produced, in which a starlike pattern of crystals formed on the surface of the solid antimony.[58] Then it was a matter of creating the *mercurius metallorum*, which was believed to be the plastic essence of metals,[59] followed by the destruction of the metals. Frederick had a great deal of experience with the initial steps. He had started working on these transformation processes many years before with the assistance of Jakob Friederich Waitz, his personal physician, and advised by Baron von Gastorff.[60] To start with, iron was used to reduce the antimony in order to create the *Spießglanzkönig* from which the *sophische Mercurius*, the basic substance for all further alchemical processing, was created through amalgamation.

This was Frederick's and Meyer's everyday routine. On Tuesday, August 3, Frederick noted: 'Made a *transparens* and *diafannisch mercurium*'.[61] This was a transparent form of mercury, incorporating the starry regulus. A liquid was produced, which was said to be an emetic, probably antimony trichloride, a Paracelsian remedy fashionable at the time.[62] The entry for August 4 read: 'Fire first thing in the morning. And then let it stand all night long. So on 5 August it began to settle, so that on 6 August the third *caput mortuum*, could be removed.'[63] The *caput mortuum* [literally: dead head or worthless remains] consisted of the remains, sometimes iron trioxide, created in the final stage of this part of the process.

The men repeated these processes in a slightly different form over the next few days. Then we read, for August 8: 'Cleaned out early. There was a lot of steam, and then took away the third *caput mortuum*.'[64] The remains were removed again. On August 9, almost as soon as they had got up in the morning, more of the translucent silver mercury was to be seen; on the next day there was even more, along with an oily substance (*materia unctuosa*).[65]

As well as Frederick and Meyer, Joseph Bürger must also have been present, either from the start, or joining them from London after a few days. During the four weeks that Frederick spent working in Amsterdam with Meyer and Bürger, he strung together a number of experiments, as planned. It seems that they built on each other, as the products of earlier experiments were used in later ones. The three men worked with different equipment and methods, using crucibles, nested retorts, and even with watery solutions that they filtered and distilled. The matter

**FIGURE 5.6**   Drawings of diamonds that Frederick wanted to purchase. ThStA Gotha, Kammer Immediate 1762, fol. 52–54. Courtesy of the Thüringisches Staatsarchiv Gotha

was even more complex. During this time, they were able to pursue only one of several possible ways of achieving their goal. Later in the autumn, and over the following year, Bürger explored two alternative paths. In London he undertook the experiments of the second path and sent Frederick the results, while delegating the third way to a friend in Scotland, who sent him the results in Hamburg, where Bürger had moved in the meantime.[66] Frederick also had the task of continuing certain experiments at home in Gotha.[67] The experiments soon went in a direction that was new for Frederick. Steps five to nine in the process involved using *Menstruum perpetuum*, an eternal solvent. Two years later, when Frederick repeated the process at home in Gotha, he noted at this stage that the '*tincturia fermentatio* and *proiectio*' were quite remarkable.[68] A closer look at the chemical diary reveals the day on which Bürger began to exert more and more influence over the direction taken by the experiments. This seems to have been on August 15, when we read in the diary: 'Work is progressing well at present, both on the universal medicine and on the *transmutation metallorum* or *lapid Phil*. The latter requires the most subtle and accurate work.'[69] What follows is no longer a daily record of the course taken by a process, but the instructions for making a medicine of drinkable gold. After all, this was the main thing that Bürger had to offer.

Bürger's interest in drinkable gold, *aurum potabile*, which he praised as his speciality, may have been connected with the roots he had put down in England

and Holland. After the death in 1670 of Rudolph Glauber, the great inventor, knowledge of his experiments with drinkable gold – building on the work of Paracelsus and Isaacus Hollandus – had reached England via men such as Johannes Moriaen and the Hartlib circle.[70] For Frederick, the search for a universal elixir was not at the forefront of his interests, and it is surprising that he took up this offer. But since his serious illness in March he may have been thinking more about his own health, and the process of making drinking gold was closely connected with the general techniques for transmuting metal.

During the busy days in Amsterdam, Frederick still found time to write to Künold and Reichardt, his councillors, every three days.[71] Of course, these letters contained not a word about his experiments in alchemy, and Frederick did not even tell Chancellor Bachoff, his close confidant, what he was really doing in Amsterdam. This shows how anxious he was to keep these activities secret. He would have left himself vulnerable to attack if word had got out about how much money and time he was spending on alchemy. Both the privy council and the people, especially the theologians, might have been annoyed and irritated. They did not understand the mixture of enthusiasm and entrepreneurial spirit that drove him.

Finally, Frederick also went shopping during his stay. He selected English chairs for his palace, bought materials and cups, and marvelled at the magnificent diamonds for sale in Amsterdam. A brochure was drawn specifically for him (Figure 5.6), and as his invoices show, he actually bought these jewels – for a considerable sum of money.[72]

## Financial matters

Paying was a problem in Amsterdam. Frederick usually issued promissory notes, which were then settled by his bankers in Frankfurt.[73] But issues arose when it came to paying Joseph Bürger. He appears to have asked Frederick to pay him the 2,000 gulden or thaler right at the start, on beginning work. Was it not too much? Frederick counted up what he had already spent on alchemy since he had started experimenting in 1684. A long list of names appears: Gastorff, Vierorth, Rothmaler, Waitz, right down to La Motte, whom he had only recently given 600 thaler (Figure 5.7).[74]

And now Bürger was asking for 2,000 thaler. Frederick, however, did not hesitate for long, and wrote out the note. But difficulties arose with the bank's disbursement. Instead of arriving in a few days, no payment arrived from Frankfurt. This was embarrassing for Frederick because he suddenly found himself without money, and he could not leave either. 'I am stuck here because of a lack of cash', he wrote to Bachoff on August 28, 'and cannot find out why, as nothing arrived by yesterday's post either. This has caused me to run up debts of more than 1,000 thaler, and has held me up here for twelve days, as [I wanted] to leave long ago.'[75] Is it true that Frederick had really wanted to leave since August 16, when the alchemical experiments had turned to the search for a universal elixir and he

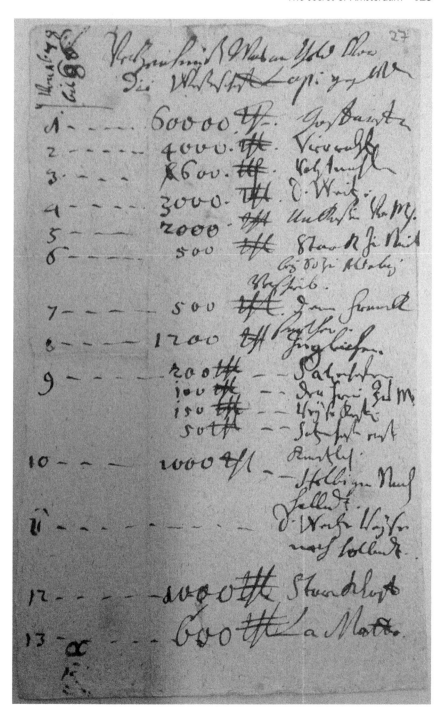

**FIGURE 5.7**    Frederick's list of sums spent for alchemists. ThStA Gotha Geheimes Archiv E XI Nr. 73★★★ (9), fol. 27. Thüringisches Staatsarchiv Gotha

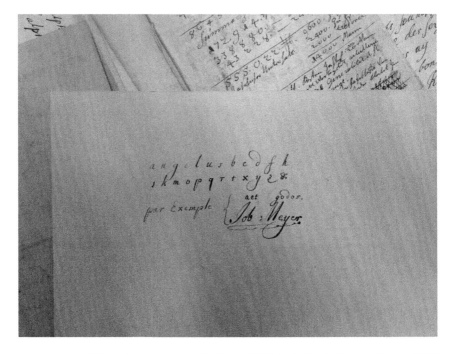

**FIGURE 5.8**    Cipher for the name Job Meyer. ThStA Gotha Geheimes Archiv E XI Nr. 73★★★ (9), fol. 29. Courtesy of the Thüringisches Staatsarchiv Gotha

was perhaps no longer involved as enthusiastically as before? We have seen that from then his diary listed only instructions, not daily observations. Or was Frederick only looking for an excuse to explain to Bachoff why he was staying on in Amsterdam?

Frederick found a banker to help him out. A financier from Antwerp advanced him the 2,000 thaler he needed to pay Bürger.[76] This was lucky because otherwise, Frederick confessed, he 'would have had to leave here with the opprobrium of the world' heaped on him.[77] But the affair also had a disadvantage: 'To stay here any longer […] would not be fitting because now everybody knows who I am.'[78] In other words, Frederick had been in Amsterdam incognito, but now the news was out that the Duke of Gotha was staying on the Elandsgracht.

## On the stock exchange

Where did Bürger incur his debts? Were they real debts, or was this merely another obfuscation so that he did not have to ask for direct payment for his expertise in alchemy? We learn from Meyer's letters that Bürger had actually fallen into debt by buying ore on the stock exchange. The stock exchange had existed since 1611; it was one of the first institutions of its kind in the world.[79] It was both a commodity exchange, where raw materials and foodstuffs arriving in the port were traded, and a stock exchange, which dealt in shares such as those of the Dutch East India Company (VOC). It was said that Bürger had received instructions from his English master to buy everything from a certain Mr. Goermann. He was to examine the goods, find out who else was buying them – at the Bast Jud house, to which we shall return – and finally to bid at the most favourable moment. He was given a free hand to make decisions, which is what tempted him to rush in.

What he should have done was to look at the ore samples the VOC provided, then buy a pound and have it examined by the metal tester Anthoni Grill, son of the alchemist of the same name.[80] Twenty-five to 30 percent should have been deducted as expenses for the smelting, and a price calculated. But Bürger had done none of this and had therefore paid far too much.[81] He claimed that he had received instructions to buy 'à tout pris' [at any price]. But the VOC had got wind of this, and therefore raised prices steeply. Meyer had attended the auction in person along with Nenibers, mint master from Cologne, perhaps acting for his other client, the prince-bishop of Trier. Nenibers had experienced something similar with artificially hiked prices when he had bid for Frederick III of Neuwied some time earlier.[82] It was too late: Bürger made a hefty loss.

Frederick was also familiar with this trade. He had been buying ore from Amsterdam's port since at least 1685. At that time he had instructed Johann Christoph Gottmann, his metals expert, and councillor Künold to buy the cargoes of ships from East Asia.[83] But now that Frederick was in Holland himself, he looked around and had Meyer track prices. Occasionally, Meyer was instructed to bid for certain goods. Shortly after Frederick's departure, Meyer wrote to him: 'The Bast Jud stocks are still doing fantastically well [;] yesterday shares for one of the ores were trading at 400 on the exchange and at the same time at 406 on another.'[84] This passage is not easy to interpret. It seems that when Meyer and Frederick were able to leave the alchemical process for a while, they visited some of the trading places that had emerged separately from the exchange and operated in competition with it. The city administration had not been able to prevent this from happening. In the Kalverstraat in particular, which ran south from the Stadhuis (town hall) on the Dam square, traders would meet in guest houses late in the evening or at night, long after the exchange had closed. Some of the traders were Jews, and they skilfully used the small differences in the official rates as quoted on the exchange (406 instead of 400) to make a profit.[85] As they wanted to make gold, Frederick and his colleagues kept a careful eye on the ores that arrived in the port. But not only on the ores: 'French wines and brandies rose by a substantial amount, made various bids, the rest were unchanged.'[86] Thus, Meyer had bought shares in brandy, probably with the duke's money, when he saw an opportunity to make a profit. For Frederick this boisterous behaviour in the expectation of profit and the chance of great wealth must have been a new and euphoric experience. Nothing of this sort happened in Germany, and especially not in Gotha. Here, by contrast, everything was possible: alchemists' gold, quick speculative wealth and a growing market for soldiers.

## Enticements of the French

In the meantime, the crisis about the Elector of Cologne's successor had come to a head. The Pope and then the emperor had come out in favour of Joseph Clemens, who was enthroned, in order to curb French expansionist ambitions on the left bank of the Rhine. Louis XIV's reaction was to endorse the Dauphin's claim to these areas, and to prepare for a military campaign.[87]

Thereupon Frederick set off south, for Brussels, where he would be closer to the messengers riding between himself and Paris. On August 28, shortly before he left, while he was still kept in Amsterdam waiting for his money, he had written to Chancellor Bachoff: 'I have asked here and there whether any subsidies are available, but everyone did the sums, and if they have no need, they will not give money.'[88] At that time, the Dutch were not interested in hiring soldiers. There was a vague hope that the Spaniards might pay the initial fee to make the business of hiring regiments more attractive for the Dutch, but Frederick ran out of time. He had to get back to Gotha, where he had long been awaited. For the commander of the three cavalry regiments to take the initiative was not an option either, as Frederick explained to the chancellor, because 'the duke would first have to win over the rulers.'[89] Apart from that, there was competition. Stuttgart also had the ear of the States General and was offering to rent them its troops. Frederick therefore had to change his strategy, and bet on a completely different card: the French.

Here Frederick's communication became confidential, and he could only speak in hints. He wrote that he had received several letters from Baron Rußwurm from Paris within a short time ('in almost three consecutive posts'),[90] and that they had been transported very quickly, in just four days. 'In them', he reported, 'the baron often and repeatedly said that the king held my person in great esteem, and that I had a good chance to make money and position myself with highly advantageous conditions, if I wanted to try.'[91] This was more than just a secret offer; Louis XIV was making urgent and repeated offers to pay Frederick a lot of money to withdraw from the Augsburg coalition and make his troops available to the French.

If his alchemical process and the stock exchange had already electrified Frederick, this took away his breath completely. How was he to deal with such an enticement to betray the Holy Roman Empire for money? In 1702 his son, Frederick II, was to do something similar and almost destroy the state of Saxe-Gotha because the imperial side found out about it.[92] This was a highly delicate matter. How was he to proceed? Frederick summoned Baron von Schwartzenstein in person – he was still there because of the trade in timber – and gave him a letter to Louis XIV, in which he politely enquired about the state of his health. Frederick then despatched Schwartzenstein to Paris with it at top speed. This was innocuous enough but sent the French king a signal that he was ready to negotiate. At the same time Frederick impressed upon Schwartzenstein that he should 'find out what this matter was really about',[93] that is, carefully enquire about the status and the seriousness of the offer, 'and then report immediately, or come back.'[94] This was express diplomacy, because the French were ready to deploy their troops. On September 24 Louis was set to declare war and occupy Cologne. At the end of August Schwartzenstein wrote from Paris that there was 'consternation in France because of actions in Cologne. And that the best conditions in the world were to be had at the present time.'[95]

Frederick awaited Louis's reply to his 'compliments letter' with trepidation. He impressed on Schwartenstein that he was to do nothing more, just to report back. It still required the king's nod. Frederick justified his actions to himself and his trusted chancellor: 'And because it was just a matter of finding out and listening, I risked it.'[96] Surely he could just explore the possible offer. Of course, Frederick's action was verging on treason. He was unable and unwilling to conduct such questionable negotiations in Amsterdam. His experiments in alchemy in a remote house on the Elandsgracht might just be acceptable but not collaboration with Holland's enemy. That is why Frederick moved to Brussels, in the Spanish Netherlands. There he could not be spied upon, as he hinted to Bachoff: 'As I still have various covert matters[,] originating […] with me, that I cannot entrust to the pen.'[97] The Dutch were also vigilant. Frederick had already considered a cipher for his correspondence with Meyer, an expanded Caesar's code, which he could use to encrypt his letters if necessary (Figure 5.8).[98] But staying in Brussels reduced the time it took messengers to get between him and Paris: 'I can have letters in three days with the post, and if a special courier is sent, he can be here from Paris in 24 hours.'[99]

And what if Louis really were to send his approval? According to Frederick, he would 'go home as quickly as possible, and consider it alone and with others.'[100] Returning to Gotha as soon as he could, he would talk there to Bachoff, his closest confidant, and discuss whether they could take this daring step and, in return for enormous sums of money, risk the emperor imposing heavy sanctions and the loud protests of the other princes. The blueprint for hiring out troops was all ready in the notebook that Frederick had filled with his scribbles in November of the previous year. 'But I ask you not to tell a soul. I have not told anyone here, not even councillor Jacobs.'[101] Jacobs was vice chancellor but not a member of Frederick's inner circle, which included only Bachoff and the diplomats Schwartzenstein and Rußwurm. Jacobs 'will be astonished at my boldness, but when he hears my reasons, he will have second thoughts when he sees that the conditions were very favourable.'[102] What reasons could one have to run so great a risk?

These reasons become apparent in the sentences that follow. It seems that Bachoff had told Frederick about the opportunity to buy up some territories in Schrylunge. This region belonged to Electoral Brandenburg but was now up for sale. This set Frederick off on another dream: 'What you report about buying […] Schrylunge, would be a salutary thing, if only we had money and the sovereignty of Electoral Brandenburg could be acquired. If things work out as I intend, we would have enough money between now and Christmas to buy another ten such counties, should they become available, and still maintain 1,000 soldiers.'[103]

**FIGURE 5.9** Familientaler Frederick I., Gotha 1691: Frederick and his six brothers. Münzhaus Dr. Busso Peus Nachfolger

Frederick adds: '*sed haec arcana sunt* [but these are secrets] and I cannot say anything so that I am not made a laughing stock if things do not work out.'[104]

In any case, Frederick already had great hopes for his experiments in alchemy. For years, he had been daydreaming about what he would do when he had 11 million thaler or more at his disposal as a result of transmuting metals into gold.[105] Added to this was the concrete prospect of receiving enormous sums of money from the French for the regiments they wanted to lease from him. Frederick thought that this argument would persuade the vice chancellor to approve the deal, and that he could then significantly expand the small territory of Saxe-Gotha-Altenburg by purchasing other territories. For years, they had been waiting for an opportunity to regain at least a little of the predominance the Ernestine princes had once enjoyed before they lost the electorship in 1547, during the Schmalkaldic war.[106] And Frederick, a risk-taking entrepreneur, would go down in history as the one who had advanced Gotha's cause. His choice of words revealed this entrepreneurial spirit: he spoke of 'grasping' the opportunity and of giving the chancellor the wherewithal to trade on the territorial market at last.[107] Between glory and ridicule ('not made a laughing stock'[108]), everything was conceivable.

## Conclusion

Soon after the middle of September Frederick was back. He went first to Schloss Friedrichswerth, which was almost finished and ready to house his collection of French portraits. It was to be inaugurated the following year.[109] On September 20 he arrived in Gotha. It became more and more clear that the trade in soldiers with France would not work. As this essay has shown, Frederick had been pursuing clandestine and dangerous business. He had been in the big world, a world in which everything was faster and more complex than in the small state of Saxe-

Gotha-Altenburg. Now, at home, he was recaptured by the situation he had somehow escaped: a decimated little territory, surrounded by other petty states with which there had been tense relations for several years. One can even say that this situation had led him to think like an entrepreneur. After his father's death in 1675, power in Saxe-Gotha had first passed to all of his seven sons in common, who were meant to rule together. When this did not work, the state was divided into seven micro-territories in 1680. As the oldest of these sons, Frederick had to try to make his share as big and powerful as possible by concluding treaties with his brothers. In the years that followed, this resulted in a number of complicated lawsuits heard by the Aulic Council (Reichshofrat), before the division was confirmed by the emperor in 1686.[110] However rosy the official version of the 'nexus Gothanus' (Figure 5.9), the association between the seven brothers and their territories, was made to look on official representations, the reality was different: disputes and debts.[111]

Frederick had tried to make up for what he had to pay out to his brothers by building up a profitable trade in subsidies. In addition, the fact that the emperor had debts for subsidies with him helped to speed up the court case.[112] At the same time, in addition to the income he derived from the forests in his territory,[113] he had tried to increase the value of the ores and mineral resources of the Thuringian Forest[114] by engaging heavily – as we have seen -- in alchemical experiments. He had invested large sums in advisers in the hope of receiving the recipe for turning base metals into gold. Everything was connected: alchemy was to produce gold from ores; the gold would make it possible to muster more regiments to be leased, and from the proceeds of both, Frederick intended to buy estates and increase the size of his state.[115] He was restless and full of enthusiasm, so much so that he sometimes lost touch with reality. In all this business, in any case, especially when acquiring occult alchemical knowledge, he had to exercise the utmost caution: nobody could find out about his laboratory work in Amsterdam; and only his chancellor could be involved in the secret negotiations with Paris. Only the less contentious issues such as the trade in timber – which did not much interest Frederick – could be officially reported back to Gotha.

Our main aim here has not been to cast light on Frederick's biography. Frederick's trip to Amsterdam has only been a means to exemplify how acting in the knowledge market of the 17th century looked from the perspective of a petty prince – a petty prince who saw himself as an entrepreneur. This knowledge market was not only in Amsterdam but also in Vienna, Paris and other places. But in Amsterdam it was particularly advanced, and through the VOC possessed global dimensions and through the stock market new financial ones. It was frequented by many princes apart from Frederick. Although a 'market' for secret knowledge had existed for a long time,[116] it took on a new dimension in the late 17th century and was increasingly interwoven with other financial activities and forces, as well as with more official markets such as art, ores or furniture. It was a transnational market, with sellers from England, Holland, Italy and Germany but also with buyers from different countries in competition with each other, without all this being openly pronounced. That made this marketplace so fragile and mysterious, even for its actors.

But the market as such has not interested us so much as the behaviour of the prince within it. Our interest has been about looking, so to speak, into Frederick's head – and heart – and seeing how the drives and the many pieces of information, wishes and various realities connected within it to form a system. Speculation, euphoria, haste, risk-taking and secrecy, as I said earlier, were the ingredients that played a role here. In contrast to the quieter conditions in Gotha, Amsterdam acted as an accelerator for the prince. It was only there, in the new situation, that everything could come out and be brought to bear, which otherwise might have emerged separately and only occasionally would have provided opportunities and options for action. The promises of the market attracted Frederick in particular: he speculated with brandy as well as with soldiers and with alchemical recipes, always driven by the prospect of a big win. That challenged him to take enormous risks.

It is a logic of outbidding that links with other logics: secret diplomacy, conspicuous consumption and patronage. In secret diplomacy, it was common practice to enter or break alliances beyond moral limits, to simulate loyalty or to offend against them. But the potential financial gain gave this political logic an economic twist. A prince had to cultivate demonstrative consumption, of course, in order to secure his authority. Frederick's shopping tours in Amsterdam were shaped by this necessity. But 'signaling' – to use an expression of the economist Michael Spence[117] – was practiced by nearly all actors in the field: the alchemist had to signal by mentioning book titles and present alchemical manuscripts to show his competence, while the French king signaled by his donation of medallions his willingness to enter into a possible secret relationship with a German prince. Many of the objects we still have today are the result of signaling. In this field, too, much had accelerated in the knowledge market of the 1680s: one gets the impression of a certain breathlessness, with which princes, scientists and agents have to seize the moment of opportunity and send out signals in many directions at the same time. Finally, the logic of patronage: Frederick offered the alchemist a protection, including a financial protection, against his creditors; he entered into a relationship of trust with him; but at the same time the relationship of giving and trust disguised (in the sense of Bourdieu) a thoroughly economic relationship in which both the patron and the client constantly looked to other actors who offered more or less cost.

From the point of view of the dynamics of emotions, the situation in emerging knowledge capitalism prizes actors who are willing to take on risks and practice essentially hazardous behaviour. Affects were the motor of the market, not only on the stock market but also in the political-economic-scientific grey area that we have considered here. Without enthusiasm and fascination, the high-risk undertaking alchemy represented would never have been possible. The loud call and the heated mood of the stock market here is instead the astonished cry, which was caused by rainbow colours in the crucible, but which often had to be suppressed so as not to irritate the neighbours. Whether or not this enthusiastic exuberance has always proved useful in the end is another question.

Much of the enthusiasm, moreover, was spent rather silently in the correspondence, in excited billets to confidants, in urgent instructions to the banker, in faltering confessions to the chancellor. What is left to us today are these letters and documents, on the one hand, and the material things on the other. Busts, paintings, medallions are still in Gotha today and are silent witnesses of the journey in 1688.

However, one wonders how the actors dealt with the many small and big disappointments that inevitably came to fruition in this inflated economy of desire. This study cannot answer that, as it only covers a short, dense section of a few weeks. But if one looks at the sequence of Frederick's alchemical advisers, which does not break even after Joseph Bürger, then the motto seems to have been after every setback: onwards and upwards!

On the other hand, we can give a more precise answer to the question of how Frederick coped with the difficulty of having to negotiate one 'market' or several 'markets', without there being a modern notion of market, and without the possibility that the demands and offers in the case of soldiers and recipes could be negotiated as openly as on the stock exchange. What is more, how could Frederick manage the system in his head, always having to relate the options of several different markets? This can be clarified by a look at his 'accounting' practices.[118] We have noted that many calculations and accounts of Frederick have been handed down in the files. At every opportunity he took ink and paper and calculated. These were not just factual calculations but very often merely fictitious speculations: if so many tons of gold are produced, if so many soldiers are rented, there would be so many gulden available. Risky and desirable economics were entrusted to the paper – and only to the paper. To nobody else. Frederick's calculations were a soliloquy.

For Frederick's decisive considerations had to take place privately. We have seen that there were different communication circles in which he was involved and different levels of secrecy.[119] With Meyer he could talk about alchemy and works of art but not about soldiers and politics; Chancellor Bachoff and Baron von Russwurm were privy to the soldier trade but probably not to the alchemical experiments. The chamber councillors Künold and Reichardt knew about the timber trade and probably also speculation on the stock market, but otherwise they were deliberately kept ignorant.[120] Not to mention Gotha's court theologians, who were suspicious of both alchemy and the sale of soldiers. Gotha never found out about the secret of Amsterdam. Around Frederick, nobody could know the whole story. One must imagine the entrepreneur as a lonely person.

*(translated from the German by Angela Davies)*

## Notes

1 The calendar question is complicated insofar as the provinces of Holland, Zeeland and Brabant had already converted to the Gregorian calendar in 1582/83, while the other provinces as well as the Protestant territories of Germany (including Gotha) still

counted on the Julian calendar, which was 10 days behind. The statements of Frederick in Gotha concerning the dates are therefore different from those of his agent Meyer in Amsterdam. I consistently use the Julian Dating here for consistency. I am grateful to Thomas Moenius, Oliver Humberg and Kai Schwahn for information and transcriptions of the letters by Meyer und Bürger; I thank Christian Wirkner, Rainer Werthmann and Thomas Moenius for the transcription of the alchemical diary and Rainer Werthmann for his help in interpreting the alchemical processes.

2 D. Margócsy, *Commercial Visions*. For the economical aspects of knowledge: M. Mulsow, "Ökonomie des Wissens."

3 Ibid. 29–73.

4 On the principles of exchange: S. Kühn, *Wissen, Arbeit, Freundschaft*.

5 Cf. B. Schmidt, *Inventing Exoticism*.

6 On the Netherlands as knowledge society: C. Lesger, *The Rise of the Amsterdam Market*. See also H. J. Cook, *Matters of Exchange*; H. J. Cook, "Sharing the Truth of Things."

7 A. Thiele, "The Prince as Military Entrepreneur?"

8 S. Kühn, *Arbeit, Freundschaft*; Mulsow, *Die unanständige Gelehrtenrepublik*, 67–86.

9 J. Mokyr, *A Culture of Growth*.

10 M. Mulsow, "History of Knowledge." On knowledge at the court M. Füssel, "Höfe und Experten."

11 See, e.g. P. Burke, *Venice and Amsterdam*; W. Frijhoff, *Geschiedenis van Amsterdam*.

12 R. Jacobson and J. Brandsch, ed., *Friedrich I. von Sachsen-Gotha-Altenburg, Tagebücher*.

13 On Gotha around 1700: A. Klinger, *Der Gothaer Fürstenstaat*; V. Albrecht-Birkner, *Reformation des Lebens*. For the subsequent period: F. Facius, *Staat, Verwaltung und Wirtschaft*. On the significance of culture in Gotha: S. Westphal, "Nach dem Verlust der Kurwürde."

14 The lengthy travel journal of 488 folio pages is still extant: Forschungsbibliothek (=FB) Gotha, Ch. A 544.

15 R. Fester, *Die Augsburger Allianz von 1686*; R. Fester: *Die armierten Stände und die Reichskriegsverfassung*; O. Heyn, "Die Ernestiner und die Reichsdefension," esp. 190–94.

16 J. A. Lynn, *The French Wars*; K. O. von Aretin, *Das Alte Reich*, 53–96.

17 Thüringisches Staatsarchiv (= ThStA) Gotha, Kammer Immediate Nr. 1759: "Herzog Friedrichs gethane Reise nach Holland nebst Reiserechnung," 1688, fol. 33–36.

18 See, e.g. September 26, 1684, when Frederick sojourned at his hunting lodge Hummelshain and harboured hopes to be able to produce in the near future gold worth 15 million thalers. From this he wanted to pay off his debts to his brothers to increase his army from just under 10,000 to 20,000 men, continue to fortify Gotha, and acquire surrounding counties, such as von Hohenstein's, to enlarge and round out his territory. ThStA Gotha Geh. Archiv E XI 98.

19 See the travel journal (footnote 14), 195ff.

20 Ibid. 217 f.

21 Travel journal (footnote 14), after 28.1.1688.

22 Frederick to Bachoff von Echt, Köln, 25.7.1688, FB Gotha Ch. A 830, fol. 119: "wegen einiger empfangener Schreiben necessitiret worden Eine postreyse nach Holland zu thun."

23 See the letter from Job Meyer to Frederick, 17.11.1687, ThStA Gotha, Geheimes Archiv EXI, Nr.73, fol. 380r. See as well the travel journal (footnote 14), 21.

24 On the loss of significance: S. Westphal, "Nach dem Verlust."

25 M. Mulsow, "Philalethes in Deutschland."

26 For the reconstruction of this episode: K. Schwahn, "Feilschen"; T. Moenius, "Herzog Friedrich I. von Sachsen-Gotha-Altenburg."

27 K. Schwahn, "Feilschen," 3 f. On Hellwig: V. Keller, "The Centre of Nature"; M. Mulsow, "Alchemische Substanzen als fremde Dinge."

28 Telgens had already worked for Johann Joachim Becher in 1671. P. H. Smith, *The Business of Alchemy*, 155.
29 Meyer to Frederick (footnote 23), fol. 385 v/386r.
30 Meyer to Frederick (footnote 23), fol. 385 v sq. In the travel diary we read that in fall 1687 Meyer still lived in the "tower of Amersfoort" on the Prinsengracht.
31 A marble statue of Venus attributed to Bartholomäus Eggers was sold at Artnet auctions.
32 The list is in Meyer to Frederick (footnote 23), fol. 386vf. and as a copy also in Kammer Immediate (footnote 17), fol. 385.
33 Meyer to Frederick, Geheimes Archiv EXI, Nr.73★★★, (2), fol. 1v.
34 Stadsarchief Amsterdam.
35 R. Lambour, "De alchemistische wereld." On Glauber in Amsterdam: J. T. Young, *Faith, Medical Alchemy*; Helmut Gebelein and Rainer Werthmann,, *Johann Rudolf Glauber*. In Amsterdam there lived for a certain period also alchemists such as Johann Joachim Becher and Daniel Crafft. We lack a general monograph about the alchemical milieu in Amsterdam.
36 Meyer to Frederick (footnote 23), fol. 381r.
37 See the silver medal (Thaler) of Frederick from 1687 on his alchemical experiments.
38 J. J. Spiess, *Kleine Beiträge*, vol. 1, 133.
39 Meyer to Frederick, ThStA Gotha, Geheimes Archiv, E XI, Nr. 73★★★ (2), fol. 5v; 23.3.1688.
40 Meyer to Frederick (footnote 39), fol. 13r; 27.4.1688, 13r.
41 On Bürger we know next to nothing. On his letters in the Gotha archive see O. Humberg, *Der alchemistische Nachlaß*. Humberg is working on an edition of the letters.
42 Meyer to Frederick (footnote 39), fol. 13v.
43 Ibid.
44 Ibid.
45 Ibid. On these alchemists: L. M. Principe, *The Secrets of Alchemy*; W. R. Newman and L. M. Principe, *Alchemy*.
46 M. Mulsow, "Pantaleon der Alchemist."
47 P. Bourdieu, *The Logic of Practice*; T. Nummedal, *Alchemy and Authority*.
48 Meyer to Frederick (footnote 39), fol. 18r.
49 Bürger to Frederick, Chelsea 7.9.1688, ThStA Gotha Geheimes Archiv E XI Nr. 73★★★.
50 See, e.g. the fictitious relationship of "Pyrophilus" to "Pantaleon" in the case of Gastorff; M. Mulsow, "Philalethes in Deutschland." See also T. Nummedal, *Alchemy*. On the "secretum anglicanum": footnote 67.
51 Frederick to Bachoff, FB Gotha Ch. A 830, fol. 121.
52 Ibid.
53 ThStA Gotha, Kammer Immediate 1762, fol. 175.
54 Meyer to Frederick (footnote 39), fol. 32r.
55 ThStA Gotha, Kammer Immediate 1762, fol. 176–177. On the Gotha administration: U. Hess, *Geheimer Rat und Kabinett*. On Künold: M. Mulsow, "Alchemische Substanzen als fremde Dinge."
56 Cf. Frederick's alchemical process notes: ThStA Gotha, Geh. Archiv, E XI Nr. 100: Diarium Chimicum.
57 Ibid. fol 1r.
58 Ibid. fol 1v. On the starry regulus: L. M. Principe, *The Secrets of Alchemy*.
59 Critical on this: W. Rolfink, *Non ens chimicum*.
60 See M. Mulsow, "Philalethes in Deutschland."
61 Alchemical diary (footnote 56), fol. 5r.
62 R. W. Soukup and H. Mayer, *Alchemistisches Gold*.
63 Alchemical diary (footnote 56), fol. 5v.
64 Alchemical diary (footnote 56), fol. 6v.

65 Ibid.
66 Bürger to Frederick (footnote 49), 2.4.1690, 271r.
67 See especially the diary ThStA Gotha GA E XI, Nr. 101 "Diarium Uber alle meine Itzo neü angefangene processe," from December 4,1689 to January 1690, and from October 20th to December 4th, 1690.
68 See a later addition to the Alchemical diary (footnote 56), fol. 11r: "Notirt. den 9. Jannary. 1690."
69 Alchemical diary (footnote 56), (no pagination), 15. August.
70 Young, *Faith*, chap. 6, pp. 183–216. See, e.g. Johann Rudolph Glauber, *Opera Chymica*, p. 273.
71 Kammer Immediate 1762 (footnote 55).
72 Kammer Immediate 1762 (footnote 55), fol. 52–54. See the travel diary of 1687 (footnote 14), p. 41 f.
73 Kammer Immediate 1759 (footnote 17), e.g. fol. 46; as well as Kammer Immediate 1762 (footnote 55).
74 ThStA Gotha Geheimes Archiv E XI Nr. 73★★★ (9), fol. 27.
75 Frederick to Bachoff (footnote 51), fol. 124.
76 Kammer Immediate 1759 (footnote 17).
77 Frederick to Bachoff (footnote 51), fol. 124.
78 Frederick to Bachoff (footnote 51), fol. 124.
79 L. Petram, *The World's First Stock Exchange*.
80 Meyer to Frederick (footnote 39), fol. 15v. On Grill: L. M. Principe, "Goldsmiths and Chymists."
81 Meyer to Frederick (footnote 39), fol. 15v.: "über die werthe auffgejagt."
82 Meyer to Frederick (footnote 39), fol. 15v.
83 M. Mulsow, "Alchemische Substanzen."
84 Meyer to Frederick (footnote 39), 9./19.9.1688, fol. 38v.
85 I am grateful to Inger Leemans for information about the alternatives to the official stock exchange. On the Jewish merchants in Amsterdam: Israel, European Jewry; Idem, Empires and Entrepots.
86 Meyer to Frederick (footnote 39), fol. 38v.
87 See on this crisis, e.g. Van der Cruysse, "Madam," 352ff.
88 Frederick to Bachoff (footnote 51), fol. 125.
89 Frederick to Bachoff (footnote 51), fol. 126.
90 Ibid.
91 Frederick to Bachoff (footnote 51), fol. 127.
92 Facius, *Staat*.
93 Frederick to Bachoff (footnote 51), fol. 127.
94 Ibid.
95 Ibid.
96 Frederick to Bachoff (footnote 51), fol. 126a.
97 Ibid.
98 ThStA Gotha Geheimes Archiv E XI Nr. 73★★★ (9), fol. 29.
99 Frederick to Bachoff (footnote 51), fol. 126a.
100 Ibid.
101 Ibid.
102 Ibid.
103 Frederick to Bachoff (footnote 51), fol. 126a/127a.
104 Frederick to Bachoff (footnote 51), fol. 127a.
105 ThStA Gotha, Geheimes Archiv E XI Nr. 98 (see footnote 22). See M. Mulsow, "Ökonomie."
106 S. Westphal, "Verlust."
107 Frederick to Bachoff (footnote 51), fol. 127a.
108 Ibid.

109 See the ¼ Thaler medal which was coined on the occasion of the inauguration in 1689 "Auf die Einweihung von Schloss und Kirche in Friedrichswerth" by Christian Wermuth. An image is in the auction catalogue of Münzhandlung Dirk Löbbers.
110 S. Westphal, *Kaiserliche Rechtsprechung*.
111 "Familientaler," Gotha 1691, with Frederick I surrounded by his six brothers.
112 See S. Westphal, *Kaiserliche Rechtsprechung*. Frederick tried to circumvent the Reichshofrat, but was not really successful.
113 A. Klinger, *Der Gothaer Fürstenstaat*, 196–98.
114 Ibid. 203–210.
115 On this knowledge economy see also M. Mulsow, "History of Knowledge," esp. 164–68.
116 D. Jütte, *The Age of Secrecy*.
117 M. Spence, "Job Market Signaling"; M. Spence, "Market Signaling;" see also K. M. Eisenhardt, "Agency Theory"; for an application on the conspicuous consumption in the Renaissance: J. K. Nelson and R. J. Zeckhauser, *The Patron's Payoff*.
118 On accounting: J. Soll, *The Reckoning*.
119 D. Gambetta, *Codes of the Underworld*.
120 On deliberately keeping people ignorant: R. N. Proctor and L. Schiebinger, *Agnotology*.

# Bibliography

Albrecht-Birkner, Veronika. *Reformation des Lebens: Die Reformen Herzog Ernsts des Frommen von Sachsen-Gotha und ihre Auswirkungen auf Frömmigkeit, Schule und Alltag im ländlichen Raum (1640–1675)*. Leipzig: Evangelische Verlagsanstalt, 2002.

Aretin, Kart Otmar von. *Das Alte Reich 1648–1806*. Vol. 2: *Kaisertradition und österreichische Großmachtpolitik (1684–1745)*. Stuttgart: Klett-Cotta, 1997.

Bernier, Francois. *Abrégé de la philosophie de Gassendi*. Paris: Langlois, 1674–1684.

Bourdieu, Pierre. *The Logic of Practice*. Cambridge: Polity, 1990.

Burke, Peter. *Venice and Amsterdam: Study of Seventeenth-century Elites*. Cambridge: Polity Press, 1994.

Cook, Harold J. "Sharing the Truth of Things: Mistrust, Commerce, and Scientific Information in the 17th Century." In *'Eigennutz' und 'gute Ordnung'. Ökonomisierungen der Welt im 17. Jahrhundert*, edited by Sandra Richter and Guillaume Garner , 273–91. Wiesbaden: Harassowitz, 2016.

Cook, Harold J. *Matters of Exchange: Commerce, Medicine, and Science in the Dutch Golden Age*. New Haven: Yale University Press, 2008.

Cruysse, Dirk van der. *'Madam sein ist ein ellendes Handwerck': Liselotte von der Pfalz – eine deutsche Prinzessin am Hof des Sonnenkönigs*. München: Piper, 1995.

Facius, Friedrich. *Staat, Verwaltung und Wirtschaft in Sachsen-Gotha unter Friedrich II. (1691–1732): Eine Studie zur Geschichte des Barockfürstentums in Thüringen*. Gotha: Engelhardt-Reyher, 1933.

Fester, Richard. *Die armierten Stände und die Reichskriegsverfassung (1681–1697)*. Frankfurt: Jügel, 1886.

Fester, Richard. *Die Augsburger Allianz von 1686*. München: Rieger, 1893.

Jacobsen, Roswitha and Juliane Brandsch, eds. *Friedrich I. von Sachsen-Gotha-Altenburg. Tagebücher von 1667–1677*, 3 vols. Weimar: Böhlau, 1998–2003.

Frijhoff, Willem, Marijke Carasso-Kok, Maarten Prak, and Piet de Rooy, eds. *Geschiedenis van Amsterdam*. 4 vols. Amsterdam: SUN, 2004–2007.

Füssel, Marian. "Höfe und Experten: Relationen von Macht und Wissen in Mittelalter und

Früher Neuzeit." In *Höfe und Experten: Relationen von Macht und Wissen in Mittelalter und Früher Neuzeit*, edited by Marian Füssel, Antje Kuhle, and Michael Stolz, 7–18. Göttingen: Vandenhoek, 2018.

Gambetta, Diego. *Codes of the Underworld: How Criminals Communicate*. Princeton: Princeton University Press, 2011.

Gebelein, Helmut and RainerWerthmann. *Johann Rudolf Glauber: Alchemistische Denkweise, neue Forschungsergebnisse und Spuren in Kitzingen*. Kitzingen: Sauerbrey, 2011.

Glauber, Johann Rudolph. *Opera Chymica*. Frankfurt: Götze, 1658.

Hess, Ulrich. *Geheimer Rat und Kabinett in den ernestinischen Staaten Thüringens: Organisation, Geschäftsgang und Personalgeschichte der obersten Regierungssphäre im Zeitalter des Absolutismus*. Weimar: Böhlaus Nachfolger, 1962.

Heyn, Oliver. "Die Ernestiner und die Reichsdefension (1654-1796)." In *Die Ernestiner: Politik, Kultur und gesellschaftlicher Wandel*, edited by Werner Greiling et al., 185–204. Weimar: Böhlau, 2016.

Humberg, Oliver. *Der alchemistische Nachlaß Friedrichs I. von Sachsen-Gotha-Altenburg*. Elberfeld: Humberg, 2005.

Israel, Jonathan I. *Empires and Entrepots: The Dutch, the Spanish Monarchy and the Jews, 1585–1713*. London: Bloomsbury, 1990.

Israel, Jonathan I. *European Jewry in the Age of Mercantilism, 1550–1750*. Liverpool: Littman Library of Jewish Civilization, 1997.

Jütte, Daniel. *The Age of Secrecy: Jews, Christians, and the Economy of Secrets, 1400–1800*. New Haven: Yale University Press, 2015.

Kathleen M. Eisenhardt. "Agency theory: An assessment and review." *Academy of Management Review* 14/1 (1989): 57–74.

Keller, Vera. "The Centre of Nature: Baron Otto von Hellwig between a Global Network and a Universal Republic." *Early Science and Medicine* 17 (2012): 570–588.

Klinger, Andreas. *Der Gothaer Fürstenstaat: Herrschaft, Konfession und Dynastie unter Herzog Ernst dem Frommen*. Husum: Matthiesen, 2002.

Kühn, Sebastian. *Wissen, Arbeit, Freundschaft. Ökonomien und soziale Beziehungen an den Akademien in London, Paris und Berlin um 1700*. Göttingen: Vandenhoek, 2011.

Lambour, Ruud. "De alchemistische wereld van Galenus Abrahamsz (1622-1706)." *Doopsgezinde Bijdragen* 31 (2005): 93–182.

Lesger, Clé. *The Rise of the Amsterdam Market and Information Exchange: Merchants, Commercial Expansion and Change in the Spatial Economy of the Low Countries*. Aldershot: Ashgate, 2006.

Lynn, John A. *The French Wars 1667–1714: The Sun King at War*. Oxford: Oxford University Press, 2002.

Margócsy, Daniel. *Commercial Visions: Science, Trade, and Visual Culture in the Dutch Golden Age*. Chicago: University of Chicago Press, 2014.

Moenius, Thomas. "Herzog Friedrich I. von Sachsen-Gotha-Altenburg (1646–1691) und der Rittmeister Johann Henrich Vierordt (1649-1685): Eine Fallstudie aus der alchemistischen Korrespondenz." *Mitteilungen der Gesellschaft deutscher Chemiker/Fachgruppe Geschichte der Chemie* 25 (2017): 31–46.

Mokyr, Joel. *A Culture of Growth: The Origins of the Modern Economy*. Princeton: Princeton University Press, 2016.

Montfaucon de Villars, Nicolas-Pierre-Henri de . *Comte de Gabalis*. Paris: Barbin, 1670.

Mulsow, Martin. "Alchemische Substanzen als fremde Dinge." In *Präsenz und Evidenz fremder Dinge im Europa des 18. Jahrhunderts*, edited by Birgit Neumann, 43–72. Göttingen: Wallstein, 2015.

Mulsow, Martin. "History of Knowledge." In *Debating New Appoaches to History*, edited by Marek Tamm and Peter Burke, 159–88 (with comment by Lorraine Daston). London: Bloomsbury, 2019.

Mulsow, Martin. "Ökonomie des Wissens, Wissen der Ökonomie und Wissensökonomie." In ,*Eigennutz' und ,gute Ordnung'. Ökonomisierungen der Welt im 17. Jahrhundert*, edited by Sandra Richter and Guillaume Garner, 295–300. Wiesbaden: Harassowitz, 2016.

Mulsow, Martin. "Pantaleon der Alchemist: Biographische Aufklärung über das Versteckspiel eines Alchemikers" (publication in preparation).

Mulsow, Martin. "Philalethes in Deutschland: Alchemische Experimente am Gothaer Hof 1679-1683." In *Goldenes Wissen. Die Alchemie-Substanzen, Synthesen, Symbolik*, edited by Stefan Laube and Petra Feuerstein-Herz, 139–54. Wolfenbüttel: Herzog-August-Bibliothek, 2014.

Mulsow, Martin. *Die unanständige Gelehrtenrepublik: Wissen, Libertinage und Kommunikation in der Frühen Neuzeit*. Stuttgart: Metzler, 2007.

Mulsow, Martin. *Prekäres Wissen: Eine andere Ideengeschichte der Frühen Neuzeit*. Berlin: Suhrkamp, 2012.

Nelson, Jonathan K. and Richard J. Zeckhauser, eds. *The Patron's Payoff: Conspicuous Commissions in Italian Renaissance Art*. Princeton: Princeton University Press, 2008.

Newman, William R. and Lawrence M. Principe. *Alchemy Tried in the Fire: Starkey, Boyle, and the Fate of Helmontian Chymistry*. Chicago: Chicago University Press, 2002.

Nummedal, Tara. *Alchemy and Authority in the Holy Roman Empire*. Chicago: Chicago University Press, 2007.

Petram, Lodewijk. *The World's First Stock Exchange*. New York: Columbia University Press, 2011.

Principe, Lawrence M. "Goldsmiths and Chymists: The Activity of Artisans within Alchemical Circles." In *Laboratories of Art*, edited by Sven Dupré, 157–79. Dordrecht: Spinger, 2014.

Principe, Lawrence M. *The Secrets of Alchemy*. Chicago: Chicago University Press, 2013.

Proctor, Robert N. and Londa Schiebinger eds. *Agnotology: The Making and Unmaking of Ignorance*. Stanford: Stanford University Press, 2008.

Rolfink, Werner. *Non ens chimicum: Mercurius Metallorum et Mineralium*. Jena: Werther, 1670.

Schmidt, Benjamin. *Inventing Exoticism: Geography, Globalism, and Europe's Early Modern World*. Philadelphia: University of Pennsylvania Press, 2015.

Schwahn, Kai. "Feilschen um geheime Papiere: Job Meyers Rolle in den Verhandlungen mit Friedrich I., Nieuwkerck und Tellgens über den Vierordtschen Nachlass." In *Alchemie und Fürstenhof*, edited by Martin Mulsow and Joachim Telle (forthcoming).

Smith, Pamela H. *The Business of Alchemy: Science and Culture in the Holy Roman Empire*. Princeton: Princeton University Press, 1994.

Soll, Jacob. *The Reckoning: Financial Accountability and the Making and Breaking of Nations*. New York: Basic Books 2014.

Soukup, Rudolf Werner and Helmut Mayer. *Alchemistisches Gold, Paracelsische Pharmaka: Laboratoriumstechnik im 16. Jahrhundert*. Wien: Böhlau, 1997.

Spence, Michael. "Job Market Signaling." *Quarterly Journal of Economics* 87, no. 3 (1973): 355–74.

Spence, Michael. *Market Signaling: Informational Transfer in Hiring and Related Screening Processes*. Cambridge, MA: Harvard University Press, 1974.

Spiess, Johann Jakob. *Kleine Beiträge zur Aufnahme und Ausbreitung der Münzwissenschaft*, vol 1. Ansbach: Posch, 1768.

Thiele, Andrea. "The Prince as Military Entrepreneur? Why Smaller Saxon Territories Sent 'Holländische Regimenter' (Dutch Regiments) to the Dutch Republic." In *War, Entrepreneurs, and the State in Europe and the Mediterranean, 1300–1800*, edited by Jeff Fynn-Paul , 170–92. Leiden: Brill, 2014.

Westphal, Sigrid. "Nach dem Verlust der Kurwürde: Die Ausbildung konfessioneller Identität anstelle politischer Macht bei den Ernestinern." In *Zwischen Schande und Ehre: Erinnerungsbrüche und die Kontinuität des Hauses. Legitimationsmuster und Traditionsverständnis des frühneuzeitlichen Adels in Umbruch und Krise*, edited by Martin Wrede and Horst Carl, 173–92. Mainz: Zabern, 2007.

Westphal, Sigrid. *Kaiserliche Rechtsprechung und herrschaftliche Stabilisierung: Reichsgerichtsbarkeit in den thüringischen Territorialstaaten, 1648–1806*. Köln/Weimar/Wien: Böhlau, 2002.

Young, John T. *Faith, Medical Alchemy and Natural Philosophy: Johann Moriaen, Reformed Intelligencer, and the Hartlib Circle*. Aldershot: Ashgate, 1998.

# 6

# LIEFHEBBERIJ

## A market sensibility

*Claudia Swan*

The seventeenth-century painting *Glorification of Commerce and Science* (Figure 6.1) serves as an articulate frontispiece to this volume on knowledge societies as affective economies. The painted figures that populate this visualization of a knowledge economy variously connect knowledge, economy and affect in a lively congregation of humans, animals and mythological personages. Art is central to this microcosm: the attributes of the liberal arts are strewn across the foreground; an ape riding in Mercury's chariot dispenses items associated with mimetic arts and play; and the painting itself owes its existence to its artist. At left, shrouded in shadow at the far end of the portico in which a group of men study the world in the company of globes and books, an artist sits at an easel: structurally, the painter and his work are crucial. The art of painting records knowledge; and art stirs affect.

In the early modern era paintings were prized commodities, and subject to the contingencies of an open market in the Netherlands. This essay explores the *liefhebber* (devotee or admirer) – a figure that emerged in that time and place – asking how knowledge of art, the market for it, and affect were configured by those identified as *liefhebbers* and in their practice of *liefhebberij*. The *liefhebber*, I suggest, embodied a market sensibility: both knowledge and affect were critical to evaluating works of art; and critical and market valuation went hand in hand with appreciation unto love for art.

## Terms

Early modern standardization of the Dutch language hinged on the publication, by Christoffel Plantin in Antwerp in 1573, of the first Netherlandish translation dictionary. The monumental *Thesaurus Theutonicae Linguae/ Schat der Neder-duytscher spraken/ Thresor du langage Bas-alman, dict vulgaireme[n]t Flameng*, one of the earliest printed translation handbooks, consists of close to 40,000

**FIGURE 6.1**    Attrib. to Jan Brueghel II, *Glorification of Commerce and Science (The Children of Mercury)*, c. 1649. Oil on canvas, 70 × 92,3 cm. Rijksmuseum Amsterdam: SK-A-3027

Netherlandish words and phrases and their French and Latin counterparts.[1] Varieties of *liefde* defined in the *Thesaurus* include blind, brotherly and passionate love, and amount to 40 related words and phrases in all. *Liefhebber* follows *liefde* and is translated as *amateur* in French and *amator, dilector* in Latin. Plantin's *Thesaurus* enumerates *liefhebbers* of money, of the public, of the arts (translated into Latin as *cultor Minervae*), of music, peace, foreigners, women, truth and wisdom (*philosophus*). Last but certainly not least is the *alder liefhebber*, lover of all.[2]

All *liefhebbers* love, but do different registers of affect apply to *liefhebbers* of women or foreigners, money or truth? What is the nature of the love of philosophers for wisdom or of *liefhebbers* of the courtly art of the pen to whom this calligraphy manual is dedicated (Figure 6.2)? The discrete histories of penmanship and philosophy suggest that not all *liefhebbers* are alike, even though, at least in the case of Plantin's treasury, the term seems stable enough. In a recent study on the amateur in historical perspective, Lisa Skogh notes that, 'Unlike the somewhat more restricted identities of the connoisseur or the virtuoso, the identity of the lover (*amator, amateur, liefhebber, Liebhaber,* etc.) looms so large that it has escaped attention'.[3]

Generally it is agreed that *liefhebbers* were learned non-professionals whose knowledge of a given subject or practice enabled them to exercise discernment. In

**FIGURE 6.2** Hans Strick after Marie Becq/Strick, Title page, *Schat oft Voorbeelt ende Verthooninge van Verscheyden Geschriften ten dienste vande Liefhebbers der hooch-loflijcker konste der Penne*, engraving, 1618. Rijksmuseum, Amsterdam: BI-1885-1328-1

many cases, early modern *liefhebberij* is explicitly associated with knowledge – and with practical value. When the Dutch merchant-voyager Jan Huygen van Linschoten (1563–1611) published *Itinerario*, an account of life and trade in the East Indies, in Amsterdam in 1596, he advertised it in a lengthy subtitle as being 'of great use and interest and also pleasing to all of those who are curious about and *liefhebbers* of what is exotic'.[4] The ornamental artistry of the title page of the *Itinerario* notwithstanding, the publication was not directly intended for art collectors or artists. Van Linschoten's appeal to *liefhebbers* is symptomatic in that it assumes that curiosity and appreciation are tied to knowledge and to use.

It is a commonplace of the literature that Henry Peacham (1578–c. 1644), English author of the *Compleat Gentleman* (1622), relies on the Dutch term *leefhebbers* to translate *virtuosi*.[5] He does so in the context of a discussion of a love (and market) for classical antiquities. Vera Keller has called attention to the significance of *liefhebberij* within the early modern history of science, noting the occlusion of the *liefhebber* in historical studies in favour of the *virtuoso*. These two terms operate across the terrains of art and knowledge production, both in current scholarship and among early modern writers. In lieu of mutually exclusive categories, Keller points to a 'mixed landscape of *virtuoso* and *liefhebber* in the early seventeenth century' and to the possibility that *liefhebbers* were as involved as *virtuosi* in the cultivation of natural philosophy.[6]

The term *liefhebber* was widely used and *liefhebberij* was variously expressed, but the most common current translation of the Dutch term *liefhebber* is amateur of art.[7] In art historical scholarship, classical references to the lover (*amator*) are often cited as etymological backdrop to the 16th-century Italian association of love with the arts and with virtue: Giorgio Vasari (1511–74) used the term *amatore* to designate 'someone who loves arts or ideas and the activities connected with them, or, alternatively, loves the practitioners of these activities.'[8] Plantin's *Thesaurus* associates the arts with knowledge in the figure of Minerva, whom the *liefhebber* of arts (*cultor Minervae*) worships.[9] Appreciation of the arts requires judgement and discernment, predicated on sensory perception. Historians of early modern art have touched on the ability of the *liefhebber* to examine, distinguish, and appreciate works of art, but few studies emphasize the nexus of taste, as exercised by *liefhebbers*, and the market.[10] It is my view that the collateral relationship between appreciation and value was in constant tension in early modern expressions and understandings of *liefhebberij*. This chapter explores practices of *liefhebberij* in early modern Dutch culture, emphasizing the closely related aesthetic, epistemological, and market values *liefhebbers* cultivated.

Many *liefhebbers* were patrons of the arts – collectors, Maecenases, or dealers – and therefore potentially involved in appraising works of art, whether in critical or in monetary terms, or both. In addition, *liefhebbers* were often described as being knowledgeable about art, having an ability to discern its qualities.[11] Discernment and evaluation involved knowledge and taste, and the practice of *liefhebberij* was more often than not social.[12] In her account of early modern *liefhebbers* of flowers, Anne Goldgar traces a community of shared tastes and interests, a microcosm bound by social and market values.[13] Knowledge of the sort Van Linschoten provided was valuable insofar as it was instrumental in the market for goods *liefhebbers* appreciated.[14] Goldgar has demonstrated the affiliation between knowledge on the part of *liefhebbers* and market value in the case of tulips, noting of the valuable merchandise exchanged and collected by *liefhebbers* that 'there is no easy line to be drawn between the supposedly artistic and selfless *liefhebber* and the apparently profit-hungry salesman'.[15] This may help to account for the efforts that were consistently made – by early modern theorists and practitioners alike – to assert the civility and social standing of the *liefhebber*. Love (for art) nor money nor knowledge alone sufficed to command respect: sociability was also a key factor in the practice of *liefhebberij* as a market sensibility.

## Who was a *liefhebber*?

From the late 16th through the early 18th centuries in the Netherlands a robust variety of individuals were called or called themselves *liefhebbers*. More often than not, the love (*liefde*) they were said to have (*hebben*) was for art or matters artistic. (Of course, archival and printed records attest to this form of love to a degree that might be implausible in the case of lovers of peace or truth, whose affective affinities are less readily preserved.) In the opening lines of his polemical address in praise of painting, *Lof der Schilder-Konst*, delivered in 1641 to the Leiden Guild of St. Luke, Philips Angel (1616–83) calls the audience of painters *lief-hebbers* – but quickly specifies he means of drink and the clinking of glasses, which he says they preferred to working at their easels. Later in the oration Angel reverts to a more conventional use of the term, where he refers to viewers of paintings as *Lief-hebberen.*[16]

To be a *liefhebber*, what form or degree of participation in an art or other practice was required? The historical record is ambiguous. The proceedings of a three-day literary festival that took place in Rotterdam in 1598 at which 60 verses were performed by members of rhetoricians' guilds was published as *Der Redenrijke constliefhebbers stichtelicke recreatie.*[17] While the title of this pamphlet ('The edifying recreation of *liefhebbers* of the art of rhetoric') suggests that all of those who participated in the recreation and performed the refrains and songs it records were *liefhebbers*, its lengthy subtitle mentions members of chambers separately from individual *liefhebbers*, indicating that a distinction pertained within the shared love for rhetoric.[18]

Beginning in the first decade of the 17th century, individuals who neither performed nor produced art, some of whom were dealers and collectors of paintings and other luxury goods, registered for membership in the Guild of Saint Luke in Antwerp as *liefhebbers* of painting. Filips van Valckenisse (1554–1614) is the best-known of several members of the Antwerp élite who were not themselves artists and who joined the painters' guild. Van Valckenisse was head of the Antwerp civic militia, a merchant, friendly with several Antwerp artists, and a collector of repute. In 1607 he was one of four men registered as *liefhebber der scilderyen.*[19] Joining the guild as a *liefhebber* rather than as a full member entailed reduced duties and fees, while providing access to the guild's members and activities.[20] Van Valckenisse and other *liefhebbers* of painting pursued, acquired, and may have traded on the knowledge of the art to which they declared their love by joining the guild.

In these same years, several individuals identified as merchants also joined the Antwerp Guild of Saint Luke: the designations 'commerce in paintings' (*neringe van scilderye*) or paintings dealer (*coopman van scilderye*) appear to distinguish outright commerce from forms of engagement denoted by the qualification of *liefhebber.*[21] While *liefhebbers* were not always ostensibly in it for the money, in at least one case a member of the guild was registered as both *coopman* and *liefhebber der scilderyen* (Jan Cooymans).[22] Records of the membership in the Guild of Saint Luke in The Hague later in the century explicitly attest to the concern among *liefhebbers* in the 1640s and '50s with sales of paintings.[23] Clearly a close connection between making and appreciating art, whether the art of rhetoric or of painting, pertained; and *liefhebbers* had a hand in establishing the value of art – a matter to which I will return.

The death of the printmaker and painter Hendrick Goltzius (1558–1617) inspired the vastly talented Sir Balthasar Gerbier (1592–1663) to compose a lengthy encomium that was published in 1620. Gerbier's *Eer ende claght-dicht* is an extraordinary record of the Netherlandish art world and of the terms according to which artists such as Goltzius, of course, and Peter Paul Rubens (1577–1640), who plays a key role, and others too, were esteemed.[24] Gerbier's lament fantasizes a funeral procession led by an art goddess identified as *teeeken-const* [sic] who is joined by Nature, the Graces, the Fates, and nymphs; Rubens is described painting a series of imaginary works in honour of Goltzius, and a bevy of Netherlandish artists pay their respects. Gerbier describes the art goddess as surrounded by thousands of *liefhebbers*.[25] All of those who come to mourn Goltzius – whether allegorical or mythological or actual, as in the case of the named artists – are *liefhebbers* in the sense of having affection for the artist.

Initially, Gerbier uses the term in the literal sense to denote an admirer. A marginal note in the text refers to an individual as a big-time *liefhebber*: '*Raeuwaerts was eenen grooten liefhebber die Cornelis met eenen Peerelen bant vereerde*' (Raeuwaerts was a great *liefhebber*, who honoured Cornelis with a pearl [head]band.'[26] Jacob Rauwert, a prominent Amsterdam-based merchant who died in 1597, was intimately associated with the Haarlem school of artists. He amassed a vast collection of paintings, prints and drawings that was publicly auctioned 15 years after his death, in 1612.[27] In addition to having been a collector, Rauwert is reputed to have studied painting with Maarten van Heemskerck (1498–1574). Gerbier mentions him in connection with the artist Cornelis Cornelisz. van Haarlem (1562–1638).[28] Rauwert's commitment to art and artists is also commemorated in dedications of two prints in which he is credited as a consummate lover of pictures and as a student of painting and a lover of engraving (Figure 6.3).[29] But if the example of Rauwert suggests that what made a person a *liefhebber* was his or her knowledge of artistic practice or the propensity and ability to collect it, elsewhere in the *Eer ende claght-dicht*, Gerbier's text demonstrates how variously and broadly the term applied: all of Goltzius's mourners were '*liefhebbers*' and later the term is used to describe any discerning viewer of works of art.[30]

A year after Gerbier's lament was published, the Antwerp-born painter Ambrosius Bosschaert (1573–1621) died during a visit to The Hague, where he had travelled to deliver a painting to a member of the court of the Stadholder Prince Maurits (1567–1625). The flower still-life painting Bosschaert made for Frederik van Schurman (1564–1623), steward to the stadholder, for which the painter was paid the remarkable sum of 1000 guilders, survives (Figure 6.4), as does an account of his death and its impact written by his daughter Maria Bosschaert: 'My father Ambrosius Bosschaert died in The Hague in the year in which the 12 Years' Truce elapsed [...] and, having died in The Hague, was buried there, to the sorrow of many *liefhebbers*'.[31] It is clear that Bosschaert's work was highly valued and well remunerated, and there is no reason to presume that his *liefhebbers* were exclusively artists. That Bosschaert's 'angelic hand' is invoked in the inscription beneath the vase in the 1621 painting may, incidentally, attest to the vocabulary *liefhebbers* relied on to appraise artistry.[32] They may or may not have known how Bosschaert painted his extraordinary *blompotten*, but they clearly knew enough to mourn the loss of his widely recognized talent.

Bosschaert's daughter invokes anonymous *liefhebbers* en passant, speaking for the currency of the term at the time within artistic circles. In his monumental *Schilder-Boeck* (1604), a founding document of the Dutch artistic tradition, the artist and

**FIGURE 6.3** Hendrick Goltzius after Cornelis Corneliszn van Haarlem, *The Companions of Cadmus Devoured by a Dragon*, engraving, 1588. Rijksmuseum, Amsterdam: RP-P-OB-102.215

author Karel van Mander (1548–1606) makes repeated mention of *liefhebbers* and 'art-loving' (*Const-liefdige*) patrons and collectors. Van Mander refers to Rauwert several times as a *Const-beminder* or lover of art.[33] In many instances throughout the *Schilder-Boeck*, *liefhebbers* are explicitly patrons: Apelles had Alexander and Jan van Eyck Philip the Good; Hans Holbein had Henry VIII, Van Mander writes; Michelangelo and Raphael had 'the art-loving popes'; and 'we have Melchior [Wyntgis]', to whom van Mander dedicated the first of the six volumes of his *Schilder-Boeck*.[34] Van Mander's text serves in this regard as a source for historical reconstruction of private ownership of art and the role of *liefhebbers* in the resurgence of the art market in the northern Netherlands after 1580. In the case of a now unknown painter, Van Mander writes that 'one finds his works here and there with *liefhebbers*' and also describes an owner of that painter's works as 'art-loving' (*Const-liefdigen*).[35] Being able to paint or otherwise produce art was not a prerequisite for being considered a *liefhebber*, however; indeed, the most consistent qualification of the close to 25 contemporary individuals Van Mander so names is that they owned works of art, and more than half of them owned more works by living artists than by older masters. This is clear from the exquisite research Marten Jan Bok has conducted on 'Art-Lovers and their Paintings' using Van Mander's

**FIGURE 6.4** Ambrosius Bosschaert the Elder, *Bouquet of Flowers in a Glass Vase*, oil on copper, 1621. National Gallery of Art, Washington DC: 1996.35.1

*Schilder-Boeck* as a source: Van Mander's account of artists past and present places significant emphasis on collectors and patrons, often called *liefhebbers*.[36]

*Den Grondt*, the opening book of the *Schilder-Boeck*, is dedicated to 'the highly esteemed, honorable, and *Const-liefdigen* Sir Melchior Wijntgis', Master of the Mint in Middelburg when the *Schilder-Boeck* was published, and a friend of Van Mander.[37] Wyntgis (?–before 1626) was a prodigious collector and Maecenas to a new generation of artists, whom Van Mander promoted. The majority of the *liefhebbers* Van Mander mentions in his *Schilder-Boeck* maintained collections; they hung their paintings in 'chambers' and 'cabinets' which they made available to others.[38] Just as he secured the position of Netherlandish artists whose lives he recorded among their ancient and Italian forbears, and advanced a critical language for the appreciation of Netherlandish art in his *Schilder-Boeck*, so too Van Mander promoted a new class of individuals to support them: *liefhebbers*.[39] The progeny of the love of art Van Mander attributed to collectors was more art, of course. One *liefhebber*, Jacques Razet (d. 1609), even made provisions to endow a fund to provide training for talented youth (male and female!) who wished to become painters or engravers.[40]

The greatest *Const-liefhebber* of the time, according to Van Mander, was the Holy Roman Emperor Rudolf II (1552–1612).[41] At the outset of the *Schilder-Boeck*, Van Mander recommends Rudolf II's court at Prague as a Mecca for artists and suggests the inextricable relationship of esteem and value, encouraging at Rudolf II's palace and elsewhere, 'in all of the *Const-camers* of powerful *Liefhebbers*, examining, taking one's time, and estimating the worth and price of all of the extraordinary, precious works in order to see what a remarkable amount one discovers'.[42] Here, as in the documents of the Antwerp Guild of Saint Luke cited earlier, *liefhebbers* occupy and embody associations between the market and criticism, value and evaluation.

Recalling that the collector van Valckenisse joined the Antwerp guild in the company of members identified as merchants, and all under the rubric of *liefhebbers*, it stands to reason that Van Mander's descriptions of works in the collections of *liefhebbers* such as Rudolf II elide economic and artistic value. Van Mander writes of the 'worth and price' (*weerde en prijs*) of the *costelijcke stucken* ('costly/worthy pieces') he recommends for close and sustained examination. A dedicatory poem printed in the *Schilder-Boeck* in honour of Van Mander also implies the relationship between qualitative evaluation and the monetary value of art among *liefhebbers*: 'Behold, examine, and investigate, you esteemed *Const-liefhebbers*/This inestimable work, of wondrous Art:/Who can prize it highly enough, that has earned such praise?'[43] Van Mander may have called out 'art-lovers' so often and in positive terms, Bok suggests, in order to foster their patronage.[44] Many of the *liefhebbers* Van Mander praised also bought and sold works of art, demonstrating the close relationship between liefhebbers as collector/patrons and the market.

## Liefhebberij

What sorts of learned, commercial and affective practices qualified the *liefhebber*? Describing *liefhebberij* as a market sensibility requires investigation of the matter of evaluation and value, with attention to where these overlap. The volume of the *Schilder-Boeck* that contains Van Mander's translations of Giorgio Vasari's *Lives* of Italian artists is dedicated to 'the honorable, highly esteemed gentleman, Bartholomeus Ferreris, painter, and *liefhebber* of the art of painting.'[45] Elsewhere, too, Van Mander identifies individuals who were practicing artists – such as Rauwert, who studied painting with Van Heemskerck – as *liefhebbers*.[46] Van Mander specifies that Munich-born Hans Rottenhammer (1564–1625), a master of cabinet paintings, was also beloved by both artists and amateurs: 'just as his paintings were esteemed by *liefhebbers*, his name was also held in estimation and to be reckoned with among artful painters.'[47] While artists and *liefhebbers* are distinct categories, they clearly shared taste and an interest in works of art. The categories 'artist' and *liefhebber* signal discrete practices but are contiguous in matters of taste.

Van Mander frequently associated admiration and value. In his life of Lucas van Leyden (1494–1533), Van Mander writes that Hendrick Goltzius owned Lucas's triptych of *The Healing of the Blind of Jericho* (1531), which was prized above all other works painted by the 'old master':

> But greatest of all of his known works is a cupboard with two doors, most exquisite and beautiful; it is now with the art-loving and richly artful Goltzius in Haarlem, who purchased it in Leiden in 1602 for a hefty price and to his great satisfaction. By dint of his knowledge of art, he [Goltzius] has a great passion and love for Lucas's works.[48]

According to Van Mander, Goltzius was as artful as he loved art. In his description of how Goltzius acquired Lucas's triptych at great cost and the pleasure he took from it, Van Mander invokes the relationship between value and affect. The subsequent comment about knowledge, lust and love drives home the point: to love a work could entail economic investment, and that love might conjoin knowledge and passion.

In his life of Goltzius, Van Mander writes at some length about an engraving Goltzius made in the manner of Dürer – a small engraving of the *Circumcision of Christ* (1594) that the artist aged and passed off as an authentic work. Goltzius's forgery, which Van Mander elegantly calls a 'disguise' or 'masquerade', was successful:

> This print then travelled, disguised and in masquerade, to Rome, Venice, Amsterdam, and elsewhere, where it was regarded with astonishment and delight by artists and knowledgeable *Liefhebbers*, some of whom bought it at great cost, happy to have gotten hold of a previously unknown work by the

artful Nuremberger. It was also quite amusing that the master [Goltzius] was everywhere prized far above himself.[49]

Goltzius's protean abilities, his mastery of the handling and manner of other artists, posed a challenge to the ability of artists and *liefhebbers* alike to discern the authorship of his work. The question of value is central here: not only was the hitherto unknown 'Dürer' very costly but for this work Goltzius was valued at more than his own worth, Van Mander notes.

Over the course of the 17th century, *liefhebbers* engaged with art and artists as patrons and collectors but also as critics of art, knowledgeable commentators or what would later come to be and are still called connoisseurs.[50] Associating *liefhebberij* with connoisseurship, with its claims to a science of attribution, captures a shared interest in value but simultaneously occludes the emotive investment that is characteristic if not constitutive of the early modern *liefhebber*. Angel's *Lof der Schilder-Konst* argues for the status of painting as a liberal art and for its qualities relative to poetry – and outlines, along the way, a series of qualifications for fine paintings that could instruct both practitioners and *liefhebbers*. It opens with a dedication to a collector, Johan Overbeeck (1617–80), 'in gratitude for your kindness in opening your art cabinet that I might satisfy the desire of my inquisitive eyes.'[51] Desire and curiosity drive the appreciation of art, in ways Angel returns to throughout his oration. In what Hessel Miedema describes as 'a dutiful genuflection' to the dedicatee, Angel asks Overbeeck to forgive the impurity of his language as he will use words painters themselves use. A diplomatic gesture to be sure, this calls attention to the authenticity of the terminology and also signals Angel's commitment to makers and interested viewers alike. The more one understands about how artists talk about their work, the more readily one can make sense of what one sees. It is worth considering whether Angel's text cultivates painters and *liefhebbers* in equal measure.[52]

Angel's *Lof der Schilder-Konst* is structured according to a series of qualities required of fine paintings that are, as Eric Jan Sluijter has pointed out, rather uncomplicated: good judgement and a steady hand are needed, as are knowledge of history and mythology and the capacity to combine compositional motifs. The desired effect of the latter is described by Angel as an 'aenghenamen bevallijcken luyster', which Sluijter translates as 'pleasantly attractive splendour.'[53] Elsewhere, Angel promotes *netticheyt* or neatness of facture of the sort that characterizes the works of the Leiden school of *fijnschilders*, Gerrit Dou (1613–75) first among them; indeed, Dou is the touchstone for much of Angel's text. In general, art should be easy on the eyes, and appealing to lovers of art; the overriding qualification for a fine painting is that it mimic nature deftly and convincingly, coming as close to nature as possible. The highest form of praise one can give is that 'the successful imitation of life is unprecedented.' Although directed to an audience of painters, Angel's *Lof der Schilder-Konst* in its printed form offers a handbook of terms and criteria according to which admirers could reflect on paintings, and according to which those works could be valued.

Especially pertinent to the matter of *liefhebberij* is the consistent emphasis on affect and on value. As, for instance, where Angel writes that one of the qualities he enumerates – *Rijckelijckheydt*, abundance or a 'pleasingly decorative richness' – 'awakens [stimulating affections] in the breasts of art-lovers (*Konst-beminders*). One sees this daily in those who enrich their paintings and works with it, drawing the delighted eye of art-lovers (*Liefhebberen*) eagerly to their works, with the result that the paintings sell more readily.'[54] Paintings should appeal to the eyes of art lovers, whose responses find structure and phrasing in Angel's text; when they do, they sell well. Dou, epitome of Angel's qualifications, secured the patronage of an 'unvergleichbarer Liebhaber' (*liefhebber* beyond compare) Pieter Spierinck (c. 1595–1652), collector and diplomat, according to rather unusual terms: for 500 florins per year Spierinck maintained right of first refusal to Dou's paintings.[55] Angel himself describes the contract; rather than discrediting the artist, it redounds to his credit that he commands such high fees and such market prestige.[56] As Sluijter has made clear, this was not a patronage relationship that prevented Dou from operating on the open market; rather, it strengthened his market power, much as did Angel's praise for his paintings in the *Lof der Schilder-Konst*.[57]

According to several theoretical treatises of the 17th century, recognizing a great work of art coincided with being able to distinguish between originals from copies. Conceptions of individual manner bore directly on considerations of authorship, and in many cases qualitative language such as Angel used to describe rendering and facture factored into considerations of authenticity. 'No separate term existed yet for forgeries', Anna Tummers writes of the 17th century, but interest in judgement and discernment of 'what is good, what is beautiful and what are copies and originals' ran high.[58] The distinction between a copy and an original (the latter often referred to as a *principael* in era sources) directly affected market value. In some cases, if a painter was very clever and made a copy indistinguishable from an original (by herself or others) the ability to do so could garner praise, but in general even copies by a painter of her own work were deemed less valuable than the original inventions.[59] It is important to bear in mind that it was standard practice for young artists to learn their craft by imitating masters' works: the distinction between original and copy pertains principally to the market for art rather than the studio arena. In principle, therefore, but also in practice, considerations on quality spoke directly to value.

In 1649 the Parisian printmaker Abraham Bosse (1604–76) published *Sentimens sur la distinction des diverses manieres de peinture, dessein, & des originaux d'avec leurs copies*, widely considered one of the first treatises of art criticism and connoisseurship.[60] Bosse's *Sentimens* is a fascinating excursus on a French variant of *liefhebbers*, the *Curieux de Tableaux*, whom he credits with having inspired the text. Impelled by the challenge of conveying knowledge of how to distinguish among works of art and how to discern originals from copies, Bosse offers up his treatise, he writes, in the spirit of resolving bitter disputes between *Curieux de Tableaux* and practitioners concerning the merits of works of art. Straight away he invokes merchants as well, among those interested in the distinction between originals and copies. Bosse even suggests that learning the art of distinction between originals and copies will improve the stature of merchants and *Curieux & connoissants*. The latter, he complains, are falsely credited with *manie*:

'Car c'est a tort qu'on repute à folie et foiblesse, d'estre amateur & connoissant de ce qui est beau & bon.'[61] It was mistaken to confuse an amateur's affective investment with chaotic emotions; being a *liefhebber* required judgement.

Throughout the text of the *Sentimens*, Bosse implicates knowledge in the assessment *and* the making of art: the knowledge of what is beautiful and good motivates the *Curieux & connoissants* no less than the knowledgeable (*'savant'*) painters and engravers he invokes. The iconography of the title page of *Sentimens* (Figure 6.5) is nowhere explicated in the text, but it is worth considering the encounter it stages among allegorical figures as a commentary on the relationship between knowledge and art and, perhaps, love. In the engraving, a female allegory of painting holds a palette in one hand and gestures with the other toward a tableau depicting Minerva; she has turned from her easel, just visible in the background, to offer her work up to the gaze of another female figure, who regards the tableau. A putto wearing a laurel crown supports the painting from below. Painting is the very embodiment of knowledge, in the figure of the goddess, and is supported by love – at least in mid-century Paris. In the subsequent century, the *Encyclopédie* will assert a clear distinction between amateur and connoisseur; the latter is not defined by his taste, but by 'a certain discernment by which he judges art'. Moreover, although not all painters are connoisseurs, the connoisseur must be a painter, according to the *Encyclopédie*.[62] The relationship between *liefhebberij,* practice, and knowledge is symbiotic in the 17th century, at least according to the sources under review here.

In his ambitious theoretical treatise *Inleyding tot de Hooge Schoole der Schilderkonst* (1678), the painter Samuel van Hoogstraten (1627–78) addresses the status and pre-disposition of *liefhebbers*, whose admiration for art, Van Hoogstraten writes, needs to be protected from deception.[63] He recommends consulting with artists directly, as judgement of art requires thorough understanding of the grounds of art. *Achting* (consideration) and *oordeel* (judgement) are crucial to the *liefhebber*, but do not necessarily come naturally. Training is needed, both Bosse and Van Hoogstraten write, to harness and to focus affective and rational capacities. For the *liefhebber/curieux*, the exercise of judgement is a requisite counterweight to affect: love and curiosity are tempered by knowledge, not least to protect market investment.[64] Van Hoogstraten, it has been noted, is particularly biting in his passing commentary on *liefhebbers*, denigrating them for their lack of knowledge. Rather than indicating a fundamental shift in the perception and relative status of amateurs or *liefhebbers*, Van Hoogstraten's critique seems to me to be symptomatic of a broadening market, in which merchant-*liefhebbers* had to prove their mettle. While in the later 18th century, especially in France, a clear distinction between amateurs and connoisseurs can be drawn according to who exercised sentimental appreciation (amateurs) and who practiced judgement and discernment (*connoisseurs*), throughout the 17th century and in the Netherlands, *liefhebberij* generally entailed both affect and knowledge and had significant market repercussions.

A lively drawing by Rembrandt van Rijn (1606–69) of a group of men weighing in on works of art in a studio setting is frequently adduced in discussions of Rembrandt's sentiments about those who judged (his) art and is regularly cited

**FIGURE 6.5** Abraham Bosse, Title page, *Sentimens sur la distinction des diverses manieres de peinture, dessein, et graueure,* engraving, 1649. Source gallica.bnf.fr/Bibliothèque nationale de France

in histories of art criticism (Figure 6.6). An asinine figure (the ears of an ass protrude from his hat) seated at left holds forth on a painting propped up before him and another image on the ground. The two works share a similar format and

**FIGURE 6.6**  Rembrandt van Rijn, *Satire on Art Criticism*, pen and brown ink with corrections in white on paper, 1644. The Metropolitan Museum of Art, NY: 1975.1.799

size, although the portrait-like image lying on the ground does not seem a sketch for the framed painting. It is tempting to try to affiliate them as original and copy, and to see the protagonist of this image as judging their relationship. In the right foreground, squatting behind the framed picture, a man in a hat wipes his naked bottom. An old, sketchily depicted figure leans in from behind a framed painting, his body bowed under the weight of a gold chain; Egbert Haverkamp Begemann associated the very large shield behind him with Minerva. While the ass's ears may suggest an association with the legend of the Calumny of Apelles, Paul Crenshaw has proposed a more immediate, personal iconography: he associates Rembrandt's satirical drawing with the publication by Constantijn Huygens (1596–1687) in 1644 – the date inscribed on the drawing – of a series of epigrams that were critical of a portrait by the artist.[65] What is legible of the inscriptions – the rhyming phrases 'dees […] van d kunst / is […] gunst' – associates art (*kunst*) with favour (*gunst*), implying both appreciation of the quality of art and estimation of its value. Did Rembrandt mean to implicate Huygens directly, and does the shitting figure embody the artist's response to criticism of his work? While a personalized interpretation of this biting sketch is not out of the question, the references to money (in the figure wearing an implausibly heavy chain) and to knowledge (by way of Minerva) are also consistent with a more general understanding, outlined in the foregoing pages, of *liefhebberij* as a market sensibility. The figures assembled by Rembrandt have been said to embody Van Hoogstraten's reservations about *liefhebbers*, whom he refers to as deluded and blind. But the critic sitting on a barrel in the drawing by Van Hoogstraten's master has the power, by way of his favour, to transform shit into gold. Imagine that the men in hats – the seated critic, the squatter and the two standing men at the far right – are all *liefhebbers*. Products of the artist are subject to the power of the *liefhebber* to influence their value by favouring them, in a context where knowledge and money are in play.

## Sociability

Most of the present discussion of *liefhebbers* and *liefhebberij* pertains to 17th-century sources. Looking ahead to the early 18th century, we note substantial consistency as regards the relationship between sociability and knowledge.[66] In 1711, more than a century after Van Mander's *Schilder-Boeck* appeared in print, Jan van Beuningen (1667–1720) received the scholar and collector Zacharias Conrad von Uffenbach (1683–1734) and his brother at his home in Amsterdam. In the published account of the Uffenbach travels, their visit is described as follows:

> On Thursday 22 May in the morning we visited Mister Van Beuningen on the Singel [...] We had met in the shop of [Nicolaes] Visscher, when my brother was buying copper [prints] and, as a *Liebhaber* of drawings, he invited us to his [house], to see his paintings, of which he was a great *Liebhaber* and *Kenner*. We saw there, in three large rooms and a small cabinet, an exceptional stock of some 150 works by the most famous painters. We examined them repeatedly, the one after the other, with pleasure, and appreciated in particular some works, in which Rubens had painted figures and Brueghel the landscapes (in which he most excelled). The paintings were all in the costliest, carved, and gilded frames [...].[67]

Van Beuningen was one of the best-connected collectors and dealers of his day. In 1713, he oversaw the auction of the paintings collection of Stadholder-King William III after the monarch's death, and over the course of his career he 'played a key role in the formation of several aristocratic picture collections in Germany and England.'[68] Van Beuningen worked for both the Dutch East India and the West India Companies and in other capacities that 'put him at the very heart of the financial world of the Republic'; he successfully cultivated a reputation as a patron of the arts, a collector and a trusted agent.[69] Koenraad Jonckheere's keen reconstruction of Van Beuningen's personal and business network, which extended to monarchy and dignitaries, demonstrates how the banker-*liefhebber* operated at the nexus of collecting and trade.

In addition to organizing major auctions of works of art, Van Beuningen offered select items in his own collection to buyers. Writing in 1710 of art and the market in Amsterdam, a contemporary observed that it was difficult to come by good works for sale from private collections except in the case of Van

Beuningen, whom he calls 'the greatest *liefhebber* in the city at present.' But 'good friends', he wrote, 'can always obtain something beautiful.'[70] Friendship – sociability – was key to acquisition in a market that operated in private spaces. The transition in the Uffenbach anecdote from shop to collection, from the Visscher print emporium to Van Beuningen's cabinet, mediated social realms and was eased by a mutual recognition among *liefhebbers* of interest and status.[71]

According to Peacham's *Compleat Gentleman*, an early 17th-century manual of refined behaviour and a guide to taste, the cultivation of virtue and social skills are essential for the *virtuoso* or *liefhebber*. As others have pointed out, learning to draw and to engage in the practice of art was an integral part of social formation and gentlemanly conduct in early modern Europe. In the explication of his dedication to Ferreris of the Italian lives in his *Schilder-Boeck*, Van Mander associates civil, honest, and ingenious European society with drawing and painting, implying that art is a bulwark against barbarism.[72] Herman Roodenburg has recommended study of the social history of beauty, with particular reference to civility and connoisseurship.[73] The figure of the *liefhebber* would play a key if motile role in this history, vying through practice of and affection for art for status and recognition based on market savvy and knowledge. In the *Compleat Gentleman* Peacham asks whether merchants can be noble – and avers that artists cannot, as they engage in labour.[74] But through the cultivation of art, *liefhebbers* could secure social status. *Liefhebberij* might thus be deemed a market sensibility with social value. It engages knowledge and discernment and taste, in the process of evaluating and valuing works of art. In the painting with which this book and this chapter open, *Glorification of Commerce and Science* (Figure 6.1), the processes and products of the market and of the knowledge economy depend on art. In the practices of *liefhebberij* as a market sensibility, knowledge and affect – often subsumed as taste but always reliant on judgement and trade – establish value.

## Notes

1 *Thesaurus Theutonicae Linguae* runs to 40,000 entries in all. F. Claes, *De Thesaurus* and F. Claes, "Über die Verbreitung." For a modern lexigraphical overview of Dutch 17th-century art historical sources that deploy the term *liefhebber*: LexArt AdGn°323761 https://lexart.fr/terms/view/1843.

2 *Thesaurus Theutonicae Linguae*, LI-LI.

3 L. Skogh, "The Varied Role of the Amateur," 490–91.

4 "Alles [is] beschreven ende by een vergadert, door den selfden [Van Linschoten], seer nut, oorbaer, ende oock vermakelijcken voor alle curieuse ende Liefhebbers van vreemdigheden." J.H. van Linschoten, *Itinerario*.

5 H. Peacham, *The Compleat Gentleman*, 105.

6 V. Keller, "Art Lovers," 547. Cf. V. Keller, "The 'Lover'," 1.1, where she proposes that *liefhebberij* be likened to fandom: "Before the modern cult of personality, such fans gathered around ideas, values, practices, and categories of objects, rather than individuals."

7 See in particular Z. Z. Filipczak, *Picturing Art in Antwerp*; J. van der Veen, "Liefhebbers, handelaren en kunstenaars"; E. A. Honig, *Painting and the Market*; M. Zell, "A Leisurely and Virtuous Pursuit."

8 P. Taylor, "The Birth of the Amateur," 502. Taylor's essay identifies *liefhebbers* as collectors (even when painters), and argues for the decline in estimation of the *liefhebber* over the course of the 17th century. The evidence seems to me rather more complex.

9 Z. Z. Filipczak, *Picturing Art in Antwerp*, cites this entry in the *Thesaurus* where she writes that the *liefhebber* "could be considered a worshipper of Minerva, the goddess of wisdom and the arts," 69–70.

10 M. Zell, "A Leisurely and Virtuous Pursuit," 349, refers to the fear of being tainted by the market, which seems more readily applicable to modern connoisseurs than to early modern *liefhebbers*.

11 As a form of amateurism akin to connoisseurship, *liefhebberij* was favoured in the early modern era but came to be understood and criticized as dilettantism in the 19th century. P. Taylor, "The Birth of the Amateur."

12 *Liefhebbers* communed with other *liefhebbers*: "The identity of the 'lover' was a means of cementing and emphasising social networks." L. Skogh, "The Varied Role of the Amateur," 493.

13 A. Goldgar, *Tulipmania* offers an important group portrait of *liefhebbers*–particularly in Middelburg–at the outset of the 17th century, of flowers and (other) strange, or exotic goods. What is particularly compelling and important about *Tulipmania* is its analysis of the value systems–economic and aesthetic–and the networks that characterized early modern *liefhebberij*.

14 "Like art, then, this [the tulip trade] was a trade that operated around networks, and these were networks not just of capital, but of knowledge." A. Goldgar, "Poelenburch's Garden," 189.

15 A. Goldgar, *Tulipmania*, 197.

16 P. Angel, *Lof der Schilder-Konst*, 3, and on spirit and the ability to compose in a fluid manner: "Soo werdt dit dan mede in een Schilder vereyscht, door dien dat hy hier door de Historien, die hy af-beeldt, de Lief-hebberen, en die ghene diese sien; te verstandelijcker kan voorstellen," 38–39. On Angel's text, see H. Miedema, "Philips Angels *Lof der schilder-konst*"; M. Hoyle and H. Miedema, "Praise of painting"; E. J. Sluijter, *De lof der schilderkunst*.

17 *Der redenrijke constliefhebbers stichtelicke recreatie* (Leiden: Henrick Lodowicxz. van Haestens and Niclas de Clerck, 1599). The topics set to elicit and inspire responses on the part of the participants were spiritual ("Hoe sal den Leerling recht oordeelen van zijns Leeraers leer"/"How shall the student judge his teacher's teachings") and political ("Waer in ons daden, boven de Romeynsche zijn te prijsen"/"In what ways are our [Batavians'] deeds more laudable than the Romans'?") Full text available at dbnl.org.

18 *Waer in begrepen zijn t' Sestich seer schoone Refereynen ende Liedekens soo Geestelijck als Politiqve opten Vraghe Ende Regel Ghepronuncieert ende ghesonghen by Diuersche Cameren ende Particuliere Liefhebbers der Rethorijcken binnen der Stede Rotterdam den acht-tienden Negenthienden ende Twintichsten Augusti ano 1599*. This distinction recurs in the introduction, in which the hosts, the *Blauwe Acoleyn* chamber of Rotterdam, also specify that the rhetoricians are not masters of their art: "Want voor ervaren Constenaers wy ons niet beromen." The following stanza reads: "Wy heten u eendrachtich, vriendtlick wel-gecomen,/Alle const-Lief-hebbers, hy sy Camer-broeder of gheen,/ Wel-coem (segh ick noch eens) heten wy alle vromen, / Die met eeren Rethorices const comen verbreen."

19 On the registration of *liefhebbers* in the chamber of rhetoric the Violieren (wallflowers or gillyflowers), associated with the Antwerp Guild of Saint Luke: P. F. Rombouts and T. F. X. van Lerius, *De Liggeren*, 440–41 (1607); Z. Z. Filipczak, *Picturing Art in Antwerp*, 51–52. On van Valckenisse's collection: E. Duverger, *Antwerpse Kunstinventarissen* I (*1600–1617*), 299–311. In 1614, when the probate inventory was drawn up, van Valckenisse owned nearly 500 paintings, some stored in rental spaces, a significant number of which were grouped as copies; he also owned *naturalia* and other luxury wares.

20 E. A. Honig, *Painting and the Market*, 202.

21 P. F. Rombouts and T. F. X. van Lerius, *De Liggeren*, I (1602) 418–19: H. Ceynen "coopman van scilderye"; B. Hertichs, "neringe van scilderye"; H. van Oosten "neringe doende van scilderye"; M. van Cleve "coomenscap doende met scildery"; P. Peetersen, den wert in Henegou "lieffhebber der scilderyen."

22 Cooymans is registered in 1607; P. F. Rombouts and T. F. X. van Lerius, *De Liggeren*, I (1602), 440. All further research into *liefhebbers* in Antwerp depends on the groundbreaking work of Z. Z. Filipczak, *Picturing Art in Antwerp*.

23 A. Tummers, *The Eye of the Connoisseur*, 179. The *liefhebbers* recorded in 1656 were granted permission to purchase works by artists from other cities but not to sell them without the express permission of the burgomasters.

24 B. Gerbier, *Eer ende claght-dicht*. D. A. Freedberg, "Fame, Convention and Insight," 240–45. Freedberg first drew critical attention to Gerbier's *Eer ende claght-dicht* and offers an unsurpassed account of it, also as a crucial source for the early appreciation of Rubens.

25 B. Gerbier, *Eer ende claght-dicht*, 1.

26 B. Gerbier, *Eer ende claght-dicht*, 7.

27 A. Bredius, *Künstler-Inventare*, V, 1734–50; The Montias Database of 17th Century Dutch Art Inventories, Inv. no. 605. M. J. Bok, "Art-Lovers and their Paintings."

28 B. Gerbier, *Eer ende claght-dicht*, 7. On Rauwert/Rauwaert as a patron of Cornelis in particular: J. L. McGee, *Cornelis Cornelisz. van Haarlem*, 219–224. Aaron M. Hyman refers to Rauwert as a patron throughout "Brushes, Burins, and Flesh."

29 Rauwert is credited as an exceptional "admirator" of paintings in the dedicatory inscription of the engraving *The Dragon Devouring the Companions of Cadmus* by Hendrick Goltzius, after Cornelis Cornelisz. van Haarlem of 1588; "Hasce artis primitias CCPictor Inuent., / Simulq[ue] HGoltz. Sculpt. D. Iacob. Raeuwerdo / Singulari Picture alumno et chalcographice / admiratori amicitiæ ergo DD. / A° 1588" ("These first fruits of art are a gift of friendship from C. C. Painter as inventor and likewise H. Goltzius as engraver, to Master Jacob Rauwert, exceptional student of the art of painting and admirer of the art of engraving"). See also the series of prints *Acta Apostolorvm* after Jan Stradanus and Maarten van Heemskerck dedicated to "D. Iacobo Ravwardo svmmo pictvrae admiratori" by his friend Philips Galle (*c.* 1582); title page (Rijksmuseum RP-P-OB-5813; http://hdl.handle.net/10934/RM0001.COLLECT. 114729).

30 B. Gerbier, *Eer ende claght-dicht*, 9.

31 "Mijn vader Ambrosius Bosschaert is gesturven in Schravenhage in 't jaer als den 12 jarigen Trebes uut was […] ende aldaer gesturven ende in Schravenhage begraven, tot droefheyt van veel liefhebbers." A. Bredius, "De bloemschilders Bosschaert," 138 and A. Wheelock, "Ambrosius Bosschaert."

32 For 17th-century concern with works by the hand of the artist, see A. Tummers, *The Eye of the Connoisseur*, Chapter 3.

33 K. van Mander, *Schilder-Boeck*, *passim*; A. Rijkhoff, "'De Liefd' tot Const," 17–26 and *passim*.

34 *Den Grondt der Edel vry Schilder-const* is dedicated to Wyntgis, mint-master and collector. On Wyntgis: M. J. Bok, "Art-Lovers and Their Paintings," *passim* and 162. K. van Mander, *Schilder-Boeck*, fol. 3v. The *rijcke liefhebbers* (fol. 93r.) in his preface to the Italian lives are surely not artists; and he inserts the term *Const-liefhebber* to qualify Agnolo Doni, who is described simply as a friend of Michelangelo in the Vasari text Van Mander translates. G. Vasari, *Le Vite* (1568) VI, 22: "Venne volontà ad Agnolo Doni, cittadino fiorentino amico suo, sì come quello che molto si dilettava aver cose belle così d'antichi come di moderni artefici, d'avere alcuna cosa di Michelagnolo" is rendered by Van Mander as "Een Const-liefhebber zijnen vriendt, genoemt Agnolo Doni, Florensche Borger, die veel fraey dinghen Antijck en Moderne hadde, was ooc lustich

wat te hebben van Michel Agnolo" (fol. 165v.) On Vasari and Van Mander, see P. Taylor, "The Birth of the Amateur," 502–504.

35 The painter is Lodewijk Jansz. van den Bos; K. van Mander, *Schilder-Boeck*, "gelijck men zijn dingen hier en daer by den liefhebbers mach sien. Hy was oock fraey van beelden, als te sien is by Const-liefdigen Melchior Wijntgis," fol. 217r. On Van den Bosch, see C. V. Verreyt, "De Schilder Lodewijk Jansz. van Valckenborch." Cf. the poem by A. van der Mijle, "Een Nieu-Jaer-Liedt."

36 M. J. Bok, "Art-Lovers and Their Paintings"; J. van der Veen, 'Liefhebbers, handelaren en kunstenaars'.

37 "Aen seer Achtbaren, Erentfesten, en Const-liefdigen Heer Melchior Wijntgis eerst raedt, en generael Meester van der Munten der vereenighde Nederlanden: nu Meester van de Munt des Landts, en Graeflijckheyt Zeelandt, mijnen besonderen Heer en goeden vrient." K. van Mander, *Schilder-Boeck*, fol. 3r.

38 K. van Mander, *Schilder-Boeck*, fol. 231v.–232r.

39 On the critical categories promulgated by Van Mander, see W. S. Melion, *Shaping the Netherlandish Canon*.

40 M. J. Bok, "Art-Lovers and their Paintings," 143 and notes 89–91. H. Miedema, *Karel van Mander*, II, 89–93.

41 Van Mander writes of a triptych by Lucas van Leyden that "Dit stucxken is te-ghenwoordich by den Keyser Rodolphus, den meesten Const-liefhebber van desen tijdt." K. van Mander, *Schilder-Boeck*, fol. 213v.

42 "[…] den teghenwoordigen meesten Schilder-const-beminder der Weerelt, te weten, den Roomschen Caesar Rhodolphus de tweedde, sien in zijn Keyserlijcke wooninghe, en oock elder, in alle Const-camers der machtighe Lief-hebbers, alle d'uytnemende costlijcke stucken, ondersoeckende, overstaende, en rekenende yeders weerde en prijs, om te sien wat mercklijcke somme hy vinden sal." K. van Mander, *Schilder-Boeck*, fol. 4v.

43 "Aensiet, insiet, doorsiet, ghy Const-liefhebbers jonst' / Dit onvolprijslijck werck, wonderlijckbare Const': / Wie cant prijsen ghenoech, waer toe veel prijs gheclancken?" Van Delmanhorst, "Een ernstlijck Lof-dicht, ter eeren des wedergheboren Apellis, ende Nederlandtschen Maronis, Caroli Vermander." K. van Mander, *Schilder-Boeck*, fol. 2v. Cf. his remarks on Jacob Grimmer: "zijn edel wercken zijn verdienstlijck by den liefhebbers over al in grooter weerden ghehouden." K. van Mander, *Schilder-Boeck*, fol. 256v.

44 M. J. Bok, "Art-Lovers and Their Paintings," 143.

45 "Den Eersamen, seer achtbaren Heer, Bartholomeus Ferreris, Schilder, en Schilderconst liefhebber."

46 In the case of Ferreris, see also fol. 214r., the Life of Lucas van Leyden: "Noch is te Leyden een cleen soet Mary-beeldeken van hem, by den Const-liefdighen Bartholomeus Ferreris, oock Schilder wesende."

47 "Soo dat ghelijck zijn schilderijen by den liefhebbers in weerden zijn, zijnen naem ooc onder den constighe Schilders weerdich is ghenoemt en gherekent te wesen." K. van Mander, *Schilder-Boeck*, fol. 296r.

48 "Maer boven al dat van hem is te sien, is een Casse met twee deuren, het uytnemenste, en schoonste, en is nu ter tijt by den so Const-liefdigen, als Const-rijcken Goltzius te Haerlem, welcken dat in 't Jaer 1602. tot Leyden om grooten prijs heeft ghecreghen, tot zijn groot verheughen, als een die tot Lucas dinghen, door de goede kennis der Const, grooten lust, en liefde heeft." K. van Mander, *Schilder-Boeck*, fol. 212v. The painting is in the collection of the Hermitage Museum, St. Petersburg (inv. no. 407).

49 "Dese Print dan dus gaende vermomt en in mascarade, te Room, Venetien, Amsterdam, oft oock elder, was by den Constenaren en verstandighe Liefhebbers met groot verwonderen en behaghen geern ghesien, oock van eenighe om grooten prijs ghecocht, wesende verblijdt te hebben becomen van den constighen Norenbergher sulcx stuck, datmen noyt meer ghesien hadde. Het was oock wis te belacchen, dat den Meester hoogh boven hem selven over al is ghepresen geworden." K. van Mander,

*Schilder-Boeck*, fol. 284v. See W. S. Melion, *The Netherlandish Canon*, 45. The print is catalogued as *Hollstein, New* (Goltzius), 11.

50 P. Taylor, "The Birth of the Amateur"; A. Tummers, *The Eye of the Connoisseur.*
51 As translated by M. Hoyle in H. Miedema "Philips Angels *Lof der schilder-konst*", 230. On Overbeeck: idem, 250.
52 T. Weststeijn, "Translating *Schilderspraeke.*"
53 E.J. Sluijter, "Didactic and Disguised Meanings?", 181.
54 P. Angel, *Lof*, 39, as translated by Hoyle, 243-244. E.J. Sluijter, "Didactic and Disguised Meanings?", 183.
55 B. Noldus, "An 'Unvergleichbarer Liebhaber'."
56 E.J. Sluijter, *De Lof der Schilderkunst.*
57 E.J. Sluijter, *De Lof der Schilderkunst*, esp. 26–30.
58 From a 1700 petition the fraternity of painters submitted to the burgomasters of Amsterdam; A. Tummers, *The Eye of the Connoisseur*, 64.
59 Ibid., 74.
60 A. Bosse, *Sentimens*. Cf. Le Blanc, "*Sentimens…*"; R. Filzmoser, "Conceptualizing the Copy"; A. Tummers, *The Eye of the Connoisseur*, 65–70. On Bosse and manner: R. Zorach, "A Secret Kind of Charm," 245ff.
61 A. Bosse, *Sentimens*, 3.
62 D. Diderot and J. d'Alembert, *L'Encyclopédie*: "*Amateur*" Vol. I (1751), 317; "*Connoisseur*" Vol. III (1753), 898. Also cited by P. Taylor, "The Birth of the Amateur," 511–512. Taylor traces the distinction to François-Marie de Marsy, *Dictionnaire abrégé de peinture et d'architecture* (Nyons: 1746).
63 S. van Hoogstraten, *Inleyding*; P. Taylor, "The Birth of the Amateur," T. Weststeijn, *The Visible World*; A. Tummers, *The Eye of the Connoisseur, passim.*
64 On Taylor's recent account, "The Birth of the Amateur," the boom and bust cycles of the art market in 17th-century Holland resulted in aspersions being cast on the *liefhebber* as an eager but unknowing amateur.
65 P. Crenshaw, "The Catalyst for Rembrandt's Satire."
66 On the long 17th century: J. van der Veen, "Liefhebbers…." Van der Veen notes that 17th-century collectors were regularly called *liefhebbers* and notes, though briefly, the sensuous investment in the goods such *liefhebbers* collected. Pleasure and sensory gratification are key. Van der Veen cites a French visitor to the home/collection of Nicolaes Witsen: "Il semble que la maison soit moins faite pour l'habitation, que pour le plaisir des yeux."
67 Z.C. von Uffenbach, *Herrn Zacharias Conrad von Uffenbach merkwürdige Reisen* Vol. II, 418.
68 K. Jonckheere, *The Auction of King William's Paintings*, 37.
69 Idem, 40, 51; on Van Beuningen, 37–54. On the extraordinary wealth of earlier *liefhebbers* and their investments in the East India Company: M. J. Bok, "Art-Lovers and Their Paintings."
70 From a letter written by Isaak Rooleeuw in Amsterdam in 1710 quoted by K. Jonckheere, *The Auction of King William's Paintings*, 44-45.
71 The matter of social comportment in collection spaces merits further study. Roelof van Gelder cites *De Geöffnete Raritäten- und Naturalien-Kammer,* 1707, a manual of comportment for owners of and visitors to collections, used by Uffenbach. R. van Gelder, "Liefhebbers" 262; Jay Tribby, "Body/Building."
72 K. van Mander, *Schilder-Boeck*, fol. 92r. "Want aenghesien in onse volck-rijck Europa, niet Barbarisch, beestelijck, maer Borgerlijck, eerlijck, en vernuftigh de Menschen zijn ghewent te leven: Soo en isser haest niet behoeflijcker noch nutter, om cleen by groot, en groot by cleen onderlinghe te gheneeren, als de voorverhaelde Teycken- oft Schilder-const."
73 H. Roodenburg, "Visiting Vermeer," 392.
74 H. Peacham, *Compleat Gentleman*, 11–12.

# Bibliography

Anonymous. *Der redenrijke constliefhebbers stichtelicke recreatie*. Leiden: Henrick Lodowicxz. van Haestens and Niclas de Clerck, 1599.

Anonymous. *Thesaurus Theutonicae Linguae / Schat der Neder-duytscher spraken / Thresor du langage Bas-alman, dict vulgaireme[n]t Flameng*. Antwerp: Christoffel Plantin, 1573.

Angel, Philips. *Lof der Schilder-Konst*. Leiden: Willem Christiaens, 1642.

Bok, Marten Jan. "Art-Lovers and their Paintings: Van Mander's *Schilder-Boeck* as a Source for the History of the Art Market in the Northern Netherlands." In *Dawn of the Golden Age: Northern Netherlandish Art 1580-1620*, edited by Ger Luijten, 136–66. Rijksmuseum: Amsterdam, 1993.

Bosse, Abraham. *Sentimens sur la distinction des diverses manieres de peinture, dessein & graveure, & des originaux d'avec leurs copies: Ensemble du choix des sujets, & des chemins pour arriver facilement & promptement à bien pourtraire*. Paris: A. Bosse, 1649.

Bredius, Abraham. "De bloemschilders Bosschaert." *Oud-Holland* 31 (1913): 137–40.

Bredius, Abraham. *Künstler-Inventare. Urkunden zur Geschichte der holländischen Kunst des XVIten, XVIIten und XVIIIten Jahrhunderts*. The Hague: Nijhoff, 1915–1922.

Claes, Frans. *De Thesaurus van Plantijn van 1573*. 's-Gravenhage: Mouton, 1972.

Claes, Frans. "Über die Verbreitung Lexikographischer Werke in den Niederlanden und Ihre Wechselseitige Beziehungen mit dem Ausland bis zum Jahre 1600." In *The History of Linguistics in the Low Countries*, edited by Jan Noordegraaf, Kees Versteegh, and Ernst Frideryk Konrad Koerner, 17–38. Amsterdam / Philadelphia: John Benjamins, 1992.

Cook, Harold J. and Sven Dupré, eds. *Translating Knowledge in the Early Modern Low Countries*. Zürich: Verlag, 2012.

Crenshaw, Paul. "The Catalyst for Rembrandt's Satire on Art Criticism." *Journal of Historians of Netherlandish Art* 5, no. 2 (2013). DOI: 10.5092/jhna.2013.5.2.9.

Diderot, Denis and Jean d'Alembert, eds. *L'Encyclopédie ou Dictionnaire raisonné des sciences, des arts et des métiers*. 17 vols. Paris: Briasson, Le Breton & Durand, 1751–1756.

Duverger, Erik. *Antwerpse Kunstinventarissen uit de zeventiende eeuw*. 14 vols. Brussels: Koninklijke Academie voor Wetenschappen, Letteren en Schone Kunsten van België, 1984–2009.

Filipczak, Zirka Zaremba. *Picturing Art in Antwerp*. Princeton, NJ: Princeton University Press, 1987.

Filzmoser, Romana. "Conceptualizing the Copy: Abraham Bosse's *Sentimens sur la distinction des diverses manieres de peinture, dessein, & des originaux d'avec leurs copies*." In *Between East and West: Reproductions in Art*, edited by Shigetoshi Osano, 95–107, Proceedings of the 2013 CIHA colloquium in Naruto, Japan, (January 2013). Cracow: IRSA, 2014.

Freedberg, David A. "Fame, Convention and Insight: On the Relevance of Fornenberg and Gerbier." *The Ringling Museum of Art Journal: Papers Presented at the International Rubens Symposium, 1982* (1983): 236–59.

Gelder, Roelof van, "Liefhebbers en geleerde luiden: Nederlandse kabinetten en hun bezoekers." In *De wereld binnen handbereik: Nederlandse kunst- en rariteitenverzamelingen, 1585–1735*, edited by Ellinoor Bergvelt and Renée Kistemaker, 259–92. Amsterdam/ Zwolle: Waanders, 1992.

Gerbier, Balthasar. *Eer ende claght-dicht: Ter Eeren van den lofweerdighen Constrijcken ende Gheleerden Henricus Goltius*. 's Gravenhage: Aert Meurius, 1620.

Goldgar, Anne. *Tulipmania: Money, Honor, and Knowledge in the Dutch Golden Age*. Chicago and London: University of Chicago Press, 2007.

Goldgar, Anne. "Poelenburch's Garden: Art, Flowers, Networks, and Knowledge in Seventeenth-Century Holland." In *In His Milieu: Essays on Netherlandish Art in Memory of John Michael Montias*, edited by Amy Golahny, Mia M. Mochizuki, and Lisa Vergara, 183–91. Amsterdam: Amsterdam University Press, 2007.

Honig, Elizabeth A. *Painting and the Market in Early Modern Antwerp.* New Haven and London: Yale University Press, 1998.

Hoogstraten, Samuel van. *Inleyding tot de Hooge Schoole der Schilderkonst: anders de zichtbaere werelt.* Rotterdam: F. van Hoogstraeten, 1678.

Hoyle, Michael and Hessel Miedema. "Philips Angel *Praise of Painting* (1642)." *Simiolus* 24 (1996): 227–58.

Hyman, Aaron M. "Brushes, Burins, and Flesh: The Graphic Art of Karel van Mander's Haarlem Academy." *Representations* 134 (2016): 1–34.

Jonckheere, Koenraad. *The Auction of King William's Paintings (1713): Elite International Art Trade at the End of the Dutch Golden Age.* Amsterdam/Philadelphia: John Benjamins, 2008.

Keller, Vera. "The 'Lover' and Early Modern Fandom." *Transformative Works and Cultures* 7 (2011): https://doi.org/10.3983/twc.2011.0351.

Keller, Vera. "Art Lovers and Scientific Virtuosi?" Special issue of *Nuncius: The Varied Role of the Amateur in Early Modern Europe* 31 (2016): 523–48.

Le Blanc, Marianne. "*Sentimens* […] d'Abraham Bosse, stratégie d'un discours sur l'art à la fin des années 1640." In *Littérature et peinture au temps de Le Sueur. Actes du colloque de Grenoble*, edited by Jean Serroy, 35–42. Grenoble: Musée de Grenoble, 2003.

Linschoten, Jan Huygen van. *Itinerario. Voyage ofte Schipvaert van Jan Huygen van Linschoten naer Oost ofte Portugaels Indien.* Amsterdam: Cornelis Claesz, 1596.

Mander, Karel van. *Het Schilder-Boeck.* Alkmaar: Jacob de Meester, Haarlem: Paschier van Wesbusch, 1604.

McGee, Julie L. *Cornelis Cornelisz. Van Haarlem (1562–1638): Patrons, Friends and Dutch Humanists.* Nieuwkoop: de Graaf, 1991.

Melion, Walter S. *Shaping the Netherlandish Canon: Karel van Mander's Schilder-Boeck.* Chicago and London: University of Chicago Press, 1991.

Miedema, Hessel. "Philips Angels *Lof der schilder-konst.*" *Oud Holland* 103–4 (1989): 181–222.

Miedema, Hessel. *Karel van Mander, The Lives of the Illustrious Netherlandish and German painters.* 6 vols. Doornspijk: Davaco, 1994–1999.

Mijle, Abraham van der. "Een Nieu-Jaer-Liedt, aen den Achtbaren, Erentvesten, ende Konst beminnenden Heere, Melchior Wijntgis." In *Den Nederduytschen Helicon*, 212–14. Alkmaar: Jacob de Meester, 1610.

Noldus, Badeloch. "An 'Unvergleichbarer Liebhaber': Peter Spierinck, the Art-dealing Diplomat." *Scandinavian Journal of History* 31, no. 2 (2006): 173–85.

Peacham, Henry. *The Compleat Gentleman.* London: [by John Legat] for Francis Constable, 1622.

Rijkhoff, Annelies. "'*De Liefd' tot Const*': Een onderzoek naar kunstliefhebbers in het *Schilderboeck* van Karel van Mander." MA Thesis, University of Utrecht, 2008.

Rombouts, Philippe-Félix and Théodore François Xavier van Lerius. *De Liggeren en andere Historische Archieven der Antwerpsche Sint Lucasgilde.* Antwerp: Julius de Koninck, 1874.

Roodenburg, Herman. "Visiting Vermeer: Performing Civility." In *In His Milieu. Essays on Netherlandish Art in Memory of John Michael Montias*, edited by Amy Golahny, Mia M. Mochizuki, and Lisa Vergara, 385–94. Amsterdam: Amsterdam University Press, 2007.

Skogh, Lisa. "The Varied Role of the Amateur: Introduction." Special issue of *Nuncius: The Varied Role of the Amateur in Early Modern Europe* 31, no. 3 (2016): 489–98.

Sluijter, Eric J. "Didactic and Disguised Meanings? Several 17th-Century Texts on Painting and the Iconological Approach to Northern Dutch Paintings of this Period." In *Art in History. History in Art*, edited by David Freedberg and Jan de Vries, 175–207. Santa Monica, CA: Getty Center for the History of Art and the Humanities, 1991.

Sluijter, Eric J. *De lof der schilderkunst: Over schilderijen van Gerrit Dou (1613–1675) en een traktaat van Philips Angel uit 1642*. Hilversum: Verloren, 1993.

Taylor, Paul. "The Birth of the Amateur." Special issue of *Nuncius: The Varied Role of the Amateur in Early Modern Europe* 31, no. 3 (2016): 499–522.

Tribby, Jay. "Body/Building: Living the Museum Life in Early Modern Europe." *Rhetorica: A Journal of the History of Rhetoric* 10 (1992): 139–63.

Tummers, Anna. *The Eye of the Connoisseur: Authenticating Paintings by Rembrandt and His Contemporaries*. Amsterdam: Amsterdam University Press, 2011.

Uffenbach, Zacharias Conrad von. *Herrn Zacharias Conrad von Uffenbach merkwürdige Reisen durch Niedersachsen Holland und Engelland*. 3 vols. Frankfurt und Leipzig: [s.n.], 1753–1754.

Vasari, Giorgio. *Le Vite de' piu eccellenti pittori, scultori e architettori […]*. Florence: Giunti, 1568.

Veen, Jaap van der. "Liefhebbers, handelaren en kunstenaars: Het verzamelen van schilderijen en papierkunst." In *De wereld binnen handbereik: Nederlandse kunst- en rariteitenverzamelingen, 1585–1735*, edited by Ellinoor Bergvelt and Renée Kistenmaker, 117–34. Zwolle: Waanders, 1992.

Verreyt, C. V. "De Schilder Lodewijk Jansz. van Valckenborch gezegd van den Bosch." *Oud Holland* 8 (1890): 235–40.

Weststeijn, Thijs. "Translating *Schilderspraeke*: Painters' Terminology in the Dutch Edition of Franciscus Junius's *The Painting of the Ancients* (1637–1641)." In *Translating Knowledge in the Early Modern Low Countries*, edited by Harold J. Cook and Sven Dupré, 163–96. Zürich: Verlag, 2012.

Weststeijn, Thijs. *The Visible World: Samuel van Hoogstraten's Art Theory and the Legitimation of Painting in the Dutch Golden Age*. Amsterdam: Amsterdam University Press, 2008.

Wheelock, Arthur K. Jr. "Ambrosius Bosschaert/Bouquet of Flowers in a Glass Vase/1621." *Dutch Paintings of the Seventeenth Century*, NGA Online Editions. Accessed March 17, 2019.

Yeager-Crasselt, Lara. "Knowledge and Practice Pictured in the Artist's Studio: The "Art Lover" in the Seventeenth-Century Netherlands." *De Zeventiende Eeuw. Cultuur in de Nederlanden in interdisciplinair perspectief* 32 (2017): 185–210.

Zell, Michael. "A Leisurely and Virtuous Pursuit: Amateur Artists, Rembrandt, and Landscape Representation in Seventeenth-Century Holland." *Nederlands Kunsthistorisch Jaarboek* 54 (2004): 334–68.

Zorach, Rebecca. "'A Secret Kind of Charm, not to be Expressed or Discerned': On Claude Mellan's Insinuating Lines." *Res: Anthropology and Aesthetics* 55/56 (2009): 235–51.

# 7

# THE SHAPING OF YOUNG CONSUMERS IN EARLY MODERN BOOK-OBJECTS

## Managing affects and markets by books for youths

*Feike Dietz*

Alexander van Goltstein was an adolescent with an enormous appetite for buying books. As appears from his diary, kept at the very beginning of the 19th century, it was sometimes impossible for him to restrain himself, even when he firmly resolved to keep a tight hand on the purse.[1] He bought some of his books without any special reason: as he wrote in his diary, he just wanted to possess them.[2]

I aim to understand how and to what extent young acquisitive consumers such as Van Goltstein were created in the early modern book market of the Dutch Republic, roughly from 1600 to 1800. This chapter will trace patterns and developments within the construction and conceptualization of young – loosely defined here as the unmarried[3] – consumers in this book market. While economic and book historians usually approach the book market from an institutionalist approach and often overlook the products themselves,[4] my focus is exactly on the books: how did they present themselves to young consumers, and how did they invite young people to develop the mental and physical need to acquire and use them? By combining close readings and insights from the histories of emotions, consumption and youth literature, I argue that books for young people marketed desire as an economic category.

The Dutch book market is a fruitful case study because of the Republic's high rate of literacy and enormous book production.[5] The market for youth literature became a flourishing literary subsystem in the late 18th century, as we know from earlier book historical research: children's books account for around 5 percent of book production.[6] Books for teenagers and adolescents, however, had already developed into commercially attractive and competitive products in the 17th century, when a dynamic youth culture manifested itself. Thanks to their prosperous economic situation, young and wealthy (male) people were able to develop a luxurious lifestyle, undertake international travel, dress fashionably and buy expensive products such as song and emblem books.[7] The digital *Liederenbank* contains around 44,000 early modern songs for the young, published from the late 16th century onwards.[8]

This commercial expansion helps us to conclude that early modern producers of youth literature were highly successful in presenting their wares as desirable and favourable. At the same time, however, early modern youth literature had to contend with its slightly controversial reputation. Many adults were concerned about youngsters – especially girls – who were inclined to read abundantly, ignoring the condition of their eyes, their physical health and their everyday activities.[9] In the 17th-century play *De romanzieke juffer* (The novel-sick lady, 1685), for example, a young female compulsive reader functioned as a warning to spectators.[10] Eighteenth-century magazines and spectators also frequently discussed copious reading practices among the young, out of concern for the youngsters' inability to manage and interpret information.[11] Such worries stemmed from a more general anxiety about irrational and untamed passions, and the desire to raise and discipline youths.[12] But despite all fears and objections, youth literature must have attracted many people. Since the success of a market depends on products which were considered morally legitimate,[13] producers of youth literature must have succeeded in presenting their products as valuable and needed. I seek to understand how.

For the English situation, some research has been done on the commercial strategies developed in the children's book market during the second half of the 18th century.[14] The expansion and commercialization of this market seems to have been – at least partly – stimulated by the changing shape of material books. John Newbery's *Little pretty pocket-book* from 1744, for example, came with a ball for boys and a pincushion for girls. The commercial strategy the publisher Newbery developed here is still used today to attract children: both in the book market and elsewhere, contemporary companies try to attract the loyalty of young consumers by supplying little toys along with their products. Newbery's method was, however, not only the result of commercial ambitions but also rooted in Locke's pedagogical program, in which playing was considered to be a vital steppingstone to effective empirically-based learning.[15] According to the literary scholar Heather Klemann, we have to understand Newbery's Lockean method as a profound strategy to make young readers aware of the capacity of domestic objects. Since Newbery also 'codifies his own books as virtuous objects in his stories', and even shaped one of his books as a ledger, he blurred the distinction between books and practical objects, turning them into things to touch, to possess, and to circulate.[16]

Dutch book producers must have developed other strategies and routes to make their wares commercially attractive. Most of Newbery's books were never reprinted or translated in the Dutch Republic,[17] while comparable toy-books were never developed there.[18] In one of the popular children's poems by Hieronymus van Alphen, the protagonist instead creates an opposition between his books and his toys: 'I exchange my hoop and my peg top for books'.[19]

Klemann's interpretation of the English cases, however, allows me to presume a fruitful relationship between the commercialization of youth literature on the one hand, and, on the other, the representation of young people's books as objects affecting the reader's body and mind. Inspired by Klemann's concept 'book-toy hybrid', I will use the term 'book-object hybrids' to denote books that fictionally represent themselves as material things and places. I argue that these kinds of discursive book-object hybrids spurred the development of young consumers who considered books as affective objects. In this way, the early modern book market created engaged consumers who used book-objects to manage their emotions, and who were gradually shaped as agents within a money-driven market culture.

## Books as objects of consumption and market socialization

The originality of my approach lies in its focus on book-object hybrids for the young both as affective instruments for market socialization and as commodities stimulating consumption. I draw on different historiographical traditions to develop such an approach: the histories of consumption, of youth literature, of pedagogy and of the book. My approach is, first of all, indebted to research on the 18th-century desire for consumer goods, substantially stimulated by Maxine Berg in the past decades.[20] I am building on Berg's idea that markets contributed to the creation of senses and tastes, and that shopping practices depended on advanced consumer knowledge and skills.[21] The early modern market is, I thus assume, based on market knowledge and affects shared by its participants. According to the economic sociologist Patrik Aspers, participants in modern markets 'do not have to go through years of socialization' to internalize such market cultures, beliefs and behaviours, 'as a general market culture is deeply entrenched in the lifeworld of most contemporary "market societies".'[22] But in the case of early modern youth literature, we are dealing with a target group which still needed to shape its attitudes and identity, and with a market which was still developing.[23]

Young people have been given little attention in the historiography of early modern consumption. According to Daniel Thomas Cook, '[t]here is virtually no place of children' in the 18th-century consumer revolution, except for some discussions of the young as an important 'vehicle for a kind of "capital investment".'[24] I aim to understand young people as consumers themselves instead of as targets of the investment of adults, taking their own thrift and consumerism seriously. According to Gary Cross, author of several books on the history of children's consumption, a gradual shift from the parents' to the children's desires only emerged from the 1930s onwards.[25] While we need to restrain ourselves from comparing 20th-century and early modern young people and their desires, I am assuming that the early modern book market also at least partly depended on children and adolescents with a certain degree of interest in reading and buying books. I aim to understand how these interests were encouraged.

In the historical literature on consumption, it is quite uncommon to focus on books as commodities. As the consumer revolution has been traditionally connected to new consumer goods (such as coffee, tea, tobacco) and luxury products (clothes, glasses, jewellery), books have been given surprisingly little attention.

Erlin has argued in favour of a pivotal role for the book in consumption studies, assuming that it combined several important functions in a consumer society: books were 'commodities' as well as important media 'for the dissemination of knowledge about and attitudes towards commodities',[26] and 'for the representation of consumption and of new consumer goods.'[27] As such, they not only participated in a consumer market but also reflected on it, and contributed to the socialization of book consumers.

This especially holds true for children's books. Within the history of pedagogy, early modern as well as more recent children's books are approached as important instruments of socialization, transmitting knowledge and moral values, and thus fashioning child subjects.[28] A good deal of research has been done on youth literature as a place to acquire practical skills and know-how. In *Affect, Emotion, and Children's Literature* and *Learning How to Feel*, scholars have read (mainly modern) youth literature as a tool for emotional socialization: by representing emotional situations and characters, books actively shape emotions and emotional skills, and help young readers to understand and redirect their own affective life.[29] Building on this approach, I will particularly focus on the construction of feelings and attitudes towards the market. As McCloskey has pointed to conceptualizations and representations of markets as driving forces for market developments, there is ample reason to take this function of books seriously.[30]

I will particularly examine the imagination and representation of young consumers and consumerism in books for the young.[31] As we assume that young children were often unable to buy books themselves,[32] I will first of all focus on marketing strategies for older adolescents with money to spend, looking particularly at the many songbooks published for this target group. Books for younger children are, however, discussed in this chapter as well. From the late 18th century onwards, they represent consumption processes of children, and as such offered a new kind of monetary education that targeted children rather than their consuming parents.[33]

This chapter will first analyse how book-objects for youths affected body and mind and helped to manage readers' desires. Towards the beginning of the 18th century, book-objects were increasingly portrayed as commodities in an economic and commercial market system: books for older adolescents were gradually marketed as experiences driven by money and pleasure, while 18th-century literature for children intended to create young book buyers.

## Books as affective book-objects

Titles are the first elements in books that establish a relationship between object and consumer: Gérard Genette considers them as objects that circulate and direct 'many more people than the text.'[34] I use Genette's distinction between 'thematic titles' ('a title that refers to subject matter') and 'rhematic titles' ('a title that refers to form'),[35] and derive from Genette's idea that rhematic titles create secondary semantic effects: titles such as 'fables', 'confessions' or 'journal' immediately relate the book to a certain category or genre.[36]

As 'thematic titles easily dominate the field nowadays', most titles of early modern books for the young were (at least partly) rhematic in character.[37] While they indeed frequently refer to their genre or book type (such as 'manual', 'instruction', 'introduction', 'songs', 'story', 'catechism'), several other books for youths present themselves by their title as a place, object or experience.[38] Books were gardens (the *lusthof* or 'pleasure garden' was quite frequent), instrumental goods (such as pin-boxes or snuffboxes), musical instruments (strings, trumpets), clothing (crowns, dresses, seam bindings), vehicles (such as tour boats), mirrors, food (fruit, fish, milk, banquets), flowers (sometimes plaited: garlands), or animals (dogs, finches). Such type of rhematic titles create meaningful connotative flavours that Gennette did not discuss: instead of a historical period or a generic context, these titles call up material forms and located realities. They in fact turn the book into a sensual practice affecting body and mind, an instrument or place to see, smell and experience. Prefaces and frontispieces often function to reinforce this presentation, inviting young consumers to consider the book as an object to touch or as an environment to explore and appropriate.

The title *Bloem-tuyntje* (Flower Garden, 1660) by Jan Claes Schaap, for example, represents the book as a garden. In a small introductory poem, the book directly addresses the reader, stimulating him to approach the book as a garden with various colors and textures, and flowers to pick.

> That I was named after a GARDEN, that was done
> Because in me, as in a garden, there are won
> Various things, that often do not have the same
> Virtue or nature, the same grace or name;
> But that are different both in texture, color and
> In merit, not identically sweet in scent.
> Let him who wants to know my inner layout
> Pick one of my dear flowers, and find out.[39]

Book and garden are here considered to be highly comparable, since they stimulate the same type of sensual experiences. The visual perception ('siet') is highlighted by the enjambment in the second line, while the book is also depicted as something to smell and touch. Since flowers can be picked, it seems possible for readers to reshape the book by their tactile practices. The dedication to Schaap's children, to whom he offers the book as his last will and testament, stimulates comparable sensual and physical experiences: 'pick, sense, smell and taste'. The herbs and flowers are compared to easily digestible milk and distinguished from 'solid food' which requires much more prudence. Schaap's children – depicted as his 'own flesh and blood' – long for this type of milk to nourish their growing up.[40] In this way, Schaap gradually merges the garden, his body and the book, turning the reading of the book into a highly physical and environmental experience.

Simultaneously, however, a certain distance between book and garden continues to exist. The 'I' in the introductory poem explicitly positions itself as an object *entitled* 'Garden': it is a book-garden hybrid instead of a natural garden. In his dedication, Schaap also discusses some vital differences between his book-garden and real gardens. While natural gardens feed the physical body, this garden attracts the soul: 'Many rich people leave their children for Gardens and Courtyards, in order to entertain their flesh: but I give you this Garden to amuse and exercise the Mind.'[41]

The frontispiece also depicts physical and mental practices as connected but not convertible (Figure 7.1). On the one hand, the reader encounters a garden to see, smell and explore. Instead of spiritual milk (as promised in the dedication) or the rich diversity of flowers and herbs (as promised in the preface), this garden is full of tulips – important commodities at the time, and functioning as symbols for economic progress and material luxury.[42]

At the same time, however, observing the garden functions as a stepping-stone to spiritual reflection. The activity of looking is visualized by the two men in the front, pointing in the direction of the tulips. These men strongly resemble a pair in another engraving made by Adriaen van der Venne and printed in the *Zeeuwsche Nachtegael* (1623), depicting how we see the greatness of God in his creation (Figure 7.2). The man with the telescope at the bottom of the garden also contributes to the representation of the activity of looking. The woman behind the garden gate, finally, looks in a mirror to link the sensual perception of the garden to the process of internal reflection.

While some people look, other people work: they sow, weed, fish and hunt for birds.[43] Whereas cultivated gardens are often opposed to rural wilderness in 17th-century iconography, now people work both in and outside the garden, using their hands, eyes and nose to achieve internal knowledge and growth. The church in the background depicts their final destination,[44] while the fisherman functions as a spiritual fisherman angling for souls – an image we could relate to Van der Venne's famous image *Zielenvisserij* (Fishing for souls, 1614).[45] The ape on the gate (also a visual motif Van der Venne often used)[46] could be interpreted as the crudity we need to overcome by our mental efforts.

The *Bloem-tuyntje* functions, to summarize, as a book-garden hybrid: a book as well as a garden, to consume, walk through and observe in both a mental and physical way. Comparable titles – *bloemhof, lusthof* (flower garden, pleasure garden) – were quite familiar in the genre of (song) books for young consumers in the 17th century. In the songbook *Brusselschen Bloem-hof van Cupido* (Brussels's Flower Garden of Cupid, 1641) by Guilelmus van der Borcht, to give another example, young readers are addressed as 'being hungry and longing for a nourishing poem' and are urged to read 'greedily', just like sheep grazing in the field.[47] Similar to the *Bloem-tuyntje*, title and preliminaries contribute to the conceptualization of the book as a desirable and sensual environment, and stimulate a specific mode of reading: readers are invited to experience and internalize their book-places.

**FIGURE 7.1**   Schaap, Jan Claesz. *Bloem-tuyntje*. Amsterdam: Jacob ter Beek, 1724, frontispiece. Special Collections, Utrecht University, shelfnumber MAG: LMY 256

*Ex minimis patet ipfe Deus.*

Niet iffer oyt van God foo cleyn en flecht gefchapen,
      Of 'twijft fijn Schepper aan ;
Men kan uyt alle dingh ghelijck met handen rapen,
      Dat God dat heeft ghedaan :                                    (den
Siet maar een plantjen aan , een ftruyckjen kleyn van waar-
      Het toont dat God daar is,
Want 'tWefen dat het heeft, koomt niet eerft uyt der aarden,
      Maar van Gods macht ghewis ;
Het Leven dat het heeft , kan niemand haar oock geven
      Dan God die boven leeft :
                                    C 3                           Wan-

FIGURE 7.2   [Anonymous]. *Zeevsche nachtegael, ende des selfs dryderley gesang: geheel anders inder vvaerheyt verthoont, als de selve voor desen by sommighe uyt enckel mis-verstant verkeerdelijck is gheoordeelt.* Middelburg: Ian Pieterss vande Venne, 1623, page 21 from part 3. Special Collections, Utrecht University, shelfnumber MAG: LMY 111

A related category of books is the book–food hybrid. Since people's constant and bodily hunger for food is far more pressing than their desire for other consumer goods,[48] this convergence between books and food stimulates the

**FIGURE 7.3**    Ingen, A. van.'*t Gespeende Diemer-baersjen. Opgeschaft voor des selfsgemaeckte slaven en slavinnen van de hedendaegsche Min. Bestaende soo in zedige, boertige als amoreuse Sangh-dichten, nevens eenige Leevertjens, Kusjes en andere Mengelrijmpjes verseld.* Amsterdam: Jan Claessen ten Hoorn, 1675, frontispiece. Special Collections, Royal Library The Hague, shelfnumber 174 H 34

idea of the book as a physical and inescapable need.'*t Gespeende Diemer-baersjen* (The Rinsed Perch, 1675), for example, is offered as fish dished up for young consumers. The frontispiece depicts the perch on a plate, as well as showing the young lovers to whom it is served (Figure 7.3).[49] These lovers, presented in the subtitle as the 'slaves of love', need to digest their meal – the book – in order to struggle out of Cupid's grasp and be protected against his destructive power.

In the *Sangh-bancquet, op-gedist in papiere schoteltjens, en voor-geset de Rotterdamse juffertjes* (Song Banquet, Dished up on Paper Plates, and Placed before Rotterdam Ladies, 1664), songs were presented as an alternative type of banquet. While it is usually highly improper to scramble for food at a banquet, this place is meant for gobbling. Rather than physical appetite, this dish will take our 'lightened lust' away.[50] Eating songs becomes a way of satisfying emotional desires.

Such rhetorical strategies were also applied to early modern catechisms, which are sometimes explicitly represented as edible or drinkable consumer products by their titles: 'milk for children', 'food for youngsters', and so forth.[51] Instead of turning the reading process into a physical practice, they rather invite their readers to distinguish the needs of the body and the needs of the mind. In the preface of Johan Reinier Kelderman's *Melk voor suygelingen en kinderen in verstand en jaren* (Milk for Babies and Older Children, 1708), the book's milk is characterized as a specific type: 'father's milk', that is spiritual milk, consisting of pen drops and biblical liquid.

> This milk for souls is sprung
> Of children at the breast,
> That first will wet the tongue,
> A first relief from thirst
> Which from a man is wrung.
> Man's milk and the brain's seepage,
> Drops from the pen, such a clear sap,
> The dew of heavenly knowledge,
> Juice from the Bible tapped
> Is here for youth's free usage.[52]

Father Kelderman's mental milk, transmitted by books, seems to be a masculine counterpart of mother's milk supplied by breasts. But at the same time, Kelderman is represented as both father *and* mother of the soul, opposed to biological fathers and mothers taking care of the child's body. As readers may conclude, youths need both female and male parents and have to consume physical as well as mental food, offered by parents within and outside the book.

Readers were not only stimulated to consume and internalize their books: they were also urged to use them as a practical object. The *Nutte tijdtquistingh der Amstelsche jonckheyt* (Useful Pastime of the Amstel Youth, 1640), is offered as an object to store in the young girls' 'sewing baskets and chests' instead of 'a bookseller's window'.[53] The songs should not be confused with endless hair-ribbons, the preliminary texts explain but rather resemble fashionable shoes.[54] Publisher and author, apparently trying to enter the daily world of young girls, present a manual for using books and songs: they are objects to carry and bring along. Their value is presented as the effect of this practice: just like feathers, the songs are very light in character, but turn into valuable ornaments when they embellish girls' heads.[55] Following this line of thought, readers were not to consume the book passively but were also urged to produce its value and meaning by their own reading practices. Media theorists generally use the term 'prosumer' to denote this type of consumers, who are actively involved in the production of their consumption goods. In our digital age, prosumers are omnipresent, but prosumerism has also emerged in the non-digital world from the second half of the 20th century onwards: McDonald's customers have to compose their meal, while IKEA shoppers put together their own furniture.[56] Although the readers of the *Nutte tijdtquistingh* did not undertake the same kind of unpaid and concrete work activities, they could be fruitfully considered as engaging, participating prosumers who spurred the desire for reading and buying books by their own production of value.

Book-object hybrids, in sum, were offered to be internalized and used. They presented themselves as mental (instead of realistic) places or objects, as well as sensual experiences to be tasted and consumed in the way natural gardens, foods and practical things need to be perceived. Titles, frontispieces and front matter clearly contributed to the invitation to perceive and consume them. In this way, affective relationships were established between books on the one hand and the bodies and minds of young consumers on the other. The consumer was shaped as a prosumer: an active and bodily engaged participant within an affective book experience.[57]

## The economy of emotions

In the 17th century, affective book-objects for (older) young people functioned as sensual practices to structure and redirect emotions. In the case of the *Sangh-bancquet* discussed previously, consuming the banquet of songs was a way of both experiencing and managing emotions. One of the songs depicts the romantic love between man and woman as a way of tasting honey. An insatiate woman describes how her lips pass the 'sweet honey dew' to the lips of the man she loves. He, however, immediately wipes the 'godly taste of nectar' with his handkerchief: emotions are stirred up as well as counterbalanced.[58]

The volume *Openhertighe herten* (Open-hearted Hearts, 1620s) – anonymously published but possibly written by Jan Jansz Starter[59] – presents itself through its title and frontispiece as a heart to open, as well as a place to find the pure affections of the heart (Figure 7.4). The depicted couple on the right holds a heart as well as a mug, to denote the activity of consumption. As their simple clothes show, this couple belongs to the lower class. On the left, a rich couple is depicted, identifiable by their clothing, headdress and fan. While the couple on the right has a heart, this couple on the left holds a book.[60] The interaction between men and women is, in this way, organized around their book as their open-hearted heart: by opening hearts, they come closer to each other and experience their love and unity.

This all encourages readers to consider their book as a heart to open, and their heart as a book to read. When they open the book, they in fact open and read their hearts, meeting their vices and virtues. The frontispiece depicts how to handle this book-heart hybrid: readers need to stick their pin into the book, and read the exposed lesson. This pin symbolizes the risk they experience while using their book as well as their heart. The reader may encounter bad vices and must manage the uncertain outcomes. But the book also helps to understand and redirect destructive emotions and behaviour and tries to develop virtuous attitudes. The book, in fact, admits to being part of the unsteady game of life and simultaneously promises to discipline the body and the mind.

Books such as the *Sangh-bancquet* and the *Openhertighe herten* help to redirect and rationalize affects within an 'economy of emotions': emotions must be structured

**FIGURE 7.4** [Anonymous]. *Openbertighe herten*. S.l.: s.n., 1620s, frontispiece. Special Collections, Royal Library The Hague, shelfnumber 2218 E 22

and exchanged, offered and returned, in order to make them valuable to those who conduct and share them. The relationship between desire and economy is sometimes imagined in a highly explicit way. As Arie Jan Gelderblom has demonstrated, (emblem) books for youth often served the 'organisation of desire' by presenting love as an economic category.[61] Gelderblom analysed how emblems invited young people to invest in their relationships by gaining profit from their love and by balancing up their accounts. The anonymous *Nieuwen Ieucht Spieghel* (A New Mirror of Youth, 1617), for example, represents the love between partners of different ages as unequal and therefore unproductive (or without offspring), a problem which could not be counterbalanced by money (Figure 7.5). Young readers of *Nieuwen Ieucht Spieghel* also learned to consider virility and virginity as 'economic assets': intercourse between a young man and woman is, for example, depicted by the taking of a pouch (Figure 7.6).[62]

These types of books, however, also develop a far more negative discourse on money. In one of the songs of the *Friesche Lusthof* (Frisian Pleasure Garden, 1621) by Jan Jansz Starter, money and property are defeated by a faithful mind,[63] while virtue is represented as the greatest wealth, making poor people rich.[64] In another song, a young man, Veelker, shelters Cupid, who has run into bad weather. When Cupid wants to thank his saviour, Veelker says: I don't want any money, but want you to trust my good intentions. Cupid explains: I will thank you for your courtesy, by offering you my courtesy as well. There is no money to exchange here, but rather services, virtues, affects.

**FIGURE 7.5**  [Anonymous]. *Nieuwen Ieucht Spieghel*. [Arnhem: Jan Jansz., 1617], emblem 41. Digital edition Emblem Project Utrecht: http://emblems.let.uu.nl/nj1617.html

'Twas out of generosity that I have sheltered
To make your trembling state easier to bear,
But not for goods or money, for those I do not care.[65]

In such a case, the 'economy of emotions' is not considered to be a market system based on money and prices but an alternative cycle of gift and reciprocity. This alternative exchange model resembles early modern gift culture, identified as a value system 'based on interactions and binding obligations', and functioning beside the economic market. Gifts were to be negotiated 'within social relations that become enmeshed in the cycle of offering and reciprocation', and were powerful instruments for creating status, honour and alliances.[66] Such alternative values were vital in early modern society, in which economic stability derived from sympathy and friendship,[67] and honour and reputation stemming from virtuous actions formed the basis of social classification.[68] As Elizabeth Honig demonstrates in her analysis of the art market, honour culture as an 'alternative site of value-creation' was no less important than economic value based on market transactions.[69]

The cycle of gift and reciprocity affected 17th-century adolescent literature in two connected but different ways. First of all, love is represented as a gift within a system based on reciprocity: virtues and affects are exchanged, and services are

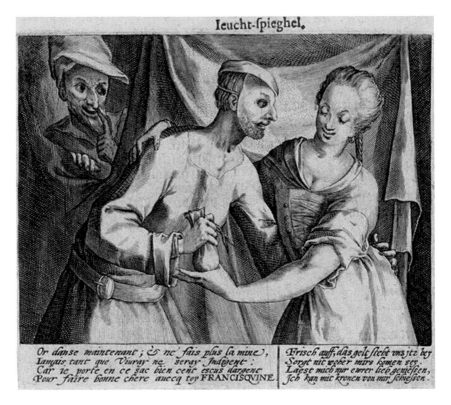

**FIGURE 7.6** [Anonymous]. *Nieuwen Ieucht Spieghel.* [Arnhem: Jan Jansz., 1617], emblem 44. Digital edition Emblem Project Utrecht: http://emblems.let.uu.nl/nj1617.html

reimbursed by virtues. In the *Vermakelijcke bruylofts-kroon* (Diverting Wedding Crown, 1659), for example, money is brushed aside,[70] and 'requited love' is presented as the intended reward:

> Soul fountain, only you
> can conquer me,
> O my lovely!
> Give me bounty,
> with your dearest counter-love.[71]

Wedding crowns are offered and should be counterbalanced by requited love,[72] while requited love is itself perceived as a physical gift in the shape of a crown: 'Crown my soul by love in return'.[73] In the *Amsteldams minne-beekje* (Amsterdam Stream of Love, 1637), requited love is also presented as a gift.[74] In the *Lof van Cupido* (Cupid's Glory, 1626) and *Apollo's Lusthof* (Apollo's Pleasure Garden, 1673), suffering lovers beg for requited love to balance their sick hearts.[75] When this cycle of offering and receiving love failed – as is the case in *Apolloos Snaaren*

(Apollo's Strings, 1664) – the lover falls into great misery and has to make heavy sacrifices.[76] The *Minneplicht en Kuysheyts-kamp* (Duty of Love and Struggle for Chastity 1625), to give a last example, introduces a repeating final line that emphasizes how good love is 'worthy' of love in return.[77]

Secondly, the book itself is part of the cycle of gift and reciprocity. In the introduction of the aforementioned *Friesche Lusthof*, the author Starter tries to gain the favour of young women and explains: as I am offering you some poems, I deserve your favour, and will thank you by writing more verses.[78] In *Apollo of Ghesangh* (Apollo or Songs, 1615), Apollo presents himself in the dedication to his young readers as divine and powerful, being the vital force behind everything in the world.[79] Poets and singers are depicted as Apollo's seeds, since he is the god of music and the arts: 'you my own offspring'.[80] By creating songs, poets place themselves in the service of their father, who, in his turn, will offer their products to the young girls adored in these texts: 'I decided to devote them to virginity.' As a result, the young girls would be able to understand and recognize the men's suffering and would offer 'reward in return.'[81] By accepting the book, readers in fact participate in a system of reciprocity and need to take the responsibility of using the book and preserving the system.

Readers are not always urged to accept this kind of responsibility. The preface of *Minne-plicht ende kuysheyts-kamp* (1625/26) even explicitly relieves its readership of this obligation.[82] The book is dedicated to the 'Dutch nymphs', who are so beautiful that everyone wants to place himself in their service, without expecting any service in return. The cycle of gift and reciprocity seems to be broken but is eventually confirmed in any case, as the nymphs' virtues are considered to be a 'reward in themselves.'[83]

In this way, the book and its young readers are presented as vital links in the chain of giving and receiving. The book invites its consumers to accept books as sensual and emotional experiences to organize affects and love within an economic system of counterbalancing and reciprocity. Reading books is a way of developing honourable love affairs and discovering truths and virtues. The book is sometimes even represented as a face or a heart in which virtues and thoughts will be discovered.[84] Consumers have to do the book a favour by internalizing and practicing its moral knowledge, and by valuing and loving it, to obtain some honour and value as well. As the books often took the shape of natural book-object hybrids (gardens, hearts, flowers, food), the implication is that the affective system to be internalized is natural and logical.

## Towards an economy of money and pleasure in adolescent literature

Adolescent literature from the later 17th century onwards saw the emergence of a more explicit connection of experiences with books to the system of economic and commercial investments. The adolescent reader gradually developed from a consumer transacting emotions to a consumer participating in a money-driven market culture: book-object hybrids were gradually marketed as commodities spurred by money and pleasure. This tendency could be clearly illustrated by several books with titles referring to Apollo. In the previous section, I discussed the early 17th-century *Apollo of Ghesangh* within the context of a cycle of offering and reciprocity. The 1660s and 1670s saw the rise of more Apollo book-object hybrids which encouraged affective interactions between books and readers. For example, the title and frontispiece of *Apolloos snaaren* (Apollo's Strings, 1664) – written by the young Pieter Elzevier, who later developed into a publisher and pornographer[85] – offered the book as a lyre to touch, play and hear.[86] In Elzevier's preface, young Amsterdam ladies ('Amstel-juffertjes') are urged to receive the songs and connect them to their body and mind: songs should be fondled by hands and experienced by tongues and throats; songs need to stir up emotions:

> but considering how early your worships have embraced all authorised and decent novelties, I make bold to offer these strings (tuned to the loveliest and latest tones) rather to you than to the matrons, so that they can rest in your soft lap, to be stroked by your sweet fingers and to be sung and warbled by your divine throats and tongues.[87]

Elzevier's next Apollo book *Den lacchenden Apoll, uytbarstende in drollige rymen* (The Laughing Apollo, Bursting out in Turdish Rhymes, 1667) clearly demonstrates Elzevier's development into an author of dirty and erotic work. The book has been dedicated to young girls, who should consider rhymes as turds, who are invited to smell and chew them, and who are encouraged to use the pages of their book as toilet paper.

By receiving (compare title page – Figure 7.7), touching and effectively using the turds and toilet paper, the girls would honour the book's request: it is their alternative mark of service in return.

> Accept then, together with other honest and merry folk, my *Laughing Apollo, or Turdish Rhymes*, read and read on, chew and ruminate our rhyming Turds, and find out what their smell, nature and properties are […]. Gracious ladies, he is proud to be able to supply you (by making this turdish booklet) with the leaves to fill the wooden dish of the shithouse, so that you may wipe yourself when your turdish shop has been gilded at the back, for in this way he can show you that he is truly your worship's humblest servant.[88]

We see comparable strategies in *Apollo's lusthof* (1673) published in the same period. The book is offered to the Amstel Nymphs as a natural place full of flowers to pick and smell. Apparently, these flowers sometimes have an erotic flavour. A man wants to thank a girl who darned his socks and invites her to his bed: 'There, I will lay the profit down in your lap'. The lady agrees: 'There you will pay for my work, if you want to, / Show your manpower'.[89] In this case, people make transactions through erotic practices instead of using money, along the lines of the system of offering and reciprocity. The affective interaction between youths and book-objects no longer takes the shape of a circulation of moral sentiments but rather encourages immoral practices of untamed passion and pleasure.

As a next step in this development, the 18th century saw the rise of Apollo book-objects that explicitly positioned themselves as commodities in an economic, money-driven system. In the case of *Apollo's prullekraam* (Apollo's Trash Stall, 1716) by Jakobus Rosseau, the book is compared to a marketplace where books were bought and circulated.[90] In his dedication to the young nymphs, Apollo extols the virtues of his goods: 'I have shepherds' tunes, farmers' drones, love songs and other whims, near my bottom, which I cannot mention, I have something to clink and to drink'.[91]

This Apollo title could be connected to the series of *Apollo's Marsdrager* (Apollo's Pedlar, 1710) by Gysbert Tysens and the several editions of *Apollo's gift*.[92] In *Apollo's kermis-gift aan de Haagsche vermaaksgesinde jeugd* (Apollo's Fairtime Gift to the Hague Young Folk, Disposed to Pleasure, 1740), the readers' favour was to be expressed by their acquisition of the book. The author thanks his paying readers, because '[n]o poetry will gain new energy without any profit'.[93] The reader is

**FIGURE 7.7** Elzevier, Pieter. *Den lacchenden Apoll, uytbarstende in drollige rymen.* Amsterdam: B. Boekholt, 1667, frontispiece. Special Collections, Royal Library The Hague, shelfnumber 174 G 44

addressed as someone who should buy this book and should continue buying in order to save the ongoing production of new songs.

Titles which name Apollo's pedlar and market stall connect books to an economy based on money and pleasure. In combination with frontispieces depicting commercial processes, such titles could be interpreted as instruments to signal the diverting nature of the books and be connected to the development of a printed popular entertainment industry.[94] This development is not specifically related to young consumers, but adolescents were often addressed and represented as agents in this culture of money and pleasure.

We trace here a development within the tradition of book-object hybrids: books were gradually adapted into commercial practices in which young readers were urged to throw themselves into a world of pleasure, passion and money. The *Vermakelyke Slaa-tuintjes* (Entertaining Lettuce Garden, 1777 – several comparable titles) differs from 17th-century book-garden hybrids in its explicit promotion of erotic love and pleasure; the pornographic *D'openhertige juffrouw* (The Open-Hearted Lady, 1680) refers by its title to the *Openhertighe herten* (1620s) but now represents desire as something to pursue instead of control.[95] And while the shepherd's crook in the *Harders stafje ofte soet vermaen* (Shepherd's Crook or Sweet Warning, 1664) functions as an instrument of discipline, 18th-century books refer to shepherd's crooks to evoke a community of rustic shepherds who drink and celebrate together.[96] Within the opening song of *Het herders-stafje, met het zingende Zwaantje* (The Shepherd's Crook with the Singing Swan, 1740s?), people spend all their money on drink, considering money as the foundation of pleasure.[97] In *Het harders-stafje, oft Het soet geselschap* (The Shepherd's Crook or Sweet Company of Shepherds and Shepherdesses, 1740)[98] solitude is compared to poverty. Money, unity and amusement turn out to be the intended purposes in these 18th-century shepherd's-crook books.

And while 17th-century titles often refer to natural objects and places, as I discussed in the third section, in the 18th century luxurious commodities and manmade places emerged. In the *Schatkamer der Nederlandsche jeugd* (Treasury of Dutch Youth, last quarter of the 18th century), the book takes the shape of a room full of treasures, which is depicted on both the frontispiece and the preface as a 'book room' ('boekkamer').[99] Books turn into treasures, and the *Schatkamer der Nederlandsche jeugd* takes shape as a place to explore such precious and valuable goods.

*De nieuwe vermakelyke Snuyf-Doos* (The New and Diverting Snuff-Box, 1766) presents the book as a highly fashionable luxury object for 18th-century upper-class men. The commercial fashion for snuff-boxes is described in the first song: consumers are driven by their own desires and pleasures, and sellers by their wish for money.

> What commerce flourishes
> Like th'ever present snuff store,
> Where each one nourishes
> His growing want for more.

All who can use their boots
Be it spinster or green youth,
Have their snuff tin about,
With snuff or oft without
[...]
Then there are those who wish
for Pompadour or Fiolet ,
And mention without anguish
It's the way my nose is set.
Thus each to his inclination
Buys for his delectation,
Will want to be supplied
With what he did decide
And all the sellers of the snuff
Care for is how you pay for the stuff.[100]

Readers are addressed as well-to-do people who want to buy diverting luxuries such as books: 'Friends, buy with pleasure this snuff-box full of amusement'.[101] This longing for fashionable luxuries is encouraged as well as criticized within the book: the book warns of the torn clothes and dirty lice hidden behind much splendour and majesty.[102] The market of money and modish luxury is ridiculed here, at the same time as it is identified as the context in which books and their consumers participate.

Young readers, to conclude, were increasingly addressed as consumers who longed for commodities, luxuries and amusement, and thus wanted and needed to spend their money on affective book-objects. By buying goods, the books promise, consumers would foster their own pleasure as well as a flourishing and fashionable book market.

## Creating sensible child consumers in the 18th century

While the adolescent book market developed into a pleasure- and money-driven market, the book market for young children took another direction in the second half of the 18th century. In comparison with the adolescent (song) books discussed previously, late 18th-century enlightened children's books were explicitly developed for pedagogical and moral purposes, and were intended to reach a public of young children who usually did not buy their own books. Title pages and prefaces did not depict young readers as acquisitive purchasers of entertainment and luxury goods, as happened in 18th-century adolescents' literature. They rather addressed the children's parents, aiming to convince them of their moral purposes and virtuous effects.

As a fascinating exception to this tendency, *De vermaarde historie van Gillis Zoetekoek* (The Renowned History of Giles Gingerbread, translated from the English, 1781) presents an image of greedy young book buyers on the preliminary pages: with outstretched arms, children try to acquire a book held by the bookseller (Figure 7.8).[103] According to the accompanying poem, this is book-seller Jasper, who sells the cherished book that everyone wants to have. Text and image can be interpreted as a commercial strategy to spur the youngsters' buying interests.

> So those who want it should not dally
> *But should accompany me,*
> *For it may soon be completely sold out.*
> Away they flew, that's all it took:
> To Jasper's, there to acquire the book.[104]

Although most enlightened children's books did not include these types of explicit marketing elements, 18th-century youth literature often used fictional techniques to teach market skills and to stimulate a youthful market culture. The Dutch material has never been studied from this perspective, but recent scholarship by Sandra Maß on German and English sources offers us some insight into this process of economic and monetary education.[105] Maß has analysed the growing numbers of books and toys developed to train children's monetary skills within schools, as well as in family environments, to argue that monetary education was intended to shape the children's body as well as emotional behaviour:

> This training was based on three intertwining elements: the construction and bodily control of needs, learning and training how to use money adequately, and finally, acquiring knowledge about money. Theoretically, this process can be classified as embodiment. Body, cognition, and emotions were combined in most elements of monetary education: the body of the child had to learn and train to use money in certain ways and to experience the appropriate feeling when confronted with money and needs, and the child had to play and read in order to strengthen this process.[106]

The competences to embody changed during the 18th and 19th centuries, Maß demonstrated. While late 18th-century and early-19th-century education was pre-dominantly dedicated to the development of a moral monetary habitus, char-acterized by benevolence and the act of donating money, the later 19th century shifted focus to the process of consumption, investment and business cycles. Spending money was then represented as 'an act of investment for an expected output, for an increase in production cycles, and an increase in profit making'.[107] Such consumption patterns were taught by books and also toys; throughout the 19th century, replicas of shops became increasingly popular as toys to train the children's monetary skills.[108]

In this chapter, I am particularly interested in the way 18th-century Dutch children's books made young people into economic agents who traded and bought

CORNELIS ᴀᴀɴᴢʏɴᴇ SCHOOLMAKKERS.

De Neef van Govert Zoetekoek
 Verkoopt, o maats! een aartig boek,
Van elk die leeren wil gezocht;
 Die 't hebben wil moet niet lang ftaan,
Maar aanftonds met my mede gaan,
 Want ftraks is 't mooglyk uitverkocht.

Toen vlogen zy, by heele hoopen
 Na Jasper, om een boek te koopen,

**FIGURE 7.8** [Anonymous]. *Proeve eener kleine historie, voor kinderen.* Amsterdam: P. Hayman, 1781, fol. *3r. Special Collections, University of Amsterdam, shelfnumber OK 78–199

books. Books sometimes function as the paper equivalent of play shops. The *Officina Scholastica of School-winkel* (School shop, 1743) is explicitly marketed as a shop which offers emblems, epigrams and other types of texts 'for sale'.[109] Journals and text collections were generally entitled 'magazijn', a term which also denotes a storehouse or warehouse (e.g. *Magazyn der kinderen* 1757, *Nieuw magazijn voor jonge juffrouwen* 1792). Such book-shop hybrids connected books and market places and thus shaped children in their role as shoppers.

The process of spending and profit-making, which Maß connected to the late 19th century, is already visible in the late 18th-century Dutch material: fictional children not only donate books to those in need but are also portrayed as buyers of books. In Willem de Perponcher's *Onderwijs voor kinderen* (Education for children, 1782), a father gives his three children each three ducats to spend. While his two sons wasted the money and became ill from the many sweets they bought, Karoline – the only girl! – wrote up a cashbook and weighed up her expenses carefully: she obtained a couple of useful things – including books – for herself, and invested some money in school books for poor children.[110] Young readers were to learn to consider books as part of a balanced pattern of spending, and to connect bad investments to physical problems.

In the case of the reading manual *Wij zijn kinderen met elkanderen; ik ben er ook bij* (We are Children Together: I am Involved as Well, 1797), fictional children buy, distribute and read books as physical commodities, in order to gain profit from them. They not only acquire knowledge from books[111] but even obtain money for their reading: when they read a book to their illiterate uncle and aunt, they are rewarded with some pennies.[112] Since they use the money to buy another book, their reading turns into profitable labour and an economic system in itself.

The title and title page of *Wij zijn kinderen met elkanderen* simultaneously contribute to the readers' engagement: young readers are invited to model themselves upon the 'I' and thus to become involved in the reading community depicted in both text and image (Figure 7.9). In the first pages of the book, children read along with the fictional children (as they all read the book and words created by the schoolmaster), and thus share in their reading pleasure:

We are *children* all *together*
We are already going to *school.*
*Hello* Teacher!
*Hello!* Children!
What is our Teacher doing?
He makes the words we read in this book.
*Hello* Miss!
Hello *Ka!* hello Anna. Sit down. – Ah, *each is sitting with her book.*
Are we not *sitting sweetly, silently* together?
O yes: that is a *joy* to *see.*
*One reads*; the *other* reads *along*; and Miss *makes* sure it is right.[113]

Wij zijn Kinderen
met elkanderen.

Ik ben er ook bij.

[ *Nieuwold, J. N.* ]

*Eerſte Stukjen.*

Tweede vermeerderde uitgaaf.

Te GRONINGEN, Bij
A. GROENEWOLT en ZOON.
1797.

**FIGURE 7.9** [Anonymous]. *Wij zijn kinderen met elkanderen. Ik ben er ook bij.* Groningen, A. Groenewolt and son, 1797, title page. Special Collections, University of Amsterdam, shelfnumber OK 06–1776

*Wij zijn kinderen* in this way contributes to the creation of an affective community around books as objects to read and as commodities to circulate – just as Maß argued that monetary education intensively targeted the children's emotions. *Wij zijn kinderen* in fact stimulates the young reader to participate in a community in which the love for books is shared and the commercial market is spurred.[114]

As could be expected from Maß' analysis, (book) market skills are represented as emotional as well as bodily. In the *Vermaarde historie van Gillis Zoetekoek* mentioned earlier, reading is represented as a physical way of consuming: Gillis learns his ABC by eating letters made of gingerbread. In this way, the book connects a mental process of internalization – reading letters – to the very literal practice of physical internalization: eating letters.[115] This connection between eating and consuming was not a new invention; in the third section, I discussed several book-food objects aiming to spur affective interactions between book and consumers. However: the consumption motif is now explicitly connected to social and economic growth. Books and letters become part of an economic system as young readers discover how Gillis' reading practices are the first step in his development to wealth and success. Gillis is dreaming about becoming a coach driver in the beginning of the story, a perspective which gradually becomes within his reach when he acquires the ability to read. With such an inquisitive attitude, his father promises, Giles will obtain a coach himself.[116]

So children's books offered youngsters several opportunities to act as sensible as well as profitable book agents, and to use the book market to improve themselves and others. In comparison to the international context analysed by Maß, Dutch children's books turn out to be quite early propagators of children as spending and profit-making book consumers.

## Conclusion

While English publishers sold objects along with their books in order to stimulate tactile book practices among the young, the Dutch market developed discursive book-object hybrids to shape active and affective youths joining the book experience. Through titles, frontispieces and prefaces, books for youths were offered as objects and places to touch and taste, to internalize and practice, and young consumers were invited to act as engaged prosumers.

This alternative route may have been the effect of the controversial reputation of a youthful reading culture. The book-object representations might have contributed to the marketing of books for youths as 'valuable' products: the book-object hybrids promised their readers to organize affects within a natural system based on offering and reciprocity, honour and cultural value. The flourishing and competitive book market for the young in the 17th century was, apparently, not spurred by the representation of highly acquisitive buyers. Market success rather depended on its reliability and moral character: using books was represented as an instrument of managing affects.

The early modern young reader gradually developed from a consumer transacting emotions to a consumer participating in a commercialized market culture. From the later 17th century onwards, the commercial role and market context of books became more visible in adolescent literature. The reputation of the book-object as a moral instrument enabled book producers to adopt successful and reliable affective strategies to serve new purposes. Book-objects – now sometimes shaped as luxury goods (such as snuff-boxes) and commercial places (such as market stalls) instead of natural gardens and nourishing foods – spurred the desire for pleasure and underlined the need to spend money and preserve commercial markets. The affective system in which readers participated was gradually shaped as a system based on money, profit and spending consumers.

Now as the books openly admitted their status as commercial products to adolescents, reading developed into a way of managing markets for children. Enlightened Dutch books for younger readers, largely published in the second half of the 18th century, were above all dedicated to the transmission of knowledge about how to make proper investments, how to use books and markets to improve oneself and others, and how to create affective communities to share the book experience. In this case, again, the affective representation of the book functioned as a way of organizing and managing affects and desires among the young, instead of just encouraging them.

The pattern I trace – from managing emotions to managing markets – cannot be detached from age categories. Books for younger children functioned as instruments for explicit market socialization, while adolescent literature generally discussed the economy of love, and spurred the interest for money and amusement. The difference could, of course, be connected to the stages of development of the age groups, as well as their specific needs. However, the question 'who actually bought these books?' should also be taken into account: buying parents might well have preferred books about market socialization above those about emotional risks.

The young consumer was a gendered consumer as well. The late 18th-century *Onderwijs voor kinderen* by De Perponcher depicted the virtuous market manager Karoline as distinct from her wasteful brothers. Femininity was in this case related to patience and charity. More dominant, however, was the connection between femininity and the body. Kelderman's catechism *Melk voor suygelingen en kinderen in verstand en jaren* (1708) opposed mother's milk to masculine mental milk, and stimulated an internal – and thus masculine! – mode of consumption. Adolescent song and emblem books were often explicitly addressed to young girls, who apparently had to be seduced into maintaining the cycle of offering and returning love and songs. While the imagination of young consumers in a way contributed to the wider dissemination of market knowledge and skills among the young, it simultaneously disciplined youths and conformed them to restricting norms.

## Notes

1 A. van Goltstein, *De vertrouwde van mijn hart*, 86. I want to thank poet and translator Han van der Vegt who translated the poems I quote in this chapter. In order to remain "true" to the literary character of the texts, we chose lyrical translations, in verse.
2 A. van Goltstein, *De vertrouwde van mijn hart*, 90.
3 Marriage was considered as the important rite of passage to adulthood. Most people married between 25 and 30. B. B. Roberts, *Sex and Drugs*, 38; E. K. Grootes, "Het publiek van de 'nieuwe liedboeken'", 77.
4 Cf. C. Rasterhoff and K. Beelen's chapter in this volume, in which they point out this problem. While my chapter focuses on the book products, Rasterhoff and Beelen's is dedicated to larger patterns of success and innovation in the book market.
5 E. Buringh and J. L. van Zanden, "Charting the 'Rise of the West'".
6 J. Salman, "Children's Books as a Commodity," 80, note 28.
7 B. B. Roberts, *Sex and Drugs*; E. K. Grootes, "Het publiek van de 'nieuwe liedboeken'".
8 E. Stronks, "'Dees kennisse zuldy te kope vinnen,'" 152.
9 M. O. Grenby, *The Child Reader*, 197–98, 203; Jacqueline Pearson, *Women's Reading in Britain*. A more general discussion on the (controversial) reputation of books in the early modern period: Adrian Johns, *The Nature of the Book*, esp. ch. 2.
10 P. Altena, "'Ben jy lui Studenten'".
11 A. Baggerman, "Keuzecompetentie."
12 P. Griffiths, *Youth and Authority*; J. H. Dekker, "Het verlangen naar opvoeden"; K. E. Carter, *Creating Catholics*.
13 P. Aspers, *How are Markets Made?*, 6; K. Healy, *Last Best Gifts*.
14 M. O. Grenby, *The Child Reader*; M. O. Grenby, *Little Goody Two-Shoes*; Seth Lerer, *Children's Literature*, ch. 5.
15 H. Klemann, "The Matter of Moral Education"; M. O. Grenby, "The Origins of Children's Literature."
16 H. Klemann, "The Matter of Moral Education," quote on 225.
17 An exception, *The Renowned History of Giles Gingerbread*, will be discussed in section 6. Newbery's *Newtonian System of Philosophy adapted to the Capacities of Young Gentlemen and Ladies* has been translated as well: Huib Zuidervaart, "Science for the Public," 253.
18 As an exception: a small number of ABC board games were developed, cf. some examples in Buijnsters and Buijnsters-Smets, *Paper-Toys*, from 139 onwards.
19 H. van Alphen, *Kleine gedigten*, 25: "Mijn hoepel, mijn priktol verruil ik voor boeken."
20 M. Berg and H. Clifford, *Consumers and Luxury*; M. Berg and E. Eger, *Luxury in the Eighteenth Century*; M. Berg, *Luxury and Pleasure*.
21 See for example: M. Berg, *Luxury and Pleasure*, ch. 7 on shopping and advertising.
22 P. Aspers, *How are Markets Made?*, 8.
23 Idem, 26, discusses the first phase in the development of markets, in which "actors" identities are in the process of formation.
24 D. T. Cook, "Children's Consumption in History," 589–90. Cook discusses N. McKendrick, J. Brewer, and J. H. Plumb, *The Birth of a Consumer Society*, as a study which discusses children as subjects of adult investment.
25 G. Cross, *Kid's Stuff*; Cross, *The Cute and the Cool*; cf. D. T. Cook, "Children's Consumption in History," 591.
26 M. Erlin, "Book Fetish," 355–56.
27 M. Erlin, *Necessary Luxuries*, 2.
28 See, e.g. chapters in Anja Müller, "Fashioning Childhood."
29 K. Moruzi, M. J. Smith and E. Bullen, *Affect, Emotion and Children's Literature*; U. Frevert, "Learning How to Feel."

30 D. McCloskey, *The Bourgeois Virtues*.

31 By focusing on the imagination and representation of young consumers and consumerism, my approach is related to for example L. Jacobson, *Raising Consumers*; D. T. Cook, *The Commodification of Childhood*; E. G. Garvey, *The Adman in the Parlor*.

32 Cf. P. Crain, "The Child in the Visual Culture."

33 Cf. S. Maß, *Kinderstube des Kapitalismus*; S. Maß, "Useful Knowledge."

34 G. Genette, "Paratexts," 75: "For if the text is an object to read, the title […] is an object to be circulated."

35 G. Genette, "Paratexts," 78.

36 G. Genette, "Paratexts," esp. 89.

37 Cf. G. Genette, "Paratexts," e.g. 86, although Genette is not very explicit about his definition of the "historical period."

38 I selected all 17th- and 18th-century titles containing the word "youth" (jeugd, jeugt, jeught) from the Short Title Catalogue of the Netherlands. After deleting all books about the young (e.g. pedagogical tracts about the education of youth, meant for adults), I was left with around 500 titles explicitly addressed to "youth" as their target group. This list is far from complete, of course: texts for young people did not always identify their target group within the title. Some bibliographies and studies on youth literature helped me to find many more titles: F.A. Snellaert, "Oude en nieuwe liedjes"; G. D. J. Schotel, *Oud-Hollandsch huisgezin*; P. J. Buijnsters and L. Buijnsters-Smets, *Bibliografie*. Schotel observes many remarkable book titles in the 17th century song culture among the young and gives many examples.

39 "Dat ik de tijtel draeg van TUYNTJE, dat geschiedt/ Om dat men juyst in my als in een Tuyntje siet / Verscheyde dingen, die niet even al te samen / En zijn in kracht en aert, in schoonheyt ende name; / Maer seer verscheydentlik van stof, fatsoen, en kleur, / En zijn ook alle juist niet even soet van geur. / Die weten wil hoe ik inwendig ben gelegen, / Die plukt een Bloempjen af, en oordeelt dan te degen." J. C. Schaap, *Bloem-tuyntje*, ★2 v. Note: I quote the 1697 reprint.

40 J. C. Schaap, *Bloem-tuyntje*, ★3 v: "Plukt, proeft, riekt en smaekt"; "sterke spijse"; "eygen vlees en bloedt."

41 J. C. Schaap, *Bloem-tuyntje*, ★3r: 'Veel rijke laten hun kinderen Tuynen en Hoven na, om haer na den vleesche in te verlustigen: maer dese Tuyn geev' ik u, om u na den Geest te vermaken en te oeffenen.'

42 Cf. A. Goldgar, *Tulipmania*.

43 The man with the game bag is hunting for birds.

44 Cf. E. Stronks, "Churches as Indicators."

45 A. van der Venne, *De zielenvisserij*, Rijksmuseum Amsterdam, SK-A-447. See for a brief discussion: Pollmann, 'No Man's Land', 260–261.

46 J. Cats, *Sinne- en minnebeelden*, emblem 42.

47 G. van der Borcht, *Brusselschen Bloem-hof*, ★★4 v: "Hongh'righ naer een voedigh dicht"; "Swelghend."

48 On food as an exceptional type of consumption goods: S. W. Mintz, "The Changing Role of Food," 261–62.

49 A. van Ingen,"*t Gespeende Diemer-baersjen*."

50 Sangh-*bancquet*, A4: "ontsteken lust."

51 For example: Naylor, *Melk voor kinderkens* (milk and food); Spitsius, *Zielvoedende melk-spys* (milk). B. Bekker, *De Friesche godgeleerdheid* combines several catechisms for children at different ages: *De Vaste Spijze der Volmaakten*; *Kinder-melk*; *Gesneeden broodt voor de Kristen Kinderen*: food, milk, cutted bread.

52 "Zielenmelk voor Zuigelingen, / Voor de kindren aen den borst, /'t Eerste voedsel aller dingen, / De eerste laefnis voor de dorst, / Ziet men van een' man ontspringen. / Mannenmellek, honingsappen / Pennedruppels, zuiver nat, / Daeu van hemelwee-tenschappen / Bybelvocht uit't harssenvat / Kan de jeugt naer lust hier tappen." J. R. Kelderman, *Melk voor suygelingen en kinderen*, s.p.

53 *Nutte tijdtquistingh*, 6: "naey-mantjes oft koffertjes"; "een Boeck-verkoopers venster." Cf. A. van Toorn, M. Spies, and S. Hoogerhuis, "Christen Jeugd," 109.

54 *Nutte tijdtquistingh*, 6, A4r + v.

55 *Nutte tijdtquistingh*, 5.

56 G. Ritzer and N. Jurgenson, "Production, Consumption, Prosumption," 14–20; G. Ritzer, *The McDonaldization of Society*; K. K. Chen, "Artistic Prosumption."

57 Cf. K. Vanhaesebrouck's chapter in this volume, on the creation of a comparable type of bodily engaged consumers within the context of theatre.

58 Sangh-*bancquet*, B6v: "soute Honingdou"; "vergode Nectar smaken."

59 M. Van Vaeck, "De *Openhertighe herten*" on the *Openhertighe herten* en the 18th-century stick books, and their relationship to Starter.

60 M. Van Vaeck, "De *Openhertighe herten*," 129; *Openbertighe herten*.

61 A. J. Gelderblom, "Investing in your Relationship"; the concept "organization of desire" is borrowed from Judith Butler.

62 Idem, 137–39.

63 J. J. Starter, *Friesche Lust-hof*, 62.

64 Idem, 99.

65 't Was uyt goedgunstigheyd dat ick u by my nam, / Om u verstramde le'en op't mackelijckst te vieren, / Maer niet om geld noch goed, dat 's tegen mijn manieren." Idem, 80.

66 Quotations: I. Krausman Ben-Amos, *The Culture of Giving*, 5. Mauss's groundbreaking essay "Essai sur le don" (1923–24) was the first to define the distinguishing characteristics of the gift culture. M. Mauss, *The Gift*. In the past few decades, the gift culture has been largely studied by historians, literary scholars and sociologists: e.g. Ben-Amos, *The Culture of Giving*; F. Heal, "Food Gifts"; Natalie Z. Davis, *The Gift in Sixteenth-Century France*; A. E. Komter, *The Gift*. It is nowadays conceptualized as an alternative value system that was not replaced by a developing economic market, as has long been assumed, but rather functioned beside it. Cf. Ben-Amos, *The Culture of Giving*, 2; L. Fontaine, *The Moral Economy*.

67 For the Dutch context: L. Kooijmans, *Vriendschap*; I. Thoen, *Strategic Affection?*

68 E. A. Foyster, *Manhood in Early Modern England*, esp. 8–9.

69 E. Honig, "Art, Honor, and Excellence," quote on 90. Cf. introduction of Michael Hutter and David Throsby, *Beyond Price*.

70 J. C. Mayvogel, *Vermakelijcke bruylofts-kroon*, 4: "t Gelt en kan geen wijsheyt geven": "Money is not able to offer wisdom."

71 "Ziels-Fonteyn, ghy alleyn, / Kunt my overwinnen, / O mijn schoone! / Wilt my loonen, / Met u lieve weder-min." Idem, 35.

72 Idem, 1 v.

73 Idem, 27: "Wilt (...) / Met weder-liefd" / "Mijn Zieltje Kroonen'.

74 *Amsterdams minne-beekje*, 73.

75 H. van Van Bulderen, *Apollo's lusthof*, 4; E. Pels de Jonge, 't *Lof van Cupido*, 99–101.

76 P. Elzevier, *Den lacchenden Apoll*, 1–5.

77 J. van den Vondel and J. van Heemskerck, *Minne-plicht*, 163–64.

78 J. J. Starter, *Friesche Lust-hof*, 20.

79 *Apollo of Ghesangh,* *2r.

80 Idem, 2: "ghy mijn eyghen-kroost."

81 Ibidem: "ick heb mijn nu bedacht / Die te vereeren aan het Maaghdelijck gheslacht"; 4: "weder-loon."

82 J. van den Vondel and J. Van Heemskerck, *Minne-plicht*, 7–9.

83 Idem, 7: "belooninge in haer eygen selfs."

84 Cf. *Openhertige herten*. Another example: Starter, *Friesche Lust-hof*, 228: "syn wesen [his face], / Waeruyt men magh het boeck van syn gedachten lesen."

85 Inger Leemans was the first to argue that author Pieter Elzevier must have been the same person as publisher and later pornographer Elzevier, who presumably wrote

*De doorluchtige daden van Jan Stront, opgedragen aan het kakhuis* (1684–1696). That means that Pieter Elzevier published the youthful love songs in *Apolloos Snaaren* when he was around 20 years old. In *Apolloos Snaaren*, we could find some careful allusions to fornication. I. Leemans, "Een verloren zoon," 79–80.

86 Several years earlier, the famous anthology *Apollo's harp* (1658) created a comparable connection to books and musical instruments by its title. This anthology was not explicitly offered to young readers but has been dedicated to the probably young Miss G.v.L. Worp: Worp suggested that this G.v.L. was Geertruid van Limborg, who married Geraerd Brandt 11 years later (in 1669). J. A. Worp, "Apollo's Harp (1658)," 303.

87 "maer echter overweegende, hoe yverich alle geoorlofde, en behoorlijcke nieuwigheden van UE. tot noch toe omhelst zijn; hebbe ick my verstout tot dese mijne Snaartjes (op d'aardigste en nieuwste toonen gestelt) UE. tot Matronen te verkiesen, ende aen UE sachte schoot op te offeren, op dat deselve daar in rustende, van UE. lieve vingeren gestreelt, en van UE vergôde keeltjes, en tongen gezongen en gequeelt mogen werden." P. Elzevier, *Apolloos snaaren*, ★3 v.

88 "aanvaart dan nevens andere ongeveynsde en vrolijke Basen, mijnen *Lacchenden Apoll, ofte Drollige Rijmen,* leest en door leest, kauwt en herkauwt onze Gerijmde Drollen, ten einde gy zien meugt van wat eur, natuur, en eygenschap sy zijn […].'t is hem eers genoeg, bevallige Juffertjes! dat hy (dit drollig Boekje gemaakt hebbende) u bladeren verschaft heeft, om het houte bakje van een Kakhuys op te vullen, en u drollige winkel van achteren vergult zijnde, daar mede af te vegen, ten eynde hy door dese middel kan betoonen, dat hy in waarheyt is U E. geringsten Dienaar' "Idem, 5–6; 7–8.

89 H. van Bulderen, *Apollo's lusthof,* 15: "Daer sal ick u de winst, in uwe schoot doen dalen"; "Daer kunt ghy, soo ghy wilt, mijn arrebeyt betalen, / Toont dan uw mannekragt."

90 J. Rosseau, *Apollo's prullekraam.*

91 Idem, A3r-A3v: "'k Heb Harders Deunen, / Boeren Dreunen / Minne-Zang en/ Nog meer Grillen, / By me Billen, / Die'k niet noemen ken; / 'k Heb om te Klinken / en te Drinken'" Cf. one of the songs in honour of pedlar "Klyn Jans" who distributed books and songs.

92 G. Tysens, *Apollo's Marsdrager* – and several other editions. *Apollo's kermis-gift aan de Haagsche vermaaksgesinde jeugd* (I used the edition from 1750, but many more editions were published); *Apollo's vastenavond-gift*; *Apollo's St Nicolaasgift.*

93 *Apollo's kermis-gift*, 5: "Want buiten winst of and're reen, / Zoo krygt geen Digtkunst nieuwe kragten."

94 J. Salman, *Pedlars and the Popular Press,* 44: "The image of the street seller is sometimes employed to signal the diverting nature of a certain work or as a means of addressing the intended audience."

95 *Vermakelyke Slaa-tuintjes;* J. Kloek, I. Leemans and W. Mijnhardt, *D'Openhertige Juffrouw.*

96 J. Adriaensz, *Het harders stafje*; *Het harders-stafje, oft Het soet geselschap*; *Het herders-stafje, met het zingende Zwaantje.*

97 *Het herders-stafje, met het zingende Zwaantje,* 4.

98 *Het harders-stafje, oft Het soet geselschap,* 91–93.

99 *Schatkamer der Nederlandsche jeugd,* I –II.

100 "Wat ziet men meer floreeren / Als Snuifwinkels by de hoop /, Daar yder met begeeren / Na toe gaat zy is goed koop /. Wat dat maar loopen kan /'t Zy Vryster of Jongman/, Die draagen al een Doos/ Al is't maar voor de loos / […] Ook zijn'er veel die koomen/, Om Pompadour of Fiolet / En zeggen zonder schroomen / Mijn Neus is daer to gezet / Zoo heeft dan elk zijn smaek /. En zijn eige vermaek / Te eisschen met fatzoen /Wat dat hy heeft van doen / Want't is de Snuifverkopers/ Maer alleen om't Geld te doen." *De nieuwe vermakelyke Snuyf-Doos,* 3–4.

101 Idem, 2: "Koop nu Vrienden met behaage, / Deeze Snuifdoos vol pleisier."

102 Idem, 60.

103 *De vermaarde historie van Gillis Zoetekoek* is published in the book *Proeve eener kleine historie*. The original text: *The Renowned History of Giles Gingerbread*, published in 1764 by the famous London publisher John Newbery (cf. the first paragraph).

104 "Die't hebben wil moet niet lang staan, / Maar aanstonds met my mede gaan, / Want straks is't mooglyk uitverkocht. - Toen vlogen zy, by heelen hoopen / Na Jasper, om een boek te koopen." *Proeve eener kleine historie*, ★3r.

105 Cf. S. Maß, *Kinderstube des Kapitalismus*; Maß, "Useful Knowledge". Cf. also Sebastian Felten's chapter in this volume on monetary socialization and coins as objects.

106 S. Maß 2017b, "Useful Knowledge," 75.

107 Idem, 83.

108 Idem, 85

109 T. van Gulpen, *Officina Scholastica*.

110 W. E. De Perponcher, *Onderwijs voor kinderen*, LI, 335 and further.

111 *Wij zijn kinderen met elkanderen*, 45.

112 Idem, 35.

113 "Wij zijn *kinderen* met *elkanderen*. / Wij gaan al weêr naar de *school*. / *Dag* Meester! / *Dag!* Kinderen! / Wat doet de Meester daar? / Hij maakt de woorden, die wij in't boekjen leezen. / *Dag* Mamezel! / Dag *Ka!* dag *Anna!* Ga *zitten* – Ha! *elk zit al met zijn boek*. / *Zitten* wij niet *stil* en *lief* by elkanderen? / Wel ja: *dat* is een *pleizier*, om te *zien*. / De *eene* leest op; de *andere* zit het *na*; en Mamezel *past op*, of't goed is." Idem, 3–4.

114 Cf. Mulsow's concept of the "Faszinationsgemeinschaft," modeled after Rosenwein's "emotional community": Mulsow, *Prekäres Wissen*, part IV. Cf. Ulinka Rublack's paper within this volume, analyzing Fugger's shaping of emotional communities in which the excitement about objects was shared and spurred.

115 Cf. P. Crain, *The Alphabetization of America*, 85–87.

116 *Proeve eener kleine historie*, 24: "zyn Vader zegt, dat hy verzekerd is, dat *Gillis* sig soo wel zal gedraegen, dat hy selve een Koets zal verkrygen."

# Bibliography

Anonymous. *Amsterdams minne-beekje*. Vol 1. Amsterdam: Ioost Hartgersz., 1637 (second print).

Anonymous. *Apollo's kermis-gift aan de Haagsche vermaaksgesinde jeugd*. Vol 2. Dordrecht: Hendrik Walpot, 1740.

Anonymous. *Apollo of Ghesangh der Musen*. Amsterdam: Dirck Pietersz., 1615.

Anonymous. *Apollo's St. Nicolaas-gift, aan Minerva. Voorzien met nieuwe en oude minneherders- en mengel-zangen*. Leiden: J. van Kerckhem, 17XX.

Anonymous. *Apollo's vastenavond-gift. Voorzien met de nieuwste en aangenaamste minne- harders- en bruylofs gezangen*. Dordrecht: Hendrik Walpot, ca. 1750.

Anonymous. *De nieuwe vermakelyke Snuyf-Doos, zynde verciert met veelderley zoort van aardige en aangename Gezangen*. Amsterdam: widow of Hendrik van der Putte, 1766.

Anonymous. *De vermakelyke slaa-tuintjes, waar in te vinden zyn de geurigste […] liederen*. Amsterdam: heirs of Van der Putte and B. Boekhout, 1777.

Anonymous. *Het harders-stafje, oft Het soet geselschap van harders en hardinnen, zingende allerhande ernstige en boertige […] liederen*. Haarlem: M. van Hulkenroy, 1740.

Anonymous. *Het harders-stafje, met het zingende Zwaantje, juigende allerhande … hardersbruilofts- en minne-zangen*. Amsterdam: widow of J. van Egmont, not before, 174X.

Anonymous. *Nieuwen Ieucht Spieghel*. [Arnhem: Jan Jansz., 1617].

Anonymous. *Nutte tijdtquistingh der Amstelsche jonckheyt*. Amsterdam: C. Danckertsz., 1640.

Anonymous. *Openbertighe herten*. S.l.: s.n., 1620s.

Anonymous. *Proeve eener kleine historie, voor kinderen.* Amsterdam: P. Hayman, 1781.

Anonymous. *Sangh-bancquet, op-gedist in papiere schoteltjens, en voor-geset de Rotterdamse juffertjes.* Rotterdam: s.n., 1664.

Anonymous. *Schatkamer der Nederlandsche jeugd.* Amsterdam: D. Schuurman, n.d. [=last quarter 18th century].

Anonymous. *Wij zijn kinderen met elkanderen. Ik ben er ook bij.* Groningen: A. Groenewolt and son, 1797.

Adriaensz, Jan. *Het harders stafje, ofte soet vermaen.* Haarlem: R. Tinneken, 1664.

Alphen, Hieronymus van. *Kleine gedigten voor kinderen,* edited by P. J. Buijnsters. Amsterdam: Athenaeum-Polak & Van Gennep, 1998.

Altena, Peter. "'Ben jy lui Studenten, zo moetje studeeren': Waarom Izabelle *De Franequer Los-Kop* niet lezen mocht." *Literatuur* 8 (1991): 11–18.

Aspers, Patrik. *How are Markets Made?* MPIfG unpublished Working Paper. Köln, 2009. https://www.mpifg.de/pu/workpap/wp09-2.pdf

Baggerman, Arianne. "Keuzecompetentie in tijden van schaarste en overvloed: Het debat rond jeugdliteratuur voor en na Hiëronymus van Alphen (1760-1840)." In *Een groot verleden voor de boeg: Cultuurhistorische opstellen voor Joost Kloek,* edited by Gert-Jan Johannes, José de Kruif and Jeroen Salman, 17–37. Leiden: Prima Vera Pers, 2004.

Bekker, Balthasar. *De Friesche godgeleerdheid.* Amsterdam: D. van den Dalen, 1693.

Ben-Amos, Ilana Krausman. *The Culture of Giving: Informal Support and Gift-Exchange in Early Modern England.* Cambridge: Cambridge University Press, 2008.

Berg, Maxine. *Luxury and Pleasure in Eighteenth-Century Britain.* Oxford: Oxford University Press, 2005.

Berg, Maxine and Helen Clifford, eds. *Consumers and Luxury in Europe 1650-1850.* Manchester: Manchester University Press, 1999.

Berg, Maxine and Elizabeth Eger, eds. *Luxury in the Eighteenth Century: Debates, Desires and Delectable Goods.* Basingstoke: Palgrave, 2002.

Borcht, Guilelmus van der. *Brusselschen Bloem-hof van Cupido.* Brussel: Guilliam Scheybels, 1641.

Buijnsters, P. J. and L. Buijnsters-Smets. *Bibliografie van Nederlandse school- en kinderboeken 1700-1800.* Zwolle: Waanders 1997.

Buijnsters, P. J. and L. Buijnsters-Smets. *Papertoys: Speelprenten en papieren speelgoed in Nederland (1640-1920).* Zwolle: Waanders, 2005.

Bulderen, H. van. *Apollo's lusthof, beplant met aerdige en soet vloeyende gesangen, bruylofts punt, en mengel dichten, voor de liefhebbers van de poësy.* Amsterdam: Barent Otto Smient, 1673.

Buringh, Eltjo and Jan Luiten Van Zanden. "Charting the 'Rise of the West': Manuscripts and Printed Books in Europe, A Long-Term Perspective from the Sixth through Eighteenth Centuries." *The Journal of Economic History* 69, no. 2 (2009): 409–45.

Carter, Karen E. *Creating Catholics: Catechism and Primary Education in Early Modern France.* Notre Dame, Ind: University of Notre Dame Press, 2011.

Cats, Jacob. *Sinne- en minnebeelden.* 3 vols, edited by H. Den, Luijten. Haag: Constantijn Huygens Instituut, 1996.

Chen, Katherine K. "Artistic Prosumption: Cocreative Destruction at Burning Man." *American Behavioral Scientist* 56, no. 4 (2012): 570–95.

Cook, Daniel Thomas. *The Commodification of Childhood: The Children's Clothing Industry and the Rise of the Child Consumer.* Durham: Duke University Press, 2004.

Cook, Daniel Thomas. "Children's Consumption in History." In *The Oxford Handbook of The History of Consumption,* edited by Frank Trentmann, 585–600. Oxford: Oxford University Press, 2012.

Crain, Patricia. *The Alphabetization of America from the New England Primer to the Scarlet Letter.* Stanford: Stanford University Press, 2002.

Crain, Patricia. "The Child in the Visual Culture of Consumption 1790–1830." In *Fashioning Childhood in the Eighteenth Century: Age and Identity. Ashgate studies in Childhood, 1700 to the present,* edited by Müller Anja, 63–79. Aldershot etc: Ashgate, 2006.

Cross, Gary. *Kid's Stuff: Toys and the Changing World of American Childhood.* Cambridge, Massachusetts and London: Harvard University Press, 1999 (second edition).

Cross, Gary. *The Cute and the Cool: Wondrous Innocence and Modern American Children's Culture.* Oxford: Oxford University Press, 2004.

Davis, Natalie Z. *The Gift in Sixteenth-Century France.* Madison: University of Wisconsin Press, 2000.

Dekker, Jeroen J.H. *Het verlangen naar opvoeden: Over de groei van de pedagogische ruimte in Nederland sinds de Gouden Eeuw tot omstreeks 1900.* Amsterdam: Bert Bakker, 2006.

Elzevier, Pieter. *Apolloos snaaren. Gestelt op de nieuwste en aardigste voysen.* Amsterdam: B. Boekholt, 1664.

Elzevier, Pieter. *Den lacchenden Apoll, uytbarstende in drollige rymen.* Amsterdam: B. Boekholt, 1667.

Erlin, Matt. "Book Fetish: Joachim Heinrich Campe and the Commodification of Literature." *Seminar* 42, no. 4 (2006): 355–75

Erlin, Matt. *Necessary Luxuries: Books, Literature, and the Culture of Consumption in Germany, 1770-1815.* Ithaca, NY: Cornell University Press and Cornell University Library, 2014.

Fontaine, Laurence. *The Moral Economy: Poverty, Credit, and Trust in Early Modern Europe.* New York: Cambridge University Press, 2014.

Foyster, Elizabeth A. *Manhood in Early Modern England: Honour, Sex and Marriage.* London: Longman, 1999.

Frevert, Ute et al., eds. *Learning How to Feel: Children's Literature and Emotional Socialization, 1870–1970.* Oxford: Oxford University Press, 2014.

Garvey, Ellen Gruber. *The Adman in the Parlor: Magazines and the Gendering of Consumer Culture, 1880s to 1910s.* Oxford: Oxford University Press, 1996.

Gelderblom, Arie Jan. 'Investing in your Relationship.' In *Learned love: Proceedings of the Emblem Project Utrecht Conference on Dutch Love Emblems and the Internet,* edited by Els Stronks and Peter Boot, 131–42. Den Haag: DANS Data Archiving and Networked Services, 2007.

Genette, Gerard. *Paratexts: Treshonds of Interpretation.* Cambridge: Cambridge University Press, 1997.

Goldgar, Anne. *Tulipmania: Money, Honor, and Knowledge in the Dutch Golden Age.* Chicago: The University of Chicago Press, 2007.

Goltstein, Alexander van. *De vertrouwde van mijn hart. Het dagboek van Alexander van Goltstein (1801–1808),* edited by J. Limonard Hilversum: Verloren, 1994.

Grenby, M.O. ed., *Little Goody Two-Shoes and Other Stories: Originally Published by John Newbery.* Houndmills: Palgrave Macmillan, 2013.

Grenby, Matthew O. *The Child Reader 1700–1840.* Cambridge: Cambridge University Press, 2011.

Grenby, Matthew O. 'The Origins of Children's Literature.' In *The Cambridge Companion to Children's Literature,* edited by M.O. Grenby and Andrea Immel, 3–18. Cambridge: Cambridge University Press, 2009.

Griffiths, Paul. *Youth and Authority: Formative Experiences in England, 1560–1640.* Oxford: Clarendon Press, 1996.

Grootes, Eddy. "Het publiek van de 'nieuwe liedboeken' in het eerste kwart van de zeventiende eeuw." In *Het woord aan de lezer*, edited by W. Van den Berg, P. J. Buijnsters, and Hanna Stouten, 72–88. Groningen: Wolters Noordhoff, 1987.

Gulpen, Theodorus van. *Officina Scholastica Of School-Winkel, Opgerecht naar Regels van de Syntaxis*. Rotterdam: Bartholomeus van der Spek, 1743.

Heal, Felicity. "Food Gifts, the Household and the Politics of Exchange in Early Modern England." *Past and Present* 199, no. 1 (2008): 41–70.

Healy, Kieran. *Last Best Gifts: Altruism and the Market for Human Blood and Organs*. Chicago: University of Chicago Press, 2006.

Honig, Elizabeth. "Art, Honor, and Excellence in Early Modern Europe." In *Beyond Price: Value in Culture, Economics, and the Arts*, edited by Michael Hutter and David Throsby, 89–105. Cambridge: Cambridge University Press, 2008.

Hutter, Michael and David, Throsby, eds. *Beyond Price: Value in Culture, Economics, and the Arts*. Cambridge: Cambridge University Press, 2008.

Ingen, A. van. *'t Gespeende Diemer-baersjen. Opgeschaft voor des selfsgemaeckte slaven en slavinnen van de hedendaegsche Min. Bestaende soo in zedige, boertige als amoreuse Sangh-dichten, nevens eenige Leevertjens, Kusjes en andere Mengelrijmpjes verseld*. Amsterdam: Jan Claessen ten Hoorn, 1675.

Jacobson, Lisa. *Raising Consumers: Children and the American Mass Market in the Early Twentienth Century*. New York: Columbia University Press, 2004.

Johns, Adrian. *The Nature of the Book: Print and Knowledge in the Making*. Chicago: University of Chicago Press, 1998.

Kelderman, Johan Reynier. *Melk voor suygelingen en kinderen in verstand en jaren; of Bekort ontwerp van de grond-leer der hervormde kerk*. Dordrecht, J. van Braam, 1708.

Klemann, Heather. "The Matter of Moral Education: Locke, Newbery, and the Didactic Book-Toy Hybrid." *Eighteenth-Century Studies* 44, no. 2 (2011): 223–44.

Kloek, Joost, Inger Leemans, and Wijnand Mijnhardt. *D'Openhertige Juffrouw, of D'Ontdelte Geveinsdheid (1680)*. Leiden: Astraes, 1998.

Komter, Aafke E. ed. *The Gift: An Interdisciplinary Perspective*. Amsterdam: Amsterdam University Press, 1996.

Kooijmans, Luuc. *Vriendschap en de kunst van het overleven in de zeventiende en achttiende eeuw*. Amsterdam: Bert Bakker 1997.

Leemans, Inger. "Een verloren zoon: Uitgever, drollige poëet en pornograaf Pieter Elzevier." *De boekenwereld* 18 (2001–2002): 70–82.

Lerer, Seth. *Children's Literature: A Reader's History, from Aesop to Harry Potter*. Chicago: University of Chicago Press, 2008.

Liebersohn, Harry. *The Return of the Gift: European History of a Global Idea*. Cambridge: Cambridge University Press, 2010.

McCloskey, Deidre. *The Bourgeois Virtues: Ethics for an Age of Commerce*. Chicago: Chicago University Press, 2006.

McKendrick, Neil, John Brewer and J.H. Plumb. *The Birth of a Consumer Society: The Commercialization of Eighteenth-Century England*. London: Europa Publications, 1982.

Maß, Sandra. *Kinderstube des Kapitalismus? Monetäre Erziehung im 18. und 19. Jahrhundert*. Oldenburg: De Gruyter, 2017.

Maß, Sandra. "Useful Knowledge: Monetary Education of Children and the Moralization of Productivity in the 19th Century." In *Histories of Productivity: Genealogical Perspectives on the Body and Modern Economy*, edited by Peter-Paul Bänziger and Suter Mischa, 74–91. London: Routledge, 2017.

Mauss, Marcel. *The Gift: Form and Reason for Exchange in Archaic Societies*. Translated by W.D. Halls. London: Routledge, 1990.

Mayvogel, Jacob Coenraetsz. *Vermakelijcke bruylofts-kroon, doorvlochten met verscheyden leersame gedichten*. Amsterdam: Jan Jacobsz Bouman, 1659.

Mintz, Sindey W. "The Changing Role of Food in the Study of Consumption." In *Consumption and the World of Goods*, edited by John Brewer and Roy Porter, 261–73. London: Routledge, 1993.

Morozi, Kristine, Michelle J. Smith, and Elizabeth Bullen, eds. *Affect, Emotion, and Children's Literature: Representation and Socialisation in Texts for Children and Young Adults*. New York: Routledge, 2017.

Müller, Anja, ed. *Fashioning Childhood in the Eighteenth Century: Age and Identity. Ashgate Studies in Childhood, 1700 to the Present*. Aldershot: Ashgate, 2006.

Mulsow, Martin. *Prekäres Wissen: Eine andere Ideengeschichte der Frühen Neuzeit*. Berlin: Shurkamp Verlag, 2012.

Naylor, James. *Melk voor kinderkens; ende spijse voor de starcke*. Amsterdam: Christoffel Cunradus, 1673.

Pearson, Jacqueline. *Women's Reading in Britain, 1750–1835: A Dangerous Recreation*. Cambridge: Cambrdige University Press, 1999.

Pels de Jonge, E. *'t Lof van Cupido. Met verscheyde vrolijcke en minnelijcke deuntjens*. Amsterdam: Christiaen Meulemans, 1626.

Perponcher, Willem Emmery de. *Onderwijs voor kinderen*. Utrecht: widow of J. van Schoonhoven, 1782.

Pollmann, Judith. "No Man's Land: Reinventing Netherlandish Identities, 1585–1621." In *Networks, Regions and Nations: Shaping Identities in the Low Countries, 1300–1650*, edited by Robert Stein and Judith Pollmann, 241–61. Leiden: Brill, 2010.

Ritzer, George and Nathan Jurgenson. "Production, Consumption, Prosumption: The Nature of Capitalism in the Age of the Digital 'Prosumer.'" *Journal of Consumer Culture* 10, no. 1 (2010): 13–36.

Ritzer, George. *The McDonaldization of Society*. Thousand Oaks, CA: Pine Forge Press, 1993.

Roberts, Benjamin B. *Sex and Drugs before Rock 'n' Roll: Youth Culture and Masculinity in Holland's Golden Age*. Amsterdam: Amsterdam University Press 2012.

Rosseau, Jakobus. *Apollo's prullekraam, gevuld met herders vryagies [...] en drink liederen*. Amsterdam: for A. Cornelis, 1716.

Salman, Jeroen. "Children's Books as a Commodity: The Rise of a New Literary Subsystem in the Eighteenth-century Dutch Republic." *Poetics* 28, no. 5/6 (2001): 399–421.

Salman, Jeroen. *Pedlars and the Popular Press: Itinerant Distribution Networks in England and the Netherlands 1600-1850*. Leiden: Brill, 2014.

Schaap, Jan Claesz. *Bloem-tuyntje*. Amsterdam: Jan Rieuwertsz, 1697.

Schotel, Gilles Denijs Jacob. *Oud-Hollandsch huisgezin*. Haarlem: A.C. Kruseman, 1867.

Snellaert, F.A. *Oude en nieuwe liedjes*. Den Haag: Martinus Nijhoff, 1864.

Spitsius, Johannes. *Zielvoedende melk-spys. Troostbloem van Gods eeuwige verkiezing en verwerping*. Amsterdam: Hendrik Burgers, 1732.

Starter, J.J. *Friesche Lust-hof*. 2 vols. Ed. Brouwer, J.H. and Veldhuyzen, Marie. Zwolle: W.E.J. Tjeenk Willink, 1966–1967.

Stronks, Els. "Churches as Indicators of a Larger Phenomenon: The Religious Side of the Dutch Love Emblem." In *Learned Love: Proceedings of the Emblem Project Utrecht Conference on Dutch Love Emblems and the Internet*, edited by Els Stronks and Peter Boot , 72–93. Den Haag: DANS Data Archiving and Networked Services, 2007.

Stronks, Els. "'Dees kennisse zuldy te kope vinnen'. Liedcultuur en de waarde van 'know how' in de vroegmoderne Republiek." *De Zeventiende Eeuw. Cultuur in de Nederlanden in interdisciplinair perspectief,* 30, no. 2 (2014): 147–67.

Thoen, Irma. *Strategic Affection? Gift Exchange in Seventeenth-Century Holland.* Amsterdam: Amsterdam University Press, 2007.

Toorn, Annemarie van, Marijke Spies, and Sietske Hoogerhuis. "Christen Jeugd, leerd Konst en Deugd." In *De hele Bibelebontse berg: De geschiedenis van het kinderboek in Nederland en Vlaanderen van de middeleeuwen tot heden,* edited by Harry Bekkering. Amsterdam: Querido, 1989.

Tysens, Gysbert. *Apollo's Marsdrager, veylende allerhande … snel, punt, schimp, en mengel-digten.* Amsterdam: H. Bosch, 1715.

Van Vaeck, Marc. "De *Openhertighe herten* en J.J. Starters *Steeck-boecxken, ofte't vermaak der jeugdelijker herten*: een opmerkelijke variante van de hartsemblematiek." *Verslagen en mededelingen van de Koninklijke Academie voor Nederlandse taal- en letterkunde* (1993): 122–52.

Vondel, Joost van den and Johan van Heemskerck. *Minne-plicht, ende kuysheyts-kamp. Als mede verscheyden aardighe en geestige nieuwe liedekens en sonnetten.* Amsterdam: Jacob Aertsz. Colom, 1625-1626.

Worp, J.A. "Apollo's harp (1658)." *Tijdschrift voor Taal- en Letterkunde* 7 (1887): 92–96.

Zuidervaart, Huib. "Science for the Public: The Translation of Popular Texts on Experimental Philosophy into the Dutch Language in Mid-Eighteenth Century." In *Cultural Transfer Through Translation: The Circulation of Enlightened Thought in Europe by Means of Translation,* edited by Stefanie Stockhorst, 231–62. Amsterdam: Rodopi, 2010.

**PART 2**

# Marketing and managing knowledge and affects

# 8

# MARKETING ARCTIC KNOWLEDGE

## Observation, publication, and affect in the 1630s

*Anne Goldgar*

Readers in the 1660s were treated to a pathetic vision when they read an account of the travails of employees of the Noordsche Compagnie, the monopoly whaling company, as they struggled to survive the winter on Spitsbergen in 1633–4. Andries Jansz and his six men, who had been ordered to investigate the possibility of year-round occupation of the whaling station in northwest Spitsbergen, did in fact survive, and Jansz's journal, which he had been required to keep by the company, was apparently published. Given the success of this first attempt, a different set of seven volunteers remained behind when the fleet departed Spitsbergen at the end of the summer of 1634. But this group, like a similar party on Jan Mayen Island the previous year, was more ill-fated: everyone in each party died of scurvy. Despite the apparently greatly shortened text ('I have left out a lot of unnecessary material on weather and winds'),[1] their abbreviated journal of merely three pages, produced by the Amsterdam publisher Gillis Joosten Saeghman, provided heart-tugging details about their deaths. The last lines written by the strongest of the men, on February 26, 1635, readers were told, recorded that 'The four of us who are still alive are lying flat in our bunks/We should eat/Was there one so brave that he could come out of his bunk to lay a fire/We cannot move for the pain/we pray to God with folded hands/that he will free us from this oppressive world/if it pleases him we are ready/because we cannot go on much longer without food or fire/and we cannot help each other/each must carry his own burden'.[2]

These words, and others in the short account, outline the horrors of scurvy, and give readers a means of grasping the state of mind of the sailors as they lay helpless, contemplating their end. Or they would, if we could be sure that these words were really in the journal rescued from Spitsbergen when the whaling fleet re-turned in the summer of 1635. But as no extant copies from the actual period remain, we cannot be certain of its contents, especially given the penchant of their republisher in the 1660s, Saeghman, for spicing up his stories with information and images sometimes irrelevant to the case, as the work of Marijke Barend-van Haeften and Garrelt Verhoeven has amply demonstrated.[3]

Saeghman's publication of this text was only one of several accounts of the three overwintering attempts by the Noordsche Compagnie on Spitsbergen and Jan Mayen Island. Saeghman himself published them all in the 1660s, but, as we will examine in detail later in this chapter, texts of the journals of the successful overwintering on Spitsbergen in 1633–4 and the unsuccessful one on Jan Mayen in the same year were published in 1634, and we must assume that Saeghman's account of the 1634–5 disaster was based on a text published in the 1630s as well. Saeghman's attention to the suffering of the sailors, and the possibility that an editor might have heightened these for effect, lead us to many questions about why a story like this might have been popular, and why it might have been even more popular if the reader could share the emotions and experiences of the participants. It also raises questions about the role of texts in commercial activity in the seventeenth century, and the role of commercial activity in texts. The attempts to winter in the Arctic in the 1630s were part of an economic venture, one which (like all economic ventures) involved knowledge – but what kind of knowledge was desired, and what kind of knowledge was produced, were perhaps special to this time and place. This chapter will examine the three overwinterings on Spitsbergen and Jan Mayen Island of the 1630s, in which 21 of the 28 men involved died, to consider the complex interplay of print and commerce, market and affect, emotion and fact, and vividness and authenticity in the period. In it we will see that for seventeenth-century readers, emotion was a way of marketing knowledge.

To understand this novel commercial venture – for no one previously had deliberately been instructed to spend the winter in the Arctic, nor to keep a record of such a stay – we have to think about its intellectual and commercial background. Economically, whaling was taking advantage of knowledge accrued during the several trips to the north made in the late sixteenth century as an attempt to find a northeast passage to China and the Indies, ending in the famous winter of 1596–7 when Willem Barents and his crew were stuck in the ice off the northeastern tip of Nova Zembla. Following the discovery of Spitsbergen by Barents on the 1596 voyage, the Noordsche Compagnie was set up in 1614 to take advantage of the large number of whales available for hunting around Spitsbergen, Jan Mayen Island, and through the arctic circle. Like the several other chartered companies, this had a rather complicated federal structure involving several towns, in particular Amsterdam, Delft, Enkhuizen, Hoorn, and others, and some competition among these.[4] Some of the early directors were important Amsterdam merchants such as Jacques Nicquet and Jacques Mercijs, although by the 1630s the company was led by somewhat less wealthy men, primarily from Amsterdam and Delft. The company had to face several renewals of its monopoly *octrooi*, including in the autumn of 1633, which might help to explain the timing of the first expedition to consider expanding its operations to the winter. Although whaling would be less possible in the winter, there were opportunities, especially on

Spitsbergen, for hunting of deer, walrus, and seal, and to protect the blubber-rendering equipment left behind over the winter from the depredations of English and Basque competitors, the latter of whom had plundered Dutch equipment on Jan Mayen Island several years earlier.[5] The author of the journal of the first, and successful, overwintering on Spitsbergen, Jacob Segersz van der Brugge, addressed a letter to the directors of the company in the published version of the journal, mentioning that the expedition was set up because they were 'alert Merchants, always eager for profit, [and therefore] keen to expand the limits of your trade and to double the possible profits.'[6]

The possibility of a successful overwintering was already before the eyes of the directors of the company, who had been discussing the possibility of year-round operations for nearly ten years. They were certainly aware of the admittedly difficult but for most survivable experiences on Nova Zembla in 1596–7. A more recent example, thought by some scholars to be a direct inspiration of this new attempt, was the accidental stranding of eight sailors from the English Muscovy Company on Spitsbergen over the winter of 1630–31. This event was memorialized by one of the sailors, Edward Pellham, in a pamphlet praising God's providence in 1631.[7] Pellham made a point of emphasizing that the Dutch on Nova Zembla were, as he put it, 'furnished with all things necessary both for life and health; had no want of any thing: Bread, Beere, and Wine they had good, and good store,' whereas 'We (God knowes) wanted all these' and had to eat 'Whale Frittars, and those mouldie too, the loathsomest meate in the world.' Although the danger of bears would have been the same for the men of the Noordsche Compagnie – ''twas a measuring cast which should be eaten first, Wee or the Beares', wrote Pellham[8] – the example of successful survival over the winter only two years earlier by those wholly unprepared for being stranded would have been an encouragement to the company, to try plans they had considered for some time.

One of the aspects of this event which makes it particularly interesting for scholars considering the relation between economics and knowledge is its character as what I would call a human experiment. Not only were the seven volunteers each on Spitsbergen and Jan Mayen asked to do their best to survive in harsh circumstances, but they were also required to keep a careful record of their experiences. Such a record stemmed of course from a familiar maritime tradition: the tradition of the logbook, which in this period was becoming more common on voyages and, as Margaret Schotte has pointed out, more standardized over the course of the seventeenth century.[9] The three journals which emerged from the overwinterings of 1633–4 and 1634–5 were made entirely on land, but they retained the character of ship's logs and echo the requirements Schotte describes, with the Admiraliteit of Amsterdam reviewing ship's logs for information from as early as 1618.[10] Van der Brugge writes of his overwintering on Spitsbergen that the directors of the Noordsche Compagnie were required 'carefully to note down everything that happened during the time they were there, and to put it in writing daily: so that one could from this decide if it was possible to put these places, up to now so barren and deserted, to the service and advantage of your honourable Society.'[11]

The commercial component here is clear – the company wished to test the possibility of year-round whaling – but I think it is fair to link this experiment, as the word suggests, to wider trends at this time to do with observation and the collecting of information. Recent work on observation has taken place chiefly in the history of science, such as the collection on scientific observation by Elizabeth Lunbeck and Lorraine Daston. However, as Barbara Shapiro pointed out nearly 20 years ago, a culture stressing facts and the observation and verification of those facts can also be found in the sixteenth and seventeenth centuries from fields as varying as law, history, journalism, geography, and religion, with law, in England at least, emerging as the earliest of these.[12] Gianna Pomata identifies in her essay in Lunbeck and Daston's collection the way *observationes* emerged in the sixteenth century as an interdisciplinary genre, developing first in medicine, with an author who is a careful observer who checks his facts against traditional information for accuracy.[13] She points out that this becomes a 'new cognitive category',[14] what Daston refers to as 'an epistemic genre', in which observation and checking via experiment defined broadly as 'recipe, trial, or just common experience' as well as an artificially-contrived experiment more akin to modern practice became familiar concepts across disciplines. Note-taking and simply paying attention became important,[15] although in Daston's view the leap from observation to conjecture to further observation did not take place until the eighteenth century.[16]

It is not difficult to apply a similar analysis to commercial practice in the Netherlands in the late sixteenth and seventeenth centuries. Clé Lesger has argued powerfully for the concentration of reliable information – which needed to be observed, collected, and checked – as a primary reason for the power of Amsterdam as a trading centre in the seventeenth century. A large group of historians, from Harold Cook to Daniel Margocsy to the authors writing in collections such as *The Dutch Trading Companies as Knowledge Networks,* or *Kennis en Compagnie,* or *Transformations of Knowledge in Dutch Expansion*, have stressed the connections of imperial expansion to a gathering of knowledge which in turn fed that expansion while changing understandings of the world at home.[17] Although at least some of this work has expressly focused on the history of science, we can see how observation, empiricism, and experiment such as that demanded of the men on Spitsbergen and Jan Mayen in the 1630's would, as Jacob Segersz van der Brugge himself observed, have direct effects on the success of commercial activity. In this sense every merchant and every commercial company was deeply invested in intellectual trends that we can see most clearly in the history of science.

As Lesger has pointed out, echoing Elizabeth Eisenstein, the press played an important role in making observations about commercial conditions reliable because they were checkable and, in the end, correctable, a point we of course can also make about the development of experiment in this period.[18] It was also, as Lesger has also stressed, increasingly important at this time for the author and publisher of information such as travel accounts to prove themselves to be reliable and trustworthy.[19] Lesger cites in particular the important publisher Cornelis Claesz, whose publication of travel journals, including the Nova Zembla account of Gerrit de Veer in 1598, launched the genre as an important component of the Dutch book trade in the seventeenth century.[20] I would argue, however, that even in the market for travel journals based on ship's logs, and indeed even in the publications of Cornelis Claesz, the question of reliability and checkability of observation depends greatly on the desired outcome on the part of the publisher. A publisher might, moreover, have multiple audiences in mind in producing these works. Both these points become only more important as we move through the seventeenth century.

Even if we look at the beginnings of this genre in the Netherlands in the 1590s, we can see certain conflicts or, at the very least, multiplicities in the interests of booksellers, authors, and others associated with both the book trade and the intellectual and cultural circles surrounding commercial expansion. As work on Cornelis Claesz, in particular by Bert van Selm and Elizabeth Sutton, has empha-sized, Claesz was deeply embedded in humanistic cultural circles keen to promote overseas trade, to find new and valuable trade routes, and to profit local merchants, as well as to spread newly-emerging knowledge about lands newly available to merchants. Around 40 percent of his stock had something to do with commerce and voyages, and he was connected closely with figures like Pieter Plancius (his com-mercial partner), Bernardus Paludanus, Reynier Pauw, Hendrick Hudde, Pieter Hasselaer, and Jan Huygen van Linschoten,[21] who were all greatly invested in the expansion of trade. We can see Claesz' motivations, or some of them, not only in his printing of both innovative and traditional works of seamanship and maps,[22] but also in the language and imagery on the title page of some of his travel journals. Linschoten's *Itinerario*, for example, which revealed new information about the successful Portuguese trade in India and the Indies, in which Linschoten had par-ticipated on Portuguese ships but which in 1596 was still unreachable by the Dutch, is matter-of-fact in its title page (Figure 8.1). It advertises the journal as 'containing a short description of the same Lands and Sea-coasts/with an indication of all the principal harbours/Rivers/points and places/which the Portuguese have discovered and made known....'[23] Although the title also advertised ethnographic, religious, and political details, it focused on the products that could be gained there ('the main Trees/Fruits/Herbs/Spices/and such goods') and 'also a short discussion of the Commerce/how and where it is carried out and can be found....'[24] The importance of commerce to this publication is underscored by the title page, which focused not on the wonders to be found in the Indies, but instead on the hoped-for investment to be found in the cities whose views graced the four corners of the image: Antwerp, Amsterdam, Middelburg, and Enkhuizen.

Nevertheless, it is evident that utility was not the only motivation for Claesz; indeed, Clé Lesger has argued that 'his motivation was *purely* commercial.'[25] Claesz said himself that 'we are in business *propter sanctum denarium*, for the round God [that is, money].'[26] The question is what would sell and to whom, an issue every bookseller had to consider. Arctic voyages provide us with an interesting counterpoint to those describing successful routes to the Indies. The voyages of

ITINERARIO,

**Voyage ofte Schipvaert / van Jan Huygen van Linschoten naer Oost ofte Portugaels Indien** inhoudende een corte beschrijvinghe der selver Landen ende Zee-custen/met aenwijsinge van alle de voornaemde principale Havens/Revieren/hoecken ende plaetsen/tot noch toe vande Portugesen ontdeckt ende bekent: Waer by gevoecht zijn / niet alleen die Conterfeytsels vande habyten/drachten ende wesen/so vande Portugesen aldaer residerende/ als vande ingeboornen Indianen/ende huere Tempels/Afgoden/Huysinge/met die voornaemste Boomen/Vruchten/kruyden/Specerijen/ende diergelijcke materialen/als ooc die manieren des selfden Volckes/so in hunnen Godts-diensten/als in Politie en Huijs-houdinghe: maer ooc een corte verhalinge van de Coophandelingen/hoe en waer die ghedreven en ghebonden worden/met die ghedenekweerdichste geschiedenissen/voorghevallen den rijt zijnder residentie aldaer.

Alles beschreven ende by een vergadert, door den selfden, seer nut, oorbaer, ende oock vermakelijcken voor alle curieuse ende Liefhebbers van vreemdigheden,

t'AMSTELREDAM.

By *Cornelis Claesz.* op't VVater, in't Schrijf-boeck, by de oude Brugghe.

Anno CIↃ. IↃ. XCVI.

FIGURE 8.1 Jan Huyghen van Linschoten, *Itinerario, voyage ofte schipvaert, naer Oost ofte Portugaels Indien inhoudende een corte beschryvinghe der selver landen ende zee-custen* (Amsterdam: Cornelis Claesz, 1596), title page. Courtesy of Koninklijke Bibliotheek, The Hague, shelfmark KW 893 G 57

Waerachtighe Beschrijvinghe

**Uan dzie seylagien / ter werelt nopt soo bzeemt ghe-**
hoozt/ dzie jaeren achter malcanderen deur de Hollandtsche ende Zeelandtsche schepen by
noozden Noozweghen/Moscovia ende Tartaria/ na de Conincksijcken van Catthai ende China, soo mede vande op-
doeninghe vande Wevgats,Nova Sembla, en van't Landt op de 80.graden/ dat men acht Groenlandt te zijn/ daer nopt mensch gheweest is ende
bande selle verscheurende Beyzen ende ander Zee-monsters ende ondraechlijcke koude/tot hoe op de laetste reyse sichtp int ys beset is/ende tholck op
76.graden op Nova Sembla een huys ghetimmert/ende 10.maenden haer albaer onthouden hebben/ende daer nae meer als 3 50.mijlen met open
clepne schupten over ende langs der Zee ghevaren. Alles met seer grooten perijckel/moepten ende ongeloofflijcke swaricheyt. Ghedaen
deur Gerrit de Veer van Amstelredam.

|NAVARCHVS HOLLANDVS| |SAMIVTA|

Ghedruckt t'Amstelredam, by Cornelis Claesz, op't Water, int Schrijf-boeck, A°. 1599.

**FIGURE 8.2** Gerrit de Veer, *Waerachtighe beschryvinghe van drie seylagien, ter werelt noyt soo vreemt ghehoort* (Amsterdam: Cornelis Claesz, 1598), title page. Koninklijke Bibliotheek, The Hague, shelfmark 76 D 6

1594, 1595, and 1596 were intended to locate and use a route through a northeast passage to China, and Linschoten's account of the first two voyages, published by Linschoten himself some years later in 1601, contained plenty of information for the purposes of those navigating the waters of the Kara Sea, including drawings of coastlines as they would be seen from ships.[27] On the other hand, the lack of success of all three voyages in getting any further than the barren and unpopulated Nova Zembla meant that most of the commercial interest of the accounts written by Gerrit de Veer, as far as Cornelis Claesz might have been concerned, was in the crew's heroic battles against inhospitable nature. The engravings on the title page of De Veer's account, published by Claesz in 1598, make a gesture to the Russians and Samoyeds encountered briefly on the way, but the main point of the pictures was the frightful nature of the ship's being shoved upwards by the ice, the struggle to build a house and survive, and the fights with savage polar bears (Figure 8.2). The title is similar; it stresses adventure: 'True Description of three voyages/ stranger than any ever heard in the world', to unimaginably polar latitudes ('at 80 degrees') to Greenland, 'where no person has ever been', fighting 'fierce ferocious Bears and other Sea-monsters and unbearable cold.'[28] In other words, the point of this story was not trade, but adventure.

The story was indeed exciting, if not always excitingly expressed, and its duration in Dutch memory testifies to this. But interestingly, recounting an adventure was clearly not the main intention of the author, Gerrit de Veer, who was one of the surviving members of Barents' crew. What he was marketing here was not only the excitement and misery his comrades had had to deal with, but also his own continued faith in the commercial value of the route tried by 1598 three times without success. His dedicatory epistle to the States-General, Raad van Staten, States of Holland, Zeeland, and West-Friesland, as well as Prince Maurits and the Gecommitteerde Raden of the Admiralty in Holland, Zeeland, and West-Friesland, makes it clear that in his view the purpose of the account was to show that it was indeed possible to travel to China via the northern route. De Veer cites the necessity of investment in the technology and knowledge necessary for trade, mentioning, in line with his own training under the master navigation teacher Robbert Robbertsz le Canu, the arts of navigation, measurement of latitude, and understanding of geography and its relationship to mathematics and astronomy. All this knowledge, he argued, brought great riches to the Netherlands, and could bring more with more investigation, and such investigation, he said, was what had happened on the three unsuccessful voyages to the Arctic. These voyages, De Veer wrote, were 'not wholly fruitless' and the route to China via the Arctic was 'not without hope.' This was the main reason for his book – 'so hebbe ick een corte beschyrvinghe … gedaen' – to explain the geography of the route, and to show why it would work. De Veer pointed out that, among other things, it was less cold at 80 degrees north in Spitsbergen than it was at 76 degrees on Nova Zembla, and that on Spitsbergen there were grass-eating animals in June, whereas it was too cold for these further south, at Nova Zembla. Thus a route further north was feasible, De Veer said, and we can see this not only as a plea for understanding from investors after the valuable cargo of the third voyage was lost, but also a set of observations, at times precise and mathematical, about why a northern passage deserved the continued confidence of all these officials, regents, and nobles.[29] Cornelis Claesz' full catalogue of travel works from the 1590s and the early years of the seventeenth century show that both utility and entertainment were features of his productions, but the illustrations of De Veer's journals alone show us the degree to which excitement and terror were the key selling point.

Claesz judged his market well, since there seemed no question in the years following 1598 of further investment in the northeastern route to China. At the same time, the memory of Nova Zembla in Dutch culture and beyond, was all about privation and adventure; even the English Muscovy Company's gunner's mate Edward Pellham remarked in 1631 that 'the world still doth [speake] of the Dutchmens hard Winter in Nova Zembla.'[30] We can see a similar pattern when we look at the logbooks required by the Noordsche Compagnie of the seven sailors left to winter on Spitsbergen and Jan Mayen in 1633–4 and on Spitsbergen in 1634–5. As I have mentioned, according to the account by Jacob Segersz van der Brugge, it appears that the company gave instructions for a full account of the conditions encountered by the men as they passed the winter, with the idea that this would inform the company of information useful in its future commercial plans. A large part of this information had to do with weather conditions, typical of logbooks at sea where wind direction and cloud were of more importance than on land. However, the availability of provisions, sighting of wildlife, ability to obtain scurvy grass (given that scurvy was the greatest danger in these arctic ventures), and danger of bears all feature in these accounts as what we can consider mainly commercial information. This was particularly true since in the case of the two overwinterings in which little wildlife was caught and scurvy grass was unavailable, the sailors all died, despite an apparently ample provision of supplies by the company, as outlined in an appendix to at least one edition of Van der Brugge's account of the successful overwintering on Spitsbergen in 1633–4.[31] Similarly, the careful tracking of the amount of ice in the harbour and the rare sighting of whales, walruses, and birds was important information for those making decisions about whether there would be future overwinterings.

This information was useful, but for a publisher looking for a wider market, it was also relatively boring. An account such as Van der Brugge's stressing information about what made an overwintering a success was appealing to one type of market; but there was another. As with Nova Zembla, accounts of disastrous overwinterings could appeal to a more popular market looking for adventure. There are two extant published accounts from 1634 of the overwintering on Jan Mayen Island in that year, which ended in the late spring with the return of the fleet to find all seven volunteers dead. One of the accounts (which I will for convenience call JM1) was published in Leiden, printed by Willem Christiaens [Van der Boxe][32] for Jacob Roels, interestingly with Christiaens' name printed much larger on the title page. Roels was mainly a vernacular publisher, although of relatively serious books, such as works of rhetoric, mathematics, history, geography, and literature.

Christiaens, a much more prolific publisher, issued works in Latin associated with the university, such as medical, theological and juridical disputations, as well as works in the vernacular, such as Philips Angel's *Lof der schilder-konst* in 1642, and a series of theological books in English. The seriousness of this output is reflected in the journal, in the form of a logbook, published after the fatal wintering on Jan Mayen in 1634. Although two accounts appeared in the same year, it is clear from the second one, published in Rotterdam (which I will refer to as JM2), that this Leiden edition (JM1) appeared first. I will also assume for the sake of argument that the Leiden JM1 version resembles reasonably closely the journal found with the seven dead sailors at the return of the fleet. I make this assumption because it is very plainly written, often with little information other than the wind and weather. Although we could assume that a serious publisher might want to publish a serious account, there is little here to inform or to give pleasure, at least to an audience seeking adventure. The most dramatic elements are not in the main text. We do learn on the title page that the sailors had all died – this is not remarked on in the text, which simply ends on April 30th with the report of a hard north wind – and the statement that the journal had been found between the legs of one of the seven sailors lying dead on the ground. Nevertheless, the journal states that it was published 'by a Lief-hebber of strange Voyages',[33] so the element of curiosity was clearly part of the intended appeal of the work. Following the title page,

# JOURNAEL

### OFTE

## UUaerachtige Beschrijvinge

### van al het gene

#### Datter voor-gheballen is op het Eplandt

# MAVRITIVS

### In *GROENLANDT.*

Beschreven

## By seben Persoonen / die Anno 1633. aldaer

ghelaeten waren om te ober-winteren/ dewelcke de heele
gheleghentheyt ban die plaetse/ en alles wat haer weder-
baren was/ neerstelijck aenghemerckt en hier
in opgheteekent hebben / tot dien tijdt toe
dat sp alle seben daer gheftorben sijn.

*Dese Copye is ghevonden tuffchen de beenen van een van*
*die feven , op het Velt doot leggende.*

Int licht ghebracht door een Lief-hebber van
vreemde Voyagien.

### TOT LEYDEN,
#### Ghedruckt by WILLEM CHRISTIAENS.

**Door** Iacob Roels, **Boeck-verkooper / woonende op de Hoogh-**
**landtsche Kerck-Graft / over het Wees-huys.** 1634.

**FIGURE 8.3** *Journael ofte vvaerachtige beschrijvinge van al het gene datter voor-ghevallen is op het eylandt Mavritivs in Groenlandt* (Leiden: Willem Christiaens [van der Boxe] for Jacob Roels, 1634), title page. Koninklijke Bibliotheek, The Hague, shelfmark KW Pflt 4345

moreover, is a poem by Christiaens addressed to all seafarers, praising them for their work in enduring difficult voyages, and pointing out, with notable national sentiment, the bravery of this Dutch company and its Dutch hearts to bear the terrible cold and wild bears of the lonely terrain of 'Groen-landt.'[34]

The title page and dedicatory poem tell us more than the contents of the volume about the messages of the market for voyages. In 1633, it is true, the Noordsche Compagnie was hoping for a new license to continue its monopoly (which may well have been the reason for this new venture). The account of the successful overwintering on Spitsbergen in the same year by Jacob Segersz van der Brugge, given that it was published by Saeghman, cannot be wholly relied upon to represent the original, but the dedication to the directors of the company (a company which no longer existed by the time of Saeghman's editions) suggests it is based on a contemporary original, and that it was seen as in the interests of the company to publish this happy account when all the sailors lived. Here the information about conditions on Spitsbergen might well have been of interest to potential investors in the various chambers of the company, and the publication could be seen as in the same vein as the intentions of Gerrit de Veer writing in 1598 about routes to China. Indeed, even the references to emotion in the journal of the successful over-wintering would have been a form of information for the company and its investors. Emotion, as the introduction to this volume suggests, is in itself a form of knowledge. In the case of the overwinterings, the ability of a sailor to withstand emotionally the hardships of a lonely and miserable Arctic winter would have been as helpful a piece of information as the availability of scurvy grass. In addition, the implicit linkage of these commercial efforts to national sentiment made such accounts useful in a more political sense. The poem in the JM1 Christiaens edition gives us some indication of an understanding similar to De Veer's: that even a tragic outcome for a sea expedition can be related as a means of promoting 'Hollandtsche' economic and political goals by turning this into a story of heroism.

But what brings us more squarely to the third aspect of our inquiries in this project – economies, knowledge, but also *affect* – are the choices a publisher with ideas different from Christiaens might have had when dealing with the more tragic case of the seven sailors who died on Jan Mayen Island in 1634 at the same time as Van der Brugge's were succeeding on Spitsbergen. Christiaens and Roels mentioned death on the title page and in the dedicatory poem but never again, and the pamphlet ends abruptly with the north wind on the 30th of April. The preface to the Leiden version also makes a claim to authority, mentioning that the death of the seven sailors on Jan Mayen was already known to the 'common people' through 'imagined Poems and sloppy Songs which can only be called imagined verses to which no credence should be given' – popular texts which unfortunately seem not to survive. (We have an English ballad describing the overwintering of Edward Pellham and crew from the English Muscovy Company, which may represent the kind of text Christiaens was describing.)[35] The Leiden text, as we have seen, also mentions the eagerness of some 'Lief-hebbers' to bring the actual text, found between the legs of the longest-lived of the sailors, into print. The reference to liefhebbers adds authority, and the location of the text gives a sense of immediacy and therefore also credit and trustworthiness. These are only small details, however, which could become lost in the subsequent text, which resembles a bald ship's log detailing mainly wind and weather. Authenticity might be an attraction, but it might not sell to a wider market.

In the same year, however, a second version of the pamphlet (JM2) was published in Rotterdam by Abraham Nering (Figure 8.4). The publisher and the author or editor working with him – the name is never revealed – made very different decisions about how to present the text, even though it is clearly based on

# IOVRNAEL.

### OFTE.

## Voyagie vande Groenlants

### Vaerders / Namelijck vande Seven Matros. die Ghebleven waren op het Eylant genaemt Mauritius om op het selfde Eylant te oberwinteren/oock om te besien hoe hem dit Lant toe soude draghen/ den gheheelen Winter.

Noch hebt ghy hier by, de Beschrivinghe van haer handel, ende wandel, oock wat sy gehoort ende gesien hebben, als Beeren, Wal-visschen ende meer andere Zeegedrochten , alles perfecktelijcken Beschreven, tot de tijt hares Overlijdens toe.

### TOT ROTTERDAM.

### By Abraham Nering, Boeckvercooper / by de Roode Brugghe/ Op het Zeeusche Veer/ inde Druckerije.

### ANNO, 1634.

**FIGURE 8.4** *Iournael. Ofte. Voyage vande Groenlandtsvaerders, namelijk vande seven matrosz. die ghebleven waren op het eylant Mauritius* (Rotterdam: Abraham Nering, 1634), title page. Koninklijke Bibliotheek, The Hague, shelfmark KW 893 G 57

the same manuscript journal as the version published in Leiden. There is still a stress on authenticity, it is true, and in the second edition of this text we find an address to the reader giving careful research as the reason for the expedition, and curiosity as a reason to read the text. This version ends with an afterword justifying the text and warning against the competition presented by the JM1 Leiden version: 'A Journal has been Printed in Leyden in which it is printed that they ate their Dog, and many such crude errors, which are simply Lies and adornments, and against which I would like to warn the gracious reader. The Author knows no correct Copies, except those printed at Rotterdam by Abraham Neringh, Bookseller at the Zeeusche Veer, by the Roo Brugghe.'[36] Here we also find a claim to authority and credit we have already noted in other examples of observation we have considered here, whether from eye-witnessing and attaching one's name to a travel journal (as in Linschoten or Gerrit de Veer) or in legal testimony or witnessing natural phenomena or experiment. By mentioning an author, and the possession of the correct text, the JM2 Rotterdam version of the Jan Mayen Island journal made an explicit bid for economic competition through the availability of better knowledge. A second edition of the JM2 text, in an afterword, also makes numerous claims to authenticity, adding, for example, the word DIE (in Dutch, thus 'that') at the very end of the text (which does not appear in the Leiden edition), stating that although we do not know the reason for the word, 'nevertheless we include it just as we found it....' The editor cites those who found the bodies and the authors of the journal: 'the men who were there themselves, and hand for hand saw it themselves....in the opinion of the Sailors....if you saw the written Copy which they themselves wrote, which is here and there in different hands, this is my *Principael* [main source], which came to hand, from which this Book itself is Printed.'[37] The afterword also frequently makes recourse to detail about the finding of the bodies and speculation about what must have happened to the sailors in their dying days and hours.

On the other hand, the fact the anonymous JM2 author was writing at all made the text inauthentic. It would be obvious to any reader that all the sailors who spent the winter at Jan Mayen Island in 1633–4 were dead, and therefore that the 'author' was no eyewitness. This is where affect comes in, and where we see the competition of a learned market (probably more appropriate to the readers of books printed by Willem Christiaens in Leiden) with a more popular one served by the publisher Abraham Nering, whose other publications were all vernacular texts concerning travel, religion, or drama. Despite decrying the JM1 Leiden version of the journal for lies and fantasies, including the cooked dog (a detail which actually also occurs in the JM2 Rotterdam text), what we find in the JM2 Rotterdam version is relatively systematic in editing the stark and undetailed material in the JM1 Christiaens version from Leiden.

As we have already noted, this type of editing was not unusual for a text of this kind, and particularly for later travel journals, such as those published by Joost Hartgers and Gillis Joosten Saeghman. As Garrelt Verhoeven points out, whenever Saeghman republished travel journals (as he published no original texts of his own), he added details to make these mainly late sixteenth-century texts fresher for a new audience.[38] Vibeke Roeper has also noted the degree to which editors might intervene between journals as they returned from sea voyages and their publication, not least because in the case of VOC texts it was not actually permitted by the company to publish. In the VOC sources she studied in her *doctoraalscriptie*, in many cases an editor was brought in to make the texts suitable for publication; sometimes the texts were put in the third person, or sections were cut, or new information added. Such editors were rarely named, and probably in many cases were the publisher himself. One such editor, according to Roeper, was Isaac Commelin, although he published anonymously.[39]

If we look at the editing of the story of the seven sailors on Jan Mayen Island in 1633–4, then, we need to ask how the text was changed between the relatively bland JM1 Leiden edition and the JM2 Rotterdam version published later in 1634. I would suggest that the changes, which for the most part add detail either unamplified or simply non-existent in the JM1 Leiden publication, add *affect* in order to improve its chances on the market. In the first place, the JM2 Rotterdam text adds human interest by mentioning far more details about the living conditions of the sailors. We hear that in November, for example, with cold freezing weather, 'they passed the time talking and discoursing/and each of us told his adventure/that he on Land and Water had done in his life… so we passed our time since we had no money to count…'[40] None of this appears in the JM1 Leiden edition. On the first of January, we hear that they wished each other a happy new year and a happy resolution to their situation, details which similarly are not in the Leiden edition and which among other things might incite sadness at the irony of the fact they would only live a few months longer.[41] The JM2 Rotterdam version speaks of the struggles they had with the weather, and their difficulties getting up the volcanic mountain that dominates Jan Mayen to see if they could catch any game. In the JM1 Leiden text, for example, the entry for January 7th reads in its entirety, 'The 7th ditto/ we had weather and wind as before; that night we had weather and wind as before.' But in the JM2 Rotterdam text we are told that 'a great deal of snow fell/yes, we had never seen so much snow/as long as we have been here up to now, we also have very sharp frost/it freezes both by day and by night/now we barely go out because of the great snow/and we shoot sometimes here and there into some pits or abysses so we can recognize them through so much snow.'[42] The fight against the elements which is also so prominent a feature in Gerrit de Veer's account of life on Nova Zembla thus reappears here, but greatly amplified from the Leiden text.

Secondly, the JM2 Rotterdam edition gives the reader more access, however falsely, to the emotions and feelings of the sailors as they suffered from cold, faced ferocious bears, and slowly died of their inability to find sources of vitamin C to cure their scurvy. Christiaens' JM1 Leiden edition makes no mention of feelings about their situation; everything is written as observation of bald facts about their environment and chiefly the weather. On November 28th, Nering's JM2 edition reports, they were 'courageous' and on December 19th cheerful;[43] but as the snow fell harder, we are told, they 'suffered' from not being able to go outdoors, and this same situation was considered 'verdrietigh' (pitiful) on January 19th.[44] On March 12th, in the first mention in either text of scurvy, we hear much more in the JM2 Rotterdam text about the sailors' relief at being able to get some 'refreshment' (that is, vitamin C) through the shooting of a bear, with many details of the killing, filleting, and eating of the bear and their hopes through this 'once again to regain our health.' The reader, of course, knows from the title page that the sailors will not become healthier, and on March 22nd the JM2 Rotterdam edition speaks again of emotions: 'our courage is rather low, as we are quite ill with Scurvy/we have little refreshment to keep us a bit on our feet....' As the sailors grow weaker, in the Rotterdam text we hear more and more emotion. On April 19th, according to Christiaens' JM1 Leiden version, once again we learn that they had a north wind, with freezing weather, with the same weather in the evening.[45] But Abraham Nering's JM2 Rotterdam edition gives the reader much more of what one might hope from a journal in which the subjects are about to die. On April 19th, his journal-keeper says 'we are getting sicker and sicker/for we now have no refreshment/so we are without hope and comfort/and those who are getting Ill there is little hope of recovery/through the little refreshment/and also through the great cold/since even when healthy/ one can hardly bear it/so much the worse if you are lying sick on our cots/still we hope for the best/awaiting the mercy of God' – and then adds, reverting to the JM1 Leiden text, 'wind and weather as before.'[46]

As we can see from these additions, the account published by Nering in Rotterdam not only gives us apparent access to the emotions of the sailors, but was intended to promote affect and emotion in readers themselves. In the first place, it could provide excitement for readers who did not normally experience the threat of polar bears prowling around outside their house. Both texts mention bears, but the Rotterdam version is much more expansive about their danger and the bloody fights the sailors had with them. On January 13th we hear from the JM1 Leiden version that 'We had wind and weather as before. We shot a Bear/and struck his head until he was stone dead.'[47] But according to the JM2 Rotterdam edition, 'We had a southeast wind again/with much snow and again we had a Bear at our Hut/and we heard some noise/so we looked immediately out of the Hut/then we saw him standing there/and confronted him/and shot him/and struck him in his head/so that he was completely dead and we then at the same time used Ropes or cords/and bound up his legs/and his throat and dragged him into our Hut and we skinned him in our Hut/because in front of the door it was no decent weather and because of the great cold/and also because of the snow/which lay so thickly....'[48] The image is much more vivid and thrilling for readers. This was only more the case when the sailors came to die, a moment which is unrecorded in the JM1 Leiden version, which simply breaks off, but which, as we have noted, ends in the JM2 Rotterdam version with one word, DIE (that). The narrator then takes over, saying that 'This little word (DIE) that just came from the pen, but that day could not receive its correct description, not knowing if he wanted to say (THAT) night we had the weather and wind as before, as he had observed so many times before, or what he wanted to express is known to good God, thus we leave it as we have found it.... [the person that wrote it] through faintness or through weakness laid the pen down, and went to lie in his cot or resting place, and ... gave up, and so fell asleep in peace, so that their end and day of death is here, as every gracious Reader can find it, who has come to read this.'[49] The account concludes with a report, again missing from Christiaens, of the feelings of the members of the fleet who returned to find the men all dead and describing the probable pain and suffering they must have experienced before dying. The editor makes explicit appeal to the reader to empathize with the emotions of the sailors who found the dead bodies, as well as of the sailors who had died: 'I urge the gracious Reader to consider, if it was not grievous for them, when they all started to become sick, that each could not help the other, especially for the one who was the last one alive....'[50]

The form of the changes made to the text in the JM2 Rotterdam edition indicate a taste for drama and emotion even in a text intended for a market for ostensibly factual material. We can see such taste in the kind of drama discussed by Karel Vanhaesebrouck in his contribution to this volume, but the understandings of it can be related much more widely to other artistic forms. This helps to explain the growing interest in disaster stories among travel journals, most famously just before the events of the 1630's with the bloody mutiny and wreck of the *Batavia* in 1629; the commander Pelsaert's account was a popular story in the seventeenth century.[51] According to Vibeke Roeper, by the 1660s most of the first editions published of sea travel journals were in the form of disaster stories.[52] From the account of the *Batavia* and of the stories of the deaths of the whalers on Spitsbergen and Jan Mayen in the 1630s, we can see that the taste for the dramatic, exciting, and tragic was already taking hold in the 1630s. The fashion for shipwreck tales, indeed, had already emerged in Iberia in the sixteenth century, as Josiah Blackmore has written in his account of the Portuguese *História Trágico-Marítima*, published as a collection in 1735–6, but already available in the sixteenth and seventeenth centuries as individual pamphlets.[53] These tales could have many meanings. Carl Thompson notes the possibility of metaphorical interpretations, given the possibility of redemption, and Jennifer Oliver has discussed in her recent book the political and religious meanings behind sixteenth-century French shipwreck tales.[54] Edward Pellham's stranding on Spitsbergen was certainly cast as a tale of religious redemption.[55] The seventeenth-century Dutch shipwreck and stranding tales have more of an air of excitement and the evocation of sympathy, however, and although Thompson suggests that it is only in the eighteenth and nineteenth centuries that we find attempts to evoke sympathy in shipwreck tales, Lawrence Goedde's discussion of storm and shipwreck scenes in seventeenth-century Dutch art posits that the images were intended to convey anxiety and and produce sympathy in the viewer.[56] The popularity of storm scenes – Goedde notes a 'dramatic increase' in their production between 1620–60, compared to other landscape paintings – indicates that the intensity of emotion they were intended to convey was popular among viewers.[57]

How do we square this longing for texts and images that incite emotion with the insistence on the truthfulness and authenticity of texts such as Nering's JM2 Rotterdam account? Nering made it clear in his afterword that he had changed his text, but he presented this as a virtue rather than as a problem. Addressing the reader, he points out that after the person designated to keep the journal had died, the narration was taken over by someone who was not trained to the office of *Boeck-houder*, although he had done his best. Nering therefore did his best, he claims, to clarify it, or to bring illumination to it, as he was, he said, asked to do by several good friends; considering that it was his office and trade (*Ampt ende Negotie*) to publish books, he could not refuse to bring it to the press, and hoped to have given contentment to his readers, who otherwise might have had to trust the lies or verses otherwise available. It is after this that Nering insists that readers should not trust his competitor Christiaens.[58] Thus the text was reliable, but it was also 'clarified' and 'illuminated': and as we have seen, these clarifications added emotion and incitements to emotion on the part of the reader.

This is less paradoxical if we consider understandings of the passions in the seventeenth century. Literature and the visual arts in the period were greatly influenced by theoretical concerns, inherited from rhetorical work of the ancients, that gave primacy in judging a work by its ability to engender emotion in the viewer or reader. In theoretical works about drama, painting, and poetry, writers and artists cited Aristotle, Cicero, Quintilian, and Seneca on the importance of *enargeia* (the conveying of naturalness) and *energeia* (the emotional response produced by art).[59] As a variety of scholars have noted, a main point of early modern artistic production was to provide emotionally laden images which were supposed to produce a reaction that affected the spectator or reader in both mind and body.[60] Thus early modern paintings and dramatic and poetic texts were considered to be particularly effective if they were persuasive and they moved their audience. The term famously used by Rembrandt about his own work in a letter to Constantijn Huygens, *beweeglijkheid*, although the subject of considerable debate, gives us access to the idea that movement (*bewegen*) of the emotions was an artist's goal.[61]

One purpose here was vividness for the sake of affective uplift. A reader or viewer was expected to react emotionally in a way that would provoke fear, sympathy, and compassion, and this identification with the figures in paintings and plays was intended to provide an improving moral insight.[62] Even in Christiaens' text about Jan Mayen Island, we can see an address to both the sympathies and moral judgement of the audience, for example in the introductory poem by Christiaens, which appealed to the national sentiment of readers who were urged to see what horrors 'a Hollands heart can bear.'[63] Similarly, Nering worked directly in his afterword to encourage the reader to imagine the painful experiences of the sailors on Jan Mayen, while the editor of the journal of the second over-wintering on Spitsbergen (whether Saeghman or an earlier editor) stressed the religious devotion of the dying sailors by portraying them in their last hours 'praying to God with folded hands.'[64] These texts were not as nakedly religious as Edward Pellham's account of the English Muscovy Company stranding on Spitsbergen in 1631, which is recounted as a case of godly deliverance, but it was evident that moral and emotional responses were expected.

To gain such responses, a certain vividness, such as the image of the Spitsbergen sailors dying in their bunks, was necessary. This too was consonant with ideas about the passions and their relationship to art. What may seem paradoxical is the relationship between an apparently invented scene and the claims to authenticity made by the editors of these texts. However, if we think about understandings of authenticity in the period, we can see ways in which this apparent conflict can be resolved. According, again, to art theory in the period, vividness could be a form of its own authenticity. Thus, as Claudia Swan has pointed out in a seminal article, artistic work said to be done *naer het leven* (after life) was not necessarily actually done from life, but could indeed mean simply having a lifelike effect, one encouraged by being done *uyt den gheest* (from the imagination).[65] Thomas Balfe and Joanna Woodall argue that *ad vivum* or *naer het leven* could be persuasive as a source of knowledge while not in fact attempting or indeed even claiming to be actually done in front of a living model. Instead, they suggest, if an image was *lifelike*, it could be considered to be true, precisely because it was persuasive. Thus vividness constituted truth, and indeed could be even more true than something copied from life which was not vivid.[66] If we extend these ideas to written texts, we could perhaps argue that the vividness of Nering's description of the fate of the sailors on Jan Mayen Island – 'that he through faintness or through weakness laid down his pen, and went to lie in his Bunk or resting-place, and thus gave himself up to God, to whom all things are known, and so fell asleep, so that his end and death-day is here, as the well-intentioned Reader shall find, who comes to read this'[67] – in some way was considered sufficiently truthful through its very conjuring of the image before the mind's eye. Nering goes into the first person to ask 'the well-intentioned Reader to consider if it was not tragic for them, when they all became so sick, that the one could not help the other, especially for the one who remained the last one living.' He suggests that this last person alive had helped the others 'on hands and feet,' though there is nothing in the text to indicate this, and in general the whole afterword consists of a set of speculations.[68] Yet authenticity is also claimed: the very truth of the passage comes from things the reader can only imagine, and which are called forth by the editor. Although Nering gives some more conventional reasons for us to trust his JM2 text, pointing out that those who were there themselves when the bodies were found had provided details, he also states that his text is more authentic than that of Christiaens precisely *because* he chose to 'explain' (*verklaren*) and 'illuminate' (*verlichten*) the text presented, it seems, with less vividness by Christiaens. In other words, the text was *naer het leven*, but it was not life. It was lifelike, and it should therefore provoke *beweeglijkheid*, movement, being moved, on the part of the reader.

In these texts we see some of the multivalent relationships of knowledge, economics, and affect. Economics prompted the actions reported here, but they also were developed and encouraged by knowledge. Observation and detail were necessary for the activities of commercial companies like the Noordsche Compagnie, or indeed to pursue trade at all, and the weighing of such observation and consideration of the issue of credibility was also an important activity for any aspirant merchant. Thus, devising a human experiment – pressing for first-hand reporting and experience – by sending volunteers to Jan Mayen Island and Spitsbergen made sense for the Noordsche Compagnie. The same consideration of credibility was true of booksellers wishing to publish books, and indeed of readers wishing to buy them: but the issues differed depending on the goals and the audience. Cornelis Claesz produced numerous eyewitness accounts of voyages to far places, coming from first-hand, named witnesses, some of whom were (or became) well-connected with scholarly circles, such as Linschoten, or came from wealthy merchant families. The credibility of these accounts was crucial, particularly if they were to be used to pursue further voyaging and trade; detailed accounts of coastlines and ports such as Linschoten's were useful, and his authority came from actually having been to the places he described.[69] But we can virtually see across the centuries the glint in Claesz' eye when he considered the potential market for the exciting adventures on what was otherwise a failed voyage to Nova Zembla: Gerrit de Veer had the advantage of having been there, which he wished to use to attract future investment, but Claesz had a better sense of the kind of market his book would attract. Similarly, the attempt to winter on Spitsbergen may have been part of an attempt at gaining investment by the Noordsche Compagnie, and the journal of that successful mission may have been a way of providing knowledge in aid of economics. But as for the (now lost) songs and ballads about the men who died on Jan Mayen, those will have had another goal: excitement, empathy, adventure, religious faith – though all themselves as well for the purposes of economic gain for the bookseller. Disaster narratives, shipwrecks and strandings, seemed to have a particular appeal, and continued to do so, not only in the Dutch market but in other European book markets and in England and America.[70] The emphasis could be on religion and the providence of God – as we see in Edward Pellham's account, or (and this was also fundamentally true of Pellham) on the sheer emotion and thrills of imagining hardship, misery, endurance, and perhaps even death. In the case of the overwintering on Jan Mayen Island, we have two contemporary and comparable texts from two rather different presses. One chose a more scholarly route, more akin to that of the humanistic circles of most of Cornelis Claesz' contemporaries (although the publication was not nearly so beautiful). On the other hand, an emphasis on excitement, emotion, and affect appears to have been the choice of Abraham Nering, the publisher from Rotterdam, who aimed at a more popular market, the same market he hoped to supersede in attacking cheap ballad versions of the story. Knowledge and information were important for sales, in other words, but by Abraham Nering, at least, affect seems to have been considered to be more so.

What is interesting is that credibility continued to be important even for those trafficking in affect. The anonymous editor of the Rotterdam text (probably Abraham Nering himself) admits that he has made changes, arguing that the person who acted as 'Boeck houder' had said himself that he was not trained to this office, and that he himself had done what he could 'to clarify, or cast light on,' what had been written in the journal, at the request of several friends. But he insisted that he was working from the actual written manuscript ('de Principael') which he was printing here, as opposed to the work being sold by 'Peddlers and Vagrants' selling 'crude Lies' to the people.[71] Emotion, affect, was what the popular market apparently wanted, but it was not what the Noordsche Compagnie wanted, so it seems not to have appeared in the original journal. The publisher Abraham Nering still needed to be credible, but what he had in his hands was too boring, and made too little appeal to the passions. So he made a commercial choice, a choice which put profit over accurate knowledge: but that choice was also, despite the apparent cheapness of this edition, consonant with understandings of the passions in the 1630s. What he published was not strictly true, but it *felt* true, and it moved the emotions, and that was what mattered. The choice for the passions was also the choice for profit. There was no need to choose between them.

## Notes

1  *Kort Journael, Van de seven Persoonen die op Spitsbergen in het Overwinteren, gestorven zijn, Anno 1634* (n.d. [1664?])
2  *Kort Journael*, 3.
3  On Saeghman and his alterations to texts: M. Barend-Van Haeften, "Van scheepsjournaal tot reisverhaal," 222–8; G. Verhoeven, "Voor Weynigh Geldt" I, 61ff. S. P. L'Honoré Naber makes the same point in his *Walvischvaarten*, xx.
4  On the Noordsche Compagnie: S. Muller, *Geschiedenis der Noordsche Compagnie*; L. Hacquebord, *De Noordse Compagnie*; L. Hacquebord, F. N. Stokman, and F. W. Wasseur, "The Directors of the Chambers of the 'Noordse Compagnie'."
5  L. Hacquebord, *Noordse Compagnie*, 47–57; J. Braat, "Dutch Activities in the North and the Arctic"; L. Hacquebord, F. Steenhuisen, and H. Waterbolk, "English and Dutch Whaling Trade".
6  J. Segersz van der Brugge, *Journael, Of Dagh-Register*, dedicatory epistle.
7  E. Pellham, *Gods Power and Providence*, "To the Reader."
8  Ibid.
9  M. Schotte, "Expert Records."
10  Idem, 294.
11  Van der Brugge, dedicatory epistle.
12  E. Lunbeck and L. Daston, *Histories of Scientific Observation*; B. Shapiro, *A Culture of Fact.*
13  G. Pomata, "Observation Rising," 50–51, 65.
14  Idem, 65.
15  L. Daston, "The Empire of Observation," 81–82, 95.
16  Idem, 104.
17  S. Huigen, J. L. De Jong and E. Kolfin, *The Dutch Trading Companies as Knowledge Networks*; L. Blussé and I. Ooms, *Kennis en Compagnie*; S. Friedrich, A. Brendecke, and S. Ehrenpreis, *Transformations of Knowledge in Dutch Expansion.*

18 C. M. Lesger, "The Printing Press and the Rise of the Amsterdam Information Exchange," 90.
19 Idem, 94–95.
20 Ibid., 94. For a masterful survey of Claesz's publishing business: Van Selm, *Een menighte treffelijcke Boecken*, 174–333.
21 C. Lesger, "The Printing Press," 95; E. Sutton, "Economics, Ethnography, and Empire," 102, 115 (both cite Van Selm for the figure of 40 percent); E. Sutton, "To Inform and Delight," 329.
22 C. Lesger, "The Printing Press," 95.
23 J. H. Van Linschoten, *Itinerario*, title page. '…inhoudende een corte beschryvinge der selver Landen ende Zee-custen/met aenwysinge van alle de voornaemde principaele Havens/Rivieren/hoecken ende plaetsen/tot noch toe van de Portugesen ontdeckt ende bekent…'.
24 Ibid.
25 C. Lesger, "The Printing Press," 95. Italics by AG.
26 *Nieuw Nederlandsch Biografisch Woordenboek* 10 (1937), col. 173, quoted in Lesger, "The Printing Press," 95.
27 J. H. Van Linschoten, *Voyagie*.
28 G. De Veer, *Waerachtighe Beschryvinge*, title page.
29 G. De Veer, *Waerachtighe Beschryvinge*, dedicatory epistle.
30 E. Pellham, *Gods Power and Providence*, dedicatory epistle.
31 J. S. Van der Brugge, *Journael, of Dagh-Register,* 47.
32 The STCN identifies this publisher as Willem Christiaens van der Boxe; the title page gives only his patronymic.
33 *Journael ofte Waerachtige Beschrijvinge van al het gene Datter voor-ghevallen is op het Eylandt Mauritius in Groenlandt….* (1634), title page and 20. Henceforth 'Christiaens edition.'
34 'Ghedicht aen alle Zee-Vaerende Luyden,' after title page, Christiaens edition.
35 *A Wonder beyond mans expectation* (1635?), Magdalene College, Pepys Ballads 1.74–75.
36 *Iournael ofte Voyagie vande Groenlants-Vaerders* (1634), 'Na-Reden.' Henceforth 'Nering edition.'
37 Nering edition, Na-Reden.
38 G. Verhoeven, 'Voor Weynigh Geldt,' I, 64.
39 V. Roeper, "Journalen ter Zee ende Reysen te Lande," 27–29.
40 Nering edition, entry for November 18, 1633.
41 Idem, entry for January 1, 1634.
42 Idem, entry for January 9, 1634.
43 Idem, entry for December 19, 1633.
44 Idem, entries for January 3, 1634; January 19, 1634.
45 Christiaens edition, 20, entry for April 19, 1634.
46 Nering edition, entry for April 19, 1634.
47 Christiaens edition, 13, entry for January 13, 1634.
48 Nering edition, entry for January 13, 1634
49 Nering edition, 'Na-Reden.'
50 Ibid.
51 V. Roeper, ed., *De Schipbreuk van de Batavia 1629.*
52 V. Roeper, "Journalen ter Zee," 32.
53 J. Blackmore, *Manifest Perdition.*
54 C. Thompson, *Shipwreck in Art and Literature*, 10; Oliver, *Shipwreck in French Renaissance Writing.*
55 E. Pellham, *Gods Power and Providence.*
56 C. Thompson, *Shipwreck*, 13; L. O. Goedde, *Tempest and Shipwreck in Dutch and Flemish Art*, xiii, 9, 45.
57 L. O. Goedde, 208, note 8.
58 Nering edition, "Na-Reden."

59  J. H. Hagstrum, *The Sister Arts*, 11–12; U. Heinen, "Huygens, Rubens and Medusa," 159–60; Aristotle, *Rhetorica* 1411b.
60  H. Roodenburg, *"Beweeglijkheid* embodied," 315.
61  Rembrandt wrote about how works concerning the burial and resurrection of Christ, completed in 1639 for Stadhouder Fredrik Hendrik, 'sijnt daer die meeste ende die naetuereelste beweechgelickheyt': L. De Pauw-de Veen, "Over de betekenis van het woord 'beweeglijkheid'"; T. Weststeijn, 'Rembrandt and Rhetoric', 114–15.
62  J. W. H. Konst, *Woedende Wraakghierigheidt*, 163; S. Dickey and H. Roodenburg, "Introduction," 9.
63  'Ghedicht aen alle Zee-Vaerende Luyden', after title page, Christiaens edition.
64  Nering edition, 'Na-Reden'; second journal in Van der Brugge, *Twee Journalen* (1660s), entry for 26 February 1635.
65  C. Swan, *"Ad vivum,"* 354–5.
66  T. Balfe and J. Woodall, 'Introduction'. in T. Balfe, J. Woodall, and C. Zittel, eds., *Ad Vivum*. I am grateful to Joanna Woodall for our conversations about this subject and for helping me along the path this article takes.
67  Nering edition, "Na-Reden".
68  Ibid.
69  M. Campbell, *The Witness and the Other World*, 3.
70  Cf. J. Sievers, "Drowned Pens and Shaking Hands"; Lincoln, "Shipwreck Narratives".
71  Nering edition, "Na-Reden".

## Bibliography

1634 Anonymous. *Iournael ofte Voyagie vande Groenlants-Vaerders/Namelijck vande Seven Matrosz. Die Ghebleven waren op het Eylant genaemt Mauritius om op het selfde Eylant te overwinteren/oock om te besien hoe hem dit Lant toe soude draghen/ den gheheelen Winter. Noch hebt ghy hier by, de Beschrivinghe van haer handel, ende wandel, oock wat sy gehoort ende gesien hebben, als Beeren, Wal-visschen ende meer andere Zeegedrochten, alles perfecte-lijcken Beschreven, tot de tijt hares Overlijdens toe.* Rotterdam: Abraham Nering, 1634.

1634 Anonymous. *Journael ofte Waerachtige Beschrijvinge van al het gene Datter voor-ghevallen is op het Eylandt Mauritius in Groenlandt….* Leiden: Willem Christiaens for Jacob Roels, 1634.

1635? Anonymous. *A Wonder beyond mans expectation, In the preservation of eight men in* Greenland *from one season to another, the like never knowne or heard of before, which eight men are come all safely from/thence in this last Fleet, 1631. whose names are these, William Fakely Gunner, Edward Pellham Gun-/ners Mate, Iohn Wise Robert Goodfellow Seamen, Thomas Ayers Whalecutter, Henry Rett Cooper,/Iohn Dawes, Richard Kellet Land men.* n.p., printed for H. Gosson, n.d. (1635?) Magdalene College, Cambridge, Pepys Ballads 1. 74–75.

1664 Anonymous. *Kort Journael, Van de seven Persoonen die op Spitsbergen in het Overwinteren, gestorven zijn, Anno 1634, in Twee Journalen/Gehouden by seven Matroosen, Op het Eylandt Mauritius in Groenlandt /In den Jare Anno 1633. en 1634. in haer Overwinteren, doch sijn al t'samen gestorven.* Amsterdam: Gillis Joosten Saeghman, n.d. [c. 1664].

Balfe, Thomas, and Joanna Woodall. "Introduction. From Living Presence to Lively Likeness: The Lives of Ad Vivum." In Thomas Balfe, Joanna Woodall, and Claus Zittel, eds., *Ad Vivum? Visual Materials and the Vocabulary of Life-likeness in Europe before 1800.* Intersections: Interdisciplinary Studies in Early Modern Culture, ed. Karl A. E. Enenkel. Leiden: Brill, 2019.

Barend-Van Haeften, Marijke . "Van Scheepsjournaal tot Reisverhaal: Een Kennismaking met Zeventiende-eeuwse Reisteksten." *Literatuur* 7, (1990): 222–8.

Blackmore, Josiah. *Manifest Perdition: Shipwreck Narrative and the Disruption of Empire.* Minneapolis: University of Minnesota Press, 2002.

Blussé, Leonard, and Ilonka Ooms. *Kennis en Compagnie: De Verenigde Oost-Indische Compagnie en de Moderne Wetenschap.* Leiden: Balans, 2002.

Braat, J. "Dutch Activities in the North and the Arctic during the Sixteenth and Seventeenth Centuries." *Arctic* 37, no. 4 (December 1984): 473–80.

Brugge, Jacob Segersz van der. *Journael, Of Dagh-Register/gehouden by Seven Matroosen, In haer Overwinteren op Spitsbergen in Maurits-Bay, Gelegen in Groenlandt, t'zedert het vertreck van de Visschery-Schepen der Geoctroyeerde Noordtsche Compagnie, in Nederlandt, zijnde den 30. Augusty, 1633. Tot de wederkomst der voorsz. Schepen, den 27. May, Anno 1634.* Amsterdam: Gillis Joosten Saeghman, n.d. 1664?.

Campbell, Mary. *The Witness and the Other World: Exotic European Travel Writing, 400–1600.* Ithaca, NY: Cornell University Press, 1988.

Daston, Lorraine. "The Empire of Observation, 1600-1800." In Elizabeth Lunbeck and Lorraine Daston, eds., *Histories of Scientific Observation*, Chicago: University of Chicago Press, 2011, 81–113.

De Pauw-De Veen, Lydia. "Over de betekenis van het woord 'beweeglijkheid' in de zeventiende eeuw." *Oud Holland* 74 (1959): 202–12.

Dickey, Stephanie S., and Herman Roodenburg, eds. *The Passions in the Arts of the Early Modern Netherlands. Nederlands Kunsthistorisch Jaarboek* 60 (2010).

Friedrich, Susanne, Arndt Brendecke, and Stefan Ehrenpreis, eds. *Transformations of Knowledge in Dutch Expansion.* Berlin: Walter de Gruyter, 2015.

Goedde, Lawrence Otto. *Tempest and Shipwreck in Dutch and Flemish Art: Convention, Rhetoric, and Interpretation.* University Park and London: Pennsylvania State University Press, 1989.

Hacquebord, Louwrens. *De Noordse Compagnie.* Zutphen: Walburg Pers, 2014.

Hacquebord, Louwrens, Frits Steenuisen, and Huib Waterbolk. "English and Dutch Whaling Trade and Whaling Stations in Spitsbergen (Svalbard) before 1660." *International Journal of Maritime History* 15, no. 2 (2003): 117–34.

Hacquebord, Louwrens, Frans N. Stokman, and Frans W. Wasseur. "The Directors of the Chambers of the "Noordse Compagnie", 1614–1642, and their Networks in the Company." In *Entrepreneurs and Entrepreneurship in Early Modern Times*, edited by Clé Lesger and Leo Noordegraaf, 245–51. The Hague: Stichting Historische Reeks 29, 1995.

Hagstrum, Jean H. *The Sister Arts: The Tradition of Literary Pictorialism and English Poetry from Dryden to Gray.* Chicago: University of Chicago Press, 1958.

Heinen, Ulrich. "Huygens, Rubens and Medusa: Reflecting the Passions in Paintings, with some Considerations of Neuroscience in Art History." In Stephanie Dickey and Herman Roodenburg, eds., *The Passions in the Arts of the Early Modern Netherlands. Nederlands Kunsthistorisch Jaarboek 60 (2010),* 151–76.

Huigen, Siegfried, Jan L. de Jong, and Elmer Kolfin, eds. *The Dutch Trading Companies as Knowledge Networks.* Leiden: Brill, 2010.

Konst, Jan W. H. *Woedende Wraakghierigheidt en Vruchtelooze Weeklachten: De hartstochten in de Nederlandse tragedie van de zeventiende eeuw.* Assen: Van Gorcum, 1993.

Lesger, Clé. "The Printing Press and the Rise of the Amsterdam Information Exchange around 1600." In *Creating Global History from Asian Perspectives*, edited by Shigeru Akita, 87–102, Osaka: Osaka University, 2008.

L'Honoré Naber, S. P. *Walvischvaarten, Overwinteringen en Jachtbedrijven in het Hooge Noorden 1633–1635*. Utrecht: N.V.A Oosterhoek's Uitg.-MIJ, 1930.

Lincoln, Margarette. "Shipwreck Narratives of the Eighteenth and Early Nineteenth Century: Indicators of Culture and Identity." *British Journal for Eighteenth-Century Studies* 20 (1997): 155–72.

Linschoten, Jan Huyghen van. *Itinerario, Voyage ofte Schipvaert/van Jan Huygen van Linschoten naer Oost ofte Portugaels Indien....* Amsterdam: Cornelis Claesz, 1596.

Linschoten, Jan Huyghen van. *Voyagie, ofte schip-vaert, van Ian Huyghen van Linschoten, van by noorden om langes Noorwegen...tot voorbij de revier Oby...1594 en[de] 1595*. Franeker: Gerard Ketel, 1601.

Lunbeck, Elizabeth, and Lorraine Daston, eds. *Histories of Scientific Observation*. Chicago: University of Chicago Press, 2011.

Müller, Samuel. *Geschiedenis der Noordsche Compagnie*. Utrecht: Gebr. van der Post, 1874.

Oliver, Jennifer. *Shipwreck in French Renaissance Writing: The Direful Spectacle*. Oxford: Oxford University Press, 2019.

Pellham, Edward. *Gods Power and Providence: Shewed, In the Preservation and Deliverance of Eight Englishmen, left by mischance in Green-Land Anno 1630. nine moneths and twelve dayes*. London: for John Partridge, 1631.

Pomata, Gianna. "Observation Rising: Birth of an Epistemic Genre, 1500-1650." In Elizabeth Lunbeck and Lorraine Daston, eds., *Histories of Scientific Observation*, Chicago: University of Chicago Press, 2011, 45–80.

Roeper, Vibeke. "Journalen ter Zee ende Reysen te Lande: De Produktie van Gedrukte Teksten over Reizen naar Oost-Indië 1596–1700." Doctoraalscriptie, University of Amsterdam, 1992. 2 vols.

Roeper, Vibeke, ed. *De Schipbreuk van de Batavia 1629*. Zutphen: Walburg Pers, 1993.

Roodenburg, Herman. "*Beweeglijkheid* Embodied: On the Corporeal and Sensory Dimensions of a Famous Emotion Term." In Stephanie Dickey and Herman Roodenburg, eds., *The Passions in the Arts of the Early Modern Netherlands. Nederlands Kunsthistorisch Jaarboek* 60 (2010), 307–18.

Schotte, Margaret. "Expert Records: Nautical Logbooks from Columbus to Cook." *Information & Culture* 48, no. 3 (2013): 281–322.

Selm, Bert van. *Een Menighte Treffelijcke Boecken: Nederlandse Boekhandelscatalogi in het begin van de Zeventiende Eeuw*. Utrecht: HES Uitgevers, 1987.

Shapiro, Barbara J. *A Culture of Fact: England, 1550–1720*. Ithaca, NY: Cornell University Press, 2000.

Sievers, Julie. "Drowned Pens and Shaking Hands: Sea Providence Narratives in Seventeenth-Century New England." *William and Mary Quarterly* 3rd ser. 63, no. 4 (October 2006): 743–76.

Sutton, Elizabeth. "Economics, Ethnography, and Empire: The Illustrated Travel Series of Cornelis Claesz, 1598–1603." PhD thesis, University of Iowa, 2009.

Sutton, Elizabeth. "To Inform and Delight: The Commodification of Travel Images in Amsterdam." *Mediaevialia* 32 (2011): 325–56.

Swan, Claudia. "*Ad vivum, Naer het leven*, From the Life: Defining a Mode of Representation." *Word and Image* 11, no. 4 (October–December 1995): 353–72.

Thompson, Carl, ed. *Shipwreck in Art and Literature: Images and Interpretations from Antiquity to the Present Day*. New York/London: Routledge, 2013.

Veer, Gerrit de. *Waerachtighe Beschryvinge Van drie seylagien/ter werelt noyt soo vreemt ghehoort....* Amsterdam: Cornelis Claesz, 1598.

Verhoeven, Garrelt. "Voor Weynigh Geldt: Leven en Werk van de Amsterdamse Boekdrukker/Boekverkoper Gillis Joosten Saeghman, 1619–1704." Doctoraalscriptie, University of Leiden, 1991. 2 vols.

Weststeijn, Thijs. "Rembrandt and Rhetoric: The Concepts of *affectus, enargeia* and *ornatus* in Samuel van Hoogstraten's Judgement of his Master." In *The Learned Eye: Regarding Art, Theory, and the Artist's Reputation: Essays for Ernst van de Wetering*, edited by Marieke van den Doel, Nastasja van Eck, Gerbrand Korevaar, Anna Tummers, and Thijs Weststein. Amsterdam: Amsterdam University Press, 2005, 111–30.

# 9

# COORDINATION IN EARLY MODERN DUTCH BOOK MARKETS

## 'Always something new'

*Claartje Rasterhoff and Kaspar Beelen*

In 1660s Amsterdam, the shop of bookseller Iohannes van den Bergh was the place to be, or so the image on the title page of *Spiegel der gedenckweerdighste wonderen en geschiedenissen onses tijds* wants us to believe (Figure 9.1). The bookseller presents a sheet to the customer and the viewer, reading *Altyt wat nieuws* (Always something new), suggesting that the latest titles were always on offer. In this case, the image, which takes up a large chunk of the title page, might have advertised the shop rather than the book (a compendium of stories narrating remarkable events). Such commercial self-fashioning could very well have been a way to showcase Van den Bergh's recent move to the Dam, an A-location right next to the Town Hall, but it also testifies to a market culture in which novelty was an important value proposition.[1]

This chapter examines this market culture by statistically measuring patterns of innovation in the Dutch market for books. Book markets serve as a reasonable proxy for knowledge markets, as they were a crucial site for commercial exchange of knowledge, ideas and information.[2] Even if it has proven difficult to tie the emergence of knowledge markets to a particular time and place, the Low Countries were certainly one of the hotspots where ideas, information, knowledge, and beliefs were heavily commoditized. The Dutch Republic presents a particularly good case with which to study the expansion of early modern knowledge economies, exactly because its book markets displayed such spectacular growth (cf. Figures 9.2 and 9.3). From this 'intellectual entrepôt' and 'bookshop of the world', Dutch publishers and merchants fulfilled an important function in the international exchange of knowledge.[3]

How the Dutch Republic became a publishing powerhouse has been well studied. A typical explanation is that circumstances on both the supply and demand sides were favourable: people had money to spend; southern-Netherlandish immigrants injected relevant knowledge, skills, and material. Plus, there was relative freedom of the press and high literacy levels; and, not insignificantly, conditions in other countries were much less favourable. An additional series of explanations for

**FIGURE 9.1**    Title page of Laurens van Zanten, *Spiegel der gedenckweerdighste wonderen en geschiedenissen onses tijds*, Amsterdam, Iohannes van den Berg 1661. Royal Library, The Hague; KVB University Library University of Amsterdam

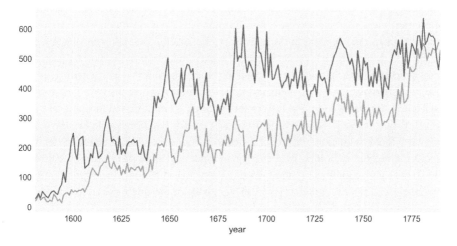

**FIGURE 9.2**    Number of titles issued annually in the Dutch Republic. The light grey line represents the Dutch titles, the dark grey line the total corpus

the deepening and broadening of the Dutch book market focuses less on circumstances and more on the mechanisms that brought demand and supply together.[4] These include product innovations that made books affordable and appealing to new consumers, and marketing and distribution innovations such as auctions, catalogues, advertisements, and stock and publishers' lists.[5] Collaboration in guilds and other

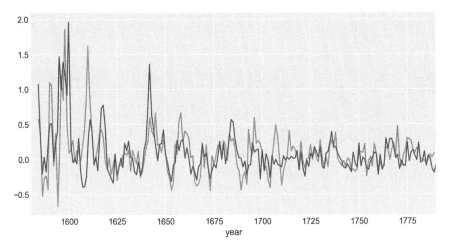

**FIGURE 9.3**   Relative growth. Percent change by four-year period. The light grey line represents the Dutch titles, the dark grey line the total corpus

more informal professional networks further reduced information asymmetries and facilitated convergence of shared practices, collectively determining the rules of the game in local markets and industries.

These observations have led historians to argue that market forces alone cannot account for observed patterns of growth and innovation in cultural industries like publishing, and that the specific organizational structure of Dutch markets for books also contributed to their success.[6] This chapter will build on this interpretation by analyzing a specific type of informal market organization, namely coordination via products – in our case books. Books were, as they still are today, important actors in knowledge markets because they carried and mediated knowledge (scientific, popular, or otherwise), but they were also actors within the book market. The texts as well as the title pages and other features of the book communicated meaning and the value of the product.[7] Printer's devices such as van den Bergh's (Figure 9.1), for instance, acted as markers of identification for bookshops and as signifiers for the books themselves, indicating eminence, genre specializations, or ideological stances.[8] Book titles also combined a cultural and commercial function; they were 'a coded message – in a market situation [...] half sign, half ad, the title is where the novel as language meets the novel as commodity.'[9]

Studies of single or small sets of publications have demonstrated how publishers and other agents in the early modern book markets used title-pages, dedications, printers' devices, prefaces, indexes, and paratext as powerful marketing strategies and means of communication with their (potential) customers, competitors, and colleagues.[10] In this volume, Feike Dietz's chapter on children's books, for instance, elucidates how these strategies were related to the emergence of new categories. The book market, then, can be seen as a site where market actors shape knowledge products and where the knowledge products themselves also shape the behaviour of market actors.

In this chapter we will expand on this methodology by analyzing information gathered from title pages at scale. To add a broader context to the individual publishers' strategies discussed elsewhere in this volume, we employ the concept of 'coordination by meaning' as a useful analytical tool for understanding commercial and cultural aspects of knowledge production and consumption in tandem. In economic theory it is often assumed that coordination between the actions of market actors is achieved through price signals. These indicate the relative scarcity and quality of goods. But in the case of product markets in which meaning, novelty, and quality play an important role (as in the case of books), decision-making is affected less by price and quantities, and more by quality and qualities.

This is not to say that price does not matter for individual decision making, but rather that, for instance, a good book is not necessarily more expensive, and that what is considered to be good is (to some extent) in the eye of the beholder. How, then, were the individual actions of book market actors coordinated beyond price, through shared meaning? How did early modern consumers and producers come to value new products, and how did their valuation practices affect overall market development? We hypothesize that, among other things, information on title pages collectively formed a cultural frame of reference and thereby coordinated supply of and demand for new (and old) knowledge.

To operationalize the quantitative study of titles and title pages as market devices, we have developed a methodological framework integrating research on early modern material culture, cultural economic theory, and methods in the digital humanities, and we have tested it on a wonderful dataset of the title pages of books produced in the early modern Dutch Republic: the Short Title Catalogue Netherlands (STCN) of the Dutch Royal Library.[11] The STCN is the Dutch retrospective bibliography for the period 1540–1800, compiled on the basis of library collections in the Netherlands and abroad.[12] Information on author, publisher, year, and place of publication, edition, etc. is included if provided on the title page, and the collation formula, subject labels, and other metadata have been added by hand.[13] Figures 9.2 and 9.3 show the number of, and relative change in, the number of titles listed in the STCN per year.[14] Limitations of the dataset have been extensively discussed elsewhere, but one major drawback deserves explicit mention: this is a *short* title catalogue, which means that in many cases we do not have full titles.[15] Our conclusions can therefore, at this point, not be more than tentative.

## Methodological framework

The relationship between the expansion of book markets and knowledge exchange has received ample scholarly attention. While growth rates in the Dutch Republic might have been above average, they testify to processes of market expansion that were both cause and consequence of a wider European phenomenon: the dramatic rise in knowledge production and consumption (more knowledge for more people).[16] During the early modern period knowledge was increasingly cherished as a public good in, for instance, the intellectual communities of the Republic of Letters, and in formal institutions such libraries, schools, universities, and cabinets of curiosities.

At the same time the commoditization of knowledge, ideas, and information was expedited by the expansion of book markets. Dutch publishers in particular responded aptly to increases in supply of and demand for new knowledge, and thus they contributed greatly to making it available more rapidly, widely, and at a larger scale than ever before.[17] Many studies of early modern knowledge production emphasize new knowledge, new products, new genres, and new consumer groups, but it has not yet been systematically assessed to what extent growth in the Dutch book market was indeed driven by the introduction of, and demand for, new products and how this might have differed across time, market segments, and place.

In order to appreciate how new knowledge, new products, or new genres could take root with consumer groups, we should consider historical research on consumer culture. Knowledge, to some extent an immaterial good, materialized in the form of printed pages, and its exchange, consequently, was part and parcel of broader changes in material culture. Across early modern Europe and beyond, household possessions and material culture became increasingly rich as consumer goods were made available and sought after in broad layers of society. Although historians debate the timing, scope, and intensity of this 'consumer revolution', there is little question that during the seventeenth and eighteenth centuries in particular, the number, quality, and variety of material goods owned by households from different economic and social backgrounds expanded significantly.[18] At the same time, consumer goods such as furniture, clothing, tableware, and mirrors, became less desirable for their intrinsic qualities – value of the raw materials, functionality, and durability – and more for intangible qualities such as novelty, fashion, and design.[19]

To explain these changes, cultural explanations interact and sometimes compete with economic and social ones. For example, historians have emphasized that the changes in consumption habits were not merely responses to changes in production and distribution methods. They were also informed by, among other things, an emerging bourgeois culture that valued pleasure, novelty, or comfort, which in turn prompted changes in the organization of production and distribution.[20] Product innovation, then, was as much about *differentiating* the goods in order to cater and appeal to specific audiences as it was about improving and replacing. As a result, differences between the products – in our case books – were often marginal, but not trivial. The emphasis on fashion and novelty as well as the marketing of small but important differences between books would have come with significant costs of learning about the expected value of the books.[21] Consumers and producers needed more than access to information available in the markets in order to present or purchase the best product; they needed a shared understanding of differences and similarities in meaning in order to buy the *right* product.[22]

That this was not just a theoretical issue is evident from the numerous morally charged remarks by intellectuals about the abundance of books and the problem of how to judge them.[23] Not only were there (too) many books, there were also (too) many different, new and conflicting authorities, opinions, and experiences. Henry Basnage de Beauval (1656–1710), editor of the *Histoire des ouvrages des savants*, spoke of the Republic of Letters being submerged in 'kind of flood and overflow.' And in 1680 German polymath Gottfried Wilhelm Leibniz complained of 'that horrible mass of books which keeps on growing […].'[24] Even if these complaints became a fashionable motif in early modern academic discourse (and scholars have observed similar outcries in other periods), other sources confirm that consumers and producers relied on an array of formal and informal institutions and devices when they try to compare, value, and assess new products.[25] Readers employed a multitude of channels and devices (apart from word of mouth) such as periodicals, *historia literaria*, lexica, bibliographies, encyclopedia, reviews, and other 'aids to erudition' that could help acquire information and facilitate judgments. On the supply side, the growing importance of intermediaries and the introduction of market devices, such as advertisements, publishers' lists, and catalogues that helped broader audiences distinguish, compare, and communicate have also been interpreted as a function of growing market complexity.[26]

Clearly, all these devices and institutions contributed to coordination in the increasingly complex markets for books and knowledge. But what they do not reveal are the more informal and unintentional processes of coordination by meaning. Economic sociologists have long pointed to the importance of standards, classifications and qualifications of goods to create order in markets.[27] Generally, however, these are often neither fixed nor well-defined, and this makes them difficult to pinpoint, much less define, especially in the early modern period when book markets and their organizing principles were in the early stages of development. Especially when standards and classifications are difficult to codify and under construction, consumers and producers tend to compare new occurrences to other occurrences in order to form judgments.[28] These comparisons are, for instance, explicit in reviews or recommendations, but we would argue that interrelations between book titles and title pages can also be understood as important instruments in making comparisons and judgments.

Consequently, book titles and other information from title pages are not only the place where we might observe novelties or innovations, but also the process of coordination. In this chapter we are experimenting with the identification of new product groups and products in data gathered from early modern Dutch title pages. Our aim in analyzing information from title pages is therefore also twofold: 1) to approximate to what extent knowledge (book) market growth was, in fact, driven by product innovation; and 2) to explore how we might interpret these patterns in relation to processes of coordination by meaning. In order to establish how novel the information, knowledge and ideas published in the Dutch Republic in the form of books were in different periods, we need to revisit the often-used but tricky concept of innovation.[29]

In theory, each newly issued title can be seen as a new product in the book market. But of course, not every title is equally novel or distinct (nor is every new invention an innovation), and publishers issued reprints, pirated editions, compendia, and serial publications such as almanacs and periodicals. More importantly, innovation is in itself a fuzzy concept, strongly shaped by present-day interpretations. Fuzzy concepts have in common that they have no formal definition and are therefore difficult to measure directly and quantitatively, because their boundaries are dependent on specific contexts and conditions. In the case of innovation, formal definitions tend to indeed be very general, whereas historical examples are highly context-specific. As a result, there are no standard procedures for measuring innovation in product markets. Therefore, we are not striving to come up with a single definition or measure, but instead are using a data-driven approach embedded in digital humanities research to approximate innovation.[30] Specifically we are combining and comparing multiple measures related to product innovation: diversity, similarity and 'burstiness'. Diversity allows us to assess just how thematically differentiated the Dutch publishing business was; similarity measures approximate novelty in relation to other titles; and the burstiness algorithm helps to establish how 'novelties' stick or resonate over time.

## Diversity

Originally developed in studies on biodiversity, diversity indices have been used on several occasions to assess the composition of product markets, mostly related to firm specialization.[31] Here, we broaden the scope to the entire STCN in order to establish levels of specialization or diversification in terms of product groups. The simplest diversity measure is known as 'richness': counting the number of types or categories in the dataset per year. In our case, richness can be expressed in terms of, for instance, subject and subject combinations, language, size, or typographical features.[32]

As was to be expected, the book market became increasingly rich over time, as evidenced by a clear upward trend in the number of different categories assigned to titles throughout the period. But this does not say anything about the relative importance of the categories. There are, for instance, 22 different formats in the STCN, but the four main formats quartos, octavos, duodecimos, and folios combined make up 97 per cent of the observations.[33] And when it comes to language (28 categories), circa 60 per cent was in Dutch, with French and Latin making up 96 per cent of the non-Dutch language books.[34] The relative distribution of titles across categories can be measured by dividing the number of titles in each different category by the total number of titles (this measure is called evenness or proportional abundance). In the year 1660, for instance, 1,023 titles were published in 13 language categories (60 per cent of titles were published in the category Dutch, 28 per cent in Latin and 6 per cent in French). By calculating the inverse of the maximum proportional abundance we can establish a diversity level: 60 per cent: $D = 1/60$, which indicates that in this year, publishers effectively published in 1.6 language categories.

In the case of subject categories (105 in total) distribution is less uneven. Take 1660, for instance, where we count 1,935 titles in 74 categories: (percentages rounded) 13 per cent in Pedagogy, 10 per cent in History (Italy), 6 per cent in

Physics, 6 per cent in Spanish Language & Literature, 7 per cent in Theology (Bible and Bible interpretation), and several other categories scoring 3 per cent or lower.[35] Here, the simple diversity measure is $D = 1/13$, indicating that in 1660 publishers were collectively publishing in 7.7 subject categories. It is important to note that subject labels are not categories ascribed by contemporaries, but by present-day bibliographers. However, preliminary tests with a classifier suggest that the subject labels correspond reasonably well to identifiable word patterns in the titles; we, therefore, have used the assigned subject labels as crude indicators of product groups.[36]

With so many different categories and years, we cannot present distributions for all. Fortunately it is possible to measure diversity mathematically, taking both richness and evenness into account. In the Simpson diversity measure, each year is treated as a population with a single diversity score; the higher the score, the higher the level of diversity (between 0 and 1). Figure 9.4 shows the trend over time. Diversity levels are high in general (between 0.8 and 0.95) and increase between the late sixteenth century and the middle of the seventeenth century, after which they remain relatively stable.[37]

These aggregations, however, obscure differences between subject categories. The STCN lists multiple subjects for most titles. The general subject category of Geography, for instance, features 69 other subjects (i.e. 'Geography & Theology'; 'Atlases & Geography'). When we calculate diversity levels for different subject categories, we find that most of them hover around 0.6–0.7, but that there are marked differences across the categories in terms of changes over time. The category of Geography, for instance, displays a steady increase, during

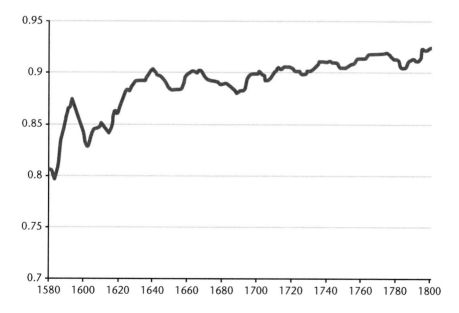

**FIGURE 9.4**  Measure of diversity #1: Simpson Index per year, 1570–1779

the eighteenth century as well. Theology shows a sharp increase early in the period, followed by a drop and then a surge to 0.65 by the close of the seventeenth century. History is stable between 0.65 and 0.70 throughout the seventeenth century and then shows a modest increase. Philosophy fluctuates between 0.4 and 0.6, and medicine has a fairly low and stable score (around 0.5) as compared to the total dataset.[38]

Admittedly, though, there are several limitations to this measure. It is fairly crude, dependent on anachronistic subject category classifications. There is, moreover, a strong imbalance in the number of observations in the early periods and the later periods, and our focus on subject does not do justice to the full range along which other product dimensions differentiation could take place. And most importantly, it does not show how new or distinctive the individual products would have been in the eyes of potential consumers.

To start redressing this latter aspect, we have introduced a second diversity method that zooms in on the titles themselves by means of the type-token ratio (TTR). The TTR compares the size of the vocabulary (the unique words) to the total length of the titles (the number of tokens in all titles taken together). For this exercise spelling normalization was required and we therefore limited the sample to the Dutch-language titles (during the seventeenth century c. 60 per cent of the total STCN sample). The text was then, to some extent, standardized to contemporary Dutch to correct for orthographic variation over time.[39] This essentially means that we limited the analysis to the market for non-ephemeral Dutch-language publications (114,795 titles). After we excluded the sizable subject categories 'state publications', 'public and social administration', and 'period documents', we arrived at a sample of 64,706 titles.[40] In these categories titles generally use the same or very similar phrases in the titles, and therefore inclusion would strongly skew the results towards lexical specialization.

The problem with lexical diversity measured as such is its sensitivity to size, which, in this case, makes it difficult to compare earlier with later periods. However, to allow for a longitudinal analysis, we computed (for each year) the TTR on smaller randomized samples of 500 words – a procedure we repeated 20 times. Moreover, we only considered longer words, since these are more likely to indicate the content of the book. Then we computed the mean and standard deviation of the yearly TTRs and plotted the results in Figure 9.5. The graph shows strong fluctuations, but the general trend is by and large similar to the one in Figure 9.4, although it also displays a marked decline during the eighteenth century.

Combined, the two diversity measures confirm that during the seventeenth century Dutch market for books became richer in terms of categories and vocabulary, but that diversity levels reached their peak roughly by the middle of the seventeenth century. This is in line with trends in the number of active publishers, which also reached a saturation point by the 1660s, whereas the total number of titles (compare Figure 9.2) continued to increase after the middle of the seventeenth century.[41] A second observation is that although expansion is observed in terms of subject diversity, the trend is not linear. The overall diversity index indicates changes from the 1620s onwards, and in several individual categories (medicine, theology) there is a pronounced, albeit small, drop in the timeline in the 1620s, after which growth rates pick up. This pattern is also consistent with previous analyses of the number of publishers and the number titles.

The fact that overall these patterns, derived from relatively crude measures, are (by and large) consistent with earlier findings suggests a relationship between informal product group formation and market expansion/contraction that is worth exploring in more depth.[42] To this end, we have further broken down the fuzzy concept of product innovation by comparing two different algorithmic forms that acknowledge the relationships *between* titles: similarity and burstiness.

## Similarity and burstiness

First we calculated the number of newly published and reprinted titles. The STCN does not systematically indicate whether a title is a reprint of an earlier publication (although in some cases it is listed). Moreover, we were not trying to identify more or less identical reprints, but instead to establish clusters of product variants. We did so by means of a similarity measure, based on the edit-distance between titles.[43] The titles were matched as full strings of characters. These were fuzzy matches, which means that titles did not have to match 100 per cent in order to be classified as a variant. Instead we used 85 per cent as a cutoff point, which is arbitrary, but works well because it allows for spelling variations not captured by the normalisation procedure (i.e. it matches *cronijcke* and *kroniek*; *colomen* and *ko-lommen*), but also for titles that are different but highly similar (i.e. *Catechismus, ofte Onderwijzinge in de christelijke lere* (1611, 1657, 1708, 1721, 1733); *Catechismus, of het Onderwijzinge in de christelijke religie* (1591); *Catechismus ofte onderwijzinge in de christelijke godsdienst* (1687);'*t Groot achter-hofken, beplant met verscheiden geestelijke liedjes* (1639) and'*t Vermeerderde achter-hofken, beplandt met verscheiden geestelijke liedjes* (1657).

Figure 9.5 shows that the ratio of titles published per year that are unique and those that are title variants oscillated between 60 and 80 per cent, with a slightly higher average for new titles in the early period. Most variants were in the categories of religious publications, such as bible editions, psalms, catechisms; but we also found multiple variants in other product groups, such as travel, songbooks, plays, and medicine. In absolute terms, the number of new Dutch-language publications increased from a few dozen in the early 1600s to c. 150 in 1650s, just over 200 in 1750s and close to 350 in 1780. The number of new titles declined between c. 1615 and 1640, whereas the number of variants stagnated, trends reflecting the stagnation observed for the total dataset in Figure 9.1.

Similarity largely measures re-use, the extent to which titles resemble each other. To inspect the other side of the coin, namely lexical inventions, we applied a different algorithm that identifies periods of increasing *influence* – with the latter concept being defined as moments that induced changes that reverberated over the subsequent years. More precisely, we applied Kleinberg's Burstiness algorithm, which monitors sudden increases in the frequency of words and the persistence of

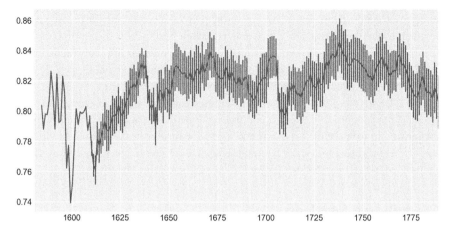

**FIGURE 9.5**   Measure of diversity #2: type-token ratio per year

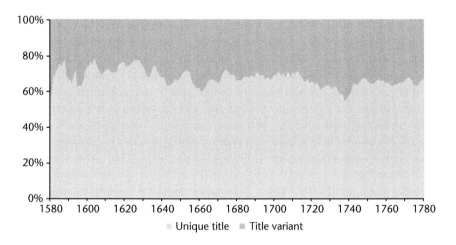

**FIGURE 9.6**   Similarity measure

these changes (their 'survival' so to say) over time.[44] We are modelling the book market as a stream of arriving data; the titles concatenated by year are the incoming items. A burst can be understood here as a time period (consecutive years) in which certain words appear (on average) significantly more than expected.[45] Burstiness models the arrival times at which certain words appear. Words that occur suddenly at high rates for certain time intervals are said to 'burst' or to be 'bursty'. Bursty words in our corpus are, for instance, *schrift* (bible/Scripture) and *anatomisch* (anatomical). Figures 9.7 and 9.8 show the relative frequency of these words and the identified bursts.

The words *anatomisch*, for example, exhibits a burst (Figure 9.7) around the middle of the seventeenth century, but only around 1700 does changing frequency constitute a sizeable burst (because the sudden increase continued for a few years). The bursts of the word *schrift* (Figure 9.8) are primarily located at the turn of the

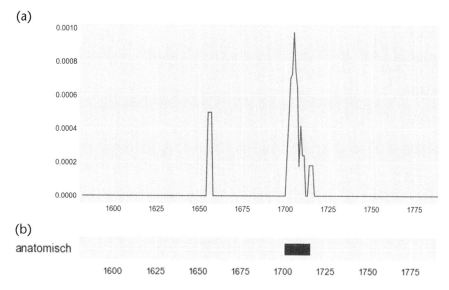

(a)

(b)
anatomisch

**FIGURE 9.7** Relative frequency of the word *anatomisch*

**TABLE 9.1** The top bursty words and their weight scores for the year 1582

| Word | Weight |
| --- | --- |
| *inhoudende* | 84.41 |
| *heilige* | 51.01 |
| *testament* | 38.73 |
| *gantse* | 29.46 |
| *bijbel* | 25.59 |

**TABLE 9.2** The top bursty words and their weight scores for the year 1756–7

| Word | Weight |
| --- | --- |
| *wetenschappen* | 19.14 |
| *natuurkundige* | 13.29 |
| *bevestigd* | 13.17 |
| *proefnemingen* | 12.93 |
| *comptoir* | 10.42 |

seventeenth century and are associated with religious vocabulary in this period (in expressions such as *heilige schrift* and in titles referring to the bible). These observations tie in with existing narratives about the book market, which note an expansion of secular topics in addition to religious vocabulary. We evaluated the

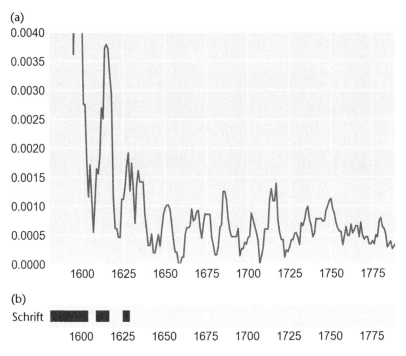

**FIGURE 9.8** Relative frequency of the word *schrift*

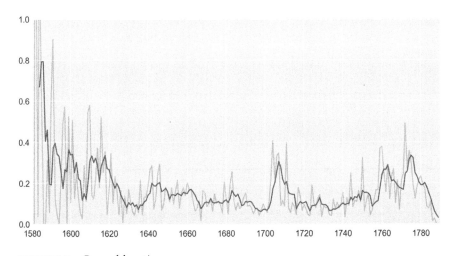

**FIGURE 9.9** General burstiness score

method further by inspecting bursty words for different time periods and for specific topics. Tables 9.1 and 9.2 compare bursty words for the year 1582 and the years 1756–7. [46]

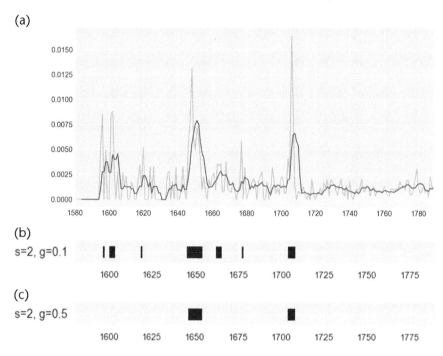

**FIGURE 9.10**  Burstiness scores for 'travel' topic

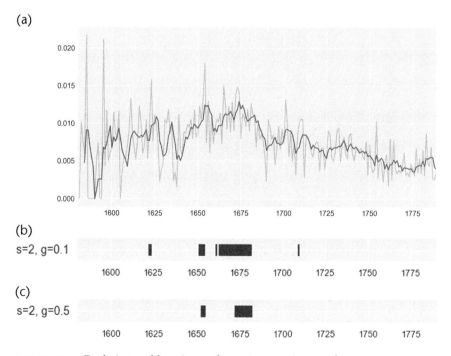

**FIGURE 9.11**  Evolution and burstiness of negative emotion words

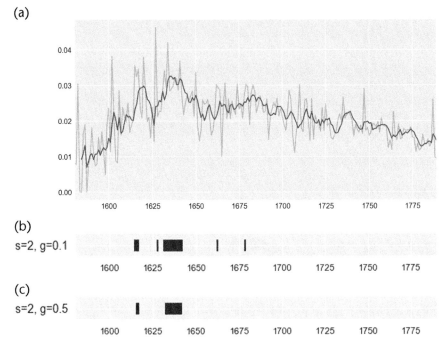

**FIGURE 9.12** Evolution and burstiness of positive emotion words

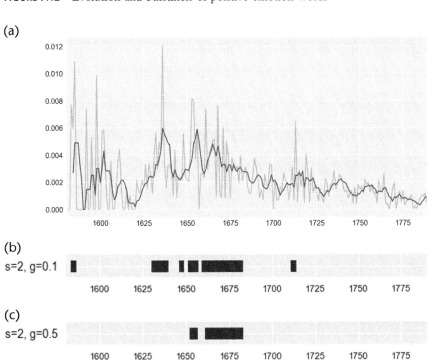

**FIGURE 9.13** Evolution and burstiness of words expressing anxiety

To detect 'influential years' – those that had an impact on the book market because they induced a change that persisted in the subsequent years – we computed the summed weight of the bursts generated in a year, which we divided by the vocabulary size. This score can be understood as the average burstiness of words in a given year. Figure 9.9 plots the scores over time. The burstiness scores present strong fluctuations, but we can make out several leaps. First of all, and fairly unsurprisingly, we see relatively high levels around or just after 1600, when growth rates in the Dutch book market were very high. (This is also due to the low number of titles published in the early years). A second burst is observed from the 1630s onwards, which is in line with the findings discussed earlier concerning a growth surge around that time. Interestingly, there are indications of further surges around the turn of and by the end of the eighteenth century.[47]

These general trends are intriguing, but for our purposes it is perhaps more interesting to use the burstiness measure to identify the emergence or development of new themes or topics. Figure 9.10 shows the evolution and burstiness of what we may call a 'travel' topic (words used are *reis, voyage, voyagien, reisboek*, and *reize*). The two graphs visualize how the found bursts depend from the parameter *gamma*, which determines the difficulty of transitioning from a non-bursty to a bursty state (for higher values, the algorithm is less sensitive to changes in the frequency of words encountered in the stream of information).

These results tie in – at least at first glance – with studies of travel literature that observe three stages in the development of travel literature: from journal (*journael*) to travelogue (*reisbeschrijving*), to imaginary travelogue (*imaginair reisverhaal*).[48] The first surge takes place around 1600s, when publishers such as Cornelis Claesz turned information reported from foreign travels into a commercial good. The second surge, in the 1660s, shows a series of small but not trivial product adaptations by the Amsterdam publisher Gillis Joosten Saeghman.[49] The surge in the early 1700s might be explained by another development in the 'genre' of travelogues: the popularization of imaginary travel stories (such as Henrik Smeeks's *Beschryvinge van het magtig Koninkryk Krinke Kesmes*).[50]

Besides inspecting topical fluctuations, we also investigated changes in the affective and emotional dimensions in book titles. By computing the presence of title words referencing emotions or affects, we could try to monitor the use of affect and emotions in patterns of differentiation in early modern Dutch book market. These results remain preliminary and require further validation. However, they tie in – to some extent – with existing knowledge about the book market and culture in the Golden Age. Most of the positive emotions are located in the first half of the seventeenth century, while the second half is characterized by higher levels of anxiety and negative emotions. The use of affective language – or rather the bursty changes therein – appears to decline in the eighteenth century.

All these figures should be treated with care. On a data level, they only cover a sample of the publications in the Dutch language, and spelling normalization is far from perfect. Moreover, the data imbalance makes comparison over time more difficult, as small changes in the early period have a great effect on the eventual score. Regarding the interpretation of the measure, burstiness helps us to compute years that proved influential, i.e. which produced changes which had an impact on what followed. But these changes cannot be straightforwardly equated with innovations, as 'new' items on the market (for example, some words appear without becoming bursty if the gaps between their occurrences are long).

It is also possible that the representation of novelty by burstiness favours resonance, and therefore leaves out smaller, short-lived, but perhaps combined meaningful innovations. These are not (fully) captured by our analyses, but could definitely be studied by means of a similar approach. More generally, product innovation of course also took the form of differentiation by design, rather than thematically as approximated by title. The aforementioned Gilles Joosten Saeghman, for instance, differentiated his publications by reprinting previous versions at relatively low prices, by adjusting the format by, for example, using two columns (a characteristic of popular literature), and by reusing many illustrations in his travelogues, based on series of woodcuts and copper engravings.[51]

## Conclusion

With this chapter we contribute to a growing body of historical literature that aims to make visible the complex interactions that help create, reproduce, and structure markets (and the relations between markets) for (new) knowledge. We proposed the concept of *coordination by meaning* as an analytical tool to bridge economic and cultural analyses of innovation, and offered methodological suggestions on how to measure such a widely used but fuzzy concept in historical research. In fact, we hope to have also demonstrated that the notion of markets is equally fuzzy; they are neither given, nor clear-cut, but made and messy: and it is worth exploring how markets come into being.

The data-driven analysis of patterns in book titles issued between 1570 and 1799 pointed us to some general and specific observations about how market formation in Dutch book market developed during the early modern period. We observed that even though market growth was to a large extent driven by the publication of new titles, a solid share of the output was not new by our measures. Presumably, many new knowledge products were product variants, distinguished less by text or topic than by other product features, adapted for specific target groups. Michael Hutter refers to this by the term 'familiar surprises': products that combine novelty and thrill with familiarity and comfort.[52]

Publishers responded to increasing competitive pressure by not only having their products stand out from the crowd, but also by making them recognizable. Innovation, then, was the product of a process of product differentiation distributed across many different entities. We hypothesize that by these acts of individual differentiation, publishers contributed collectively to coordination in the book market and spurred the development of product groups that themselves became distinguishable from one another. Knowledge and ideas resonated through the product variants not only chronologically, but also geographically and socially.

This, in turn, also supported the rise of large and complex knowledge markets. Consequently, publishers and other print agents did not only introduce commercial innovations, or maintain knowledge in book form so that it could be exchanged or consumed. By collectively – albeit perhaps unintentionally – classifying knowledge, and by influencing perceptions, they also added to epistemic innovation in what we may consider the field of knowledge exchange.

Within the constraints of this chapter and our approach we could not analyze the full range of actors, channels, and devices in processes of differentiation of the early modern book market. Nor could we assess systematically the impact of emotional and affective marketing and communication on consumers' purchasing decisions, nor of consumers' preferences and signals on publishers' strategies. Still, these analyses on an aggregate level provide clues and suggestions for how consumers and suppliers could value and compare novelty through books themselves, and how we might study this with the help of digital methods. Methodologically, the chapter reflects on the application of such computational (or digital) methods, questioning how concepts from the humanities can be matched with algorithms and the scores they produce. The relation between calculation and interpretation is often not straightforward, and we, therefore, inspected the corpus from multiple angles, using a wide range of different techniques to trace historical patterns in the STCN.

Even though the chapter takes a more computational approach, it remains firmly embedded in history: the focus on patterns does not discard the need for a coherent narrative, which flows from a close knowledge of the data and their (historical), and ties together the otherwise disconnected experiments. Looking at the past from such a hybrid perspective – merging multiple computational methods and interpreting them in the light of the historian's contextual knowledge – opens up, we believe, a fruitful common ground, where the humanities and the computational sciences can meet. It creates new opportunities for innovative interdisciplinary research.

## Notes

1 On this move: B. Hekman, "Een drukker aan de drank," 20.
2 J. L. Van Zanden, *The Long Road.*
3 P. G. Hoftijzer, "The Dutch Republic."
4 C. Rasterhoff, *Painting and Publishing.*
5 On the art market: M. J. Bok, "Paintings for Sale."
6 Ibid.; M. Prak, "Painters, Guilds, and the Art Market."
7 M. M. Smith, *The Title-Page*; J. Barchas, *Graphic Design*; R. Chartier, *The Culture of Print.*
8 A. Pettegree, *Reformation.*
9 Translation by Franco Moretti. F. Moretti, "Style, Inc.".
10 Cf. A. Silva, Marketing Good Taste'. Dutch examples include: D. van Netten, "Een boek als carrièrevehikel"; G. Verhoeven and P. Verkruijsse, eds., *Ioumael ofte Gedenckwaerdige beschrijvinghe*; P. Dijstelberge, "De vorm van het Boek in de Gouden Eeuw."
11 Unfortunately, we could not use the full texts of the books, because these are not yet digitized at scale. Cf. Digitale Bibliotheek voor de Nederlandse Letteren (DBNL): https://www.dbnl.org/.
12 All books have been described book-in-hand, and titles are transcribed and abbreviated from the typographical title page. Consider also counterparts in other countries, such as the STCV and of course the USTC. By the end of 2015 the database contained more

than 206,000 titles and over 520,000 copies. The data is also available as linked open data in rdf. W. Beek, R. Hoekstra, F. Maas, A. Meroño-Peñuela, and I. Leemans, 'Linking the STCN'; F. Maas, 'Innovative Strategies'.
13 Copies from the same print run are recorded, but not entered as separate titles.
14 It also possible to generate approximations of the number of pages with a collation parser developed by Leon van Wissen. www.github.com/LvanWissen/CollationParser.
15 M. Van Delft, "Kwantitatief onderzoek op basis van de STCN." Although there are some significant limitations to the scope of the dataset (no information on print runs, many false or incomplete imprints, abbreviated instead of full titles), estimates are that a significant share of titles produced in the Dutch Republic have survived the test of time and made it into the STCN.
16 J. L. Van Zanden, *The Long Road*.
17 D. Van Netten, *Koopman in kennis*; Stronks. "Dees kennisse zuldy te kope vinnen."
18 W. Ryckbosch, "Early Modern Consumption History"; M. Berg and H. Clifford, eds., *Consumers and Luxury Consumer Culture*; J. Brewer and R. Porter, eds., *Consumption and the World of Goods*.
19 C. Rasterhoff, "Markets for Luxury Goods"; C. Fairchilds, "The Production and Marketing of Populuxe Goods"; T. Hine, *Populuxe*. Cissie Fairchilds has described this aspect by means of the twentieth-century term *populuxe*, which she introduced into historical research in her analysis of the popularity of cheap copies of items used by the aristocracy in eighteenth-century France – such as umbrellas or fans.
20 Ibid; J. De Vries, *The Industrious Revolution*; J. De Vries and A. van der Woude, *The First Modern Economy*.
21 On coordination through meaning see E. Dekker, "Exemplary Qualities: Market Coordination and the Valuation of Singular Products" (August 30, 2015). https://ssrn.com/abstract=2653373 or ttp://dx.doi.org/10.2139/ssrn.2653373. See also.
22 N. De Marchi and H. Van Miegroet, "Art, Value, and Market Practices."
23 C. Wellmon, *Organizing Enlightenment*; A. Blair, *Too Much to Know*; H. Cook, *Matters of Exchange*, 15; A. Goldgar, *Impolite Learning*.
24 A. Goldgar, *Impolite Learning*, 57–8.
25 See also B. De Munck and D. Lyna, eds., *Concepts of Value*.
26 C. Rasterhoff, *Painting and Publishing*; J. M. Montias, 'Art Dealers'.
27 P. Aspers and J. Beckert, eds., *The Worth of Goods*; M. Hutter and D. Throsby, eds., *Beyond Price*.
28 Based on Dekker, "Exemplary Qualities."
29 Innovation is a hot but elusive topic in present-day creative industries such as the publishing industry. See for instance Hutter et al., "Innovation Society Today."
30 Many thanks to Ivan Kisjes and Leon van Wissen, who helped with cleaning and normalizing the data used for this chapter.
31 See an exciting historical study by art historian Matthew Lincoln in which he employs it to assess levels of specialization among early modern Netherlandish print publishers. Lincoln, *Modeling the Network*.
32 For sake of space, we leave out other characteristics of the title page, such as publisher, typography, and author.
33 P. Dijstelberge, "e vorm."
34 R. Mathis and M. A. Mathis, "Books in Foreign Languages."
35 Note that all "History" categories together make up a little over 20 percent of total number of publications.
36 The classifier is an algorithm that tries to identify to which of a set of categories (sub-populations) a new observation belongs. It does so on the basis of a training set of data containing observations (or instances) whose category membership is known. In our case, we had a classifier predict which subject labels fit best with a (Dutch) title. Almost all titles in the STCN have one or more subject labels, and the classifier is therefore multilable. Overall, the predictive quality was high, which suggests that there is indeed a relationship between the bibliographical subject categories and features of the title. Moreover, words in the title seem to be relatively important to assigning the right subject labels to the right title. Therefore we use it here to assess the scope of subjects in

which publications were issued and how this changed as the market expanded. The following features were included in the analysis: Title (in case of STCN this is almost always the shortened title); Author(s); Year of publication; Publisher(s); Typographical features (typography, but also other elements of the title page as noted in STCN); Size; Collation formula (translated into measure of number of pages through the collation parser). We used a sample of normalized Dutch titles without potential double counts (almost 90,000 out of c. 200,000) in the STCN. www.github.com/LvanWissen/.

37  Simpson Diversity Index on the basis of frequency counts. Formula: $D = N(N - 1)/ \Sigma n$ $(n - 1)$. D = diversity index; n = the total number of titles of a particular subject category; N = the total number of titles of all subject categories; $\Sigma$ = sum.

38  While the number of multilable medicine categories increased (high richness), most publications still fell in a small number of categories (low evenness).

39  For dealing with spelling variation we used a tool called VARD2 (http://ucrel.lancs.ac.uk/vard/about), and took other preprocessing steps such as tokenizing, lowercasing, and adjoining. See also Wijckmans and Kisjes, "Adapting a Spelling Normalization Tool."

40  This in itself is informative, because it shows that more than forty per cent of all 'unique' titles were administrative or otherwise ephemeral publications.

41  C. Rasterhoff, *Painting and Publishing*, part I.

42  Ibid.

43  The Levenshtein distance measures the distance between two strings, in this case two titles.

44  J. Kleinberg, "Bursty and Hierarchical Structure."

45  On bursts as a visual aid in historical text mining, see also: P. Huijnen et al., "A Digital Humanities Approach."

46  The list only includes words directly derived from the book titles. We excluded words that are artefacts of the STCN corpus, such as the word "volume", which originally appeared as one of the bursty words for this year, but is actually an STCN category added by the creators of the corpus. The appearance of "volume" as bursty word refers to the explosion of serial publications in this period (a phenomenon well-described in the existing literature).

47  Correlation: yearly = 0.628 (p < 0.001), 3-yearly weighted average = 0.729 (p < 0.001). Robustness check: possibility of correlation depending on settings parameters, so played around with, patterns and correlations seem to be relatively robust.

48  M. Barend-van Haeften, "Van scheepsjournaal tot reisverhaal."

49  G. Verhoeven, "En koopt er geen."

50  P. J. Buijnsters, *Imaginaire reisverhalen.*

51  G. Verhoeven, "En koopt er geen."

52  M. Hutter, "Familiar Surprises," 204.

# Bibliography

Short Title Catalogue, Netherlands (STCN), https://www.kb.nl/en/organisation/research-expertise/for-libraries/short-title-catalogue-netherlands-stcn (site last accessed January 6, 2019; data-dump from June 2017).

Aspers, Patrik, and Jens Beckert, eds. *The Worth of Goods.* Cambridge: Cambridge University Press, 2010.

Barchas, Janine. *Graphic Design, Print Culture, and the Eighteenth-Century Novel.* Cambridge: Cambridge University, 2003.

Barend-van Haeften, Marijke. "Van Scheepsjournaal tot Reisverhaal: Een Kennismaking met Zeventiende-eeuwse Reisteksten." *Literatuur* 7 (1990): 222–28.

Beek, Wouter, Rinke Hoekstra, Fernie Maas, Albert Meroño-Peñuela, and Inger Leemans. "Linking the STCN and Performing Big Data Queries in the Humanities." *Digital Humanities Benelux Conference*, June 12–13, 2014.

Berg, Maxine, and Helen Clifford, eds. *Consumers and Luxury Consumer Culture in Europe, 1650–1850*. Manchester: Manchester University Press, 1999.

Blair, Ann. *Too Much to Know: Managing Scholarly Information before the Modern Age*. New Haven and London: Yale University Press, 2010.

Bok, Marten Jan. "'Paintings for sale'": New Marketing Techniques in the Dutch Art Market of the Golden Age.' In *At Home in the Golden Age: Masterpieces from the Sor Rusche Collection*, edited by Marten Jan Bok, Martine Gosselink, and Marina Aarts, 9–29. Zwolle: Waanders, 2009.

Brewer, John, and Roy Porter. eds. *Consumption and the World of Goods*. London: Routledge, 1993.

Buijnsters, Piet J. *Imaginaire Reisverhalen in Nederland gedurende de Achttiende Eeuw*. Groningen: Wolters-Noordhoff, 1969.

Chartier, Roger, ed. *The Culture of Print: Power and the Uses of Print in Early Modern Europe*. Princeton: Princeton University Press, 1989.

Cook, Harold. *Matters of Exchange: Commerce, Medicine, and Science in the Dutch Golden Age*. New Haven and London: Yale University Press, 2007.

De Marchi, Neil, and Hans van Miegroet. "Art, Value, and Market Practices in the Netherlands in the Seventeenth Century." *The Art Bulletin* 76, no. 3 (1994): 451–64.

Dekker, Erwin. "Exemplary Qualities: Market Coordination and the Valuation of Singular 22Products." (August 30, 2015). Available at SSRN: https://ssrn.com/abstract= 2653373 or http://dx.doi.org/10.2139/ssrn.2653373.

Delft, Marieke van. "Kwantitatief onderzoek op basis van de STCN: Mogelijkheden en Aandachtspunten." *Jaarboek voor Nederlandse Boekgeschiedenis* 16 (2019): 63–80.

De Munck, Bert, and Dries Lyna, eds. *Concepts of Value in European Material Culture, 1500–1900*. Aldershot: Ashgate, 2015.

Dijstelberge, Paul. "De vorm van het Boek in de Gouden Eeuw." blogpost October 28, 2013. http://boekindegoudeneeuw.blogspot.com/2013/10/de-vorm-van-het-boek-in-de-gouden-eeuw.html (last accessed January 6, 2019).

Fairchilds, Cissie. "The Production and Marketing of Populuxe Goods in Eighteenth-Century Paris." In *Consumption and the World of Goods*, edited by John Brewer, and Roy Porter, 228–48. London: Routledge, 1993.

Goldgar, Anne. *Impolite Learning: Conduct and Community in the Republic of Letters, 1680–1750*. New Haven and London: Yale University Press, 1995.

Hekman, Bauke. "Een drukker aan de drank: De neergang van Johannes van den Bergh, drukker-boekverkoper te Amsterdam." *Fumus* 11 (2013): 20–24.

Hine, Thomas. *Populuxe*. New York: Alfred A. Knopf, 1986.

Hoftijzer, Paul G. "The Dutch Republic, Centre of the European Book Trade in the 17th Century." *European History Online (EGO)*, published by the Leibniz Institute of European History (IEG) (2015): http://www.ieg-ego.eu/hoftijzerp-2015-en (last accessed January 6, 2019).

Hutter, Michael. "Familiar Surprises: Creating Value in the Creative Industries." In *The Worth of Goods*, edited by Patrik Aspers, and Jens Beckert, 201–220. Cambridge: Cambridge University Press, 2010.

Hutter, Michael, Hubert Knoblauch, Werner Rammert, and Arnold Windeler. Innovation Society Today *Historical Social Research/Historische Sozialforschung* . Special Issue: Methods of Innovation Research: Qualitative, Quantitative and Mixed Methods Approaches. (2015) 40, 3 (153) 30–47.

Hutter, Michael, and David Throsby, eds. *Beyond Price. Value in Culture, Economics and the Arts*. Cambridge: Cambridge University Press, 2008.

Huijnen, Pim, Fons Laan, Maarten de Rijke, and Toine Pieters. "A Digital Humanities Approach to the History of Science: Eugenics Revisited in Hidden Debates by Means of Semantic Text Mining." *Social Informatics* 8359 (2013): 70–84.

Kleinberg, Jon. "Bursty and Hierarchical Structure in Streams." *Data Mining and Knowledge Discovery* 7, no. 4 (2003): 373–97.

Lincoln, Matthew. *Modeling the Network of Dutch and Flemish Print Production, 1550–1750.* PhD diss., University of Maryland, 2016.

Maas, Fernie. "Innovative Strategies in a Stagnating Market Dutch Book Trade 1660–1750." project report 2013, Vrije Universiteit Amsterdam. http://www.centrefordigitalhumanities.nl/files/2013/09/ReportSTCN.pdf

Mathis, R., and M-A. Mathis. "Books in Foreign Languages: Publishing in the Netherlands, 1500-1800." In *Specialist Markets in the Early Modern Book World*, edited by Richard Kirwan, and Sophie Mullins. Leiden: Brill, 2015, 294–311.

Montias, John Michael. "Art Dealers in the Seventeenth-Century Netherlands." *Simiolus* 18 (1988): 244–56.

Moretti, Franco. "Style, Inc. Reflections on Seven Thousand Titles (British Novels, 1740–850)." *Critical Inquiry* 36, no. 1 (2009): 134–58.

Netten, Djoeke van. *Koopman in kennis: De uitgever Willem Jansz Blaeu in de geleerde wereld 23(1571–1638).* Bijdragen tot de Geschiedenis van de Nederlandse Boekhandel, new series 15. Zutphen: Walburg Pers, 2014.

Netten, Djoeke van. "Een boek als carrièrevehikel: De zeemansgidsen van Blaeu." *De Zeventiende Eeuw* 27, no. 2 (2011): 214–31.

Pettegree, Andrew. *Reformation and the Culture of Persuasion.* Cambridge: Cambridge University Press, 2009.

Prak, Maarten. "Painters, Guilds, and the Art Market during the Dutch Golden Age." In *Guilds, Innovation and the European Economy 1400–1800*, edited by Stephan R. Epstein, and Maarten Prak, 143–71. Cambridge: Cambridge University Press, 2008.

Rasterhoff, Claartje. *Painting and Publishing as Cultural Industries: The Fabric of Creativity in the Dutch Republic.* Amsterdam: Amsterdam University Press, 2016.

Rasterhoff, Claartje. "Markets for Luxury Goods." In *Cambridge Companion to the Dutch Golden Age*, edited by Geert Janssen, and Helmer Helmers, 249–67. Cambridge: Cambridge University Press, 2018.

Ryckbosch, Wouter. "Early Modern Consumption History: Current Challenges and Future Perspectives." *BMGN- Low Countries Historical Review* 130, no. 1 (2015): 57–84.

Silva, Andie. *Marketing Good Taste: Print Agents' Use Of Paratext To Shape Markets And Readers In Early Modern England.* PhD diss., Wayne University, 2014.

Smith, Margaret M. *The Title-Page. Its Early Development, 1460–1510.* London: British Library, and New Castle, Del.: Oak Knoll Press, 2000.

Stronks, Els. "'Dees kennisse zuldy te kope vinnen': Liedcultuur en de waarde van 'know how' in de vroegmoderne Republiek." *De Zeventiende Eeuw* 30, no. 2 (2014): 147–67.

Verhoeven, Garrelt. "'En koopt er geen dan met dees fraaie Faem': De reisuitgaven van Gillis Joosten Saeghman." *Literatuur* 9, no. 6 (1992): 330–38.

Verhoeven, Garrelt, and Piet Verkruijsse, eds. *Iournael ofte Gedenckwaerdige beschrijvinghe vande Oost-Indische Reyse van Willem Ysbrantsz. Bontekoe van Hoorn. Descriptieve bibliografie 1646–1996.* Bijdragen tot de geschiedenis van de Nederlandse boekhandel, new series 1. Zutphen: Walburg Pers, 1999.

Vries, Jan de. *The Industrious Revolution: Consumer Behavior and the Household Economy, 1650 to the Present.* Cambridge: Cambridge University Press, 2008.

Vries, Jan de, and Ad van der Woude. *The First Modern Economy.* Cambridge: Cambridge University Press, 1997.

Wellmon, Chad. *Organizing Enlightenment: Information Overload and the Invention of the Modern Research University.* Baltimore: Johns Hopkins University Press, 2015.

Wijckmans, Tessa , and Ivan Kisjes. "Adapting a Spelling Normalization Tool Designed for English to 17th Century Dutch." paper presented at DH2018, June 26–29, 2018, Mexico City. https://dh2018.adho.org/en/adapting-a-spelling-normalization-tool-designed-for-english-to-17th-century-dutch (last accessed January 6, 2019).

Zanden, Jan Luiten van. *The Long Road to the Industrial Revolution: The European Economy in a Global Perspective, 1000–1800*. Leiden: Brill, 2009.

# 10

# THE SPECTACLE OF DISSECTION

## Early modern theatricality and anatomical frenzy

*Karel Vanhaesebrouck*

In the history of the theatre of the Low Countries, or in Dutch cultural memory at large, the work of Vondel takes up a dominant position, as an aesthetic and intellectual reference, but also as an important *lieu de mémoire* incarnating the complex cultural identity of the Dutch Republic.[1] This central position in historiography is no coincidence, as his work seems to incarnate the gradual classicization of early modern theatre and, thus, the development of theatre into a harmonious, well-balanced and – first and foremost – discursive form of art. However, if one has a closer look at theatre practice itself (so not only at the production of *texts*), you will discover all kinds of spectacular practices eagerly exploiting the gory techniques of late medieval mysteries while at the same time exploring new techniques of baroque artifice. Some of the stories represented were utterly violent and thrived on the early modern public's fascination for abject corporality and physical violence. In this violent type of theatricality, the poetical, discursive dimension is of secondary importance as it seeks to immerse its public in a liminal experience, deliberately obscuring the distinction between the presented fiction and the public's lived reality. Not discourse but bodies take centre stage in this theatre.

In this chapter I will investigate how this particular type of theatricality related to other forms of public display of the human body in which 'extreme bodies' take centre stage: execution prints and anatomical lessons, on the verge of spectacle, emotion, and knowledge production. I will thus discuss the interconnections between violence, technique, emotions, and physicality in seventeenth-century theatre, by analyzing how theatre exploited the anatomical frenzy of its public. On the basis of several historical examples we will show how this culture transformed throughout the century in a fundamental way and how this transformation impacted the relation between art (more specifically: theatre) and early modern science and knowledge culture. We will put forward the notion of 'spectacle' as a pivotal term to explain how knowledge was gradually commercialized, functioning in a market populated by avid consumers who were at the same time enthusiastic spectators. On the basis of a number of case studies we will explain how the Dutch Republic developed an affective economy in which the basic commodity was not a material object but an embodied experience.

One of the basic strategies deployed by all kinds of cultural entrepreneurs in this new visual market was the graphic representation of bodies and of physical violence. Playwright and theatre director Jan Vos was without a doubt one of the people who perfectly understood the basic principles of this new economy, developing theatre into a genuine cultural industry. Vos' theatre exploited desire and curiosity, played on crowd emotions and sought to produce mass effect. On the basis of our analysis of one of Vos' iconic tragedies, we will describe how early modern theatre made ample use of other representations to produce a performative, affective impact on the spectator. We will do so by focusing on the spectacular, on-stage demonstration of physical violence, of bloodshed, and torture. This spectacle of violence should be understood as an integral part of a broader, baroque culture of spectacle in which the idea of dissection, of opening up and disintegrating bodies functioned as a central *topos*. The ambition of the present text is anything but exhaustive. Its aim is not to present an overview of early modern theatre culture in the Netherlands nor to present an in-depth analysis of Jan Vos' theatre work. Nor will it provide the reader with an integrated perspective on the practice of anatomy as an emerging scientific discipline or discuss acquainted cultural phenomena such as the anatomical theatre and atlas as emanations of the concomitant academic *habitus*. On the basis of a limited number of documented case studies, inside and outside the theatre, we will demonstrate how these examples may help us to understand the changing relationship between science, theatricality, spectacle, and commercialization in the Dutch Republic.

## Affective spaces and the beholder

Early modern theatre culture functioned as an affective space in which bodies, emotions, and objects collided. In his 2012 article 'Affective spaces: a praxeological outlook', Andreas Reckwitz explains how historical research has systematically insisted on the connection between modernity and rationalization, assuming that 'emotions are by and large neutralised in modern spheres of social action.'[2] That assumption led, so he continues, to the stubborn myth of an affect-neutral modern sociality. As an alternative he proposes to focus on the complex intertwinement if space and emotions, which are 'material and cultural at the same time'.[3] The realm of the social is by definition messy, multi-layered, and unstable, rather than being grounded in a gradual evolution towards normative order and rationality; it is a 'partly reproductive, partly ever-evolving network' which is grounded both in practices and in implicit knowledge comprising human bodies as well as artefacts.[4] The realm of the social is thus constituted by a whole series 'of interconnected "doings" […] and the implicit knowledge they share.' Exactly this relation (and sometimes tension) between practices and implicit knowledge will prove to be of crucial importance in the present contribution. We will demonstrate how ideas about the inside of the body, but also about the cultural representation of violence inflicted on the body outside of the theatrical realm, also inform the circulation of energies within the theatre; how, in other words, one cannot understand what happens onstage without bringing in the cultural context which enables the codes proper to theatre to function. Spectators mobilize implicit knowledge to understand and to be affected by what they see, through the circulation of artefacts and practices in a rapidly expanding economy of spectacle.

The theatre stage is the locus *par excellence* where emotions are tightly tied up with bodies. Actors incorporate emotions, use their bodies to re-present (literally: to make present again). These representations of emotions simultaneously impact the body of the onlooker, the essence of theatre being the simple fact that both production and reception (or: encoding and decoding) happen at the same time.[5] After the play, the same spectator will describe his emotions by referring to his bodily sensations: 'cold sweat broke out', 'this or that scene was really chilling', etc. Bodily images and emotions function within a specific historical context and are thus anything but ahistorical concepts. They are cultural practices, just as theatre is a cultural practice. A body on a stage always has a concrete emotional impact on its onlooker, and that effect is in turn translated into a body image. Each of these steps functions within a specific context. Therefore, theatre – and we will come back to this point – is a socio-symbolic practice: on the stage physically present bodies symbolize specific emotions and this process of symbolization can only function within a specific social context, i.e. the affective space called theatre.

In *Pain and Compassion in Early Modern English Literature and Culture* Jan Frans van Dijkhuizen explains that the concept of pain was a permanent subject of discussion. He not only analyses how early modern literature both imagined and shaped the Christian experience of pain (and the intended emphatic effect that went with it), but also connects these literary and cultural strategies to the medical and philosophical discussions of pain of that era, showing how these were also part of a broader cultural horizon. In early modern England, Van Dijkhuizen convincingly explains, pain was not in the first place connected to the one suffering the pain, but with the compassion experienced by those who witness this pain. Put in other words: the essence of the historical experience of pain is not be found in the body of the victim but in the eye of the beholder.

In his foreword to the volume *Beholding Violence in Medieval and Early Modern Europe*, W.J.T. Mitchell defines the notion of 'beholding' as 'a kind of space- and time-travel.'[6] Exactly this idea will prove to be of central concern to understand the intertwinement of early modern theatre culture in the Dutch Republic (more specifically: the cruel violence of early modern tragedies) and its surrounding cultural context, and more precisely the transformation of the relation or tension between both. Beholding, Mitchell explains, is not just a synonym for 'observing, witnessing, viewing, watching, even reading or interpreting'; it may include all of these, but 'it incorporates them into a complex process that combines fascination (literally, 'a binding') with a certain distance or detachment.' Exactly this double bind, between binding and detachment, will prove to be the very nexus of the fundamental transformation which we will attempt to describe in the following pages. It will have as a consequence that this critical distance will be gradually replaced by – or rather: will be taken to coexist with – a rapidly expanding swirl of representations facilitated by a new cultural and commercial infrastructure (prints, cabinets, atlases, etc.). This infrastructure will transform knowledge into spectacle and thus into commodities to be consumed. This coexistence of critical distance on the one hand and the desire to lose oneself in one's experience as a spectator,' between attachment and detachment, holding and being held at the same time'[7] defines the position of the beholder.

## Realcore

In the seventeenth century the human body was a product as well as a spectacle, and an object of knowledge. This body was eagerly 'staged' in different cultural practices: executions, prints, anatomical theatres, playhouses, the true object of spectacle being the inside of the body. The theatrical culture of the Dutch Golden Age functioned thanks to an obstinate inquisitiveness or *curiositas*: the spectator was not only looking for new knowledge about the human body, but his curiosity was also an object of commercialization.[8] The fascination of the early modern spectator with the inside of the human body took shape in the event of anatomical dissections.[9] During dissections the body was literally laid open, layer after layer, as if it was a land to be explored, with the help of a series of techniques that did not only allow both 'performers' and 'spectators' to understand reality, but also obscured that same reality by penetrating deeper and deeper into it, to the point where the viewer could lose his self. Within this context Jonathan Sawday links dissection to pornography: the body as an object without identity, as a complex of fragments, an object pleasurably ogled by the spectator and his libido sciendi. Sawday quotes Linda Williams's well-known book *Hard Core: Power, Pleasure and 'the Frenzy of the Visible'* in which she connects the pornographic look, as a 'drive for knowledge', with the body as an object, as a spectacle.[10] Below, I will explain how this beholder was invited through all kinds of extra-theatrical representations to critically analyze what he saw in the hope of coming to a better understanding of the complex reality of the human body, while at the same time being invited to take pleasure in this same body as a spectacle to be consumed.

The early modern spectator in Europe understood violence on stage because he or she had been witness to violent events outside the theatre, directly (in public space) or indirectly (in print).[11] In the Golden Age masses of representations of executions and other types of public violence were circulating. A famous example was without a doubt Jacques Caillot's series *Les Grandes misères et malheurs de la guerre* (1633), of which one of the sets was re-published in Dutch between 1677 and 1690 as *De droeve Ellendigheden van den Oorlogh*. The Dutch knowledge economy proved to be a potentially profitable market for printers, engravers, designers, and the like.[12] One of their preferred topics was public executions or other violent events that had taken place in public space.

Executions were a form of *realcore* theatre. They turned the public space into a spectacle, as well as a tribunal, enabling the spectators to steal a glance at the battered, mutilated, or opened-up body of the condemned. In *Seeing Justice Done: The Age of Spectacular Punishment in France*, Paul Friedland describes how the execution evolved in the course of the sixteenth and seventeenth centuries, in most Western European countries, from a ritual to a simple spectacle and how the people participating 'in a ceremony that held profound personal meaning to them' became what Friedland aptly describes as 'penal voyeurs' of 'a form of spectacle in which one could watch the suffering of another out of simple curiosity and without actually taking part or sharing the traditional communal ritual of healing and redemption.'[13] Executions functioned along the same lines as theatre plays. Spectators were desperate to obtain a good spot to watch people die on the scaffold. In some cases seats were even sold at the windows of the houses looking out onto the square where the scaffold was located[14]: 'the new penal voyeurs [...] could gaze out at the real-life drama unfolding beneath them, and they could take it all in – the suffering of the patient, the compassion of the crowd – as if they were all characters in a magnificent spectacle, to which they themselves were not participants but spectators'.[15]

Executions and other forms of violent dramatics in the public space became events that were marketed, for instance via the distribution of prints. Both executions (moments of juridically sanctioned violence inflicted on a condemned body by the powers that be), and unexpected or uncontrollable eruptions of publicly displayed violence (such as the lynching of political protagonists), greatly fascinated the people. From a historical point of view lynchings were quite rare and exceptional events. However, in most cases they had a profound impact on the memorial culture of a nation or a group, as the same event was constantly being reiterated through accounts of all kinds, most importantly visual representation in prints and paintings. One of these rare events that had a profound impact on the Dutch cultural imagination was without a doubt the lynching of the De Witt Brothers on August 21, 1672. In his publication *Ooggetuigen van de Gouden Eeuw* René van Stipriaan extensively quotes Joachim Oudaen (1628–1692), a potter from Rotterdam and also a numismatist and poet (he wrote, among other things, *De Haegsche Broedermoord*), who describes what happened to the corpses after the brothers had been lynched and hanged[16]:

> Now the corpses had to suffer. Someone cut the fingers off the hands, another the noses off the faces, the lips off the mouth, the ears off the heads, the tongues from the mouth, the toes off the feet, and everything was then sold to the bystanders, one item cheaper, another more expensively. [...] As the trade in fingers, toes, noses, ears, lips, etcetera, went ahead spectacularly, the private parts were not spared: everything else was sold out.[17]

Oudaen also describes how De Witt's private parts were sold: Johan de Witt's penis was cut into three. The brothers' corpses became merchandise, curiosities. Their clothes too were dealt with: 'Those who had earlier stolen large parts of the clothes or shirts sold small pieces to whoever showed interest. Bloody cloth was the most expensive.'[18]

The lynching was not only a real spectacle taking place in the public space: it also fed the fascination of the broad public with the reality of violated bodies, which paradoxically became reality for most citizens through the use of theatrical techniques. The utterly dramatic display of public violence was immediately taken up by the atelier of Romeyn de Hooghe, who right after the event started to put out broadsheets describing the horrific event in both words and images.[19] De Hooghe had the absolute talent to capitalize on the violence of history and understood the desire of avid spectators who acted at the same time as consumers in a rapidly expanding market of visual paraphernalia. The De Hooghe prints circulated widely as they were eagerly copied and reprinted.[20]

The many representations of public violence (especially executions) make eager use of theatrical techniques, or more precisely, explicitly insist on the theatrical nature of the event, by representing the spectators themselves, by making the *mise en scène*, the techniques deployed to theatricalize the event, visible, and by addressing the onlooker himself as a spectator. A representation of the execution of the conspirators against Maurits at the Groene Zoodje in 1623 (attributed to Nicolaas Van Geelkercken) (Figure 10.1) shows the scaffold on the left, surrounded by a mass of spectators, and, on the right, the proclamation of the punishment in the inner town court.[21] At the bottom we see the condemned behind bars, the beheading and the mutilation of a body, the three condemned and their grieving widows. The spectator is invited to scan the print and to reconstruct the story. The print uses theatrical techniques to create a time-based experience.

Similarly, the print made by Claes Jansz. Visscher (Figure 10.2) depicting the same historic event reads as a real early modern comic.[22] Once more, the scaffold surrounded by the public is central, with to the right in the same drawing the three suspects in the clothes in which they were taken prisoner (so they feature twice in the same drawing). The smaller prints underneath the main print show small scenes: carrying away the body (C), quartering and drawing the body (D), cutting open the decapitated body (B) and (E) smashing to pieces the conspirators' pistols. The fifth box is blank, as if the spectator's imagination can add yet another scene to the timeline.[23]

The public is the main subject in nearly all these prints; the looking is central. In a print by Dirk Everson Lons from 1623 (Figure 10.3) the public takes up nearly the whole picture. When we put all these engravings together, they represent a sort of phenomenology of the spectator's interest in public space. In all of these prints the same theatrical techniques are used again and again to turn the picture into an experience. The artist creates a narrative plot (the print thus gets a temporal dimension) and at the same time works with simultaneity: events that happened

**FIGURE 10.1** The execution of the conspirators against Prince Maurits, 1623. Attributed to Nicolaas Van Geelkercken. Rijksmuseum Amsterdam: RP-P-1968-283

one after the other are represented next to one another. It is impossible for the spectator to register everything at the same time. Such prints intend to involve the absent public (what really happened?) but, at the same time, construe historical

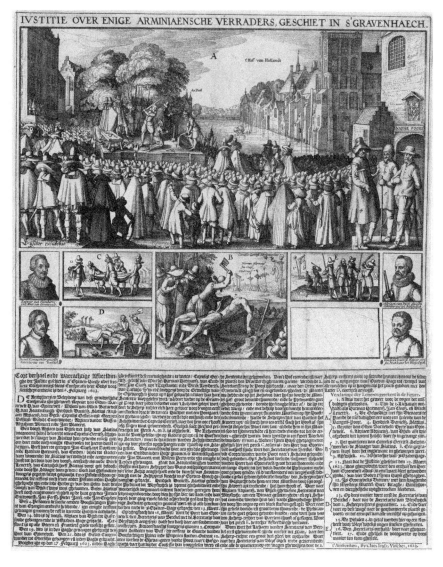

**FIGURE 10.2** Execution of Reinier van Oldenbarneveldt, David Coorenwinder and Adriaan Van Dijk, 1623, by Claes Jansz. Visscher. Rijksmuseum Amsterdam: RP-P-OB-81.043

reality: they shape the ways in which the spectators remember the event, no matter whether they were present or not. But above all these prints testify to a structural fascination with abject corporality, and together they form a catalogue of early modern cruelty that consciously appeals to the eager look of the spectator. These pictures are spectacles: they are fundamentally theatrical (they make ample use of theatrical techniques) *and* they have a performative effect (they *make* history). At

**FIGURE 10.3** Execution of Reinier van Oldenbarneveldt, David Coorenwinder and Adriaan Van Dijk by Dirk Everson Lons, 1623. Rijksmuseum Amsterdam: RP-P-OB-81.040

the same time they invite to self-reflect, they have the spectator think about his role in history. The real subject of these pictures is therefore the spectator: his reflection on looking and the importance of looking for the construction of public space, of reality and memory.

All these prints are aimed at creating an embodied experience; they draw the spectator inside and demonstrate, at the same time, what techniques are used to do so. This leads us to the underlying hypothesis of this contribution: theatricality functioned as a structuring principle of early modern culture,[24] including in the Dutch Republic. Of course, we are not saying anything new here. More important is the following proposition: precisely this commercialization, the functioning of objects in a market, enabled what was theatrical to turn into a spectacle. We will see how extra-theatrical practices used theatrical strategies, by engrafting onto a dramatic plot structure and thus enabling reflection and critical distance. At the same time this commercialization put this distance under pressure: there was less room for reflection, only a swirl of images, a spiral of violence, that we will later also find in the theatre plays of Jan Vos. First, we will discuss anatomy, specifically anatomical cabinets, anatomical atlases, and anatomical lessons, in which we find comparable theatrical techniques.

## The frenzy of anatomy

In anatomical cabinets, atlases and classes art, knowledge and spectacle converge. The Dutch 'artist of death' Frederik Ruysch is without a doubt the most adequate example of this typically early modern convergence.[25] Ruysch was not only a scientist, but, maybe even in the first place, also a director: in his cabinet, preparations became true mise *en scènes*. Ruysch succeeded, in his own words, to

> Render deceased bodies in such a natural way, so that they cannot be distinguished from a living and sleeping human being, all limbs, that are motionless in deceased people, nearly moving as in a living human being. Moreover, the dead produce a rather unpleasant smell; but these bodies are nice to smell.[26]

The production of factual scientific knowledge was probably a secondary role of anatomical cabinets. In the first place, they were spectacles, in every sense of the word, and thus meant to function on the spectacle market, the experience itself, the beholding, becoming merchandise. In the cabinet of Ruysch the preparations became a true spectacle: Ruysch embellished details with lace or damask, or rested a baby's head on a placenta, as if it were a pillow.[27] The cabinet gave shape to a new corporality (the inside of the body as a newly explored terrain), but also capitalized on the same affective dimensions that were part of the theatre of cruelty of the seventeenth century: fascination, awe, and horror. In another preparation – they almost seem to be theatrical installations – we see two skeletons of foetuses embracing one another comfortingly. Ruysch combined his scientific spectacles with typical baroque vanitas elements such as plumes or strings of pearls (for which he based himself on the Leiden anatomical theatre) and thus invited the spectator to reflect upon life and death.

The same theatrical techniques also featured in the anatomical atlases from the period, such as Govert Bidloo's *Anatomia Hvmani Corporis* (with drawings by Gerard de Lairesse) (1685; Figure 10.4 shows the 1728 edition). First the bodies were laid open for the spectator as true *mise en scènes*. In addition the atlas forms a kind of time experience: the viewer follows the course of the anatomical lesson but never gets a complete survey of the different parts. Such atlases also consciously capitalized on the affects of the spectator, such as horror and fascination. Bidloo was a clever marketer; his atlas was his visiting card. It had to advance his career, but at the same time it had to function within an economy of spectacles and affects of which the aforementioned prints were part. Therefore Bidloo consciously opted for a theatrical approach. He provided the illusion that the spectator was looking over the shoulder of the anatomist, at close quarters, so the viewer would see all the details in real life. In his drawings De Lairesse clearly showed that these are specific, individual bodies. Hair or other physical details reminded the spectator that the represented parts originated from a specific body, a specific life. The body which was laid open became a mirror of the body of the spectator, from which it was impossible to distance oneself. Bidloo and De Lairesse used ropes, nails and other supporting parts to stage-manage the body as best as possible, as if the corpse posed or laid itself open for the spectator.

Even more so than in the atlas, in the anatomical lessons the inside of bodies were turned into a spectacle. On July 21, 1687, the English painter Thomas Person visited the anatomical theatre in Leiden on his tour in the Dutch Republic, the Southern Netherlands, and France. It was summer, so there were no anatomical lessons (they were only organized in winter, for obvious reasons), but Person, full of awe, did describe the skeletons and the other 'wondrous works of the creator', and the anatomical theatre as 'a theatre of horrors'.[28] In the seventeenth century there were 16 anatomical theatres in the Netherlands.[29] They played a crucial part in the development of science. The anatomical lesson was an experience-oriented practice in which careful observation, the handling of instruments, and the theoretical explanation of what you encounter were central. At the same time this anatomical lesson was part of the judiciary system (the anatomical lesson as additional punishment for the condemned),[30] and of the early modern culture of collecting (the anatomical theatre was simultaneously an exhibition room for exotics and naturalia). But above all anatomical theatres warranted the cultural spread of knowledge via spectacle. Just as with the prints and the anatomical atlas, the spectator is also here invited to exchange his exegetic look (looking for explanations) for an exploring look (looking for experiences).[31] The anatomical theatre was a room of *display*, of dead bodies, of the physician's skills, of fancy dress, but also of curiosities, just like the public execution, 'which likewise united magistrates and the general public, and combined horror and reflection upon mortality, entertainment and learning, music and the display of power.'[32]

In Amsterdam one could attend an anatomical lesson with a ticket costing six or seven stivers.[33] The first public dissection in Amsterdam took place in 1550 on the body of the thief Suster Luydt. In 1556 Philip II granted the surgeons permission

FIGURE 10.4 Plate 28 from Govert Bidloo, *Ontleding des menschelyken lichaams* (Utrecht: Jacob van Poolsum 1728), with printed illustrations designed by Gerard de Lairesse. Utrecht University Open Access, https://dspace.library.uu.nl/handle/1874/283576

to open up the corpse of a condemned criminal once a year. From 1587 onwards that same guild organized public dissections in the former chapel of the Saint Margaretha convent by the Lesse. They shared a floor with the chamber of rhetoric 'In liefde bloeyende'. In 1619 the surgeons moved to the low building (laaggebouw) (the former Saint Anthony Gate) and in 1639 moved back to the building by the Nes (which the chamber of rhetoric had left in the meanwhile). By the end of the century the building was too dilapidated to cope with the great public interest, so the anatomical lesson moved once again to the St.-Anthonies-Waag after a drastic renovation.[34]

The new Theatrum Anatonicum (or the 'snijburg', 'cutting castle') had room for 500 spectators, with a revolving table in the middle for maximum visibility.[35] 'Several lights in the roof shine directly on the cutting table', Nicolaas ten Hoorn writes in his *Wegwijzer door Amsterdam* from 1713. The visitor could read the translation of a Latin verse of Caspar Barlaeus underneath the dome: 'Wrongdoers harmful to the human race / Can still be useful after they have been killed.'[36] The anatomy book of the surgeons' guild provides a good idea of the way an anatomical lesson was conducted, for instance via the enumeration of the receipts and expenses for the anatomical demonstrations between 1699 and 1702.[37] The bills in the book refer to expenses not only for the remuneration of officials, or the cost of light, but also for more pleasurable commodities such as wine, biscuit, meat and beer. The list of expenses for the dissections conducted between March 26 and 31, 1702 even mentions 'half a lamb.'[38] In the theatre the public was required to respect quite a number of rules, as the regulations of the Order of Surgeons (1605 and 1625) teach us: no laughing, no talking, no quarrelling or sneering, and no stealing.[39] There was a fine of minimum six guilders for stealing parts of the body.[40] The minutes of the guild mention disturbances more than once. Dissections were announced in the *Amsterdamsche Courant*. On average a public lesson yielded two hundred florins for a male body, and three hundred and fifteen florins for a female body. Sumptuous dinners were often organized along with the anatomical lesson.[41] So the anatomical lesson as a theatrical event brought together three types of spectacles: the execution, the public dissection and the semi-public banquet.

In the anatomical lesson, just as in the executions prints, horror, reflections on death and mortality, entertainment, instruction and the display of power all convened in a festive spectacle, driven by the carnivalesque curiosity of the public. Not clinical distance but immersive theatricality was central in what Sawday calls 'the spectacular culture of dissection.'[42] At the same time the anatomical lesson as a spectacle was the expression of a new form of knowledge, aimed at experience instead of being based on the respect for texts and authority. That is why in representations of anatomical theatres the spectator is central, just like in the execution prints. In *The Body Emblazoned* Sawday meticulously describes the title page of Vesalius' *De Humani Corporis Fabrica* (1543) and shows how everybody is watching everybody else, just like in early modern theatre.[43] It is no coincidence that the artist chose the typical theatre architecture of that period as a background and that the spectator who holds the book looks Vesalius straight in the eyes, as he lays open the body on the dissection table.

## Staging bodies in Jan Vos, *Aran en Titus*

Due to a lack of sources it is difficult to prove whether or not the public for all of these different cultural practices was the same, and how much executions, anatomic lessons, and theatre plays shared the same audience. On the basis of a documented case in Montpellier Paul Friedland, asking if 'anatomy theatres and executions were both caught up in a rising tide of spectacularity', cautiously asserts that 'it does not seem too much of a conceptual leap to imagine that the same crowd at the same time might have felt a similar curiosity about public executions, which also allowed spectators to look at the corpse of a stranger in a similar setting.'[44] The early modern Dutch economy of spectacle was probably characterized by the same mobility of people from one (commercialized) cultural practice to the other, bringing the vulgarized understanding of what bodies look like on the inside from the realm of justice or anatomy to the theatre and the other way around. Probably a smaller group bought prints representing violent scenes from recent history and one can assume, based on a simple economic reality, that not everybody who was fascinated by the spectacle of anatomy owned an anatomical atlas, or had the chance to visit an anatomical cabinet. However, all of these practices functioned within a new capitalist economy of emotions, in which emotions, in this case horror, but also curiosity, or plain voyeurism, were bought and sold as commercial products. All of these entrepreneurs, printers, anatomists, illustrators, exploited the same strategy: embodiment and emotional involvement.

The history of anatomy in the Dutch Republic cannot be disconnected from the history of theatre (and more specifically the graphic representation of violence), as both theatre and anatomy capitalized on the very same emotions. Anatomy made ample use of theatrical strategies, while Senecan horror theatre exploited the anatomical imagination the spectators brought with them to the playhouse. Theatrical techniques enabled anatomists to stage their 'performances', live or in print. One of the most famous examples of this is Govert Bidloo himself: Bidloo wrote several plays, he was one of the members of the art society Nil Volentibus Arduum (founded in 1669), and acted between 1681 and 1688 as one of the directors of the Amsterdam theatre.[45] Early modern theatre functioned as a laboratory where techniques were tested and where artists experimented with the blurry line between reality and fiction, between presence and representation, between the real and make-believe. Conversely, theatre artisans eagerly exploited spectacular techniques that were developed outside of the theatre, permanently insisting on the importance of 'display' or 'spectacle' as the backbone of early modern public space.

Dutch theatre has traditionally been labelled as classicist in nature, partly due to the central, canonical position of Vondel in literary history and education: the spectacular baroque was said to have had little impact on Dutch theatrical culture.

This traditional view however, has been increasingly questioned. In his publications on Vondel, Frans-Willem Korsten insists on the baroque aspects of this presumably classicist playwright.[46] Moreover, the traditional presumption of the classicist nature of the Dutch seventeenth century ignores the consistent presence of translations and adaptations of (often utterly violent) Spanish plays in the Amsterdam theatre, as one can assess in the CREATE database,[47] developed by a team from the University of Amsterdam, mapping all the plays staged at the Amsterdam theatre between 1637 and 1800.[48] The case of Govert Bidloo can teach us that, when it comes to violence and the spectacle of the body, the boundaries between 'classicist' and 'baroque' or 'spectacular' blur. Although he was a former member of the French-classicist art society Nil Volentibus Arduum, Bidloo's theatrical output and interest seem to have been quite spectacular, as is demonstrated, for instance, by his musical play *Het zegepraalende Oostenryk, of the verovering van Offen* (*The victorious Austria, or the conquest of Buda*) (1686), which he wrote immediately (within three weeks) after the historical event.[49]

In the theatre from that same period symbolically violated corpses seem to have haunted the repertoire. Theatre formed an integral part of the early modern 'culture of dissection'. Especially during the first half of the seventeenth century this tendency was in vogue, first of all under the influence of the Senecan horror tragedy, which was introduced in the Netherlands relatively late: in 1600 *Den Spieghel des hoochmoets* by Jacob Duym, an adaptation of Seneca's *Troades*, was included in *Een spieghelboek* and staged by a Flemish theatre group.[50] These Senecan tragedies are always characterized by the same basic ingredients: high-placed figures, rhetorical language, and a great dose of gruesome events with an unhappy ending. Abundance (*copia*) and variety (*varietas*) are the most important dramaturgic principles as the play develops according to an episodic sequence of loose building blocks rather than a tight plot. In many of these plays the body, either wounded or opened-up, takes up a central spot, for instance in *Haaghse broedermoord* by Oudaan, *Hierusalem verwoest* or *Gysbrecht* by Vondel, *Veinzende Torquatus* by Brandt, *Trazil* by Van der Goes, and *Aran en Titus* by Jan Vos,[51] which premiered on 20 September 1641 in the recently opened Amsterdam theatre and which would be represented about 100 times between 1641 and 1665.[52]

On January 3, 1638 the Amsterdam theatre, built by Jacob Van Campen, opened its door with the staging of Vondel's famous play *Gysbrecht van Aemstel*. Up to that date, no other town in the Dutch Republic possessed an official theatrical institution solely devoted to the representation of theatre plays.[53] Therefore the Amsterdam theatre was one of the city's showpieces, officially initiating the professional spectacle economy in Amsterdam.[54] The design of the new theatre is the perfect metaphor for the position of the Dutch Republic as a central node in the rapidly expanding international network of information and knowledge, as international influences were swiftly adapted to local needs. Van Campen's design was, to name just one example, 'clearly inspired by the theatre from Antiquity as well as by the Italian reception of that same heritage, symbolized by Palladio's

**FIGURE 10.5** Title plate of the 5th edition of Jan Vos, *Aran en Titus* (1656) (Amsterdam: Jacob Lescailje, 1661). Leiden University

famous Teatro Olimpico (1585).'[55] This combination allowed Van Campen to present a building that aligned with recent trends, while at the same time symbolically connecting Amsterdam to Ancient Rome.

The tragedy programming of the Amsterdam theatre consisted of tragedies that more or less fitted in with the Senecan tradition, but at the same time capitalized on the public's eagerness for revengeful violence. The Amsterdam playwright Jan Vos perfectly understood the public's enthusiasm for graphic spectacle. Always putting 'seeing' before 'saying',[56] he reached the provisional climax of spectacularization. Even if theoretically the didactic aspect prevailed in his work, in practice the stimulation of emotions more and more clearly became a goal in itself.[57] His *Aran en Titus* turned out to be a gigantic success, and the play became the classic example of the Seneca-inspired visually oriented horror theatre with excessive violence. There is indeed something for everyone: chopped-off hands and heads, rapes, murder, manslaughter, corpses served and eaten by a mother, and so on. The title plate of Vos' tragedy efficiently sums up the theatrical horror. We are at the end of the story, the cannibalistic meal has just been finished (see the dishes in the foreground). Thamera has just eaten the flesh of her two sons. Both had raped Rozelyna (Lavinia in Shakespeare's *Titus Andronicus*), daughter of Titus, and then cut off her tongue and hands. She enters with the dish and is finished off by her father (she lies in the foreground). Meanwhile, Thamera is screaming. Aran rushes in and falls in a fire. We also see Titus who has lost his left hand. Emperor Saturninus, who will kill Titus, is killed in his turn by Lucius, son of Titus, with the assistance of his uncle Marcus Andronicus (to the right of the emperor). Between Thamera and Lucius we probably notice Askanius, son of Lucius (who has nothing to do with the scene). To the left a balcony with a trapdoor from which flames and smoke could emerge. The engraver brings together two different scenes from the end and compresses the dramatic time to reach a maximum spectacular effect (indeed, the print had to make the book attractive as merchandise).

We only have an incomplete idea of how these horrors were represented on stage. Sometimes certain events were told, not shown. Still, many scenes demand that the physical violence is effectively shown: the dangling corpse of Bassanius (II,8), two crushed dead bodies in a pit (idem), Titus cutting off his hand (III,4), the heads of two brothers being brought in (III,5), and, as a prologue to the final horror, the fifth scene of the fourth act: Titus cuts his enemies' throats, asks Rozelyna to collect the blood in a dish, then realizes she has no hands. He then asks her to bite out their hearts from their bodies with her teeth and spew them in their faces:

> Come over here with a plate
> Here Rozelijn, come over here and take your revenge on this villain
> while I tear open this cruel chest with a knife
> How are you standing there? What's wrong? Don't you have hands
> Tear open his diaphragm with your blooded hands
> The chest ripped open, you owe this to your terrible fate
> There, spit the murderous heart into the face of the murderer.[58]

We know that in many European theatres the *striking effects* of the late medieval mystery plays were used: fake blood, prostheses, pyrotechnics, and so on.[59] Thanks to the studies of, among others, Hunninger, we have precise information as far as the theatrical architecture and the use of space (for instance revolving panels) are concerned. At the same time we still lack many details about the technical aspects of the theatre of the early seventeenth century, especially regarding the representation of violence.

In his article 'The Politics of Mobility' Helmer Helmers explains that this violence also has political implications, just like the prints we referred to earlier.

Just as with Nero in *Britannicus* by Jean Racine, the personal desires of the emperor prevail over his public responsibility as a sovereign. Other characters make the danger that lurks around the corner more explicit. Jan Vos has Thamera say: 'Woe to them who prevail their lust over holy justice', and a little later: 'The king belongs to the common interest, the common interest does not belong to the king.' The answer of Saturninus is the answer of an absolute monarch: 'The will of the sovereign can lawfully speak here.'[60] The warning Vos gives to his spectators is therefore clear, as Helmers rightly states in his analysis of the play: 'lustfulness in a powerful emperor [...] resulting in tyranny.'[61] Helmers describes how *Aran en Titus* should be read as a political warning against too much display of power, a warning that must have been music to the ears of the Amsterdam regents at a time when they had to withstand the increasing power of the House of Orange. In this context Vos also uses the motive of rape, as a metaphor for the violation of sovereignty, the *body politic*.

The performative effect of tragedies such as those of Jan Vos cannot be separated from the representations of violence outside the theatre, which we discussed earlier. Indeed, precisely these representations facilitate the performative effect of such plays; they informed the expectations the seventeenth-century public took along to the theatre. More specifically concerning the anatomical theatre: the fact that part of the public saw opened-up bodies with their own eyes, in real life or via prints, made an embodied experience of theatrical violence possible. The spectator brought knowledge about bodies and about violence inflicted on bodies that he had gathered during extra-theatrical activities into the theatre itself. Events such as public executions, or dissections in the anatomical theatre, or objects such as prints depicting the recent past's violent moments, enabled the spectator to transform the theatre into an affective space and to become a beholder who was able to manage the ontological complexity of theatre itself, i.e. the co-presence of performers and spectators. The 'culture of dissection' functioned as a structuring regime that made sure horror in theatre was actually experienced physically, even if the mode of representation is evidently artificial and therefore implausible, also for the then spectator. That is why Barlaeus writes in his foreword of the edition of *Aran en Titus*: 'I am alike dazed and overwhelmed in mind'.[62]

## Embodied experience and spectacle

With all of these cultural practices, ranging from execution prints over anatomy to theatre, a new commercial market was gradually taking shape, a market in which affective experiences were consumed (hence: affective economies). In his seminal article on this history of consumption, anthropologist David Graeber explains that etymologically speaking to consume meant 'to seize or to take completely over', and from the fourteenth century even 'to destroy': 'it meant destroying something something that did not have to be (at least quite so thoroughly) destroyed'.[63] Capitalism thrives on endless production fuelled by consumption: if we consume, we destroy and thus we desire. Indeed, Graeber explains, 'modern economy (as opposed to traditional hedonism which was based on the direct experience of pleasure and thus limited by saturation and boredom) thrives on dreams and fantasies, on desire, on daydreaming about 'what having a certain product would be like.'[64] Despite the insight that desire is rooted in fantasies, he explains, with the expansion of the free market in the sixteenth and seventeenth century a real commercial industry developed, trading in emotions by exploiting consumer desires, with its own infrastructure and distribution mechanisms: prints, atlases, theatres. In the early modern period there was a genuine market of imaginary goods, of affect and emotions, in which knowledge economy, science and commercial culture became increasingly inseparable and emotional experience functioned as the ultimate commodity.

Indeed, in every single one of these cultural objects or practices the embodied experience was central. They all are part of a rapidly expanding cultural industry whose most important mechanism was the accumulation of similar experiences. Spectacle culture thrives in a continuous, cross-medial stream of impulses, stimulating affective engagement, a sort of frenzy, with the depicted or represented realities. The execution, the prints, the anatomical lesson, the anatomical atlas: they all tried to involve the public physically and sensually in the event, through the marketing of emotions. Every time bodies became an object of spectacle and therefore also a commercial product. Every single one of these cultural objects was therefore consciously overwhelming, but, at the same time, wanted to stimulate the spectator towards analysis via that same spectacle. These cultural objects thus simultaneously invited experience and interpretation. Hence, it is no coincidence that Jan Vos himself, in his introduction to his *Medea* explicitly (and in contradiction with the then prevailing moral laws in theatre theory) asserts: '… that the representation of the murder of men, if executed skilfully, has the potential to move the people's mind by the sight of it.'[65]

The early modern notion of spectacle is characterized by two apparently contradictory mechanisms. On the one hand the spectacle functions thanks to the commercialization of the human body, a marketable object that has to satisfy 'clients' in their inquisitive search for knowledge, but also lust, horror, and excitement. On the other hand, the early modern spectacle is also constructing, re-inventing reality. It studies the very conditions of reality but at the same time questions this reality via the representation of unknown worlds, in this case the inside of our body.

The early modern spectacle regime was characterized by the paradoxical interaction of theatricality and performativity. Theatrical techniques made it possible to install a breach with daily life and to turn reality into a stage (with the accompanying scenography, role-playing, and dressing) in order to be able to look at reality and also at one's own body with a different eye. At the same time the early modern spectacle was fundamentally performative: it aimed to have an impact on that same reality via a simulation of the real and especially on the collective imagination this reality follows. The spectator is always 'inside' and 'outside' and is invited to move temporarily out of his own body or out of his own reality.

Throughout different cultural expressions we have demonstrated how early modern visual media deployed techniques from theatre, and how theatre itself, as a reaction to this phenomenon, became more and more spectacle, developing itself into a commodity for the market, as part of a new industry of entertainment. The same gradual shift can be observed within anatomy, or, more specifically, the anatomical lesson turned into theatre and subsequently into spectacle: it developed from a strictly scientific exploration into a true commercial activity, prioritizing individual, embodied experiences over centralized didactics.

Similarly, plays depicting gory violence, both verbally and visually, such as *Aran en Titus*, aimed at immersing the spectator into an embodied frenzy of awe and horror and thus gave ample room to the individual experience of the spectator, who is invited to leave behind his disbelief and to eagerly enjoy the gruesome details of the depicted scene, shivering from horror and sheer enthusiasm, often simultaneously. Vos' theatre is not about controlling or centralizing the gaze of the spectator, i.e. ensuring that all spectators experience the play in a similar way. On the contrary, his play embraces spectacle by giving priority to the individual experience of every single spectator, as he perfectly knew how to position himself within the rapidly expanding market of spectacular representations of bodies and violence. Artists and artisans invented new strategies to respond to the growing demand of early modern consumers. These were curious to get a closer look at the violence they heard of, witnessed or, at worst participated in, while at the same time longing for a codified spectacle which would enable them to situate the very same violence and to cope with it.

## Notes

1 I would like to thank all members of Working group III: "Knowledge and the Market: Affective Economies of the Global Knowledge Society Project," especially PI Inger Leemans. All of them have been utterly generous in sharing their comments, advice and material with me. This article has also greatly benefited from the input of the colleagues with whom I have the pleasure to participate in the FWO/NWO project *Imagineering Violence, Techniques of Early Modern Performativity in the Northern and Southern Netherlands (1630–1690)*: Frans-Willem Korsten, Inger Leemans, Yannice de Bruyn, Michel Van Duijnen, and especially Kornee van der Haven who commented on an earlier version of the present article. A crucial part of the theoretical insights of this article is based on a co-authored article, which will be published in the *Journal of Cultural History*: "Imagineering, or What Images do to People: The Spectacle of Violence in the Seventeenth-century Dutch Republic."
2 A. Reckwitz, "Affective spaces," 245.
3 A. Reckwitz, "Affective spaces," 247.
4 A. Reckwitz, "Affective spaces," 248.
5 This is the reason why authorities have always been suspicious of this art form, of which the flux of energies and interpretations is so difficult to control.
6 W. J. T. Mitchell, "Foreword," xvi.
7 W. J. T. Mitchell, "Foreword," xviii.
8 P. Burke, *What is the History of Knowledge?*, 17–18.
9 J. Van Dijck, "Digital Cadavers"; C. Quigley, *Dissection on Display*.
10 J. Sawday, *The Body Emblazoned*, 11–12.

11 The volume by C. Bouteille-Meister et al., *Corps sanglants* illustrates the widespread circulation of representations of violence, death, suffering, martyrdom in different media throughout the sixteenth and seventeenth century, in different European countries.

12 E. Kolfin, *Gedrukt tot Amsterdam*; Rasterhoff, *The Fabric of Creativity*.

13 P. Friedland, *Seeing Justice Done*, 119.

14 In *Les histoires tragiques de nostre temps* (1614), François de Rosset describes how in every execution there are "the well-to-do spectators who have paid for the privilege of renting windows overlooking the square, the penal corollary of the theatrical loges." P. Friedland, *Seeing Justice Done*, 140.

15 P. Friedland, *Seeing Justice Done*, 141.

16 J. Oudaan, "Aantekeningen van de Moord- en mishandelinge der Heeren Cornelis en Jan de Witt den 20 Augusty 1672 in's Gravenhage, door een oor- en ooggetuyge opgesteld." This report was collected in the manuscript *Stukken en Aantekeningen wegens [...] het verschrikkelijk ombrengen van de H(e)ren Jan, en Kornelis de Wit, verzameld [...] door K.van Alkemade (en) P. van der Schelling*. Mss Royal Library The Hague, published in: R. Van Stipriaan, *Ooggetuigen*, 232–37.

17 R. Van Stipriaan, *Ooggetuigen*, 235.

18 R. Van Stipriaan, *Ooggetuigen*, 236.

19 See for example: Romeyn de Hooghe, *Depiction and True Story of the [...] Deaths of Johan and Cornelis de Witt* (1672). Rijksmuseum Amsterdam, RP-P-OB-77.136; Romeyn de Hooghe, *Murder on Johan and Cornelis de Witt* (1672). Rijksmuseum Amsterdam, RP-P-1905–6609. See also: Hale, "Political Martyrs."

20 Sometimes these copies were anonymous, in other cases they were the work of artists like Jan Luyken and Bernard Picart. I would like to thank Michel Van Duijnen who indicated this utterly fascinating network of visual representations on the death of the De Witt brothers.

21 The execution of the conspirators against Maurits, 1623, attributed to Nicolaas Van Geelkercken. Rijksmuseum Amsterdam, RP-P-1968-283.

22 Execution of Reinier van Oldenbarneveldt, David Coorenwinder and Adriaan Van Dijk, 1623, by Claes Jansz. Visscher. Rijksmuseum Amsterdam, RP-P-OB-81.043.

23 In another version of the same print the comic is enlarged with more scenes and even different representations of executions of conspirators against Maurits (27 February, 29 March, 5 May 1623) are depicted together. Rijksmuseum Amsterdam, RP-P-OB-81.021A

24 See also H. S. Turner, *Early Modern Theatricality*.

25 L. Kooijmans, *Doodskunstenaar*.

26 J. C. C. Rupp, "Theatra Anatomica," 27. Original quote from Ruysch *Alle de ontleedgenees-en heelkundige werken*, Vol. 2, "*Tot de leser*," 9: "Het natuurlijk wesen zoodanig wedergegeven aan de afgestorven lighaamen, dat men se van een levendig en slapend mensch niet kan onderscheyden, zijnde alle ledematen, die in afgestorven menschen onbeweeglijk zijn in deze nauw beweeglijk als een levende mensche. Daarenboven geven de dooden wel haast een onaangename reuk van haar; deze integendeel zijn aangenaam van reuk."

27 J. V. Hansen, "Resurrecting Death."

28 R. Van Stipriaan, *Ooggetuigen*, 60.

29 J. A. M. Slenders, *Het Theatrum Anatomicum*; H. Cook, *Matters of Exchange*.

30 F. Egmond, "Execution, Pain and Infamy."

31 H. Cook, *Matters of Exchange*, 77.

32 F. Egmond, "Execution, Pain and Infamy," 121.

33 W. S. Heckscher, *Rembrandt's Anatomy*, 32.

34 J. V. Hansen, "Resurrecting Death," 665.

35 A. Mooij, *De Polsslag*, 79 *passim*.

36 "Kwaaddoeners, schadelijk aan't menschelijk geslacht / Verstrekken nog tot nut als zij zijn omgebragt."

37 Het Anatomieboek van de Chirurgijnsgilde: Stadsarchief Amsterdam Inventaris 366: Archief van de Gilden en het brouwerscollege.
38 See also J. A. M. Slenders, *Het Theatrum Anatomicum*, 174–75.
39 J. A. M. Slenders, *Het Theatrum Anatomicum*, 91.
40 W. S. Heckscher, *Rembrandt's Anatomy*, 28.
41 J. V. Hansen "Resurrecting Death," 667; J. Van Dijck, "Digital Cadavers," 39; C. Quigley, *Dissection on Display*, 149.
42 J. Sawday, *Body Emblazoned*, 62.
43 J. Sawday, *Body Emblazoned*, 66.
44 P. Friedland, *Seeing Justice Done*, 130.
45 K. Haven, *Achter de Schermen*, 172.
46 Korsten *Sovereignty* and, more recently Korsten, *A Dutch Republican Baroque*.
47 http://www.create.humanities.uva.nl
48 Cf. K. J. Jautze, "Spaans theater in de Amsterdamse Schouwburg."
49 R. Knoeff, "Govert."
50 K. Porteman and M. B. Smits-Veldt, *Een Nieuw Vaderland*, 160.
51 On J. Vos: Geerdink, *De Sociale Verankering*.
52 *Treur- en blijspelen die op de Amsterdamschen schouwburg vertoond zijn*; Archief Huydecoper, nr 163 (392). Apart from Vondel's *Gysbrecht*, another Senecan play featuring excessive violence appeared to be prominently succesfull: *Veinzende Torquatus* by Geerardt Brandt. The play premiered on October 6 1644 and was presented 41 times between 1644 and 1665.
53 W. M. H. Hummelen, *Inrichting en Gebruik*.
54 K. Porteman and M. B. Smits-Veldt, *Een Nieuw Vaderland*, 375.
55 T. Paepe, "Computervisualisaties," 147.
56 J. Vos, *Toneelwerken*, 60
57 K. Porteman and M. B. Smits-Veldt, *Een nieuw vaderland*, 379.
58 'Komt herwaarts met een bekken. / Hier Rozelijn, kom hier, wreek u van 't schellemstuk / Terwijl ik met dit mes de wreede borst opruk. / Hoe staatge dus? wat is 't? ontbreekt het u aan handen? / Scheur Quiro 't middelrif, met uw' bebloede tanden, / Uit de 'opgesnede borst, uw' ramp heeft u verplicht. / Daar, spuw 't moordadig hart in 's moorders aangezicht.' J. Vos, *Aran en Titus*, IV, 5, verses 1896–1902) (translation KV).
59 K. Vanhaesebrouck, "Barok en Classicisme," 133.
60 "Wee hen die 't heilig recht door minlust oversteigeren"; "De Vorst is om 't gemeen;'t gemeen niet om de vorst"; "De vorstelijke wil mag hier als wettig spreken".
61 H. Helmers, "The Politics of Mobility," 357.
62 "ik sta gelijk bedwelmt en overstolpt van geest."
63 D. Graeber, "Consumption," 491–2.
64 D. Graeber, "Consumption," 495.
65 "ik geloof dat de nagebootste menschemoordt, alsze stark uitgebeeldt wordt, de gemoederen van het volk door het zien kan bewegen." J. Vos, *Alle de gedichten*, c3.

# Bibliography

## Manuscript

*Anatomieboek van de Chirurgijnsgilde*. City Archive Amsterdam, Inventory n° 366: Archief van de Gilden en het brouwerscollege, 6, 294.
Archive Balthasar Huydecoper, Utrecht Archive 67 Archive Family Huydecoper, nr 163 (392). *Treur- en blijspelen die op de Amsterdamschen schouwburg vertoond zijn*.

# Print

Alvarez, Natalie. "The Bodies Unseen: The Early Modern Anatomical Theatre and the *Danse Macabre* of Theatrical 'Looking'". Web Publication, 2011. www.janushead.org/Alvarez.pdf.

Bouteille-Meister, Charlotte, and Kjerstin Aukrust, eds. *Corps sanglants, souffrants et macabres XVIe-XVIIe siècle*. Paris: Presses Sorbonne nouvelle, 2010.

Braembussche, Antoon van den, and Angelo Vermeulen. *Baudelaire in cyberspace. Dialogen over kunst, wetenschap en digitale cultuur*. Brussel: ASP, 2008.

Brockbank, William. "Old Anatomical Theatres and what Took Place therein." *Medical History* 12 (1968), 371–84.

Burke, Peter. *What is the History of Knowledge?*. Cambridge: Polity, 2015.

Cook, Harold. *Matters of Exchange: Commerce, Medicine and Science in the Dutch Golden Age*. New Haven & London: Yale University Press, 2007.

Cook, Harold. "Amsterdam: entrepôt des savoirs au XVIIe siècle." *Revue d'histoire moderne et contemporaine* 55 (2008), 19–42.

Crombez, Thomas, Jelle Koopmans, Frank Peeters, Luk Van den Dries, and Karel Vanhaesebrouck, eds. *Theater: Een Westerse geschiedenis*. Leuven: LannooCampus, 2015

Dackerman, Susan, Claudia Swan, et al., eds. *Prints and the Pursuit of Knowledge in Early Modern Europe*. Cambridge Mass.: Harvard Art Museums, 2011.

Davids, Karel. *The Rise and Decline of Dutch Technological Leadership: Technology, Economy and Culture in the Netherlands, 1350–1800*. Leiden: Brill, 2008.

Dijck, José Van. "Digital Cadavers and Virtual Dissection." In *Anatomy Live, Performance and the Operating Theatre*, edited by Maaike Bleeker, 29–48. Amsterdam: Amsterdam University Press, 2008.

Dijkhuizen, Jan Frans van. *Pain and Compassion in Early Modern English Literature and Culture*. Rochester: D.S. Brewer, 2012.

Egmond, Florike. "Execution, Pain and Infamy: A Morphological Investigation." In *Bodily Extremities: Preoccupations with the Human Body in Early Modern European Culture*, edited by Florike Egmond, and Robert Zwijnenberg, 92–128. London/New York: Routledge, 2003.

Fischer-Lichte, Erika. *Ästhetik des Performativen*. Frankfurt am Main: Suhrkamp, 2004.

Friedland, Paul. *Seeing Justice done: The Age of Spectacular Capital Punishment in France*. Oxford: Oxford University Press, 2012.

Geerdink, Nina. *De sociale verankering van het dichterschap van Jan Vos (1610–1667)*. Hilversum: Verloren, 2012.

Goldfarb, Hilliard. "Callot and the Miseries of War: The Artist, his Intentions, and his Context." In *Fatal Consequences: Callot, Goya, and the Horrors of War*, edited by Hilliard Goldfarb, and Revi Wolf, 13–26. Hanover: Hood Museum of Art, 1990.

Graeber, David. "Consumption." *Current Anthropology* 52 (2011), 489–502.

Hale, Meredith. "Political Martyrs and Popular Prints in the Netherlands in 1672: The Murders of Jan and Cornelis de Witt in the Early Modern Media." In *Selling and Rejecting Politics in Early Modern Europe*, edited by Martin Gosman, and Joop Koopmans, 119–34. Leuven/Paris/Dudley: Peeters, 2007.

Hansen, Julie V. "Resurrecting Death: Anatomical Art in the Cabinet of Dr. Frederik Ruysch." *The Art Bulletin* 78 (1996), 663–79.

Haven, Kornee van der. *Achter de schermen van het stadstoneel: theaterbedrijf en theaterpolemiek in Amsterdam en Hamdburg 1675–1750*. Zutphen: Walburg Pers, 2008.

Heckscher, William S. *Rembrandt's Anatomy of Dr. Tulp*. New York: New York University Press, 1958.

Helmers, Helmer. "The Politics of Mobility: Shakespeare's *Titus Andronicus*, Jan Vos's *Aran en Titus* and the Poetics of Empire." In *Politics and Aesthetics in European Baroque and Classicist Tragedy*, edited by Jan Bloemendal, and Nigel Smith, 344–72. Leiden: Brill, 2016.

Holzapfel, Amy Strahler. "The Body in Pieces: Contemporary Anatomy Theatres." *PAJ: Journal of Performance and Art* 30, no. 2 (2008), 1–16.

Hoorn, Nicolaas ten. *Wegwijzer door Amsterdam*. Amsterdam: s.n., 1713.

Huisman, Tim. *The Finger of God: Anatomical Practice in Seventeenth-Century Leiden*. Leiden: Primavera Press, 2009.

Hummelen, Wim M.H., *Inrichting en gebruik van het toneel in de Amsterdamsche schouwburg van 1637*. Amsterdam: Noord-Hollandsche Uitgeversmaatschappij, 1967.

Ingham, Karen. "Tissue to Text: Ars Moriendi and the Theatre of Anatomy." *Performance Research* 15 (2010), 48–57.

Jautze, Kim J., Leonor Á.Francés, and FransBlom. "Spaans theater in de Amsterdamse Schouwburg (1638-1672): Kwantitatieve en kwalitatieve analyse van de creatieve industrie van het vertalen." *De Zeventiende Eeuw* 32 (2016), 12–39.

Knoeff, Rina. "Govert Bidloo (1649–1731). Onbemind maakt onbekend." In *De kaper, de kardinaal en andere markante Nederlanders*, edited by Jetze Touber, and Marjan Brouwer, 85–94. Rotterdam: Uitgeverij Verloren, 2010.

Kolfin, Elmer, and Jaap van der Veen, eds. *Gedrukt tot Amsterdam: Amsterdamse prentmakers en -uitgevers in de Gouden Eeuw*. Zwolle/Amsterdam: Waanders, 2011.

Kooijmans, Luuk. *De doodskunstenaar: De anatomische lessen van Frederik Ruysch*. Amsterdam: Bert Bakker, 2004.

Korsten, Frans-Willem. *Sovereignty as Inviolability: Vondel's Theatrical Explorations in the Dutch Republic*. Hilversum: Verloren, 2009.

Korsten, Frans-Willem. *A Dutch Republican Baroque*. Amsterdam: Amsterdam University Press, 2017.

Mitchell, William John Thomas "Foreword." In *Beholding Violence in Medieval and Early Modern Europe*, edited by Allie Terry-Fritsch, and Erin Felicia Labbie. Surrey: Ashgate, 2012.

Mooij, Annet. *De polsslag van de stad: 350 jaar academische geneeskunde in Amsterdam*. Amsterdam/Antwerpen: Arbeiderspers, 1999.

Nierop, Henk van, Huigen Leeflang et al., eds. *Romeyn de Hooghe: De verbeelding van de late Gouden Eeuw*. Zwolle/Amsterdam: Uitgeverij Wbooks, 2008.

Paepe, Timothy de. "Computervisualisaties van de theaterarchitectuur in de Lage Landen (1600-1800)." In *Theater*, edited by Thomas Crombez et al., 120–44.

Porteman, Karel, and Mieke B. Smits-Veldt. *Een nieuw vaderland voor de muzen: Geschiedenis van de Nederlandse literatuur 1560–1700*. Amsterdam: Bert Bakker, 2008.

Quigley, Christine. *Dissection on Display: Cadavers, Anatomists and Public Spectacle*. Jefferson, North Carolina: McFarland, 2012.

Reckwitz, Andreas. "Affective Spaces: A Praxeological Outlook." *Rethinking History* 16 (2012), 241–58.

Rasterhoff, Claartje. *The Fabric of Creativity in the Dutch Republic: Painting and Publishing as Cultural Industries, 1580–1800*. Amsterdam: Amsterdam University Press, 2012.

Roemer, Gijsbert M. van de. "Het lichaam als borduursel: Kunst en kennis in het anatomisch kabinet van Frederik Ruysch." In *Body and Embodiment in Netherlandish Art/ Lichaam en lichamelijkheid in de Nederlandse kunst*, edited by Ann-Sophie Lehmann, and Herman Roodenburg, 217–40. Zwolle: WBooks, 2008.

Rupp, Jan C.C. "Matters of Life and Death: The Social and Cultural Conditions of the Rise of Anatomical Theatres, with Special Reference to Seventeenth-Century Holland." *History of Science* 28 (1990), 263–87.

Rupp, Jan C.C. "Theatra Anatomica. Culturele centra in het Nederland van de zeventiende eeuw." In *De productie, distributie en consumptie van cultuur*, edited by Kloek Joost, and Wijnand Mijnhardt, 13–36. Amsterdam: Rodopi, 1991.

Sawday, Jonathan. *The Body Emblazoned: Dissection and the Human Body in Renaissance Culture*. London/New York: Routledge, 1995.

Slenders, J.A.M. *Het theatrum anatomicum in de Noordelijke Nederlanden 1555–1800*. Nijmegen: Instituut voor Geschiedenis der Geneeskunde, 1989.

Stipriaan, René van. *Ooggetuigen van de Gouden Eeuw in meer dan honderd reportages*. Amsterdam: Prometheus, 2000.

Turner, Henry S., ed. *Early Modern Theatricality*. Oxford: Oxford University Press, 2013.

Vanhaesebrouck, Karel. "Barok en Classicisme." In *Theater*, edited by Thomas Crombez et al., 120–144.

Vos, Jan. *Alle de gedichten van den poëet Jan Vos*, 2 vols. Amsterdam: J.L., 1662.

Vos, Jan. *Aran en Titus of wraek en weerwraek*, 17th ed. Amsterdam: Wed. Gijsbert de Groot, 1699.

Vos, Jan. *Toneelwerken*, edited by. W.J.C. Buitendijk. Assen/Amsterdam: Van Gorcum, 1975.

Williams, Linda. *Hard Core: Power, Pleasure and the Frenzy of the Visible*. Oakland: University of California Press, 1989.

Zuidervaart, Huib. "Het in 1658 opgerichte theatre anatomicum te Middelburg. Een medisch-wetenschappelijk en cultureel convergentiepunt in een vroege stedelijke context". *Mededelingen van het Koninklijk Zeeuwsch Genootschap der Wetenschappen*, 2009, 73–140.

# 11

# RUBBED, PRICKED, AND BOILED

## Coins as objects of inquiry in the Dutch Republic

*Sebastian Felten*

In this chapter, I will explore early modern coins as objects of inquiry. They had a face value (just like dollar bills today), but hidden in the material, removed from the senses of sight and touch, there was the intrinsic value of the precious metals they contained. To find out whether these two values were in sync or not involved knowledge work at many points of a coin's life-cycle: when it was mined and minted; repeatedly when it changed hands as a medium of exchange; and at the end of its life when it was demonetized and melted down, perhaps to be minted afresh. Silver and gold moved around the globe, but often haltingly, because it was repeatedly rubbed against touchstones, pricked with sharp tools, and boiled in a furnace to find out its worth. To make metallic money work as a medium of exchange, a store of wealth, and a measure of value, early modern users – that is everybody from muddy-footed peasants to starchy-collared stock traders – needed to know their coins. People scrutinized their design, learned what they weighed and they ought to weigh, their official valuation and their market value. Sometimes they went to considerable lengths to find out what the exact precious metal content was. This was the most important information, but also the one that took the most effort, time, skill, and special equipment to obtain. In a practical sense, the knowledge work that established the value of early modern money was never quite done.

The possible mismatch between appearances and the substance of a coin created a space of anxiety, as early modern people were always at risk of being shortchanged. Evelyn Welch observed that in Renaissance Italy, 'coins, like people, had names and reputations and required close scrutiny as well as an element of trust. A coin that was reliable at one moment might lose its value at another.'[1] The cameralist Julius Bernhard von Rohr advised his readers in a handbook for 'prudent' living in monetarily diverse eighteenth-century Germany that they make themselves familiar with as many coins as possible. 'Such knowledge is not only very necessary for daily life', he writes in a chapter on how to gain money, 'but it also offers you great opportunity: namely, when you obtain a certain rare coin from people who do not know their value, and then sell it on to connoisseurs and collectors [Kennern und Liebhabern].'[2] Like Rohr, I will in this chapter emphasize that the possible mismatch between appearances and substance was also a space of opportunity, that governments, money-changers, metallurgical experts, and even ordinary users could exploit to their own advantage. This twin story of anxiety and opportunity offers a fresh view on money in early modern Europe and its standardizations in the nineteenth century. The emotional dimension of money has been investigated before, but this often concerned passions aroused by the *quantity* of money: for example, how medieval and Renaissance thinkers were concerned with avarice, which was considered an unreasonable passion for more money; and how early modern and Enlightenment thinkers suggested that 'interest of gain' is a passion that can be harnessed to keep more violent passions at bay.[3] Departing from this well-trodden path of modern economic thought into the thicket of early modern money's production and use, I want also begin to turn our attention to the emotional response that *quality*, that is the material properties of concrete kinds of money, could elicit in people. Viewed from this vantage point, testing coins was not only a tool for decision-making but also for the management of emotion; and precise minting was not only a more rational way of producing coin but it also made users less anxious about the value of their money.

To make this argument, the chapter proceeds in several steps. In the first section, I introduce the idea that coins have a 'life' to illustrate how they were continually tested for weight and composition as globally mined metals made their way into the mints and markets of the Netherlands, and from there back into the world. In the second section, I add more depth to the idea that the possible mismatch between appearances and substance created a space of opportunity for metallurgical experts. Section three explores the interaction of metallurgical experts in the Dutch Republic, drawing upon the papers of one prominent family of assayers, jewellers, gold- and silversmiths. In the fourth section, I use this archive to suggest that ranking of expert opinions was one method by which early modern people determined the value of coins in an ad-hoc fashion even if different experts had divergent testing results. Section five suggests that regular, official coin testing was a 'ceremony of measurement'[4] that not only created 'stable pieces information'[5] as Simon Schaffer and Harold Cook have suggested but also served to counter ill feelings and deflate passionate discourse. In the sixth section, I widen the perspective from the smallish circle of metallurgical experts to the great mass of 'ordinary' money users in the Dutch Republic. By retracing the affective and intimate ways in which a Reformed preacher and his wife handled coins, I suggest that scrutiny of, and familiarity with, minute details of coins in circulation were an important life skill in a monetarily diverse environment and therefore widespread. The final section shows how coin reforms in the nineteenth century replaced the by then embarrassing diversity inherited from earlier centuries with highly uniform coinage. Scrutiny of coins was centralized in government offices, allowing the general public to unlearn their monetary skills. While the quantity of standardized money continued to arouse strong emotions, its material quality was henceforth of lesser import. The space of anxiety and opportunity, so characteristic of early modern money, was being reduced to a minimum.

## Mines, markets, mints

An artwork attributed to Romeyn de Hooghe, *The Allegory of Coinage*, can give us many visual cues for this twin story of anxiety and opportunity (Figure 11.1). Not much is known about this undated painting, though the provenance from the Royal Mint in Utrecht might suggest that it was commissioned by the general-masters of the mint who supervised coinage in the old Republic.[6] A female figure, Coinage herself, is at the centre of a crowded tableau that shows the transformation of ores into bullion and of bullion into specie. The life of a coin began in a mine, as is shown on the left half of the canvas, where half-clad figures produce ores from a rockface.[7] Their state of undress may suggest unfree and abundant labour in America or in ancient Greece, but the two furnaces, smoking busily in the middle ground, give away the capital intensity and technological sophistication that mining had typically reached by the time the painting was made.[8] Much of the silver and gold that entered the market around 1700 was the product of mining

**FIGURE 11.1** Romeyn de Hooghe, *Allegory of Coinage*, ca. 1670–1708, oil on canvas, 135 cm × 178 cm. Rijksmuseum Amsterdam

complexes with a high division of labour, and reliant on expert interventions that distinguished ore veins in their surrounding rock, and determined the amount of metal in the ores.[9]

One miner in De Hooghe's painting, bent by awe or hard labour, hauls metalliferous rocks towards the foreground, echoing other depictions of Holland attracting treasure.[10] Transformed in the furnace, bars of copper, gold, and silver are scattered at the feet of Coinage. Much of the silver produced in the Americas arrived on the Amsterdam market through roundabout channels during the time when the Dutch were at war with Spain, and in straightforward ways after the peace of 1648. In the second half of the seventeenth century, an estimated 148 to 180 tons arrived from Cádiz every autumn, on the 30 to 50 ships of the silver fleet; 'for the city as for the Bourse, this was an important event'[11]. These precious metals arrived in all sorts and shapes: 'silver *barros, barratones,* ingots of gold and silver; also dishes, plates, jugs and all works of silver and gold; all sorts of Spanish *reales, quart d'écus, testoons,* and *francs*; all sorts of English money, or whatever billion or specie it may be'.[12] This at least was how a group of traders described what they sought to import when they asked for permission from the authorities in 1650.

Much of the actual trading took place in the north-eastern corner of the Bourse of Amsterdam, near the exit to the Dam, precisely opposite from the stockbrokers: 'Entering from the *Beurssluis,* one first finds, on the left, between and around pillars no. 2 and 3, German Jews who trade and change all sorts of gold and silver, coined and uncoined.'[13] But as the city council complained in 1684, there were also 'Jews and others who are brazen enough to stand near the Bourse or on other marketplaces, or walk past some houses to buy up, sell, or change specie'[14]. Just like silversmiths and goldthread makers, masters of the mint were obliged to buy their raw material from licensed traders or the Exchange Bank and not, as happened often enough, through less official channels.[15] But whichever way they obtained their material, for it to be money rather than a commodity, it had to be 'struck according to a fixed standard of weight and fineness'.[16] This involved weighing and testing at many steps in the process.

Weighing was mainly a way to determine how much mass coins were missing due to clipping, wear and tear. This could be done in batches, using bags and large balances, or individually with hand-held models like this one (Figure 11.2). The hand-coloured copper engraving glued into the lid of the box shows a professional money handler with a balance in his hand. The inscription says that this balance was sold 'above the Bourse in Amsterdam', presumably in one of the shops on the first floor.[17] This testifies to the fact that bourse was one locale in which monetary expertise was concentrated in the Dutch Republic, just as in the Exchange Bank, the many mints of the country, moneychangers' offices, as well as workshops of assayers, refiners, jewellers, gold- and silversmiths.

In *Allegory of Coinage,* utensils for testing coins are depicted prominently on the left to the female figure. One method exploits the fact that alloys with different ratios of gold, silver, and copper left streaks of different colours on the black touchstone, which could be compared to a set of standardized needles. A

**FIGURE 11.2** Johannes Linderman (III), Coin balance, wood and brass, 140 mm × 68 mm × 39 mm, ca. 1775. Münzkabinett der Staatlichen Museen zu Berlin, object number: 18201790

more precise method was the fire assay, for which a small sample was placed on a high-precision balance (shown here in a protective glass case) before and after it was heated in the furnace. Also note the rooster, an attribute of Mercury, the god of trade, science, and the arts (represented here by the winged figure and the snaked staff), which seems to be scrutinizing a bar of silver from up close. The wakeful creature may point to the assayers and refiners at the mints who determined the value of the raw material and added silver or gold until the alloy was up to standard, and continuously controlled the finished product.[18]

Many of these coins were used for foreign trade and shipped to the Baltic, the Levant, and the Far East. Gold followed more complicated trade routes, but most of the silver originating from America eventually found its way to China.[19] Indeed, Dutch coin production has been described as a 'refining export industry'[20] that imported raw materials and exported a finished product, as was common in other branches of the Republic's economy.[21] But this did not mean that the scrutiny was over once the coins were released into circulation. More knowledge work was required as they passed from hand to hand, so that they could effectively mediate between wants and needs. Coins were knowledge-intensive at birth, and remained objects of inquiry throughout their life.

## Anxiety and opportunity

Consider this little snippet of early modern life from the Amsterdam notarial record. In 1683, shopkeeper Sander Ambrosius wanted to change a gold dollar but was told by the Jewish moneychanger it was not 'good' money. Sander disbelieved him, and forced him to cut it open, but was proven wrong by a silversmith who, upon inspecting the coin, confirmed the moneychanger's verdict. At this point, Ambrosius 'became so angry' that he forced the shopkeeper Jacobus de Hen, from whom, presumably, he had received the dollar, out of the shop, where he attacked him with a knife 'without any reason'.[22] Coins were made to smoothe the exchange of value, yet this duplicitous specimen caused suspicion, anger, and almost bloodshed in the street. De Hen's opportunity to shortchange him (if this is what happened) caused Ambrosius' anxiety. This, again, was an opportunity for the moneychanger, who made a living from pronouncing the value of coins his clients came across. Ambrosius' anxiety that the moneychanger might lie became the silversmith's opportunity to help, or to collect a fee for himself.

Assayers, goldsmiths, and jewellers – these occupations often overlapped in individuals – could be both forgers and critics. 'There are fraudsters who know how to apply a coating of gold on lead and other base metals, to make rings, buttons, and coins', the author of a goldsmithing handbook explained; 'I have seen my own father buy such buttons that were filled with white lead'.[23] He mentioned these rogue practices only so that honest goldsmiths would be able to detect the fraud. But was it possible to make sure that the know-how in his book was not used precisely for such illicit practices? Similarly, assayers working at the mint could make sure the alloys were spot on, but they also could help produce coins that were substandard. Most commonly, however, they helped the master of the mint to 'tickle the remedy', as the French put it: to aim as close as possible at the lower end of the margin of error, called the remedy, that the coin tariffs allowed, without overstepping the line and incurring a fee.[24]

The increased mechanization that began in the last quarter of the seventeenth century made it easier to reach this goal. The introduction of the screw press, the numismatist Gerardus van Loon wrote in his magnum opus on Dutch coins and medals, made for much more regular coins. Like other newly invented things of recent times, it quite literally 'jacked up' modern civilization above the level of the ancients; coins now were truly high-tech objects.[25] The reverse of a medal commemorating an inspection of the mint in Medemblik not only showed off the new screw press – still relatively new in the Netherlands, and an expensive investment after all – it also drew the fine line between legitimate profit and fraud: 'A good shepherd shears his sheep; he doesn't flay them (Figure 11.3).' Precise production (for the weight) and precise assaying (for the fineness) were key,

**FIGURE 11.3** Commemorative medal of an official inspection at the mint of Westfriesland in Medemblik (reverse), 1746. Silver, diameter 50.5 mm, Teylers Museum, Haarlem

because masters of the mint wanted to hit that sweet point as closely as possible. In sum, then, forgers and mints producing substandard coins, wilfully or not, made the coins in circulation ontologically unstable; they could always turn out to be something other than they pretended.

## Metallurgical experts

For money-changers, assayers, jewellers, and gold- and silversmiths, the ambiguity of coins was a resource to exploit, as they had skills that made their claims about metallic objects trustworthy and authoritative. These experts, though many of them not directly involved in minting, were 'members of the coinage state', as the States-General admonished them in a congenial turn of phrase.[26] For a family of jewellers, gold- and silversmiths, burghers of The Hague, lawyers, and government officials, this was particularly pronounced. The possible mismatch between face value and intrinsic value provided opportunity over generations to build a reputation as experts and to secure family income. A cache of documents, now preserved at the National Archive in The Hague allows us to retrace their aspirations. It is now split into family papers and an official archive, though this distinction would not have been clear at the time.[27] 'I, Johan Emants, was appointed [...] assayer-general of the mint of this country, in the stead of my father-in-law M[arcellus] Bruijnsteijn'[28], was noted proudly in the family book on July 8, 1707. Here, Johan also noted the births of his daughters, which he missed because he was travelling to inspect a mint. As assayer-general, he, his father-in-law as well as his son and great-son advised the Dutch central government in technical aspects of coinage, an office that was as respected as it was well-paid.

Johan Emants (1678–1742) was appointed only eight days after Marcellus resigned due to old age, which implies that he must have learned what was needed for the job during his assistantship, which had lasted for several years. Apart from hands-on instruction by his father-in-law, the collection suggests that the family developed its own paper-based practices of transmission. First, they preserved papers that were 'shed' by their activities themselves: corre- spondence, written-down calculations that were necessary to reverse the sampling, and reports that contained the final results but also indications about the methods used. When Marcellus Emants (1706–1792) sorted his father's estate, he placed some of the documents in folders. The title of one of them, 'Diverse examinations, calculations and equivalencies of coins by grandfather Bruinsteyn', neatly sums up the character of this collection: a trove of ex- perience and information that had accreted over time, valuable enough to be passed down the generations.[29]

Second, they created recipe collections. A recipe book in an eighteenth-century hand covered a wide range of topics useful for keeping the family prosperous. Some of them concerned health: a diet to treat kidney stones, a recipe for Paracelsus' famous *elixir proprietatis*, cough syrup, and a mixture to ward off the plague. Others concerned know-how needed to carry out public office: instructions on how to write letters in cyphers, notes about paying taxes, and importantly, the finer points of the procedures by which the central government monitored the mints of towns and provinces with minting rights. Particularly rich, however, is the collection of recipes about manipulating metals and acids. In a tangible example of transgenera- tional knowledge-transmission, a piece of a seventeenth-century recipe was pinned onto an eighteenth-century iteration of the recipe 'To extract gold from silver while leaving the silver intact'. In these recipe collections and descriptions of procedure, how-to knowledge was formulated more explicitly than in the paper trail of their activities.[30]

A third way of keeping knowledge available in the family was to define 'what a good assayer-general should know',[31] outlining an ethos of high precision that manifested in a deep control of tools and techniques, and in knowledge about the precise legal specifications of each coin type. One cluster of the desired skills re- volved around the command over materials, which was the foundation of their trade. Using tools was not enough, as an assayer-general had to be able to make and repair them, too. An assayer-general had to not only know how to use the touchstone but also how to make the testing needles. He had to know how to use cupels to pull base metals from molten alloys, and also how to manufacture them from bones. He should know how to add lead as a solvent and how to refine it so that it was fit for the task. An assayer had to know how to examine the scales, detect the flaws even in a seemingly good scale, and be able to mend them. He had to know how to calibrate the weights by adding or removing tiny specks of material. He had to know how to handle acids to test metals in addition to being able to test whether the acid itself was reliable. The list did not have propositions to be learned nor did it explain how to do things (which was sometimes spelled out in the recipe book). Rather, it defined a state of expertise that members of the family should aspire to throughout their life.

Fourth, they documented active research. The list of what a good assayer-general should know contained one hefty item to this effect, and this time it seems safe to assume that it was indeed a desideratum rather than a matter of fact. Above all, the list said, they 'should know the fineness of all gold and silver coins that have ever been struck in the Netherlands, so that when they encounter them, they know whether their weight and alloy is good or not. They must know the same about all foreign coins, especially those that are imported, and be able to make the same report on them.'[32] Some of Bruijnesteijn *Diverse examinations* were indeed the result of research into the country's monetary past. In a loose sheet titled 'Comparison of the old money, one against the other', we find the following entry about the English noble coin:

> At the time of Charles V, an English noble was counted as two old *schilden* p. 395. In 1667, these English nobles were counted as 11 guilders by the magistrate of Amsterdam. Ibidem 395. It was found that the same sort was worth 3 gold guilders in 1413, and 6 guilders and 13 stivers in 1594. Ibidem p. 396.

The source for this entry was a work by Antonius Matthaeus III (1635–1710), a legal historian at Leiden University and correspondent of the scholars Nicolaas Witsen (1641–1717) and Gijsbert Cuper (1644–1716), all of whom shared an interest in the money of the past.[33] Bruijnesteijn entry anchors the English gold coin, which was still in circulation, in a network of valuations at four different points in time, and most importantly, it established links to the Republic's money of account, the guilder. Another entry adds more nodes to this network: 'In a letter of 1456 and 1457: The English gold noble, weighing 5/2 *engels*, reckoned as 13 shillings and 4 pence.'

While the first entry was drawn from a book that Bruijnesteijn or Emants could have happened to own, this information was taken from a manuscript collection of town privileges kept at the Leiden university library.[34] Other entries point to the consultation of institutional archives, such as the information extracted from a tithe book of the church in Herwijnen (Gelderland) that an Arnhem guilder was worth 15 stivers. Others again look like the result of sheer serendipity: 'An old valuation of money found in the estate of the old Willem van Tuyll of Bruijnesteijn and Gijsbert Pieck'.[35] In the work of the assayer-general, the laboratory practices of the fire assay were thus blended with more bookish modes of historical research. The collection itself was a personal archive that was begun by Marcellus Bruijnesteijn, continued by his son-in-law, who passed it on to his own son Marcellus Emants (1706–1792). For the Emants family, keeping the chain of knowledge transmission intact paid off. A household journal reveals that the salary of ƒ 1500 that Marcellus Emants received for his service as assayer-general accounted for 23 per cent of his household's total income.[36]

## Assessing the truth by ranking expert opinions

The case of the Bruijnesteijn-Emants is particularly well-documented, but similar processes of knowledge production and transmission will have helped other families gain and retain their position on a market of metallurgical experts. But if there was a market of experts who could produce object-based proof about the value of money, how did people find out whose claim was true? Remember that even the angry shopkeeper Ambrosius sought out two experts before he pulled a knife on his fellow. One way to assess the truth of a matter was to compile and rank opinions, and the Bruijnesteijn-Emants papers can, again, give us important clues as to how this was done.

In April 1698, Marcellus Bruijnesteijn received a polite request and a stubborn piece of silver from Anthoni Grill III (1664–1727), scion of a wealthy family of silversmiths, assayers and alchemists who had spread from Augsburg to Amsterdam and finally Stockholm.[37] Grill had taken the assayers' exam with Bruijnesteijn, who was his senior by 15 years, and he may have possibly learned from him. He ended up in the service of the Exchange Bank of Amsterdam and approached Bruijnesteijn from there:

> I'm sending to you a silver bar and kindly ask you to make an assay of it, as we have had diverging results. Jan Siewerts Out [the Bank's chief assayer] found it to have 5 *penningen* 4 *grein* [430.556 per mille], but neither I nor others, nor the mint of Dordrecht, where the bar has already been sent to, have found it to be less than 5 *penningen* [416.667 per mille]. I personally found it to contain 4 *penningen* 23 3/4 *grein* [415.798 per mille], but I believe that it contains more. Therefore I'm compelled to turn to you and kindly request that you examine the bar to give us a final decision.[38]

This letter sings an interesting tune. The dominant theme is that one assay alone rarely settled the matter, as the results tended to diverge.[39] However, this melody was accompanied by a more subtle theme of personal and institutional authority. The result by Sieuwert Jansz Out carried extra weight since he was the chief assayer of the Bank, and could not be cast aside, even though a number of other assayers had had different results. Presumably they were more junior and not members of an institution, and perhaps even belonged to those sloppy practitioners that Grill complained about to Bruijnesteijn.[40] Grill doubted his own result which differed from Jansz's. The only way ahead seemed to summon the highest authority of the Republic, the assayer-general Bruijnesteijn.

Since its founding in 1609, the Exchange Bank of Amsterdam carried out the work of moneychangers with the 'autoriteyt' of an institution, and in addition offered safe-keeping and transfers like a cashier.[41] Its employees received coins, evaluated them, and converted them into their own money of account, the Bank guilder, at a discount called the agio, which they credited to their clients' accounts. 'Now the credit in the books of the bank, which is every day transferable at the bank, answers every purpose of coin, either for payment or loan', the British political economist James Steuart pointed out in 1767, 'and the proprietor has neither the trouble of receiving the species, nor any risk from robbery, or false coin.'[42] The Bank's money of account, at least looked at from across the Channel, 'stood like a rock in the sea, immoveable by the fluctuating proportion between the metals.'[43]

This detachment was achieved by assaying, which for the Bank was an accounting tool, as it allowed them to make sure that the value in their books would have an equivalent in the gold and silver that they stored in their vaults. The Bank employed its own assayers, who were important figures, as they were responsible for linking the sums in the books to gold and silver, or, as their instruction put it, 'to estimate the true value' of specie and bullion that merchants deposited. They were thus each paid a handsome salary of f 750 per year, plus income from 'own work and industriousness'. But their vigilance extended beyond the walls of the laboratory on the ground level of the new city hall, as they were to keep an eye and an ear out for 'foreign, prohibited, and counterfeited coins that may circulate in the community' and to warn the commissioners about them.[44]

This is precisely what Anthony Grill (III) and Sieuwert Jansz Out were doing in 1697. The elusive silver bar was likely connected to the mint of Harderwijk, whose master Lambertus de Ridder was troubling the Bank, the central government in The Hague, the government of Gelderland (and, presumably, ordinary users of money) by producing substandard coins.[45] In 1697, Adriaan Backer, one of the Bank's commissioners had already written to Bruijnesteijn that he and his colleagues had come across 'lion dollars, minted this year in the Province of Gelderland, whose content seems us to be a little too low', requesting him 'to make an assay of these four attached lion dollars, so that we can regulate ourselves as to which [silver] content we should write down [in our books]'.[46] In August that year, he wrote that it had come to his attention that the mint in Harderwijk was processing silver bars that were below the statutory fineness – a possible explanation for their substandard products and possibly the reason why in the following April, the Bank had subjected the same silver bar to the scrutiny of a range of assayers whose credentials differed as much as their results, and eventually turned to Bruijnesteijn.[47]

A note in Bruijnesteijn's personal papers may explain why Grill and Out believed that he could settle the matter. A 'good' assay worthy of an assayer-general, it says, was one 'to the most extreme grade [in de uijterste graat], that is, […] such a close assay [soo nouw assaieren] that nobody else can extract more from a sample'. The law may allow ordinary town assayers a margin of error of a quarter of a grein.

An assayer-general, however, by careful testing, and even more careful testing of the testing apparatus, must be able to keep his error from the actual content (*de rechte gehalte*) under one eighth of a *grein*, or 0.434 per mille.[48] In one of his responses to Backer in 1697, he emphasises that his results may differ from those of other assayers, 'because there are assayers who take (if silver is to be tested) only 5 *engels* (7.72 g) lead [as a solvent] per cupel [...] although the same should be 7 1/2 *engels* (11.58 g)'. Less trustworthy assayers also take smaller samples, and do not control the temperature of the crucible, which is the cause of divergent results.[49] In other words, the assayer-general took additional steps to control all conditions of the test, which helped make the results more authoritative and less contestable. This and the authority vested in their office made them rank high when opinions were compiled from various assayers.

A book Sieuwert Jansz published in 1681 was testimony to his expertise, and also a way to monetize it (Figure 11.4). The title page shows a well-lit, orderly workshop. An assistant is working at the furnace, while an elderly assayer is weighing out the sample. His expensive dress and his advanced age seek to instil trust in the accuracy of the work. At the same time, the book itself is a telling example of the little tools of knowledge that early modern people used to navigate the monetary diversity of their time: books that were not for reading but could be handled like a tool. The purpose of the tables was to determine the mass of gold or silver (and hence value) contained in an object such as a bag full of coins when both the weight and the purity of that object is known. This involved some mental acrobatics or written calculation, which the tables helped avoid or simplify.

## Testing as management of affects

While in the case of the stubborn silver bar several tests were combined in an ad hoc fashion, there were also fixed procedures that arranged people, objects, and actions in highly choreographed 'ceremonies of measurement'.[50] These occasions – called trial of the pyx in England, *Probationstage* in the Holy Roman Empire, and *muntbusopening* in the Dutch Republic – were designed to keep chains of custody intact, to minimise tampering, and thus forestall conflict. In the Netherlands, they served to align the production of coins across the nine to fourteen independent mints of the confederates, from mighty Holland to the tiny town of Zwolle.[51]

The obverse of the medal discussed above depicts a *muntbusopening* of the province of West-Friesland in Medemblik. A council in The Hague, consisting of the general-masters of the mint and the assayer-general, was charged with co-ordinating monetary policy across the Republic and would visit every mint within the space of two to five years. The medal shows ten officials sitting at a round table, ensuring mutual control and visibility. Depicted are presumably the master of the mint, whose coins are being examined, Teunis Kist (1704–1781); the delegation from The Hague, and representatives of the cities Hoorn, Enkhuizen en Medemblik, whose coats of arms we see at the top, along with those of the States

Uytgerekende

# TAFELEN
# In't Gout en Silver;

Gereduceert uyt Marken Troys, in Marken Fijns.

.MITSGADERS,

*Den Prijs ende Waerdy van 't selve, in Guldens,*
*Stuyvers ende Mijten; na de kours en ordre in de respective*
*Munte van de Nederlanden gebruyckelijck.*

Van nieuws Gecalculeert, vermeerdert en verbetert door
*Sieuwert Jansz. Out,* Affayeur.

*Nootsakelijck allen Koopluyden, Munte-Meesters en anderen*
*in 't Goudt en Silver handelende.*

t'AMSTERDAM,

By MARCUS WILLEMSZ. DOORNICK, Boeckverkooper op
den Middeldam, in 't Kantoor Inck-vat, 1681.

**FIGURE 11.4** Title page of Sieuwert Jansz Out, *Uytgerekende Tafelen In't Gouten Silver* (Amsterdam: Willem Doornick, 1681)

FIGURE 11.5   Commemorative medal of an official inspection at the mint of Westfriesland in Medemblik (obverse), 1746. Silver, diameter 50.5 mm, Teylers Museum, Haarlem

of West-Friesland. The circumscription alludes to the long tradition of minting in Medemblik (Figure 11.5).

The sample box, or *muntbus*, at the bottom, has just been opened; it had received every 500th coin that was produced during the audited period. The rooster, as in de Hooghe's painting, may signal alertness, but it was also the personal mark of this particular master of Teunis Kist. The contents of the box are scattered across the table, and people are engrossed in different steps of the examination: some are counting coins and some are weighing them. One figure seems to be checking the warden's account, while the inkpot and pen hint at the paper trail this visit will leave. It may also refer to the complex written calculations assayers relied on to reverse the multiple steps of sampling and to make the results gained from minuscule specks of matter eloquent about large batches of coin. As other measurement rituals, the *muntbusopening* demanded 'careful attention to a sequence of performative actions without which the measure loses value.'[52] If unbroken, the described sequence allowed the assayer to create reliable, public knowledge about large numbers of coins produced in the mints of the Republic. 'Agreed-upon methods of testing', Harold Cook writes, 'produced stable pieces of information from material objects, and this information was in turn circulated in the form of marked pieces of metal'.[53] In other words, what made the results legitimate, and the information trustworthy, was not the testing method itself, nor the authority of the involved people alone, but the procedures in which people and their actions were embedded.

While this interpretation by Schaffer and Cook is highly plausible, I would like to draw attention to another function that these ceremonies might have had in a world when the materiality of money harboured anxiety, and the quality of coins was closely linked to the reputation of their makers. In such a world, ceremonial tests also served to counter ill feelings and to deflect the impression that passions ruled instead of reason. Their pomp and circumstance could help prevent messy situations such as one which unfolded around a batch of rixdollars that the general-masters had found wanting, yet importantly not during an official inspection of the mint but by consulting their very own Marcellus Bruijnesteijn.[54] When the coins' maker Dr. Gerhard van Harn, master of the mint of Nijmegen, was informed in July 1704 that the general-masters had proposed the demonetisation of his coins, he was evidently upset. In a fiery pamphlet, he sought to restore his reputation by attacking not only coin council but also the Bank of Amsterdam whom he suspected of being behind the verdict. The strange behaviour of the general-masters, he wrote, makes one think 'that either a great passion, or a secret interest lurks behind it': this was nothing but a plot to bring down the imperial mints[55] so that the Bank and their henchmen Anthoni Grill and the VOC could mop up more silver to export with a profit, to the detriment of the country that was deprived of a means of exchange.[56] In an earlier pamphlet, he found their reasoning ridiculous, in fact no reasoning at all: 'the passions of the general-masters of the mint made it impossible for them but to put themselves blindly out of reasonable discourse and to surrender to private passions and perhaps through this and by inspiring false thoughts, achieve their goal to overthrow the master of the mint.'[57] In yet another, he berated the general-masters for the way in which they formed their opinion: that they 'did not know their duty, that they violated their instruction, because they sent two lads to visit the mint [...], whereas their instruction obliges them to visit in person. After all, they enjoy an annual allowance of $f$ 600 for travel'.[58] He expressed his firm belief that the magistrate of Nijmegen would never allow that the town's prerogative and privilege of minting, for which they had been fighting so persistently, to be ceded to the 'interested passions' of the council.[59] But to no avail. In May 1705, a Haarlem newspaper informed their readers that the States-General was about to send a resolution across the country 'by which some struck dollars of 30 stivers, coins of Nijmegen, especially those of 1703 and 1704, are prohibited to use and declared bullion' (Figure 11.6).[60] This meant that owners of these coins were not allowed to use them as money but rather treat them as uncoined metal. The regular route out of circulation would have been a moneychanger or the exchange banks, which would have cut them up, paid the owner, and reinserted them as raw material into the stream of precious metals (perhaps to be reborn as better coins).

In order to enter the crucible and transform into a new self, deviant coins had be spotted in the mind-boggling diversity of Dutch circulation. While multiple monies were probably the normal state of affairs for 'the majority of human beings

**FIGURE 11.6**   Silver dollar of the mint of Nijmegen, 1704. Diameter 35.6 mm. Teylers Museum, Haarlem (obverse and reverse)

through most of history',[61] the phenomenon was particularly visible in trading regions like the coastal rim of the Netherlands where around 1600, money-changers handled 800 to 1000 different coin types.[62] Gerhard van Harn's deviant rixdollar was only one variation of one of these types—the rixdollar with an official weight of 10 *engels* 11 *aas* (15.968 g) and a purity of 11 *penningen* 1/2 *grein* (918.402 per mille).[63] To those who understood its visual language, it told readily that it was a silver ('arg[entea]') dollar (note the armoured man) worth '30 st[uiver]', or *f* 1:10, made in '1704' at the imperial (eagle) mint of Nijmegen (coat of arms and 'civ[itatis] noviomag[ensis]). The rough execution and slightly decentred stamp (now difficult to see due to wear and clipping of the edges) gave the coin away as produced in the traditional way, by striking a stamp on a disk, and not pressed with the screw-press which was still a novel technology in the Republic. It even contained a clue that Dr. Gerhard van Harn was the responsible master of the mint (the moor's head next to the man's shin).[64]

## Everybody a 'liefhebber' of coins?

Psychologists tell us that people are very selective in how they perceive coin; in the hustle and bustle of exchange, 'details escape us.'[65] By design, early modern coins offered themselves up for such parsimonious perception. The armoured man might have been enough for an experienced user to recognize the coin's value, making the '30 st' redundant and the place-name irrelevant. But then, all clues could become significant, even and especially the miniscule moor's head that gave away the dubious maker. The maker's mark was also the primary identifier for certain coins the Dutch exported to the Baltic, as the general-masters learned in 1763. For a number of years, money users in Poland had already been refusing gold ducats, 'coined in West-Friesland, marked with a chicken or a rooster; and when the master of the mint of that province changed the mark into a little boat or barge, the Poles were not dissuaded from the prejudice'. The rooster, of course, was the mark of Teunis Kist, whose medal in celebration of his spotless audit in 1743 was described above. In their report, the general-masters consulted their archive, and upon perusal of the various inspection reports, they could reassure the States-General that 'there has never been any defect with his ducats, either in their weight nor in their alloy.' The Polish rumours, they wrote, were thus 'ungrounded and born from a spirit of jealousy'.[66]

Singling out specific coins such as the demonetized rixdollar or the doubtful ducat from the motley mix that washed through people's money chests needed the discerning eye of a connoisseur that today is only found among numismatists. This last point hints at how early modern coins could break through the cycle of birth and rebirth: demonetization as prized collectibles. This process seems to be visible in the household of Henrietta Dijlli and Arnoldus Monhemius, a Reformed preacher in the rural east of the Netherlands. This was not the house of an Amsterdam merchant. Monhemius lived removed from the hustle and bustle of the maritime provinces in a remote pocket that the Dutch call the Achterhoek, or 'back corner' of their country. But the inventory drawn up upon Henrietta's death in 1733 reveals that coins were everywhere, and that there was a startling diversity of coins, too.[67] The way they were stored suggests that they were in various states of demonetization. Some of these coins were more clearly money, especially those in the 'ordinary' money chest, where the author of the inventory named Stumph came upon substantial amounts of small cash denominated in stivers and minted in the Dutch Republic, and similar amounts of silver and copper money denominated in Cleves *Reichstaler* and minted in the neighbouring German principalities of Münster and Cleves. (He also found an old medal showing 'the pope, cardinals and Mons. Devil', perhaps kept there for good luck.) The '20 old rixdollars that had been presented to the children on some New Year's Days' already have a different flavour: they could be used as money but were singled out as special from the common circulation of mutually replaceable coins. Also infused with affect was the 'old rixdollar in a small box that had a heart on one side', kept along the New-Year's gift in a small chest. Two five-stiver-pieces and the *groschen* did not have such qualifying descriptions, but their location is conspicuously intimate: they were tucked away in the chest of the late mother of the home, and shared their 'square wooden box, clad in silver and topped with a mirror' with an engraved ring, clasps for clothing and shoes, and 'some old, broken trinkets'.

Nosing around in Arnoldus and Henrietta's house suggests a different way of thinking about money-users' involvement with monetary diversity. Coins were tucked away in drawers and chests, kept with the linen, in small boxes, as souvenirs. These were remnants of a doux commerce of a different kind, and almost fragrant with personal affection. Objects that would otherwise be legal tender dropped out of circulation, and joined another class of objects: personal, individual, perhaps even unique.[68] But how clear, really, was the boundary between a cold space of monetary exchange and a warm sphere of coin-shaped collectibles? Did not everyone on Dutch marketplaces collect different kinds of coins in their purses, handle them often, and learn what was special about them? Did not everybody have to be able to judge quality work? In other words, was not every user of this intriguingly diverse money a bit of a connoisseur-collector – 'Liebhaber'[69] as Rohr described them, or 'liefhebbers', as they would be called in Dutch?[70]

## Nothing to know about money

Collecting coins was a popular pastime among eighteenth-century citizens, though they did not usually collect domestic coins.[71] This changed in the nineteenth century, when it became clearer that the new Kingdom of the Netherlands would finally do away with the motley mix of Republican and Batavian specie that they had inherited from the past, and whose physical state deteriorated daily under the onslaught of clippers.[72] Agnites Vrolik, the chief controller of the reform, remembered with horror the shameful state of Dutch currency in the 1830s: 'Everybody hurried to get rid of the disfigured pieces that he had been forced to accept. [...] [E]mbarrassed in front of foreigners, one looked at the misshapen and maimed piece that represented the once highly esteemed Dutch guilder.'[73]

The reminting began in 1843, reached a peak in 1848 and was completed by 1851. In a first step, the Royal Mint in Utrecht – since 1806 the only mint in the Northern Provinces[74] – was substantially expanded to prepare it for continuous melting and minting for years on end. The new coins were produced with greater technical precision than ever before, as the Royal Mint in Utrecht had been equipped for the task with state-of-the-art machinery.[75] In addition, 'a number of persons, seated around a table, each of them with an accurate balance in front of them and a file in their hand' controlled the punched-out disks before they were stamped, 'piece by piece filing away from each disk exactly as much as they were too heavy on the balance'. Unlike the Republican mint masters who had been given some leeway, the Royal Mint would not allow a deviation greater than the fivehundreth part from the statutory weight.[76] The new machines and their helpers calmly and unremittingly shaped fresh coins from old ones, in unimaginable numbers and unprecedented precision. If coins had a lifecycle, Republican coins perished en masse during the 1840s.

This made it more urgent to preserve some of them as reminders of a glorious past. The recoinage meant above all things that the Dutch had to part from the 'own private coin museum' that everyone was carrying around in their purse.[77] One direct link to the Republican past was being severed, moving from everyday experience to the cabinets of coins collections. In early 1849, when the overhaul was drawing to a close, newspapers called 'lovers and collectors of coins' to attend the 'the most important auction' of their day to save a monument of Dutch national history from too great a dispersion.[78] The 4,782 coins and medals on display in an auction house in the Keizersgracht had been gathered by the late Pieter Verkade of Leiden. Together, they chronicled an 'important part of the history of the fatherland' when one axis of world trade had run through the wetlands of Holland until eventually it tilted further to the English Southwest.[79]

The increasingly cold touch of the high-tech machines at the Royal mint, and the increasingly warm touch of numismatists were part of a larger shift away from the monetary regime that based value in amounts of precious metals and towards the regime that makes the notes in wallets desirable to strangers despite their material worthlessness. There was an unprecedented concentration of scrutiny in one place, the Royal Mint in Utrecht. The high precision of the new production methods reduced the space between face value and intrinsic value, limiting both the anxiety and the opportunity that it afforded. This allowed the materiality of the coins to 'flicker'[80] out of view, and to become more clearly a symbol than an embodiment of value – an important step, I believe, on the road to fiat money.[81] Finally, monetary literacy was transformed into the arcane, specialist knowledge that only coin enthusiasts would have. Ordinary users could relax their eyes and blissfully unlearn monetary skills that had been so important in the centuries before.

Georg Simmel, making sense of the new monetary order around 1900, in which governments in so-called civilized countries increasingly dispensed with anchoring the value of money in precious metal, described the vanishing point of this development. In its ideal form, he wrote, money is an 'absolute means' that does not have any distinguishable quality other than being fungible, or tradable into something else.[82] Really-existing 'monetary media' – the material form in which people handle money – can be placed on a spectrum of fungibility, but the stuff that is most clearly money does not seem to have any material properties at all.[83] Dollars on the screens of traders, perhaps the most evocative symbol of the modern economy, appear uniform and placeless, as trading floors go online and offline, following the sun around the globe.[84] Prices may cause a rollercoaster of emotion on the trading floor, but the medium used to express prices has ended up being a rather drab thing. We know it 'better, than any other thing; because there is absolutely nothing to know about it, it cannot conceal anything from us.' It cannot do what even 'the most miserable thing can do: harbour surprises, or disappointment.'[85]

## Notes

1  E. Welch, "Making Money," 80.
2  "Mache dir allerhand / so wohl currente, als auch rare Müntzen bekandt. Denn es ist solche Erkäntniß dir nicht allein im gemeinen Leben höchst nothwendig / sondern du kanst auch auch bißweilen einen grossen Vortheil haben / wenn du von Leuten / die den Valorem einer gewissen raren Müntze nicht wissen, solche Geld-Sorten ein-wechselt / und sie hernach bey den Kennern und Liebhabern wieder unterbringest." J. B. von Rohr, *Einleitung zu der Klugheit zu Leben*, 186.
3  A. O. Hirschman, *The Passions and the Interests*.
4  S. Schaffer, "Ceremonies of Measurement."
5  H. J. Cook, *Assessing the Truth*.
6  The Rijksmuseum attributes the painting to Romeyn de Hooghe. Compare P. J. J. van Thiel et al., *All the Paintings of the Rijksmuseum*, 289; and the inventory card made by Remmet van Luttervelt, kindly shared with me by Caroline Wittop Koning and Lieke van Deinsen. W. H. Wilson, "The Art of Romeyn de Hooghe," 299, follows Hofstede De Groot, "Kritische opmerkingen," 115, who rejects the painting as too dissimilar to

the paintings in the townhall of Enkhuizen whose authorship is confirmed by archival sources. M. van Eikeman Hommes and P. Bakker, "Hoogachtbaarheid en ontzaglijke grootheid," 222–43, discuss De Hooghe's painterly work in general but do not mention *Allegory of Coinage*. Van Lutterveld notes the provenance from the Royal Mint in Utrecht in 1884, to where the painting was returned on loan in 1904.

7  The idea of a coin's life is taken from A. Appadurai, *Social Life*.

8  Compare the images in S. Lauffer, "Bergmännische Kunst," 37–68; and Theodor de Bry's well-known engraving of miners in Potosí, reproduced, for example, in Sievernich, *America de Bry*, 286.

9  Exemplary for central European mining: Bartels, *Vom frühneuzeitlichen Montangewerbe zur Bergbauindustrie*. For mining in Spanish America: Bakewell, *Silver Mining and Society in Colonial Mexico*, and by the same author *Miners of the Red Mountain*.

10  A prominent version of the theme can be found on the tympanum of the western facade of the Amsterdam city hall, executed by Artus Quellinus, which shows the four continents offering treasures to an allegory of Amsterdam. The group representing America comprises three scantily clad miners and a man lugging an amphora.

11  J. G. van Dillen, "Amsterdam," 196. Attman, *American Bullion*, 30, estimates the import of silver at 7–8 million rixdollars, which contain 25.69155 g of silver per unit (H. E. van Gelder, *De Nederlandse Munten*, 246). See also Dehing, *Geld in Amsterdam*, 242–43.

12  '[…] silvere barros, barratones, lingotten oft staven van goudt en silver, item schotels, teljoren, lampetten ende alle wercken van silver en goudt, alle soorten van Spaensche realen oft matten, cardecus testoenen en francken, alle soorten van Engels gelt, ofte wat billioenen speciën het zoude mogen wesen […]' J. G. van Dillen, *Bronnen*, no. 127, before 25 March 1650, 103.

13  "Inkomende van de Beurssluis zyde, soo vind men voor eerst op de linkerhand tusschen en omtrent de Pilaaren N°.2. en 3: De *Hoogduitsche Jooden*, handelende en wisselende in alderhande goud en silver gemunt en ongemunt." J. Le Moine L'Espine and I. Le Long, *Koophandel*, 9. For a floor plan, see M. van Nieuwkerk, *Bank of Amsterdam*, 79.

14  "Dat mede gene Joden nogte anderen sig zullen verstouten dagelijks aen de Beurs of op eenige andere marktplaats te staen, ook aen eenige huysen om te loopen om op te soeken of in te wisselen of te verwisselen eenige specië," April 6, 1684. J. G. van Dillen, *Bronnen*, 228. Some of the trading locales around the Bourse building are described in J. Le Moine L'Espine and I. Le Long, *Koophandel*, 13–14.

15  For the material economy of gold and silver, see, for example, J. G. van Dillen, *Bronnen*, nos. 281, 282, and 284, November 29, 1683–April 8, 1684, 216–27. For the Amsterdam silver market in relationship to the mints, see M. S. Polak, *Historiografie*, 190–240.

16  'Geld is gemunt Metaal, door publycque Autoriteyt op een vaste voet van swaarte en fijnte geslagen, en op valeur en prijs gestelt.' Phoonsen, *Wissel-styl*, 1.

17  Compare this contemporary description: 'Boven op de Beurs syn verscheide Kraamen, een Laakenhal, en veel Tapyten te koop.' J. Le Moine L'Espine and I. Le Long, *Koophandel*, 13.

18  For a detailed general discussion, J. Williams, "Mathematics, Part I" and "Mathematics, Part II." For the Dutch Republic, see A. Scheffers, *Om de kwaliteit van het geld*, vol. 2, 110–13.

19  See J. De Vries, "Connecting Europe and Asia," especially the figure on 76; D. O. Flynn and A. Giráldez, "Born with a 'Silver Spoon'"; and D. O. Flynn "Cycles of Silver".

20  H. E. van Gelder, *De Nederlandse Munten*, 122.

21  J. de Vries and A. van der Woude, *The First Modern Economy*, ch. 8.

22  'dat Sander Ambrosius mede Winckelier een seekere goudt een Rijxdaelder presenteernde [t]Wisselen welcke Rijxdaelder de Joodt zeyde niet goet te zijn waerop Sander Ambrosius tegen Joodt' zeyde dat die goet was, & dat hij die vrij door kappen soude, maer wilde de Joodt dat niet doen, tot dat ten laetsten de Joodt door het hart

aenstaen van Ambrosius versaeten genoeg saem gedwongen de Rijxd. door kapen ditzij het sodan aen een silversmit latende sien bevonden wiert niet goet te zijn, waerop Sander Ambrosius soe quaet wierdt dat hij [...] sonder Reden daertoe te hebben de producent buijten de deur eijst gelijck hij buijten het huis gegaen zijnde daedlijck zijn Mes uijttrock & de producent daermede grieven wilde.' Stadsarchief Amsterdam, 5075, no. 4544, p. 391, September 7, 1683.

23 W. van Laer, *Weg-wyzer*, 9.

24 F. C. Spooner, "On the Road to Industrial Precision," 15.

25 'Totdat eyndelyk, in't midden der zeventiende eeuwe, het schroeven van't geld zynde uytgevonden, de muntkonst daardoor tot de hoogste volmaaktheyd is opgevyzeld.' G. van Loon, *Beschryving*, 336.

26 'In alle welcke als litmaeten den staet vander Munte / verspreyt ende uytgedeelt is.' Anonymous, *Beeldenaer*, fol. A ii recto. This ordinance was foundational for the currency system of the Republic. Most members of the 'coinage state' were given detailed instructions and required to swear an oath. See A. Scheffers, *Om de kwaliteit van het geld*, vol. 2, *passim*. For a detailed analysis of how standards were kept (or not) among gold- and silversmiths, see Schoen, *Tussen hamer en aambeeld*.

27 Nationaal Archief (henceforth NL-HaNA), The Hague, 3.20.15 and 1.01.44, nos. 56–61.

28 NL-HaNA 3.20.15, no. 14, 8.

29 NL-HaNA 1.01.44, no. 56.

30 NL-HaNA 3.20.15, no. 24. For the role of recipes for research in the household, see Leong, "Collecting Knowledge for the Family."

31 NL-HaNA 1.01.44, no. 56, undated note 'Memorie van t'geene noodig is, dat een goet assaijeur Generael vande munten dient te weten.'

32 Ibid.

33 NL-HaNA, 1.01.44, no. 56, undated note 'Vergelijking van't oud Geld, 't een tegen het ander'; A. Matthaeus, *Fundationes*. On the correspondence between Witsen and Cuper, see M. Peters, "Nicolaes Witsen and Gijsbert Cuper" and more recently, H. J. Cook, *Assessing the Truth*. There is another clue that Bruijnesteijn-Emants were in contact with numismatic circles, as their recipe book contains a method of making impressions of medals.

34 It can still be accessed there: *Ordonnanties, Keuren,... van verschillende Noord-Nederlandsche steden en gewesten betreffende burgerlijke zaken*, Leiden UB. Other sources of the *Comparison* are A. Matthaeus, *De nobilitate* and *Veteris Aevi Analecta*, and J. van Heemskerk, *Batavische Arcadia*, perhaps in the 4th edition.

35 NL-HaNA 1.01.44, no. 56, undated note "Een oude valuatie van gelde gevonden in den sterffhuijsen van[de] ouden Wilhelm van Tuijl tot Bulckensteijn en[de] Gijsbert Pieck."

36 The balance sheet for 1755 is reproduced in A. Scheffers, "Ego-documenten," 160.

37 I. H. van Eeghen, "Het Grill's Hofje," and L. M. Principe, "Goldsmiths and Chymists."

38 '[...] Ick ben UEd. geobligeert voor de Beleefthede aen mij betoont a costi sijnde, hope gelegentheijt te vinde om UEd. Eenige dienst te connen doen, ick heb aen UEd. van daegh gesonden Een Baar Zilver, en versoecke Ued. van de selve geliefst Een Essaij te maecken, terwijl hier verschil in de selve is en Sr. Jan Sieuwerts Out die de selve geassajeert heeft op 5 pen. 4 gr. daer ick, nogh andere, nogh Op de Munt van dort daer de selve al geweest is, die nogh op geen 5 pen. maer schaers gevonden hebben, ick voor mij heb hem gevonden op 4 pen. 23 3/4 gr. sigh niet daer in wil laeten vinden maer staende houdt datse soo veel en nogh meerder hout, dies Ben ick genootsaeckt mij aen UEd. te addresseren, versoeckende denselven te Examineren en ons desisie daer in te geven [...].' NL-HaNA, 1.01.44, no. 56, Anthoni Grill to Marcellus Bruijnesteijn, Amsterdam April 23, 1698.

39 This was normal and the reason why 'good' assayers have long been repeating even their own tests: "Note also that whenever the money is tested by assay in order that the judgment of the test may be more certain, at least three impeccable assays should be made, lest through overheating or otherwise the silver should have spurted out from

one of the assays and lest from draughts or a failure of the fire, the assay should have cooled, or by the fall of coals or if any other way the assay or silver should have been diminished." Note on Assaying in the Red Book of the Exchequer, fol. 264, c. 1300. Edited and translated in C. Johnson, *De Moneta*, 81.

40 'Is van Amsteldam gekomen Anthoni Grijll en heeft mij geseijt als dat het tot Amsteldam ginck soo slecht met assaieurs als oijt,' NL-HaNA, 1.01.44, no. 56, note by Marcellus Bruijnesteijn, April 18, 1698.

41 J. G. van Dillen, *Bronnen*, 7. Dehing, *Geld in Amsterdam*.

42 J. Steuart, *Inquiry*, 293.

43 Ibid. 307.

44 "Nieuwe instructie voor de beide essaijeurs der Wisselbank", August 1, 1673, edited in J. G. van Dillen, *Bronnen*, 173–4. The other assayer, Grill's predecessor was Jan Grell (no relation). The assaying laboratory was located on the ground floor of the new city hall, next to the hall of the tellers. See the reproduction of a floor plan in M. van Nieuwkerk, *Bank of Amsterdam*, 125.

45 S. P. Haak, "Rijksmunten."

46 'Alsoo ons inde wisselbancq voorcomen. Leeuwendaelders inde provincie van Gelderland in dese jare 1697 geslagen, de welcke ons als wat beschaart synde int gehalte voorcomen, soo is myn versoeck of UEd de goedheyt belieft te hebben van van dese vier nevensgaande leeuwendaalders een assay te maken, op dat wij ons daar na souden kunnen reguleeren, ons der selver gehalte over te schryven, waar mede UEd. sult verobligeeren.' NL-HaNA, 1.01.44, no. 56, Adriaan Backer to Marcellus Bruijnesteijn, Amsterdam, May 9, 1697.

47 Ibid., Adriaan Backer to Marcellus Bruijnesteijn, Amsterdam, August 23, 1697.

48 NL-HaNA 1.01.44, no. 56, undated note "Memorie van t'geene noodig is, dat een goet assajeur Generael vande munten dient te weten."

49 Ibid., Marcellus Bruijnesteijn to Adriaan Backer, April 21, 1697 (draft).

50 S. Schaffer, "Ceremonies of Measurement."

51 Compare C. E. Challis, *New History*; H. Witthöft, 'Münzordnungen', and M. S. Polak, *Historiografie*.

52 S. Schaffer, "Ceremonies of Measurement," 338.

53 H. J. Cook, *Assessing the Truth*, 36.

54 NL-HaNA 1.01.44, 56. Gerhard Harn was later tried for producing sub-standard coins, like Lambertus de Ridder who was discussed above. S. P. Haak, "Rijksmunten."

55 Deventer, Kampen and Zwolle had defended their privileges as mints of the Holy Roman Empire when the Republic was founded, and had reasserted them in the years and decades before this incident. See S. P. Haak, "Rijksmunten."

56 G. van Harn, *Consideratien*.

57 'Dogh de passien van de Generaelmrs laten niet ander toe als sigh ten eenemael blin-delingx buijten sloth van reden over te geven aen particuliere driften off misschien daerdoor haer oogmerk mogten bereijken, en door inboeseming van verkeerde ge-dagten, den Muntmr in de exercitie van de Munt over hoop mogten werpen.' G. van Harn, *Aen de Edele*, 8. Van Harn taps into the venerable trope of passions overpowering reason here, which is discussed by James, *Passion*.

58 '[…] dat de Generael Meesters Haere plight niet weten, en haere Instructie te buyten gaen, mits dat sy twee Keerls tot visitatie deser Munte hebben herwaerts gesonden […] daer deselve volgens Haer instructie verplight syn, in Persoon selfs de Munte te gaen visiteren, waer voor deselve yder oock en jaerlycx Tracatament van ses hondert guldens tot Reysgelt genieten.' G. van Harn, *Aen de Edele*, 3. The "two lads" Matthys Dop and Hendrik Derkingh made an incriminating deposition before the magistrate, who dis-tanced themselves from Harn in a pamphlet of their own: Moorreés et al., *Kort en waerachtich*, appendix K.

59 G. van Harn, *Consideratien*, 12.

60 Anonymous, Oprechte Haerlemse. no. 21, May 26, 1705.

61 A. Kuroda, "What is Complementarity," 7.
62 H. E. van Gelder, "Nederlandse Manualen." A fraction of that diversity can be experienced numismatic collections. See British Museum Collections Online (http://www.britishmuseum.org/research/collection_online, last visited on January 4, 2018) or the online catalogue of the Münzkabinett Bode-Museum (http://www.smb-digital.de/), last visited on January 4, 2018).
63 M. S. Polak, *Historiografie*, vol. 2, 70.
64 S. P. Haak, "Rijksmunten," 407. This makes them similar to hallmarked products of artisans and manufactories. See B. de Munck and D. Lyna, *Concepts of Value*.
65 K. Soudijn, *Naar het u lijkt*, 6.
66 J. G. van Dillen, *Bronnen*, 413–14. They do not tell us whose jealousy. Perhaps of other masters of the mint?
67 Erfgoedcentrum Achterhoek en Liemers, Doetinchem, 3029, no. 118, May 1, 1733.
68 V. A. Zelizer, *Social Meaning*.
69 J. B. Rohr, *Klugheit*, see introduction above.
70 See Claudia Swan's chapter in this volume.
71 P. Beliën, "Waroom verzamelde."
72 C. de Graaf, "Muntmeesters"; M. van der Beek, *Muntslag*, 21–22.
73 A. Vrolik, *Verslag*, 8. For a recent discussion of the emotional involvement of national populations with their money, see E. Helleiner, "Macro-Social."
74 P. Dehing and M. 't Hart, "Linking the Fortunes," 41.
75 A. Vrolik, *Verslag*, table 5 in the appendix. For a detailed account of the currency overhaul and a description of the apparatus, see M. van der Beek, *Muntslag*.
76 Anonymous, "Hoe het nieuwe Geld gemaakt wordt."
77 Ibid.
78 Anonymous, "Binnenland."
79 Anonymous, "Binnenland." See also H. Brugmans, "Verkade."
80 B. Jardine, "State."
81 T. J. Sargent and F. R. Velde, *Big Problem*.
82 G. Simmel, *Philosophie*, ch. 2.
83 For an account of modern monetary diversity, V. A. Zelizer, *Social Meaning*. For the spectrum of fungibility, see her "Fine tuning." For the neo-Simmelian distinction between monetary media and perfect money, see N. Dodd, "Simmel's Perfect Money" and by the same author "Reinventing."
84 K. Knorr Cetina, "How Are Global Markets Global?"
85 G. Simmel, *Philosophie*, 362.

# Bibliography

*Manuscript sources*

Amsterdam, Stadsarchief, 5075 'Archief van de Notarissen ter Standplaats Amsterdam', no. 4544 Johannes Backer, p. 391, September 7, 1683.
Nationaal Archief (NL-HaNA), The Hague, 3.20.15 'Familiearchief Emants', no. 14, 1.01.44 'Generaliteitsmuntkamer', nos. 56–61.
Erfgoedcentrum Achterhoek en Liemers, Doetinchem, 3029 'Rechterlijk Archief van de Heerlijkheid Lichtenvoorde, 1614–1811,' no. 118 'Stukken betreffende de tuteele, 1729–39,' May 1, 1733.

*Print*

Anonymous, *Beeldenaer, ofte Figuer-boeck*. The Hague: Hillebrandt Iacobsz., 1606.

Anonymous, 'Binnenland.' *Nieuwe Amsterdamsche Courant/Algemeen Handelsblad*, The Hague: Hillebrandt Iacobsz., no. 5359, January 29, 1849.

Anonymous, *Oprechte Haerlemse Dingsdaegse Courant*. no. 21, May 26, 1705.

Anonymous, "Hoe het nieuwe Geld gemaakt wordt." *Provinciale Overijsselsche en Zwolsche Courant*, March 12, 1847.

Appadurai, Arjun, ed. *The Social Life of Things: Commodities in Cultural Perspective*. Cambridge: Cambridge University Press, 1986.

Attman, Artur. *American Bullion in the European World Trade, 1600–1800*. Göteborg: Kungl: Vetenskaps- och Vitterhets-Samhället, 1986.

Bakewell, Peter. *Miners of the Red Mountain: Indian Labor in Potosí, 1545–1650*. Albuquerque: University of New Mexico Press, 1984.

Bakewell, Peter. *Silver Mining and Society in Colonial Mexico: Zacatecas, 1546–1700*. Cambridge: Cambridge University Press, 1971.

Bartels, Christoph. *Vom frühneuzeitlichen Montangewerbe zur Bergbauindustrie: Erzbergbau im Oberharz, 1635–1866*. Bochum: Deutsches Bergbau-Museum, 1992.

Beek, Marcel van der. *De muntslag ten tijde van Koning Willem II: Ontwerp en productie van Nederlandse munten 1839–1849*. Utrecht: Het Nederlands Muntmuseum Utrecht, 1999.

Beliën, Paul. "Waroom verzamelde Pieter Teyler penningen en munten: De numismatische collectie." In *De idealen van Pieter Teyler: Een erfenis uit de Verlichting*, edited by Bert Sliggers, and Jaap Vogel et al., 92–113. Haarlem: Gottmer, 2006.

Brugmans, Hajo. "Verkade (Pieter)." In *Nieuw Nederlandsch Biografisch Woordenboek*, edited by P.C. Molhuysen, and P.J. Blok, Vol. 4. Leiden: Sijthoff, 1918.

Challis, C. E., ed. *A New History of the Royal Mint*. Cambridge: Cambridge University Press, 1992.

Cook, Harold J. *Assessing the Truth: Correspondence and Information at the End of the Golden Age*. Leiden: Primavera Pers, 2013.

Dehing, Pit. *Geld in Amsterdam: Wisselbank en wisselkoersen, 1650–1725*. Amsterdam: Verloren, 2012.

Dehing, Pit, and Marjolein 't Hart. "Linking the Fortunes: Currency and Banking, 1550–1800." In *A Financial History of the Netherlands*, edited by Jan Luiten van Zanden, Joost Jonker, and Marjolein 't Hart, 37–63. Cambridge: Cambridge University Press, 2010.

Eeghen, Isabella Henriëtte van. "Amsterdam, marché mondial des métaux précieux au XVIIe et au XVIIIe siècle." *Revue Historique* 152, no. 2 (1926): 194–201.

Dillen, Johannes Gerard van. *Bronnen tot de Geschiedenis der Wisselbanken (Amsterdam, Middelburg, Delft, Rotterdam)*. Vol. 1. The Hague: Nijhoff, 1925.

Dodd, Nigel. "Reinventing Monies in Europe." *Economy and Society* 34, no. 4 (2005): 558–83.

Dodd, Nigel. "Simmel's Perfect Money: Fiction, Socialism and Utopia in The Philosophy of Money." *Theory, Culture & Society* 29, no. 7–8 (2012): 146–76.

Eeghen, I. H. van. "Het Grill's Hofje." *Jaarboek van Het Genootschap Amstelodamum* 62 (1970): 49–86.

Eikeman Hommes, Margriet van, and Piet Bakker. "Hoogachtbaarheid en ontzaglijke grootheid: De burgemeesterskamer van het stadhuis van Enkhuizen." In *Romeyn de Hooghe: De verbeelding van de late Gouden Eeuw*, edited by Henk van Grabowsky Nierop, Janssen Ellen, Leeflang Anouk, Huigen, and Garrelt Verboeven, 222–43. Zwolle: Waanders, 2008.

Flynn, Dennis O., and Arturo Giráldez. "Born with a 'Silver Spoon': The Origin of World Trade in 1571." *Journal of World History* 6, no. 2 (1995): 201–21.

Flynn, Dennis O. "Cycles of Silver: Global Economic Unity through the Mid-Eighteenth Century." *Journal of World History* 13, no. 2 (2002): 391–427.

Gelder, H. Enno van. "De Nederlandse manualen 1586–1630." *Jaarboek voor Munt- en Penningkunde* 65 (1978): 39–79.

Gelder, Herman Arend Enno van. *De Nederlandse munten: Het complete overzicht tot en met de komst van de euro*. 8th ed. Utrecht: Het Spectrum, 2002.

Graaf, Cor de. "Muntmeesters en muntschenners, vervalsers en wisselaars: Muntgewichten en muntweegapparatuur in de Nederlanden." In *Gewogen of bedrogen: Het wegen van geld in de Nederlanden*, 57–99. Leiden: Rijksmuseum Het Koninklijk Penningkabinet, 1994.

Haak, Sikko Popta. "De rijksmunten in Gelderland tot het begin der 18e eeuw." *Bijdragen en mededelingen Gelre* 15 (1912): 361–409.

Harn, Gerhard van. *Aen de Edele en Achtb. Heeren van de Magistraet der Stadt Nymegen*. (Knuttel 15239). S.l.: S.n., 1704.

Harn, Gerhard van. *Consideratien van den munt-meester Gerhard van Harn: Over het Concept-Placaet tot het vorder Billioneeren van den Nymeegsen Daelder*. (Knuttel 15251). S.l.: S.n., 1704.

Helleiner, Eric. "The Macro-Social Meaning of Money: From Territorial Currencies to Global Money." In *Money Talks: Explaining How Money Really Works*, edited by Nina Bandelj, Frederick F. Wherry, and Viviana A. Zelizer, 145–58. Princeton: Princeton University Press, 2017.

Heemskerk, Johan van. *Batavische Arcadia*, 4th edition. Amsterdam: Johannes van Ravesteyn, 1663.

Hirschman, Albert O. *The Passions and the Interests: Political Arguments for Capitalism Before Its Triumph*. Princeton: Princeton University Press, 1997.

Hofstede De Groot, Cornelis. "Kritische opmerkingen omtrent oud-hollandsche schilderijen in onze musea." *Oud Holland* 22, no. 1 (1904): 111–120.

James, Susan. *Passion and Action: The Emotions in Seventeenth-Century Philosophy*. Oxford: Clarendon Press, 2001.

Jardine, Boris. "State of the Field: Paper Tools." *Studies in History and Philosophy of Science Part A* 64, no. Supplement C (2017): 53–63.

Johnson, Charles, ed. *The De Moneta of Nicholas Oresme and English Mint Documents*. Auburn: Ludwig von Mises Institute, 2009.

Knorr Cetina, Karin. "How Are Global Markets Global? The Architecture of a Flow World." In *The Sociology of Financial Markets*, edited by Karin Knorr Cetina, and Alex Preda, 38–61. Oxford: Oxford University Press, 2005.

Kuroda, Akinobu. "What Is the Complementarity among Monies? An Introductory Note." *Financial History Review* 15, no. 1 (2008): 7–15.

Laer, Willem van. *Weg-wyzer voor aankoomende goud en zilversmeeden*. Amsterdam: Fredrik Helm, 1721.

Lauffer, Siegfried. "Bergmännische Kunst in der antiken Welt." In *Der Bergbau in der Kunst* edited by Heinrich Winkelmann, 37–68. Essen: Glückauf, 1958.

Le Moine L'Espine, Jacques, and Isaac Le Long. *Den Koophandel van Amsterdam*. Amsterdam: Andries van Damme en Joannes Ratelband, 1714.

Leong, Elaine. "Collecting Knowledge for the Family: Recipes, Gender and Practical Knowledge in the Early Modern English Household." *Centaurus* 55, no. 2 (2013): 81–103.

Loon, Gerard van. *Beschryving der Nederlandsche historipenningen, of beknopt verhaal van 't gene sedert de overdracht der heerschappye van keyzer Karel den vyfden op koning Philips zynen zoon, tot het sluyten van den Uytrechtschen vreede in de zeventien Nederlandsche gewesten, is voorgevallen*, edited by C. van Lom, I. Vaillant, P. Gosse, R. Albertsen, and P. de Hondt. The Hague, 1723.

Matthaeus, Antonius. *De nobilitate, de advocatis ecclesiae, de comitatu Hollandiae et diocesi Ultraiectina.* Amsterdam: Apud Janssonio-Waesbergios, & Felicem Lopez, 1686.

Matthaeus, Antonius. *Fundationes et fata ecclesiarum: quae et ultrajecti, et in ejusdem suburbiis, et passim alibi in dioecesi.* Leiden: Vidua S. Schouten, 1703.

Matthaeus, Antonius. *Veteris Aevi Analecta Seu Vetera aliquot Monumenta, Quae hactenus nondum visa.* Leiden: Haaring 1698.

Moorreés, Hendrik, Wilh, Knippinck, W. v. Loon, and Peter Jossolet. *Kort en waerachtich verhael van't geene eenige tijt herwaerts is voorgevallen, ontrent het gaen der rycks-munte binnen de stad van Nymegen.* (Knuttel 15243). S.l.: S.n., 1704.

Munck, Bert de, and Dries Lyna, eds. *Concepts of Value in European Material Culture, 1500–1900.* Farnham: Ashgate, 2015.

Nieuwkerk, Marius van, ed. *The Bank of Amsterdam: On the Origins of Central Banking.* Amsterdam: Sonsbeek, 2009.

Peters, Marion. "Nicolaes Witsen and Gijsbert Cuper: Two Seventeenth-Century Dutch Burgomasters and Their Gordian Knot." *Lias: Sources and Documents Relating to the Early History of Ideas* 16, no. 1 (1989): 111–51.

Phoonsen, Johannes. *Wissel-Styl Tot Amsterdam.* Amsterdam: Daniel van den Dalen, 1688.

Polak, Menno Sander. *Historiografie en economie van de 'muntchaos': De muntproductie van de Republiek (1606–1795).* Amsterdam: NEHA, 1998.

Principe, Lawrence M. "Goldsmiths and Chymists: The Activity of Artisans within Alchemical Circles." In *Laboratories of Art: Alchemy and Art Technology from Antiquity to the 18th Century,* edited by Sven Dupré, 157–80. Cham: Springer, 2014.

Rohr, Julius Bernhard von. *Einleitung zu der Klugheit zu leben, Oder Anweisung, wie ein Mensch zu Beförderung seiner zeitlichen Glückseligkeit seine Actiones vernünftig anstellen soll.* Leipzig: Johann Christian Martini, 1715.

Sargent, Thomas J., and François R. Velde *The Big Problem of Small Change.* Princeton: Princeton University Press, 2002.

Schaffer, Simon. "Ceremonies of Measurement: Rethinking the World History of Science." *Annales. Histoire, Sciences Sociales: English Edition* 70, no. 2 (2015): 335–60.

Scheffers, Albert. "Enkele ego-documenten met numismatische inhoud." *De Beeldenaar* 18, no. 4 (1998): 156–69.

Scheffers, Albert. *Om de kwaliteit van het geld: Het toezicht op de muntproductie in de Republiek en de voorziening van kleingeld in Holland en West-Friesland in de achttiende eeuw.* 2 vols. Voorburg: Clinkaert, 2013.

Schoen, Peter. *Tussen hamer en aambeeld. Edelsmeden in Friesland tijdens de Gouden Eeuw.* Hilversum: Verloren, 2016.

Sievernich, Gereon, ed. *America de Bry 1590–1634: Amerika oder die Neue Welt. Die 'Entdeckung' eines Kontinents in 346 Kupferstichen.* Berlin: Casablanca, 1990.

Simmel, Georg. *Philosophie des Geldes.* Munich: Duncker & Humblot, 1907.

Soudijn, Karel. *Naar het u lijkt: Munten, penningen en waarnemingspsychologie.* Utrecht: Geldmuseum, 2008.

Spooner, Frank C. "On the Road to Industrial Precision: The Case of Coinage in the Netherlands (1672-1791)." *Economisch- en Sociaal-Historisch Jaarboek* 43 (1980): 1–18.

Steuart, James Sir. *An Inquiry into the Principles of Political Oeconomy.* Vol. 2. London: A. Millar and T. Cadell, 1767.

Thiel, Pieter J.J. van, Cornelius Joannes de Bruyn Kops, and Arthur François Emile van Schendel. *All the Paintings of the Rijksmuseum in Amsterdam: A Completely Illustrated Catalogue*. Amsterdam: Rijksmuseum Gary Schwartz, 1976.

Vries, Jan de. "Connecting Europe and Asia: A Quantitative Analysis of the Cape-Route Trade, 1497–1795." In *Global Connections and Monetary History, 1470–1800*, edited by Dennis O. Flynn, Arturo Giráldez, and Richard von Glahn, 35–106. Aldershot: Ashgate, 2003.

Vries, Jan de, and Ad van der Woude. *The First Modern Economy: Success, Failure, and Perseverance of the Dutch Economy, 1500–1815*. Cambridge: Cambridge University Press, 1997.

Vrolik, Agnites. *Verslag van al het verrigte tot herstel van het Nederlandsche muntwezen van het jaar 1842 tot en met 1851*. Utrecht: Gieben & Dumont, 1853.

Welch, Evelyn. "Making Money: Pricing and Payments in Renaissance Italy." In *The Material Renaissance*, edited by Michelle O'Malley, and Evelyn Welch, 71–84. Manchester: Manchester University Press, 2007.

Williams, J. "Mathematics and the Alloying of Coinage 1202–1700: Part I." *Annals of Science* 52, no. 3 (1995): 213–34.

Williams, J. "Mathematics and the Alloying of Coinage 1202–1700: Part II." *Annals of Science* 52, no. 3 (1995): 235–263.

Wilson, William Harry. 'The Art of Romeyn de Hooghe: An Atlas of European Late Baroque Culture.' PhD thesis, Harvard University, 1974.

Witthöft, Harald. "Die Münzordnungen und das Grundgewicht im Deutschen Reich vom 16. Jahrhundert bis 1871/72." In *Geld und Währung vom 16. Jahrhundert bis zur Gegenwart*, edited by Eckart Schremmer, 45–68. Stuttgart: F. Steiner, 1993.

Zelizer, Viviana A. "Fine-Tuning the Zelizer View." *Economy and Society* 29, no. 3 (2000): 383–389.

Zelizer, Viviana A. *The Social Meaning of Money*. New York: Basic Books, 1994.

# 12

# THE AMSTERDAM STOCK EXCHANGE AS AFFECTIVE ECONOMY

*Inger Leemans*

In 1723, the Dutch broker Roeland van Leuve climbed the stairs of the Amsterdam Stock Exchange. He was writing a description of the city of Amsterdam, in the form of a long poem, and chose the bourse as the epicentre of the city, which made it pretty much the centre of the universe (Figure 12.1). Van Leuve knew the bourse intimately: he used to be a successful merchant in silk, velvet, and other luxury textiles. Unfortunately, over the years, he had become more reckless, investing his capital in shares and derivatives and losing most of it during the South Sea Bubble or *Windhandel* of 1720. The city of Amsterdam generously put him on the payroll as a broker, so he could continue to work on the bourse floor, albeit in a much humbler capacity.

For his eulogy on the city of Amsterdam, Van Leuve chose the perspective of a tourist, climbing up to the first floor of the bourse building, to look down on the exchange floor, marvelling at this 'beehive where the whole world gathers its treasures'. The metaphor of the beehive Van Leuve copied from the famous Dutch poet Joost van den Vondel, who described the exchange as the pounding heart of the international economy and as a beehive of cupidity:

> Cupidity fills up the ample galleries
> Around the square, that hive of bees,
> An excellent smell, won from the land.[1]

Van Leuve also sees the bourse as 'the axis of the country, around which everything revolves', and as the centre of world trade. This staple market also functioned as the post and news office of the mercantile world. No wonder, he says, that the bourse had become the envy of many rulers, who fell in love with this 'auricle of the heart of state'.[2] Van Leuve thus described the bourse in terms of knowledge and affects – a site dedicated to the exchange of goods and

**FIGURE 12.1** Frontispiece of Roeland van Leuve's, *Waerelds Koopslot of de Amsterdamse Beurs*, Engraving J. Folkema (1723). Courtesy of Stadsarchief Amsterdam, 010097005668

information, to industriousness, greed, and envy. The success of this 'Global Castle of Commerce' depended on the combination of firstly the freedom and tolerance typical for the Dutch Republic, secondly the wise rule of the Amsterdam regents, and last but not least: the desire for profit (*winzugt*): 'In hope of profit, each one Mercury obeys; / In lust for gold they sweat to give him honour; / And diligently serve his altar of commerce.'[3] Van Leuve's eulogy introduces us to the idea that the Amsterdam exchange not only was a site of trade and information, it could also be seen as an *affective economy*. In this chapter, I will outline this idea by discussing the Amsterdam exchange as a knowledge hub, and secondly by analyzing the exchange in terms of emotions and embodiment, to argue that affects played an important role in the organization of this marketplace.

## Knowledge economies and the history of emotions

Stock exchanges have a low status in the history of knowledge studies. Most textbooks on the history of knowledge and histories of knowledge societies have little interest in the economic aspects of knowledge cultures.[4] The study of knowledge economies developed as a separate branch, within the fields of economic history and sociology.[5] While studies of *knowledge economies* analyze knowledge markets, commoditization, intellectual property rights, and human capital, histories of *knowledge societies* tend to focus on the production, adaptation, and dissemination of knowledge through institutions and locations such as monasteries, libraries, schools, universities, and (royal) academies. Stock exchanges do not seem to have attracted particular interest in either of these research fields.[6] This is regrettable, since stock exchanges did play an important role in the marketing and distribution of knowledge. In this chapter, I will make a plea for studying stock exchanges in the context of the development of knowledge societies in the early modern period. I will argue that the Amsterdam bourse functioned as an important centre for the emerging Dutch knowledge economy.

This centre of knowledge and trade can be seen as an 'affective economy'. This concept is informed by behavioural economics and the history of emotion. Since the 1990s, various disciplines have taken a so-called 'affective turn'. Economists, historians, anthropologists, and so forth study the production, expression, and transmission of emotions and the determining role emotions and affects play in political, economic, social, cultural, and individual processes. Behavioural economics is a fairly new branch in economics, which seeks to move beyond the bias toward rationality of mainstream economics. It rethinks financial and economic processes from a psychological perspective, spurring interest in the 'animal spirits' that drive economic processes, researching how hope, fear, risk loving/aversion, or euphoria influence market participation.[7]

Historical research on the early modern period cannot simply project the concepts generated in behavioural economics back in time, as the modern conception of emotions as irrational impulses 'from the underbelly' does not correspond with the early modern notion of the passions as effects on the body, which could be triggered from both within or outside of the body.[8] While researching market-emotion negotiations we need to take bodily expressions and locations into account. Market behaviour is an affective practice, communicated through the body, and shaped by locations which can be seen as affective spaces.[9]

Although the fast-expanding research field of the history of emotions, so far, has taken little interest in markets and economics, it can bring in new perspectives in behavioural economy, for instance by analyzing market places as affective communities, formed by 'groups in which people adhere to the same norm of emotional expression and value – or devalue – the same or related emotions.'[10] Emotions in these market places are emotives: performative means of communication which help to transform situations.[11] Studies in the history and philosophy of emotions have also underlined that, in the early modern period, the passions were not seen as separate from rationality and morality, but as ethical and social factors. Emotions are not merely irrational impulses, but also instruments of appraisal, knowledge, and action: one learns to understand the world through emotions and sensory engagements. Passions may form the basis of informed actions.[12] The concept of 'affective economy' thus analyses emotion-market negotiations by considering the role of bodies, locations, performativity, ethics, and cognition.

## The Bourse as a knowledge hub

Since its foundation in 1611, the Amsterdam Bourse was the central location for international trade: a global marketplace, where goods from all over the world were exchanged. In *Handel in Amsterdam* (2001), Clé Lesger stressed the importance of information and information networks for the development of the market. What made Amsterdam so successful as a commercial centre in the 17th century, according to Lesger, was not so much the fact that the city was able to store goods from all over the world, but that it grew into 'a great staple of news.' The commercial expansion of Amsterdam can be explained by the amount and quality of the news provision in this city, and the fairly stable and frequent connections with other European locations. On the basis of this information network, the Amsterdam market was able to stabilize price fluctuation and regulate supply and demand.[13]

If we take a closer look at the bourse building we will see that information might be too narrow a term. The term knowledge might be more suitable. Although it is hard to make a clear distinction between concepts of information and knowledge – historians of knowledge usually state that information is 'raw' and knowledge is 'cooked'[14] – the term 'knowledge' seems more apt to stress the level of aggregation, and of the depth and diversity of the types of information produced, sold and exchanged at the bourse. This brings us to a second aspect: at the bourse, knowledge was commodified. It materialized in various commercial goods. A walk across the bourse floor and around the bourse building can help to clarify this.

The first type of knowledge we happen upon is the information exchanged by the merchants and brokers on the bourse floor: 'solid information was the life-blood of their daily management practices.'[15] Merchants and merchant houses functioned as information networks, connected across different areas. At the Amsterdam bourse, their information network was supported by advanced services. Under the arches of the exterior of the bourse, 34 houses were rented out, among other things to post offices, runners, and notaries. The Amsterdam city board installed a bourse commissaire to oversee the bourse floor, and to enforce regulations. For a few pennies, the post runners could hire the bourse commissaire to call out the expected departure times across the bourse floor, so that merchants could hand in their letters.[16] The bourse commissaire offered his services through a personal 'business card' (Figure 12.2).

A guild of over three hundred brokers was assigned to broker deals at the bourse. From 1613 onwards, they helped to compile the official price list, published weekly to keep merchants up to speed with the pricing of the hundreds of products on sale and the exchange rates. This list was distributed all over Europe. Conscription cost four guilders annually.[17] These commercial information services helped to ensure that information could be collected, compared, and evaluated. Still, merchants continued to rely on their private networks and their personal connections with the trading companies to acquire information and to make investment decisions.[18]

The bourse was embedded in a network of legal services. At the notary offices under the arches and surrounding the bourse, merchants could file contracts, register formal agreements, and get legal advice. The bourse was also the place where official announcements were made: civic charters were posted on the bourse walls and proclaimed on the bourse floor. Depictions of the bourse also show how the walls were used for all kinds of advertisements and announcements, of the sale of houses, auctions, or foreclosures.

What is more, the bourse was one of the major centres for the book market. A large variety of book shops found their home in and around the bourse. Between 1613 and 1700 more than 70 publishers and booksellers set up shop in the adjacent arches of the building, in the *Beursstraat*, *Beurssteeg*, and on the bourse lock (Figure 12.1). In the beginning of the century, booksellers came and went, but after a while they seem to have settled, even setting up family businesses, with widows and heirs taking over the shop. Especially in the second half of the century, the bourse seems to have developed into a *bibliopolis*, catering to the international public around the exchange.

What were the knowledge products these booksellers brought to the bourse public? Did the proximity to the exchange favour certain specializations? An exploration of the bourse publishers' stock shows a large variety of knowledge products, some of which directly linked to the location.[19] News is of course essential for market organization. The bourse housed Jan van Hilten, 'the city's

**TABLE 12.1** Booksellers and publishers around the Amsterdam exchange (beurs, beurs-straat, beurssluis, beurssteeg). Sources: Short Title Catalogue of the Netherlands (STCN), Bibliopolis (bibliopolis.nl), newspaper advertisements (delpher.nl)

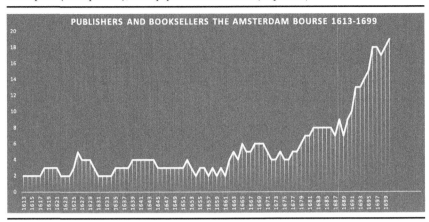

leading newspaperman.'[20] He distributed Dutch newspapers and newspapers from other European trade zones, such as Italy and Germany. Van Hilten put out a constant stream of broadsheets, with political news accompanied by transcripts of relevant documents, news about the victories and defeats of the Dutch sea heroes, or about new discoveries, for instance of a mine in Brasil in 1639. In the bourse street Jacob Vinckel printed the *Dutch Mercurius*, a yearly news outlet with much interest in trade-related news.

The bourse not only functioned as a news centre; it was also a space where opinions were formed. The evaluation of the news was perhaps just as essential as the gathering of facts. The bourse printers published pamphlets commenting upon recent events. These pamphlets were also distributed on the bourse floor, or pasted on the pillars, sometimes to the chagrin of the city council or the other bourse visitors. As the Amsterdam notarial acts are currently being digitized, it has become feasible to track what was happening on the bourse floor in more detail. Here we can learn about fights between bourse visitors about libels and public announce-ments on the bourse, as in the case of Samuel Coster who, when walking in the bourse in 1617, found a scandalous libel on one of the north pillars implicating him personally. He got in a fight trying to remove the pamphlet. After the bourse commissaire had removed the pamphlet, it was pasted on a different pillar by someone else.[21] Some pamphlets explicitly mentioned that they were hung at the bourse (and sometimes also that the Amsterdam regents had ordered their re-moval).[22] Soon after the opening of the exchange in 1611, publishers who were not located around the bourse were already printing pamphlets with an indication on the title page that the publication was to be sold on the bourse floor.[23] A travel account of a Silesian student visiting the Amsterdam bourse describes how newspapers were read aloud as sermons, and how the constant influx of news from all over the world led to heated political debates.[24]

**FIGURE 12.2** Business card of the bourse janitor Johannes de Paepe. Stadsarchief Amsterdam, BMAB00010000026_001

The bourse bibliopolis was a cosmopolitan knowledge hub.[25] The international merchant crowd attracted immigrants and internationally oriented publishers such as Bruyning (Browning) and Swart, catering specifically to the market of the English merchants and visitors, and keeping everyone informed about the political and religious developments in England.[26] After 1685, the French connection was strengthened with renowned Huguenot publishers such as Desbordes, De Lorme, and De la Feuille, who all flocked around the bourse.

The international marketplace required a variety of skills, such as the mastering of different languages. The Dutch poet Jeremias de Decker, in a poem that was attached to the wall of the exchange, expressed his wonder about this cosmopolitan space which also functioned as a school for all languages:

> This edifice rises to the skies, from Amstel's ground,
> And every day, all kinds of folk can be found,
> It is a park, where Moor and Norman do their trade,
> where Jews and Turks and Christians do pray,
> It is a school of languages, with wares from all sources.
> It is the bourse, supplying the world's bourses.[27]

The bourse printers helped to avoid Babylonian confusion by publishing French, Italian, English, and Latin dictionaries and grammars. International merchants who were new to the city, and tourists in general, could also buy maps and descriptions of Amsterdam at the exchange.

As expected, the bourse printers also provided all kinds of useful merchant handbooks, such as instruction books on law and accounting, or books like *Wisselstyl tot Amsterdam* (1681): everything a prudent merchant needed to know about the exchange of money. In 1683, a company of bourse booksellers published a Dutch translation of *Le parfait négociant* of Jacques Savary. Another dominant genre is the almanac, which helped merchants keep track of their activities. Here we see that the bourse began to function as a metaphor for the planning of time. From 1615 on we already find comptoir almanacs with a depiction of the bourse on the title page (Figure 12.3). Later, this image would become a mark of the genre.[28] Other merchant handbooks such as the *New Interest Book* (1702) by De L'Espine and Grauman (Figure. 12.4) also chose the exchange as a defining image.

The fact that publishers like city printer Jan Rieuwertsz choose the bourse as location to set up shop shows that the exchange was truly developing into a knowledge hub, an important centre of the public sphere, with an interesting correlation, or tension between state regulation, commercial interests, and heterodox thought. Rieuwertsz not only published the official announcements of the city board, but he was also responsible for the publication of many of the most infamous radical philosophical and theological works. He was the main publisher of Spinoza, Lodewijk Meyer, and Antoinette Bourignon. One of the new ideas advocated in these radical philosophical works was the acknowledgement of desire as the driving force of human behaviour,[29] an assumption that was embraced in

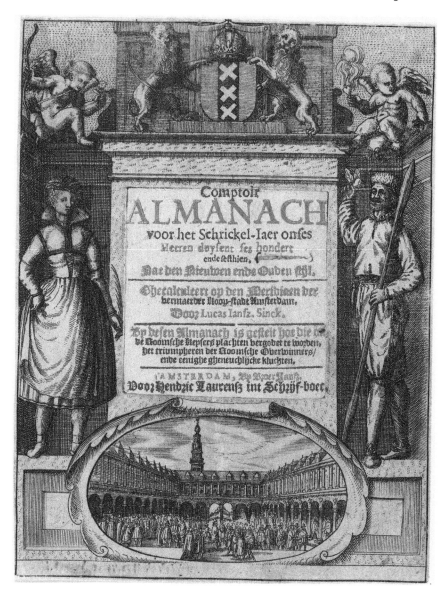

**FIGURE 12.3** Title page of the *Comptoir Almanac* for 1616. Rijksmuseum Amsterdam, RP-P-OB-80.807

economic discourse, as already indicated by Van Leuve's praise of *winzugt*. Rieuwertsz' bookshop functioned as a meeting centre for those interested in heterodox thought and critical discussions.[30] Soon the bourse attracted other early Enlightenment publishers such as Daniel van Dalen, one of the publishers of the *Boekzaal van Europe*, the first learned journal in the Dutch language.[31] Fransicus van den Enden's radical democratic treatise *Vrye politijke stellingen en consideratien*

**FIGURE 12.4** Title page of the *New Interest Book* (1702) by L.M. de L'Espine and J.P. Grauman, featuring the bourse. Stadsarchief Amsterdam, 010097005679

(1665) was advertised as being printed for the author and 'sold in the bourse street'. The bourse was thus not only a market for commercial information brokers, it was also a site for knowledge production and the formation of public opinion, where new bodies of critical thought were developed.

The exchange also developed into an instrument of socialization, helping new groups to participate in the knowledge market, or in the market in general. Journals in the vernacular (such as the *Boekzaal*) introduced readers to the world of letters. Around the building, official letter writers set up shop to assist the less literate in reading or writing letters. When new knowledge-intensive products were invented, the bourse helped to train people in handling them. Such was the case with the fire extinguisher, invented by Jan van der Heyden in 1672. The instrument was regularly tested or 'drilled' on the exchange floor, to prevent the dangerous situation if 'inexperienced people would blindly operate this artful machine.'[32]

## Knowledge about affect

The above examples suggest that the developing modern economy of the Dutch Republic was strongly connected to the development of the knowledge market. Merchant culture depended on news and the gathering of information, the formation of opinion, and training in commercial techniques and language skills through publications dealing with useful knowledge. Knowledge brokers expanded this market by developing new knowledge products and by attracting new groups to the market. The term 'useful knowledge', however, might be misleading in that it restricts our view of the skill-related knowledge products we would deem of interest for business.[33] The example of Jan Rieuwertsz, whose shop was called 'In the book of martyrs', shows that theological reflection, mathematical reasoning, and critical philosophy were also closely connected to the mercantile system. Biblical names were common around the bourse. Bourse bookseller Steven Swart first published *The Interest of England* (1663) under the imprint 'The two merchants', but after that his sign became 'In the crowned Bible'. Swart published English grammars, dictionaries and news-related publications, but also English-language 'merchant self-help books' with titles derived from their daily activities. *Happy Merchandise or Wisdoms Excellency Darkly Discovered, or Rather Greatly Obscured by Words Without Knowledge* (1672) helped merchants understand that the wisdom of God is a more profitable merchandise than silver or luxury goods. In *Spare-minutes; Or Resolved Meditations and Remeditated Resolutions* (1677), Arthur Warwick tries to induce merchants to spare a minute to reflect on sayings such as 'for he is not rich that hath much, but hee that hath enough.'

Swart's publications show that the merchant economy not only depended on technical training, but also on moral and emotional skills. This might also be the reason why bourse publishers showed such interest in poetry and drama. In the early decades of the exchange, the most expensive shop was run by Cornelis Lodewijksz. van der Plasse, under the sign 'In the Italian Bible'. Van

**FIGURE 12.5** Pieter Hendricksz. Schut, Bird's eye view of the bourse and its shops and offices (1662–1668). Printed by: Nicolaes Visscher (I). Rijksmuseum Amsterdam, RP-P-1904-1345.

der Plasse founded a shop in office supplies, selling paper, pencils, ledgers, and almanacs. He also published a newspaper, and editions of the Bible – a guaranteed source of income. On this foundation he started to publish novel literary works by famous Dutch authors such as Samuel Coster, Karel van Mander, P.C. Hooft, and Gerbrand Adriaensz Bredero.[34] The internationally oriented publisher Abraham Wolfgang, who in his imprints positioned himself 'at the entrance of the exchange, near the bourse tower', established a long-running series of French plays. Connections with the Amsterdam theatre – another important space of the Dutch knowledge economy[35] – were formalized when Jacob Lescaile, the city's official theatre printer, set up shop at the bourse in 1713. By then it was clear that the public of the bourse overlapped with that of the theatre. Merchants visited the theatre to watch themselves being enacted.[36] During the 1720s crisis the Amsterdam theatre put the bourse on stage to explain the complex financial world of stock trading to the lay public, and to urge those engaging in trade to reflect on the balance between commercial and moral values.[37]

The interrelation between the Amsterdam bourse and the theatre indicates the importance of cultural discourse for commercial development. During the seventeenth century, Dutch discourse gainsaid the classical and Christian anxieties about commercial citizenship, and embraced the ideal of the honest merchant, a 'good heart', trustworthy and sensitive, although challenged by the enticements of the market. Through this cultural discourse, the Dutch Republic developed a positively tuned commercial variant of the classical ideal of civic virtue. The merchant ought to balance his affects: his passionate desire for profit and prosperity and his affection for his household, for which he was responsible. Merchants were supposed to aspire to a higher goal in their commercial private enterprises: while honourably pursuing his self-interest, the merchant should strive for wisdom, moral leadership, a fatherly sensitivity, and the prosperity of the nation.[38] The Amsterdam exchange embodied this code of honour; a portion of all fines collected by the bourse commissaire was donated to the civic welfare system.

The Dutch Republic developed a remarkably positive discourse that celebrated trade as vital to its economic growth and as central to the Republic's self-image.[39] Knowledge came to be regarded as an important instrument in this cause. A famous example of this development is *Mercator sapiens*, the inaugural lecture by the Dutch poet and scholar Caspar Barlaeus on the occasion of the opening of the Amsterdam Athenaeum Illustre in 1632. In this lecture, Barlaeus advocated a strong connection between knowledge and commerce. Academies ought to school merchants in the classics and in philosophy, to provide them with moral instruction, and to observe and study commerce. Learned merchants are happier and wiser, Barlaeus said, and make decisions that are both profitable and moral. A prosperous city therefore also requires an institution of higher education.[40] Barlaeus thus helped to enrich the traditional ideal type of the Christian merchant, and the later variant of the neo-Stoic merchant – measuring material gain against spiritual wealth – with the ideal of a wise merchant with a firm philosophical knowledge base.[41] Later in the century, however, the neo-Stoic ideal of counteracting passions with reason was side-tracked by images, poems, plays, and treatises, which depicted passions such as the desire for profit, or the fear of risk or loss of honour, as important driving forces for market behaviour.

During the seventeenth century, then, the Amsterdam stock exchange developed into a knowledge hub, where information was accumulated, evaluated, and distributed. Knowledge was commodified in stable and reproducible forms, new bodies of knowledge were produced, and new groups of knowledge consumers were attracted to the market. The mercantile knowledge market not only accumulated and sold technical knowledge but also moral instruction and training in the balancing of affects.[42] As moral treatises and literary texts advocated the balance between commercial and moral values on an individual and a national level, the public appreciation of merchants and commerce improved over time.[43]

## The bourse as affective economy

One of the pressing questions in both the study of knowledge economies and in histories of consumer culture is why and how the process of early modern market development actually took place. Why did the demand, or the need, for knowledge and goods increase? Economic historians have presumed direct connections among the accumulation of wealth, the import of new foodstuffs and luxury goods, and the desire to consume. When wealth grows, and supply is ample, demand will apparently rise and people will consume more. Histories of consumer culture pay more attention to cultural factors. They stress that consumption helped to establish social status, which was urgent in the early modern period, as traditional identity markers were challenged through urbanization, the decline of the power of the church and transitions in the social strata.[44] Historians of knowledge economies also embrace this cultural approach, although here culture is sometimes merely a factor obstructing the increase of consumption.[45] Originally, the eighteenth century was highlighted as the age of the Consumer Revolution and the development of knowledge economies. In this volume we push these fundamental shifts back to the beginning of the early modern period, and seek to understand how consumer desire is actually created.[46] How were people – market players and consumers – 'trained' to buy and sell more, and to trade in more diverse and luxurious goods? Returning to Roeland van Leuve's eulogy of the bourse: how did this building develop into the 'global castle of commerce', a beehive, attracting profit seekers? What affective strategies were employed by the Amsterdam regents and merchant community to make the bourse a successful marketplace?

The first point to stress is that the exchange was a hybrid marketplace. Merchants formed only part of the crowd in the bourse. The building was open to the general public. While official mercantile negotiations there were limited to specified hours (the exact time shifted, but generally one or two hours at the end of the morning and one hour at the beginning of the evening), the bourse functioned as an open marketplace for the rest of the day. The general public, attracted by the shops under the arches around the exchange, was free to enter through the two gates, one on the side of the Dam Square, and the second above the Amstel at the Rokin, to stroll across the bourse courtyard, or to climb the stairs to the first floor of the building (Figure 12.5). Here they could find the very first 'shopping mall' in Amsterdam. This roofed market featured the cloth hall, where only Dutch cloth was sold, and small shops where visitors could purchase carpets, paintings, clocks, watches, ebony knives, and other luxury goods from all over the world. The shops specifically targeted women as customers, selling jewels, cutlery, clothes, textiles, and bonnets. Women also ran shops. In the 1630s for instance, Trijntje Wouters had a linen shop on the first floor and Annetje Jans sold children's hats.[47] If the customers grew weary of shopping, they could look down on the busy beehive of merchants on the bourse floor, and get new inspiration for commercial zeal.

The mercenary world thus functioned as a context and an incentive for consumer behaviour. This also worked the other way around: merchants themselves would visit the shops, to spend some of the profit they made on the floor of the exchange. This is yet another sign of the fact that markets thrive on selling trifles next to bulk goods.[48] This strategy may also have been used because the goods traded on the exchange were in some sense imaginary: merchant transactions on the bourse floor did not require any physical exchange of goods. It was even forbidden to bring more than samples to the exchange. The merchant's appetite for trade on the bourse floor was thus fanned by the display of gadgets and luxury products on the first floor. In the shops, as on the bourse floor, passions could rise when deals did not go according to plan. The archives tell us about conflicted negotiations, for instance, the Hamburg merchant who wanted to return his ill-fitting camel hair trousers, but got into a fight with the reluctant and aggressive shop owner, who stabbed his client in the head with his scissors.[49]

The fight in the cloth shop might be a sign of problems this innovative shopping zone faced, as it was not a natural success. Just as with the exchanges in Antwerp and London, Amsterdam struggled to attract enough customers to its shopping mall. According to Roeland van Leuve this was because 'In Amsterdam is ample choice / Of shops, stuffed with precious goods / Why then seek those upwards / When all you have to do now is pass along them in the street?'[50] Lesger has suggested that the dark shopping mall did not correspond with the taste of the shoppers, who preferred the light and open shopping streets such as the Warmoesstraat and later the Kalverstraat.[51] To attract more shoppers new triggers for arousing desire were set in place: in one of Job Andriesz Berckheyde's bourse paintings, we see how the shop owners displayed their goods – clocks, paintings – on the wall near the bourse entrance, under the Linen Hall sign (Figure 12.6). The painting also features a sign with two fencing men at the entrance: a reference to the fact that the bourse also housed a fencing school. Citizens could train their fighting skills at the exchange. The civic guards also used the courtyard for their military exercises.

The exchange thus functioned as an affective economy where shops, assisted by the cafés, coffee shops, and wine sellers around the exchange, tried to enhance consumer behaviour. The bourse's challenge was to attract crowds of shoppers during the day, while getting the merchants and the city brokers in and out at the specified bourse hours in an orderly fashion. As both merchants and brokers had the tendency to linger after the bourse bell had sounded the end of trading, the city repeatedly issued ordinances to forbid the brokers to dawdle around the exchange before and after opening hours.[52] The Amsterdam magistrates had their own chamber at the bourse, in the bourse tower. Here, according to Van Leuve, they could oversee the floor and also engage in trade themselves.[53]

The Amsterdam regents effectively engaged in the regulation of affect. Arousing desire had to be balanced with discouraging overly passionate, violent or else uncontrolled behaviour. Thus we can read the long list of bourse bylaws as a balancing act. While the early modern market thrived on risky behaviour, actual

**FIGURE 12.6** Job Andriesz Berckheyde, The Amsterdam Stock Exchange, ca. 1675–1680. Städel Museum, Frankfurt am Main

games of chance (e.g. card games) were forbidden, and playing children were chased off the floor during bourse hours. The women we see selling oranges, lemons, and apples at the bourse entrance in Berkheyde's painting (Figure 12.6) were not allowed to make use of wagons for their goods. They could only offer the fruit in small baskets.[54] It was forbidden to shout or curse on the bourse floor. Knives, swords, and guns were also explicitly forbidden. When things got out of hand, the bourse commissaire would step in, levy fines, and when necessary demand the clothing of the perpetrator as collateral. And for the truly unruly merchants and visitors, the Amsterdam regents had a prison cell installed in the corner of the bourse.[55] These regulations remind us that physical conflict and violence were constitutive elements of early modern trade.

## Imagining the economy

Job Berkheyde's painting (Figure 12.6) is not only interesting for what it displays, but also because it demonstrates painters', engravers', poets', and other artists' interest in the early modern economy. Berckheyde himself made at least three different paintings of the bourse, and they are just a drop in the ocean of depictions of the Amsterdam exchange. From the opening of its doors, the bourse was glorified in poems by some of the Netherlands's most famous authors: P.C. Hooft, Joost van den Vondel, Jeremias de Decker, and Jan Vos. Artists designed engravings and paintings of the building and its visitors. These depictions were sold at and around the bourse, to citizens and visitors.[56] They were also printed in travel guides, almanacs, and chorographies. The Getty Provenance Database reveals where the bourse images could end up: in the canal houses of rich merchants, but also in the homes of a physician, a textile salesman, a grocer, and of several widows of painters, trying to sell their husband's stock.[57]

The depictions celebrate the bourse as a crowded and attractive marketplace. They show men and women strolling from shop to shop, gazing at shop windows, buying products and socializing with other citizens. They explore commercial desire by depicting the bourse as a bright open space, with a mixed and lively crowd of merchants in wealthy, colourful clothes. Sometimes the merchants lure the viewer to the bourse floor. The famous painting by Emanuel de Witte (Figure 12.7) opens up to a lively bourse floor, crowded with merchants from different cultural backgrounds, all engaging in trade through embodied negotiations. The main character, centre stage, is a wealthy, fashionable merchant with a shiny red cape, who directs the visitor's gaze along his outstretched arm toward the wondrous action on the bourse floor.

In one of the early engravings of the bourse, merchants are holding exotic animals – a parrot and a monkey – while negotiating deals.[58] This visual detail is dramatized in Jasper Lemmers' farce *The Farmer-merchant* (*De boere koopman*), printed by Jacob Lescaile in 1682 and staged at the Amsterdam theatre. The farce, again, is an example of the close connection between the theatre and the bourse, and of the knowledge intensity of trade. Not only does the farmer in this farce underestimate the commercial skills needed to become a merchant (he thinks being able to read, write and calculate should suffice), more importantly he does not understand normal practice: when to attend the bourse, when to listen to the bourse bell, who can accompany you (not your wife), how to navigate the crowded floor, how to bargain, and how to recognize fake claims (such as 'this parrot can speak all languages'). In the end, the farmer is tricked into buying the parrot and the monkey, which turn out to be boys in disguise.

**FIGURE 12.7** Emanuel de Witte, The Courtyard of the Beurs in Amsterdam (1653). Museum Boijmans van Beuningen Rotterdam. Wiki commons

In the depictions of the bourse commercial knowledge is shown as being performed through merchants' bodies. These bodies seem to know exactly what to do: lift your hat to acknowledge your colleague; raise the hand before the chest to explain your position, point in a certain direction to indicate information from outside; lift both hands before the chest to indicate your standpoint; stand arms akimbo to show you will not yield to the other's position; shake hands when the deal is made. Through these images, viewers learn to see commercial enterprise as a lively and civilized society, attractive through its colourful and exotic qualities, and trustworthy through the contained movements of the traders. The bourse depictions thus helped to conceptualize the early modern economy, while celebrating trade as an organized society and attracting new actors to the market.

## Navigating the passions in the stock market

Up to now, we have treated the bourse as a single affective space. In reality, this affective economy had different sectors. On the bourse floor, every sector of trade was assigned a specific place. The pillars were numbered, so that merchants could find their targeted area (Figure 12.8). Maps of the numbered sections were sold to

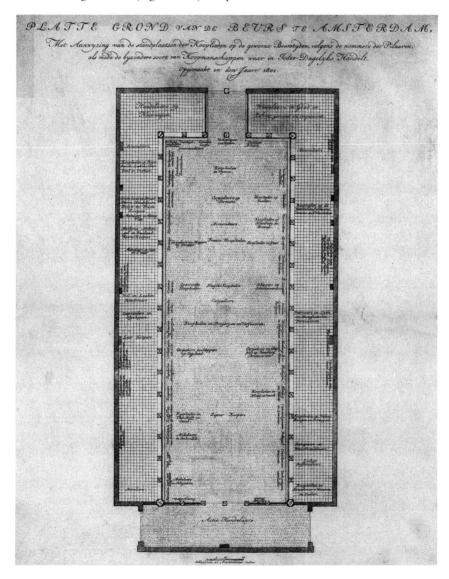

**FIGURE 12.8**    Map of the Amsterdam bourse floor. Stadsarchief Amsterdam, 010056917856

the visitors. These different trading spaces could show different affective dynamics. The paintings pick up on this: they show different pockets of traders: pairs of traders sitting on the benches under the arches, or leaning against the fences, engaging in quiet conversation, or small groups standing in the middle of the courtyard, negotiating with hand signs that mostly stay below the waistline. In the far corner of the bourse, the dynamic is quite different: here are traders crowding together, making more agitated signs: this is the corner of the stock traders.

The Amsterdam exchange was the very first *stock* exchange. From the day of the opening in 1611, VOC stocks were traded on the bourse floor. In the course of the seventeenth century, a complex and modern trading system was developed, with obligations, stocks, derivatives, short selling, and bear syndicates.[59] With the introduction of new, cheaper financial products, new groups were attracted to the market. These financial products challenged both traders and the public. They did so in terms of knowledge: stocks and derivatives are knowledge-intensive products, not self-explanatory, and unstable, since the products and strategies keep changing all the time.[60] Shares are also challenging at the level of affects and the moral economy. According to Roeland van Leuve, stock traders face different challenges, including on the psychological level. Because they operate in a trade that is very fast and 'have to be able to endure great losses in a single moment', they have to acquire specific affective qualities like constancy and perseverance.[61]

The stock market thus formed a direct threat to the delicate balance of the mercantile affective economy. Contemporary authors acknowledged this and tried to solve the issue. The most systematic approach was offered by the Portuguese-Jewish author Joseph de la Vega, in his treatise on stock trading: *Confusion de Confusiones* (1688). Scholars quarrel over De la Vega's exact intentions in this book: is it an investor handbook, an entertaining moral treatise, and/or a book meant to address the ambivalence and complexity of trade?[62] I would say that De la Vega combined these aims to present a 'science of stock trading'. In order to fully understand this new phenomenon, Vega states, one needs to be knowledgeable about many divergent fields: philosophy, ethics, law, medicine, navigation, rhetoric, biology, mathematics, astronomy, and physics. This is one of the reasons why *Confusion de Confusiones* is such a captivating work: because De la Vega tries to incorporate all these different kinds of knowledge, while acknowledging that in the end, the practice still eludes analysis. A second reason is that, to help explain this confusion, De la Vega analyses trade as an affective economy.

The tract is written in the format of a dialogue between a trader, a philosopher and a speculator, who try to make sense of the dynamics of the trade in 'actions', and the operation of the passions in trade processes. De la Vega connects with the early Enlightenment philosophy of the passions (compare Descartes, Hobbes, and Spinoza), by assuming *desire* to be a central driving force for human action, at least when it comes to commerce. This desire is envisioned in terms of lust, love, and addiction: 'Shares resemble evil desire, for those who have started to enjoy their favours, cannot disentangle from its caresses'.[63] The market is divided into two groups with specific emotional styles: *liefhebbers* and *contramineurs*, or as we would call them, bulls and bears. *Liefhebbers* love trading; they trade on hope. *Contramineurs* trade on fear. The exalted levels of ecstasy and despair on which both groups act urge the philosopher to adjust his vision of human behaviour: 'I have learned from philosophy that humans are reasonable, but these creatures are without reason.'[64]

Here, De la Vega makes an interesting turn. First he pictures an ideal type of an ordered trade floor where traders 'discard their passions, calmly listen to all parties, enquire about their motivations, contemplate their reasons and tricks, and choose the option that seems most profitable'.[65] However, the pace of the stock market does not allow for these careful strategies of decision-making. When chances of profit evaporate in the blink of an eye, how can it be wise to take the time to ponder and quarrel?[66] Jobbers and brokers therefore need to act on their passions and intuition. Passions do not need to be suppressed; they should be put to work. A successful investor is knowledgeable about his own passions and those of his colleagues. He is a scholar and master of emotions, navigating the waves of enthusiasm, fear and panic in the trade arena. He should be able to control his emotions, but he should not strive to be a stoic. Greed, anxiety, anger, and joy can be very instrumental trade passions, if one uses them well.

De la Vega's treatise thus bears witness to the early modern transition from passions to emotions, by which emotions are valued as positive actors, essential to our welfare.[67] The treatise also presents an interesting example of the transition of the concept of knowledge, as described by Susan James. In seventeenth-century philosophy knowledge becomes more closely connected to emotion, as in the conception of knowledge the ability to act presumes volition, and volition is interpreted as a passion.[68] Although it is impossible to draw only one conclusion from *Confusion de Confusiones*, we can also place De la Vega's book, just like Van Leuve's poem, at the transition from passions to interest, as described by Hirschman. These texts seem to come to terms with the desire for profit that drives market behaviour, acknowledging *winzugt* as a productive affect. However, the authors do not rationalize self-interest, nor do they praise it as the instrument to contain the unruly passions. As Hirschman moves from Spinoza to Mandeville, he seems to have missed this body of texts and images, in which interest is an embodied desire (a passionate love or lust), and knowledge and action are connected through strong passions.

## Conclusion

The Dutch Republic was one of the earliest examples of an advanced knowledge economy, in which knowledge was commoditized, and commoditized knowledge acquired an important role in economic and social processes. The Amsterdam Stock Exchange formed a central location for this development. It functioned as a knowledge hub for the world of commerce, not only because it functioned as a centre for news, the formation of opinions and commercial knowledge, but also because it helped to attract and socialize new groups of people into the market of knowledge and of knowledge-intensive products such as equities and derivatives.

This knowledge hub can be described as an affective space. Affects played a central role in the organization of bourse life, in the day-to-day practices of the commercial communities in and around the building. The building was organized to incite desire, for products and for profit; to create trader and consumer enthusiasm, but also to regulate excessively passionate behaviour and to avoid violent clashes. The regulation of affect was engineered through the organisation of the building – by the roofed shopping floor, or by ordering trade around pillars – through regulations and law enforcement, but also through an advanced public discourse, in textual, visual, and performative form. Authors like Van Leuve and De la Vega helped to develop a natural philosophy of trade, by describing the trade floor as an affective economy, in which passions functioned as embodied knowledge on which merchants could act. Historians of knowledge economies, of emotions, and of consumption history should therefore take exchanges and the collective imaginations that developed around them into account.

## Notes

1 "Gewinzucht propt de breede en lange galerijen, / Die brommen in 't vierkant, gelijck een korf, vol byen, / En uitgelezen geur, gewonnen op het velt." J. van den Vondel, *Inwydinge*, 82.
2 'Die Bykorf, daar 't Heelal zyn schatten in vergaard'; 'Dies is de as van 't land, waar 't al op draayt en wend'; 'dat daar werd gedreven/De grootste handel, die ter waereld is bekent'; 'Die hartkolk van den Staat, die veeler Vorsten min Ontstak.' R. van Leuve, *'s Waerelds Koopslot*, 47–48, 58, 93.
3 "Op hoop van winst is elk voor God Merkuur gereet; De goutzucht doet hier staag, met vollen yver swoegen/ En dienen't Koop-altaar van hem met meer genoegen." R. van Leuve, *'s Waerelds Koopslot*, 5–6, 53.
4 P. Burke, *What is the History of Knowledge?*; S. Lässig, "The History of Knowledge." Cf. the introduction to this volume.
5 J. Mokyr, *A Culture of Growth*; J. L. van Zanden, *The Long Road*.
6 Burke has a paragraph on stock exchanges in part I of his *Social History of Knowledge*.
7 G. A. Akerlof and R. J. Shiller, *Animal Spirits*.
8 G. Paster, *Reading the Early Modern Passions*; R. C. Solomon, *Not Passion's Slave*.
9 A. Reckwitz, "Affective Spaces."
10 B. Rosenwein, *Emotional Communities*.
11 W. M. Reddy, *The Navigation of Feeling*; J. Plamper, *The History of Emotions*
12 M. Scheer, "Are Emotions a Kind of Practice"; S. James, *Passion and Action*.
13 Lesger contests the concept of the staple market as a useful model for the organization of the early modern bulk trade and suggests to replace this concept with the idea of a centre for information. C. Lesger, *Handel in Amsterdam*, 16–17. Cf. J. de Vries and A. van der Woude, *The First Modern Economy*, 691–2; S. Huigen et al., *The Dutch Trading Companies*; I. Kopytoff, 'The Cultural biography of Things'.
14 P. Burke, *What is the History of Knowledge?*
15 H. J. Cook, "Assessing the Truth."
16 [Anonymous], *Extract uytet registre*. P. Scheltema, *De Beurs van Amsterdam*, 16. J. Jonker and K. Sluyterman, *Thuis op de Wereldmarkt*.
17 G. De Clercq, *Ter Beurze*, 94. H. Klompmaker, *Handel in de Gouden Eeuw*, 79. J. J. MacCusker and C. Gravesteijn, *The Beginnings*.

18 L. Neal, "The Rise of a Financial Press"; L. Neal and S. Quinn, "Networks of information"; L. Petram, *The World's First Stock Exchange*, 175–77; R. C. Michie, *The London Stock Exchange*.

19 This exploration is primarily based on the information in the *Short Title Catalogue of the Netherlands* (STCN) and www.bibliopolis.nl. As the publications I will refer to in the paragraphs below are easy to find in these catalogues, I will not add full title descriptions.

20 Hilten's *Courante uyt Italien, Duytslandt* (founded by his father Caspar van Hilten) was one of the most important, long-running Dutch newspapers. M. van Groesen, "(No) News"; A. Der Weduwen, *The Development of the Dutch Press*.

21 Stadsarchief Amsterdam, Notary Act 114686 (1617). For the digitization project of the Amsterdam notary acts: www.velehanden.nl and https://notarieel.archief.amsterdam.

22 *Eysch van de burgeren te Amsterdam, aende Beurs geplackt, en door last van den Schepenen afgescheurt* (1672).

23 In 1613, printer Marten Jansz. Brant added on the title page that he would sell his pamphlet *Een nieu liedeken* on the bourse floor.

24 C. Brugmans, *Onder de loupe*, 64–65.

25 M. C. Jacob, *Strangers*, ch. 3.

26 P. G. Hoftijzer, *Engelse boekverkopers*.

27 "Hier heft zich uit den grond des Amstels na de wolcken, / Een Plaets, die 's middags krielt van allerhande Volcken; / Een Wandelperk, daer Moor met Noorman handel drijft; / Een Kerck, daer Jode, Turck en christen in vergaeren, / Een aller Taelen School, een Merktveld aller Waeren, / Een Borse, die all's Weerelds Borsen stijft." J. De Decker, *Alle de rym-oeffeningen*, 190. We find the same wonder for the global bourse floor with its mixture of languages in Le Jolle, *Description de la ville d'Amsterdam*, 74–87.

28 Zaagman's comptoir almanacs were the most famous. J. Salman, *Populair Drukwerk*, 327.

29 S. James, *Passion and Action*.

30 P. Visser, *Godtslasterlijck*; J. Israel, *Radical Enlightenment*, 189–90, 278–83, 288–90.

31 J. J. M. Baartmans et al., *Intellectual Emancipation*.

32 Laurens Scherm, *Demonstratie van de slangbrandspuiten op het binnenplein van de Beurs te Amsterdam* (ca. 1690). Rijksmuseum Asmterdam, RP-P-AO-25-10A.

33 For a critical evaluation of the concept of "useful knowledge" see B. De Munck, "Knowledge and the Early Modern City."

34 H. Borst et al., "Analytische Bibliografie." van der Plasse also published Barthelomeus de las Casas's book on the Spanish tyranny in the West Indies.

35 On the role of the theatre in the early modern knowledge society, see Vanhaesebrouck's chapter in this volume, and A. van Bruaene, 'The Theatrum'.

36 I. Leemans, "New Plays."

37 I. Leemans, "Verse Weavers."

38 A. Weststeijn, *Commercial Republicanism*; S. Pincus, "Neither Machiavellian Moment"; D. Sturkenboom, *De Ballen van de Koopman.*

39 G.-J. Johannes and I. Leemans. "'O Thou Great God of Trade'"; D. Sturkenboom, *De Ballen van de Koopman.*

40 C. Barlaeus, *Mercator Sapiens*; C. Secrétan, *Le 'Marchand Philosophe'.*

41 S. Rauschenbach, "Elzevirian Republics"; M. Keblusek, "Mercator Sapiens".

42 M. C. Jacob and C. Secretan, *The Self-Perception.*

43 D. Sturkenboom, "Staging the Merchant."

44 Cf. M. Berg, *Luxury and Pleasure;* M. Berg and E. Eger, *Luxury in the Eighteenth Century;* J. Brewer and R. Porter, *Consumption and the World of Goods;* J. Brewer and F. Trentmann, *Consuming Cultures;* D. Roche, *A History of Everyday Things;* P. H. Smith and P. Findlen, *Merchants and Marvels;* P. Stearns, *Consumerism.* The chapter by Rasterhoff and Beelen in this volume also highlights that consumer goods became desirable for intangible qualities such as novelty and fashion.

45 J. Mokyr, *Culture*, provides a list of cultural biases that have to be overcome in order for knowledge economies to freely develop.

46  L. Jardine, *Worldly Goods;* J. L. van Zanden, *The Road.*
47  P. Scheltema, *De Beurs*, 21; J. G. van Dillen, *Bronnen*, vol. II (1612–1632) Den Haag 1933. vol. III 1633–1672.
48  Cf. the chapter by Vera Keller in this volume.
49  J. G. van Dillen, *Bronnen* II, 215 (18 June 1615).
50  'In Amsterdam is al te groote keurs, / van winkels opgepropt, met overdierbre waaren, / Dan dat men die juist zou om hoog gaan zoeken, daar men / in vollen overvloed die loopt voorbij langs straat'. R. van Leuve, *'s Waerelds Koopslot*, 55.
51  C. Lesger, *Handel in Amsterdam*, 89, 97–98. C. Lesger and J.H. Furnée, *Landscape of Consumption*, 5.
52  J. G. van Dillen, *Bronnen*, 2, 342. Later they also started to ban prostitutes from lingering around the bourse.
53  R. van Leuve, *'s Waereld Koopslot*, 116 (4 Octobre 1619).
54  Bylaws of the city of Amsterdam 19 December 1674, *Vervolg van de handvesten, privilegien, octoyen etc.* Amsterdam: O. Smient 1683, 1091.
55  I. Leemans, "The Economics of Pain."
56  The city board explicitly forbid painters to hang around the bourse to sell their products. J. G. van Dillen, *Bronnen*, 508 (21 October 1623).
57  Getty Provenance Index Database. http://www.getty.edu/research/tools/provenance.
58  Published by Boëtius Adamsz. Rijksmuseum Bolswert RP-P-OB-67.488 See also the edition by Jodocus Hondius I, 1611. Rijksmuseum RP-P-AO-25-5.
59  L. Petram, *The World's first Stock Exchange.*
60  A.L. Murphy, *The Origins of English Financial Markets.*
61  R. van Leuve *'s, Waerelds Koopslot.*
62  J. Israel, "Een merkwaardig literair werk," 160; L. Petram, *The World's first Stock Exchange*; J. Cardoso, *Confusión de Confusiones*, 123.
63  J. de la Vega, *Confusión de Confusiones*, 174. 'Acties hebben veel weg van den boozen lust, want zij die eenmaal begonnen zijn haar gunsten te genieten, kunnen zich niet losmaken van haar liefkoozingen'.
64  'Waarom wagen zij zich aan zulke gevaarlijke kwantiteiten en zulke hachelijke operaties? […] Ik heb van mijn philosophen geleerd, dat er redelijke wezens bestaan, maar ik bemerk, dat degenen, die gij mij schildert, redelooze wezens zijn.' J. de la Vega, *Confusión de Confusiones*, 67–68.
65  '[…] hartstocht af te leggen, kalm beide partijen aan te hooren, informeeren naar hun argumenten, hun redenen wikken, hun scherpzinnigheden overdenken, de berichten tegen elkaar afwegen […] en zich te neigen tot hetgeen wel het voordeligst lijkt […].' J. de la Vega, *Confusión de Confusiones*, 106–107.
66  'in een oogwenk de gelegenheid voorbijgaat, hoe kan het dan verstandig zijn door twistgesprekken weg te dringen, wat toch al in een oogwenk verloren gaat?.' J. de la Vega, *Confusión de Confusiones*, 127.
67  T. Dixon, *From Passions to Emotions.*
68  S. James, *Passion and Action.*

# Bibliography

Anonymous. *Extract uytet registre vande willekeuren der stadt Amstelredamme […]. Aengaende d'ordonnantie ende keure vande beurs deser stede.* Amsterdam: M. Colijn, 1611.
Akerlof, George A. and Robert J. Shiller. *Animal Spirits. How Human Psychology Drives the Economy, and Why it Matters for Global Capitalism.* Princeton: Princeton University Press, 2009.

Baartmans, Jacques and Jan de Vet. *Intellectual Emancipation during the Early Enlightenment: The Ambitions of a Pioneering Periodical from Rotterdam.* Nijmegen: UB, 2013.

Barlaeus, Caspar, *Mercator Sapiens: Oratie gehouden bij de Inwijding van de Illustere School te Amsterdam op 9 januari 1632.* Translated and edited by S. van der Woude. Amsterdam: Amsterdam University Press, 1967.

Berg, Maxine, *Luxury and Pleasure in Eighteenth-Century Britain.* Oxford: Oxford University Press, 2005.

Berg, Maxine, and Elizabeth Eger, eds. *Luxury in the Eighteenth Century: Debates, Desires and Delectable Goods.* Basingstoke: Palgrave Macmillan, 2003.

Borst, Henk, Cor van der Kogel, Paul Koopman, and Piet Verkruijsse. "Analytische Bibliografie en Literatuurgeschiedenis: Wonen in het Woord – Leven in de Letter." *Literatuur* 5 (1988): 332–41.

Brewer, John, and Roy Porter, eds. *Consumption and the World of Goods.* London/New York: Routledge, 1994.

Brewer, John, and Frank Trentmann, eds. *Consuming Cultures, Global Perspectives: Historical Trajectories, Transnational Exchanges.* Oxford/New York: Berg, 2006.

Bruaene, Anne-Laure van. "The Theatrum as an Urban Site of Knowledge in the Low Countries, c. 1560–1620." In Knowledge and the Early Modern City: A History of Entanglements, edited by Bert De Munck, and Antonella Romano, 33–57, Abingdon/New York: Routledge, 2019.

Brugmans, Grietje. *Onder de Loupe van het Buitenland.* Baarn: Hollandia, 1929.

Burke, Peter. *What is the History of Knowledge?.* Cambridge and Malden: Polity Press, 2016.

Burke, Peter. *A Social History of Knowledge. Vol. 1 and 2.* Cambridge and Malden: Polity Press, 2000 and 2012.

Clercq, Geert de, ed. *Ter Beurze: Geschiedenis van de Aandelenhandel in België, 1300–1990.* Brugge: van de Wiele; Antwerpen: Tijd, 1992.

Cook, Harold J. *Assessing the Truth: Correspondence and Information at the End of the Golden Age.* Leiden: Primavera Pers, 2013.

Cook, Harold J. "Amsterdam, entrepôt des savoirs au XVIIe siècle." *Revue d'histoire moderne et contemporaine* 55 (2008) 2: 19–42.

Decker, Jeremias de. *Alle de rym-oeffeningen van Jeremias de Decker.* Amsterdam: Stokinck, 1726.

Dillen, Johannes Gerard van. *Bronnen tot de Geschiedenis van het Bedrijfsleven en het Gildewezen van Amsterdam. Vol. 2 (1612–1632).* Den Haag: Instituut voor Nederlandse Geschiedenis, 1933.

Goetzmann, William N. Catherine Labio, Geert Rouwenhorst, and Timothy Young. *The Great Mirror of Folly: Finance, Culture, and the Crash of 1720.* New Haven: Yale University Press, 2013.

Groesen, Michien van. "(No) News from the Western Front: The Weekly Press of the Low Countries and the Making of Atlantic News." *The Sixteenth Century Journal* 44 (2013): 739–60.

Hart, Marjolein 't, Joost, Jonker, and Jan Luiten van Zanden, eds. *A Financial History of the Netherlands.* Cambridge: Cambridge University Press, 1997.

Hoftijzer, Paul. *Engelse Boekverkopers bij de Beurs: De Geschiedenis van de Amsterdamse Boekhandels Bruyning en Swart, 1637–1724.* Amsterdam/Maarssen: APA Holland University Press, 1987.

Huigen, Siegfried, Jan de Jong, and Elmer, Kolfin, eds. *The Dutch Trading Companies as Knowledge Networks.* Leiden and Boston: Brill, 2010.

Israel, Jonathan. *Radical Enlightenment: Philosophy and the Making of Modernity 1650–1750*. Oxford: Oxford University Press, 2001.

Jacob, Margaret C. *Strangers Nowhere in the World: The Rise of Cosmopolitanism in Early Modern Europe*. Philadelphia: University of Pennsylvania Press, 2006.

Jacob, Margaret C., and Catherine Secretan, eds. *The Self-Perception of Early Modern Capitalists*. New York: Palgrave Macmillan, 2008.

James, Susan. *Passion and Action: The Emotions in Seventeenth-century Philosophy*. Oxford: Clarendon Press; New York: Oxford University Press, 1997.

Jardine, Lisa. *Worldly Goods: A New History of the Renaissance*. New York: Nan A. Talese, 1996.

Johannes, Gert-Jan and Inger Leemans. "'O Thou Great God of Trade, O Subject of My Song!' Dutch Poems on Trade 1770–1830." *Eighteenth Century Studies* 51 (2018): 337–56.

Jonker, Joost and Keetje Sluyterman. *Thuis op de Wereldmarkt: Nederlandse Handelshuizen door de Eeuwen heen*. Den Haag: Sdu Uitgevers, 2000.

Keblusek, Marika. "Mercator sapiens. Merchants as Cultural Entrepreneurs." In *Double Agents: Cultural and Political Brokerage in Early Modern Europe*, edited by M. Keblusek, and B. Noldus, 95–109. Leiden/Boston: Brill 2011.

Klompmaker, Hendrik. *Handel in de Gouden Eeuw*. Bussum: van Dishoeck, 1966.

Kopytoff, Igor. "The Cultural Biography of Things: Commoditization as Process." In *The Social Life of Things: Commodities in Cultural Perspective*, edited by Arjun Appadurai, 64–91. Cambridge: Cambridge University Press, 1986.

Lässig, Simone. "The History of Knowledge and the Expansion of the Historical Research Agenda." *Bulletin of the Ghi* 59 (2016): 29–58.

Leemans, Inger. "The Economics of Pain. Pain in Dutch Stock Trade Discourses and Practices 1600-1750." In *The Hurt(ful) Body: Performing and Beholding Pain, 1600-1800*, edited by K. van der Haven, and K. van der Vanhaesebrouck, 273–99. Manchester: Manchester University Press, 2017.

Leemans, Inger. "'New Plays resemble Bubbles, we must own.' Staging the Stock Market, 1719–1720." In *Comedy and Crisis: Pieter Langendijk, the Dutch, and the Speculative Bubbles of 1720'*, edited by Joyce Goggin and Frans Blom. Liverpool: Liverpool University Press, 2020.

Leemans, Inger. "Verse Weavers and Paper Traders. Speculation in the Theater." In *The Great Mirror of Folly: Finance, Culture, and the Crash of 1720*, edited by William Goetzmann, and Catherine Labio, et al., 175–190. New Haven: Yale University Press, 2013.

Leemans, Inger and Gert-Jan Johannes. *Worm en donder. Geschiedenis van de Nederlandse literatuur 1700–1800. De Republiek*. Amsterdam: Bert Bakker/Prometheus 2013.

Leuve, Roeland van's. *Waerelds Koopslot of de Amsteldamse beurs, bestaande in drie Boeken met zeer veele Verbeeldingen [...] vercierd*. Amsterdam: J. Verheyden, 1723.

Lesger, Clé. *Handel in Amsterdam ten tijde van de Opstand: Kooplieden, Commerciële Expansie en Verandering in de Ruimtelijke Economie van de Nederlanden, ca. 1550-ca. 1630*. Hilversum: Verloren, 2001.

MacCusker, John J. and Cora, Gravesteijn. *The Beginnings of Commercial and Financial Journalism: The Commodity Price Currents, Exchange Rate Currents, and Money Currents of Early Modern Europe*. Amsterdam: NEHA, 1991.

Michie, Ranald C. *The London Stock Exchange: A History*. Oxford and New York: Oxford University Press, 1999.

Mokyr, Joel. *The Gifts of Athena: Historical Origins of the Knowledge Economy*. Princeton: Princeton University Press, 2004.

Mokyr, Joel. *A Culture of Growth: The Origins of the Modern Economy.* Princeton: Princeton University Press, 2016.

Munck Bert De. "Knowledge and the Early Modern City: An Introduction." In *Knowledge and the Early Modern City: A History of Entanglements,* edited by Bert De Munck, and Antonella Romano, 1–30. Abingdon / New York: Routledge, 2019.

Murphy, Anne L. *The Origins of English Financial Markets: Investment and Speculation before the South Sea Bubble.* Cambridge: Cambridge University Press, 2009.

Neal, Larry. "The Rise of a Financial Press: London and Amsterdam, 1681–1810." *Business History* 30 (1988): 163–78.

Neal, Larry and Stephen Quinn. "Networks of Information, Markets, and Institutions in the Rise of London as a Financial Centre, 1660–1720." *Financial History Review* 8 (2001): 7–26.

Paster, Gail Kern, Katherine Rowe, and Mary Floyd-Wilson, eds. *Reading the Early Modern Passions: Essays in the Cultural History of Emotion.* Philadelphia: University of Pennsylvania Press, 2004.

Petram, Lodewijk. *The World's First Stock Exchange: How the Amsterdam Market for Dutch East India Company Shares became a Modern Securities Market, 1602–1700.* Utrecht: ICG, 2011. http://hdl.handle.net/11245/2.85961.

Pincus, Steve. "Neither Machiavellian Moment nor Possessive Individualism: Commercial Society and the Defenders of the English Commonwealth." *The American Historical Review* 103 (1998): 705–36.

Pocock, John G.A. *The Machiavellian Moment: Florentine Political Thought and the Atlantic Republican Tradition.* Princeton: Princeton University Press, 1975.

Plamper, Jan. *The History of Emotions. An Introduction.* Oxford: Oxford University Press, 2015.

Rauschenbach, Sina. "Elzevirian Republics, Wise Merchants, and New Perspectives on Spain and Portugal in the Seventeenth-century Dutch Republic." *De Zeventiende Eeuw* 29 (2013): 81–100.

Reckwitz, Andreas. "Affective Spaces: A Praxeological Outlook." *Rethinking History* 16 (2012): 241–58.

Reddy, William M. *The Navigation of Feeling: A Framework for the History of Emotions.* Cambridge/New York: Cambridge University Press, 2001.

Roche, Daniel. *A History of Everyday Things: The Birth of Consumption in France, 1600-1800.* Cambridge, Cambridge University Press, 2000.

Rosenwein, Barbara. *Emotional Communities in the Early Middle Ages.* Ithaca: Cornell University Press, 2006.

Salman, Jeroen. *Populair drukwerk in de Gouden Eeuw: De Almanak als Lectuur en Handelswaar.* Zutphen: Walburg, 1999.

Scheer, Monique. "Are Emotions a Kind of Practice (and is that what makes them have a History)? a Bourdieuian Approach to Understanding Emotion." *History and Theory* 51 (2012): 193–22.

Scheltema, Pieter. *De Beurs van Amsterdam.* Amsterdam: Portielje, 1846.

Secrétan, Catherine. *Le 'Marchand philosophe' de Caspar Barlaeus. Un éloge du commerce dans la Hollande du Siècle d'Or. Étude, texte et traduction du Mercator sapiens.* Paris: Champion, 2002.

Smith, Pamela H. and Paula Findlen, eds. *Merchants and Marvels: Commerce, Science, and Art in Early Modern Europe.* London: Routledge, 2001.

Solomon, Robert C. *Not Passion's Slave: Emotions and Choice.* Oxford: Oxford University Press, 2003.

Stearns, Peter N. *Consumerism in World History.* Florence: Routledge, 2001.

Sturkenboom, Dorothée. *De Ballen van de Koopman: Mannelijkheid en Nederlandse Identiteit in de Tijd van de Republiek.* Gorredijk: Sterck & De Vreese, 2019.

Sturkenboom, Dorothée. "Staging the Merchant: Commercial Vices and the Politics of Stereotyping in Early Modern Dutch Theatre." *Dutch Crossing* 30 (2006): 211–28.

Vega, Joseph de la. *Confusión de Confusiones.* Translated by G.J. Geers. Ed. M.F.J. Smith. Den Haag: Nijhoff, 1939.

Visser, Piet. *Godtslasterlijck ende Pernicieus: De Rol van Boekdrukkers en Boekverkopers in de Verspreiding van Dissidente Religieuze en Filosofische Denkbeelden in Nederland in de tweede helft van de Zeventiende Eeuw.* Amsterdam: AD&L, 1996.

Vondel, Joost van den. *Inwydinge van 't Stadhuis t'Amsterdam.* Edited by S. Albrecht, et al. Muiderberg: Coutinho, 1982.

Vries, Jan de and Ad van der Woude. *The First Modern Economy: Success, Failure and Perseverance of the Dutch Economic Performance.* Cambridge: Cambridge University Press, 1997.

Weduwen, Arthur der. *The Development of the Dutch Press in the Seventeenth Century (1618–1700).* Dissertation University of St Andrews, 2015.

Weststeijn, Arthur. *Commercial Republicanism in the Dutch Golden Age: The Political Thought of Johan and Pieter de la Court.* Leiden: Brill, 2012.

Zanden, Jan Luijten van. *The Long Road to the Industrial Revolution: The European Economy in a Global Economy.* Leiden: Brill, 2009.

# INDEX

For Product Safety Concerns and Information please contact our EU
representative GPSR@taylorandfrancis.com Taylor & Francis Verlag GmbH,
Kaufingerstraße 24, 80331 München, Germany

Printed and bound by CPI Group (UK) Ltd, Croydon, CR0 4YY
01/05/2025
01858356-0001